SO-BIE-214

Color in the Classroom

Montante Family Library
D'Youville College

Color in the Classroom

How American Schools Taught Race,
1900–1954

ZOË BURKHOLDER

JUL 1 3 2012

OXFORD
UNIVERSITY PRESS

OXFORD
UNIVERSITY PRESS

Oxford University Press, Inc., publishes works that further
Oxford University's objective of excellence
in research, scholarship, and education.

Oxford   New York
Auckland   Cape Town   Dar es Salaam   Hong Kong   Karachi
Kuala Lumpur   Madrid   Melbourne   Mexico City   Nairobi
New Delhi   Shanghai   Taipei   Toronto

With offices in
Argentina   Austria   Brazil   Chile   Czech Republic   France   Greece
Guatemala   Hungary   Italy   Japan   Poland   Portugal   Singapore
South Korea   Switzerland   Thailand   Turkey   Ukraine   Vietnam

Copyright © 2011 by Oxford University Press, Inc.

Published by Oxford University Press, Inc.
198 Madison Avenue, New York, NY 10016

www.oup.com

Oxford is a registered trademark of Oxford University Press

All rights reserved. No part of this publication may be reproduced,
stored in a retrieval system, or transmitted, in any form or by any means,
electronic, mechanical, photocopying, recording, or otherwise,
without the prior permission of Oxford University Press.

Library of Congress Cataloging-in-Publication Data
Burkholder, Zoë.
Color in the classroom : how American schools taught race, 1900–1954
/ Zoë Burkholder.
      p.   cm.
Includes bibliographical references and index.
ISBN 978-0-19-975172-3
1. Race—Study and teaching—United States—History—20th century.
2. Racism—Study and teaching—United States—History—20th century.
3. United States—Race relations—History—20th century. I. Title.
HT1506.B87   2011
305.80071—dc22   2011004602

1 3 5 7 9 8 6 4 2

Printed in the United States of America
on acid-free paper

HT
1506
.B87
2011

To Dexter and Hollis

CONTENTS

ACKNOWLEDGMENTS

This book has benefited from conversations with friends, family, and colleagues in history, anthropology, and education over the past several years. I am deeply indebted to these folks for making the research and writing of this book a pleasurable, and in many ways, collaborative experience. My greatest debt is to Jonathan Zimmerman, who has read and commented on countless drafts and offered his boundless enthusiasm, support, advice, and critique along the way. My colleagues and the dean at the School of Education and Human Services at Montclair State University have helped me complete the final stages of research and writing for this book since 2009. I would like to say a special thank-you to Ada Beth Cutler, our outstanding dean, and to Jeremy Price, the chair of the Department of Educational Foundations, both of whom have shown tremendous generosity in supporting my research in every way possible, including a very warm and genuine interest in my personal development as a scholar and as a teacher. My colleagues Jaime Grinberg, Tyson Lewis, Helenrose Fives, Alina Reznitskaya, Mark Weinstein, David Kennedy, Kathryn Herr, Maughn Gregory, Brian Carolan, Nicole DiDonato, Jamaal Matthews, and Tamara Lucas have ensured that my first years as an assistant professor have been productive and enjoyable. Thanks to our department administrator, Brenda Godbolt, who keeps our department running smoothly, and to the future teachers at Montclair State, whose passion for studying the history of education serves as a constant source of inspiration. A Faculty Student Research Grant from Montclair State University allowed me to benefit from the tireless research assistance of MSU students Kyle Benn and Jordan Helin. Thank you, Kyle and Jordan, for your thoughtful and insightful research and writing assistance.

I also owe a tremendous debt of gratitude to the Charles Warren Center for Studies in American History at Harvard University. As a fellow at the Warren Center in 2008–2009, I was able to do additional research and writing for this book as part of a year-long colloquium on "Race-Making and Law-Making in the

Long Civil Rights Movement." This fellowship was directed by Evelyn Brooks Higginbotham and Kenneth Mack, two of the most impressive scholars I have ever met, who helped me think more critically about how my scholarship fit into the historical literature on the long civil rights movement. I also benefited enormously from the advice and assistance of the other fellows at the Warren Center: Rachel Devlin, Thomas Guglielmo, Scott Kurashige, Peniel Joseph, Kevin Mumford, Clarissa Atkinson, and Matthew Countryman. Also at Harvard University, Julie Ruben, Andrew Kahrl, Tina Collins, and Mary Dudziak were kind enough to read and comment on various drafts of this book. Arthur Patton-Hock and Larissa Kennedy ensured that we all had an especially productive year in Cambridge.

At New York University I benefited from the rigorous academic training and personal kindness of Lisa Stulberg, Marcelo Suarez-Orozco, James Fraser, Daniel Walkowitz, Harold Wechsler, Joan Malczewski, Brett Gary, and Martha Hodes. I also had the pleasure of working with Sarah Bennison, Diana D'Amico, Jonna Perrillo, Patricia Haggler, Heather Lewis, Bethany Rogers, Erich Dietrich, Afrah Richmond, and Jeffrey Snyder. Archival research for this book was funded by in part by a grant from the Steinhardt School of Culture, Education, and Human Development at NYU. A generous Fellowship on Dissertation Research Related to Education from the Spencer Foundation supported my graduate research and put me in contact with a network of leading historians including Evelyn Brooks Higginbotham, Bruce Schulman, and Betty Anderson. Through professional meetings and conferences, I have been lucky enough to gain critical feedback from some of the best scholars in American educational history including Jeffrey Mirel, Sevan Terzian, Eileen Tamura, James D. Anderson, Adam Fairclough, Thomas Sugrue, Leah Gordon, Natalia Mehlman-Petrzela, Yoon Pak, Ruben Donato, Linda Heywood, Charles Dorn, Mary P. Ryan, Eric Goldstein, and Barbara Beatty.

This book grows out of my academic interest and training in anthropology. My undergraduate studies in anthropology at the University of Virginia were shaped by the thoughtful teaching of the late James Deetz, as well as Adria Laviolette, Jeffrey Hantman, and Richard Handler. At the University of California, Berkeley, where I did my graduate work in anthropology, I was profoundly influenced by my wonderful advisor, Laurie Wilkie, as well as Margaret Conkey and Ruth Tringham. Anthropologists at both of these institutions emphasized the important connections between scholarship about the past and political issues in the present, especially public education and outreach. I am deeply indebted to all these scholars, and I hope this book reflects the best possible insights from the discipline of anthropology.

This book would not have been possible without the knowledge and support of the outstanding librarians and administrative staff at the following institutions: YIVO Institute for Jewish Research in New York, NY; Amistad Research

ACKNOWLEDGMENTS

This book has benefited from conversations with friends, family, and colleagues in history, anthropology, and education over the past several years. I am deeply indebted to these folks for making the research and writing of this book a pleasurable, and in many ways, collaborative experience. My greatest debt is to Jonathan Zimmerman, who has read and commented on countless drafts and offered his boundless enthusiasm, support, advice, and critique along the way. My colleagues and the dean at the School of Education and Human Services at Montclair State University have helped me complete the final stages of research and writing for this book since 2009. I would like to say a special thank-you to Ada Beth Cutler, our outstanding dean, and to Jeremy Price, the chair of the Department of Educational Foundations, both of whom have shown tremendous generosity in supporting my research in every way possible, including a very warm and genuine interest in my personal development as a scholar and as a teacher. My colleagues Jaime Grinberg, Tyson Lewis, Helenrose Fives, Alina Reznitskaya, Mark Weinstein, David Kennedy, Kathryn Herr, Maughn Gregory, Brian Carolan, Nicole DiDonato, Jamaal Matthews, and Tamara Lucas have ensured that my first years as an assistant professor have been productive and enjoyable. Thanks to our department administrator, Brenda Godbolt, who keeps our department running smoothly, and to the future teachers at Montclair State, whose passion for studying the history of education serves as a constant source of inspiration. A Faculty Student Research Grant from Montclair State University allowed me to benefit from the tireless research assistance of MSU students Kyle Benn and Jordan Helin. Thank you, Kyle and Jordan, for your thoughtful and insightful research and writing assistance.

I also owe a tremendous debt of gratitude to the Charles Warren Center for Studies in American History at Harvard University. As a fellow at the Warren Center in 2008–2009, I was able to do additional research and writing for this book as part of a year-long colloquium on "Race-Making and Law-Making in the

Long Civil Rights Movement." This fellowship was directed by Evelyn Brooks Higginbotham and Kenneth Mack, two of the most impressive scholars I have ever met, who helped me think more critically about how my scholarship fit into the historical literature on the long civil rights movement. I also benefited enormously from the advice and assistance of the other fellows at the Warren Center: Rachel Devlin, Thomas Guglielmo, Scott Kurashige, Peniel Joseph, Kevin Mumford, Clarissa Atkinson, and Matthew Countryman. Also at Harvard University, Julie Ruben, Andrew Kahrl, Tina Collins, and Mary Dudziak were kind enough to read and comment on various drafts of this book. Arthur Patton-Hock and Larissa Kennedy ensured that we all had an especially productive year in Cambridge.

At New York University I benefited from the rigorous academic training and personal kindness of Lisa Stulberg, Marcelo Suarez-Orozco, James Fraser, Daniel Walkowitz, Harold Wechsler, Joan Malczewski, Brett Gary, and Martha Hodes. I also had the pleasure of working with Sarah Bennison, Diana D'Amico, Jonna Perrillo, Patricia Haggler, Heather Lewis, Bethany Rogers, Erich Dietrich, Afrah Richmond, and Jeffrey Snyder. Archival research for this book was funded by in part by a grant from the Steinhardt School of Culture, Education, and Human Development at NYU. A generous Fellowship on Dissertation Research Related to Education from the Spencer Foundation supported my graduate research and put me in contact with a network of leading historians including Evelyn Brooks Higginbotham, Bruce Schulman, and Betty Anderson. Through professional meetings and conferences, I have been lucky enough to gain critical feedback from some of the best scholars in American educational history including Jeffrey Mirel, Sevan Terzian, Eileen Tamura, James D. Anderson, Adam Fairclough, Thomas Sugrue, Leah Gordon, Natalia Mehlman-Petrzela, Yoon Pak, Ruben Donato, Linda Heywood, Charles Dorn, Mary P. Ryan, Eric Goldstein, and Barbara Beatty.

This book grows out of my academic interest and training in anthropology. My undergraduate studies in anthropology at the University of Virginia were shaped by the thoughtful teaching of the late James Deetz, as well as Adria Laviolette, Jeffrey Hantman, and Richard Handler. At the University of California, Berkeley, where I did my graduate work in anthropology, I was profoundly influenced by my wonderful advisor, Laurie Wilkie, as well as Margaret Conkey and Ruth Tringham. Anthropologists at both of these institutions emphasized the important connections between scholarship about the past and political issues in the present, especially public education and outreach. I am deeply indebted to all these scholars, and I hope this book reflects the best possible insights from the discipline of anthropology.

This book would not have been possible without the knowledge and support of the outstanding librarians and administrative staff at the following institutions: YIVO Institute for Jewish Research in New York, NY; Amistad Research

ACKNOWLEDGMENTS

This book has benefited from conversations with friends, family, and colleagues in history, anthropology, and education over the past several years. I am deeply indebted to these folks for making the research and writing of this book a pleasurable, and in many ways, collaborative experience. My greatest debt is to Jonathan Zimmerman, who has read and commented on countless drafts and offered his boundless enthusiasm, support, advice, and critique along the way. My colleagues and the dean at the School of Education and Human Services at Montclair State University have helped me complete the final stages of research and writing for this book since 2009. I would like to say a special thank-you to Ada Beth Cutler, our outstanding dean, and to Jeremy Price, the chair of the Department of Educational Foundations, both of whom have shown tremendous generosity in supporting my research in every way possible, including a very warm and genuine interest in my personal development as a scholar and as a teacher. My colleagues Jaime Grinberg, Tyson Lewis, Helenrose Fives, Alina Reznitskaya, Mark Weinstein, David Kennedy, Kathryn Herr, Maughn Gregory, Brian Carolan, Nicole DiDonato, Jamaal Matthews, and Tamara Lucas have ensured that my first years as an assistant professor have been productive and enjoyable. Thanks to our department administrator, Brenda Godbolt, who keeps our department running smoothly, and to the future teachers at Montclair State, whose passion for studying the history of education serves as a constant source of inspiration. A Faculty Student Research Grant from Montclair State University allowed me to benefit from the tireless research assistance of MSU students Kyle Benn and Jordan Helin. Thank you, Kyle and Jordan, for your thoughtful and insightful research and writing assistance.

I also owe a tremendous debt of gratitude to the Charles Warren Center for Studies in American History at Harvard University. As a fellow at the Warren Center in 2008–2009, I was able to do additional research and writing for this book as part of a year-long colloquium on "Race-Making and Law-Making in the

Long Civil Rights Movement." This fellowship was directed by Evelyn Brooks Higginbotham and Kenneth Mack, two of the most impressive scholars I have ever met, who helped me think more critically about how my scholarship fit into the historical literature on the long civil rights movement. I also benefited enormously from the advice and assistance of the other fellows at the Warren Center: Rachel Devlin, Thomas Guglielmo, Scott Kurashige, Peniel Joseph, Kevin Mumford, Clarissa Atkinson, and Matthew Countryman. Also at Harvard University, Julie Ruben, Andrew Kahrl, Tina Collins, and Mary Dudziak were kind enough to read and comment on various drafts of this book. Arthur Patton-Hock and Larissa Kennedy ensured that we all had an especially productive year in Cambridge.

At New York University I benefited from the rigorous academic training and personal kindness of Lisa Stulberg, Marcelo Suarez-Orozco, James Fraser, Daniel Walkowitz, Harold Wechsler, Joan Malczewski, Brett Gary, and Martha Hodes. I also had the pleasure of working with Sarah Bennison, Diana D'Amico, Jonna Perrillo, Patricia Haggler, Heather Lewis, Bethany Rogers, Erich Dietrich, Afrah Richmond, and Jeffrey Snyder. Archival research for this book was funded by in part by a grant from the Steinhardt School of Culture, Education, and Human Development at NYU. A generous Fellowship on Dissertation Research Related to Education from the Spencer Foundation supported my graduate research and put me in contact with a network of leading historians including Evelyn Brooks Higginbotham, Bruce Schulman, and Betty Anderson. Through professional meetings and conferences, I have been lucky enough to gain critical feedback from some of the best scholars in American educational history including Jeffrey Mirel, Sevan Terzian, Eileen Tamura, James D. Anderson, Adam Fairclough, Thomas Sugrue, Leah Gordon, Natalia Mehlman-Petrzela, Yoon Pak, Ruben Donato, Linda Heywood, Charles Dorn, Mary P. Ryan, Eric Goldstein, and Barbara Beatty.

This book grows out of my academic interest and training in anthropology. My undergraduate studies in anthropology at the University of Virginia were shaped by the thoughtful teaching of the late James Deetz, as well as Adria Laviolette, Jeffrey Hantman, and Richard Handler. At the University of California, Berkeley, where I did my graduate work in anthropology, I was profoundly influenced by my wonderful advisor, Laurie Wilkie, as well as Margaret Conkey and Ruth Tringham. Anthropologists at both of these institutions emphasized the important connections between scholarship about the past and political issues in the present, especially public education and outreach. I am deeply indebted to all these scholars, and I hope this book reflects the best possible insights from the discipline of anthropology.

This book would not have been possible without the knowledge and support of the outstanding librarians and administrative staff at the following institutions: YIVO Institute for Jewish Research in New York, NY; Amistad Research

Center at Tulane University in New Orleans, LA; American Philosophical Society Library in Philadelphia, PA; Library of Congress Manuscript Division in Washington, DC; Municipal Archives in New York, NY; Archives and Special Collections at Vassar University in Poughkeepsie, NY; Tamiment Library and Robert F. Wagner Labor Archives, New York University, New York, NY.; Immigration History Research Center, University of Minnesota in Minneapolis, MN; Research Library of the Balch Institute for Ethnic Studies at the Historical Society of Pennsylvania in Philadelphia, PA; the Schlesinger Library on the History of Women in America at Radcliffe College in Cambridge, MA; American Museum of Natural History Archives, New York, NY; City of Boston Archives, West Roxbury, MA; and the New York Public Library in New York City. I met dedicated and informed librarians at each of these institutions, and my research would not have been possible without their generous assistance. I would like to say a special thanks to David Ment, Dean Rogers, Erika Gottfried, Gail Malmgreen, Kristen Mable, and Daniel Necas.

Three anonymous reviewers offered invaluable feedback on an earlier draft of this manuscript, I am extremely grateful that they took the time and energy to offer such careful criticism. This book would not have been possible without the informed and thoughtful critique of my editor at Oxford University Press, Susan Ferber, who helped me improve this book in more ways than I could possibly count.

I owe a special thanks to my kind, intelligent, and tremendously supportive parents, Christina Miesowitz Burkholder and Ervin Burkholder. My sister, Tai Burkholder, has been a pillar of strength, optimism, support, love, and entertainment for the past ten years in New York City. I would like to say a special thanks to my extended family, all of whom expressed genuine interest in my research and various forms of edible, financial, and emotional support. Their love and encouragement has meant more than I can say.

Finally, I am fortunate to be married to the world's smartest and most generous scholar—Chris Matthews. Chris's research, especially his community-based historical archaeology, is an outstanding example of what meaningful academic work looks like at its absolute best. Thanks, Chris, for your love and support. My children, Dexter and Hollis, have grown up alongside this book, joining me on research trips, fellowships, and now a full-time tenure-track job in New Jersey. I'm not sure if there is a foolproof way to write a book, but if there is, I think sharing your life with two people as fun, spontaneous, loving, and deeply intelligent as Dexter and Hollis must be it. This book is dedicated to Dexter and Hollis, my muses, with gratitude and love.

Color in the Classroom

Introduction: The Social Construction of Race in American Schools

> In Germany today, even the scientist can teach only those things which agree with Hitler's ignorant prejudices. There is no excuse, however, for ignorance or prejudice in our educational world, which is free to teach the truth.
>
> —Franz Boas, 1939

> [Teachers] need to see that, in spite of its terrible potency in the world today, racism is vulnerable.
>
> —Ruth Benedict, 1946

> The cure for prejudice is scientific investigation, straight thinking, and proper education.
>
> —English Teacher, 1947

Just before Christmas break in 1943, eighteen elementary students from P.S. 6 in Manhattan assumed their places on stage for the musical *Meet Your Relatives*. Catering to incessant government demands for tolerance education, the purpose of this play was to popularize the anthropological definition of human race and its message of racial equality. As the curtain opened, twelve "eminent scientists" dressed in cap and gown stood in two rows on either side of an illustrated chart mounted in the center of the stage. Six children, wearing folk costumes from around the world, stood in front of the scientists and recited their opening lines:

FIRST CHILD: You have heard many ideas since you were born on the question of Race, Religion, and Nationality. We all know Hitler's pet ideas on the superior, super-duper Aryan race. I don't have to tell you what he thinks of *you* or *me*—or DO I?

SECOND: Don't smile. He isn't the only one with pet ideas and pet hates. Why even here in our own democratic America, there are some people who are all mixed up on the subject of Race, Religion, and Nationality.

THIRD: Did you know that there are some people in *our own* country who think there is something very 'specially superior about belonging to the White Race? They actually think that the yellow, the black, and the red races are inferior—DO YOU?

The answer was an emphatic no, and the entire cast called out, "Well, we feel that all these ideas and hates are the bunk—and this morning we are out to DeBunk the Bunk—"

FIFTH: We are going to clear up the whole mess once and for all—
ALL: And we are going to clear it up scientifically![1]

Under the direction of their teacher, Alice Nirenberg, the students did just that, reciting for the audience the scientific definition of human race as delineated in the recent publication of *The Races of Mankind* by the anthropologists Ruth Benedict and Gene Weltfish. This small, illustrated pamphlet challenged Nazi racial propaganda by asserting the relative equality of what scientists in the 1940s understood as the three races of humankind: Mongoloid, Negroid, and Caucasian. *The Races of Mankind* promised to lay out the "facts that have been learned and verified" concerning human biological differences.[2] As "scientific" lessons on race, these anthropological materials were widely understood to be not only apolitical, but representative of an indisputable truth that stood in pointed contrast to pseudoscientific Nazi racial propaganda.

During World War II, many American teachers believed that fighting racial prejudice constituted a valuable contribution to the war effort and participated in a massive effort to teach racial tolerance in order to help secure democracy and promote world peace. By 1946, educators bragged that in addition to appreciating minority groups, "Students are also learning the positive facts of race and culture which provide the scientific basis for belief in the equality of men."[3] Their students agreed, noting the impact that factual information and "proper education" had on racial prejudice. As one student explained, "With clear thinking instead of ignorance, we can eliminate much of the misunderstanding that brings prejudice. By our experiences we see the result obtained by the correct education."[4] Scientific "facts" were supposed to wipe out the "ignorance" that led to racial bigotry. In this sense, teaching scientific facts about racial egalitarianism served to reform the very meaning of a "proper" and "correct" education.

Swept up in the same social and political currents, in 1939 America's most prominent anthropologists became convinced that they could wage a deliberate campaign to undermine racism in the United States. Drawing on dominant social science paradigms of how racial prejudice was formed and reproduced, these activist scholars believed that by promoting a more egalitarian conception of human race they would wipe out irrational racial prejudice. To accomplish this visionary task, they turned to the nation's largest and most powerful institution dedicated to knowledge production and social reproduction—public schools. Because social scientists understood racial prejudice to be the result of both inaccurate information and faulty socialization, schools were the most logical site of reform. Not only did public schools allow activists to reach out to millions of Americans in virtually every corner of the nation, they also housed the only group social scientists believed had the capacity to completely re-form their basic understanding of racial difference—children.

Color in the Classroom tells the story of one of the most audacious antiracist initiatives ever undertaken in American history—the joint effort by anthropologists and educators to revise what they called "the 'race' concept" in American schools during World War II. In doing so, it examines two distinct but overlapping historical processes—an anthropological movement to reform racial discourse in schools during wartime, and a longer process of the social construction of race in American classrooms from the turn of the twentieth century through the historic *Brown v. Board of Education* ruling in 1954. While historians have long recognized the important role that anthropology, among other social sciences, played in the Supreme Court's decision to outlaw racial segregation in the public schools, this study is the first to reveal that anthropologists worked directly with teachers as early as 1939 to fight racial prejudice and reform the democratic ideal through the institution of public schools.

This analysis focuses on the dominant educational discourse on race as articulated by the nation's leading white educators working in prominent teaching organizations at the city, state, and national level. During the era under consideration here, all of these teaching organizations were either exclusively white or run by white leaders. African American teachers were relegated to second-class citizenship within these prominent teaching associations, or they chose to work through black teaching associations. These black teaching associations were tremendously important sites of professional development and educational activism for black teachers; however, they did not have the financial backing, institutional support, or political power to influence broader national trends in the way teachers taught about race.

This dominant educational discourse on race was one of many that influenced the social construction of race in twentieth-century America, but it had an especially powerful influence because it was produced through the nation's single largest institution of knowledge production, elementary and secondary schools. This understanding of race can be located in professional teaching journals such as the *English Journal, Elementary English Review, Social Education, Social Studies, Science Teacher, American Biology Teacher, Journal of the NEA,* and *High Points of the Bulletin of the City of New York.* Published on a regular basis, these teaching journals feature firsthand accounts of classroom practice. They defined current pedagogical trends and kept teachers up to date on "professional" teaching practices, including the appropriate way to teach about racial others, who was racially distinct, and what this racial distinction meant. Editors had the power to select certain articles for publication and reject those that were undesirable or inappropriate. The way teachers spoke about race in these journals does not represent the full range of discussion, but is taken to reflect what prominent teacher association leaders wanted teachers to internalize and perform.[5]

With the help of anthropological texts like *The Races of Mankind,* racial discourse in American schools underwent a paradigmatic shift during the span of World War II. The most significant part of this transformation was the introduction of the scientific concept of race, as delineated by the twentieth century's leading antiracist anthropologist, Franz Boas, into American teachers' everyday language. This anthropological definition of race not only narrowed the boundaries of who was identified as a racial minority, but also introduced a new concept—culture—to explain the diversity of human life on earth. As this book shows, American teachers modified and translated these concepts as they put them into practice in their classrooms. Some teachers employed the anthropological definition of human race to challenge racism and social inequality, thereby creating some of the most critical antiracist pedagogy of the twentieth century. This critical antiracist pedagogy was more the exception than the rule. Most teachers simply translated an essentialist understanding of human "race" into a softer language of "culture" that continued to define minority individuals according to the supposedly natural or inherent characteristics of their group. In doing so they constructed culture as a foil to race in a way that recast the most damaging aspects of early twentieth-century racialist thinking into a more acceptable, but equally reductionist, discourse of cultural diversity.

It was the "scientific" quality of *The Races of Mankind* and other anthropological texts that made antiracist teaching materials accessible to teachers like Alice Nirenberg during World War II. Pressured to teach tolerance for racial minorities as part of the war effort, teachers were looking for a strategic way to teach racial equality in what could be, despite institutional support, a volatile and unstable environment. Explosive racial conflicts over jobs, housing, and military service left many white Americans edgy about questions of racial equality for the nation's African American, Asian American, and Latino citizens. What is more, before World War II many Americans still believed that an individual's biological race determined his or her potential for behavior, morality, health, and intelligence. In general, they did not restrict their conception of race to three main categories delineated by anthropologists, but instead followed outdated scientific models or pseudoscientific claims that ranked racial "stocks" such as Alpine, Mediterranean, and Nordic based on their supposed proximity to the Anglo-Saxon ideal.[6]

The anthropological definition of race thus challenged American students' most basic, deeply held beliefs about the nature of human difference. One teacher reported "the apparent relief and surprise of the Negro children in her class as they read *The Races of Mankind*."[7] In contrast, white students sometimes felt compelled to share the reasons they disliked "Negroes," "Japs," Italians, or Jews, among other "racial" minorities. It was not uncommon for a teacher to deliver a lesson on racial tolerance, only to have a student jump out of his seat and shout, as one New Jersey student did after a lesson on the Japanese: "The only solution is to get a tommy-gun and kill them off. The rest is nonsense. There is no room for idealism in this war."[8]

The more Americans performed highly visible, yet reprehensible, acts of racial prejudice during wartime, the more intellectuals and educational reformers dedicated themselves to improving antiprejudice education. "With science as his shield, the educator must bridge our 'great divides,'" proclaimed the African American philosopher Alain Locke to teachers in 1940.[9] Locke, like other scholars dedicated to social justice, believed that "science" with its neutral and authoritative armor would literally shield teachers from criticism as they waged an educational war on racism.[10]

Following the lead of Franz Boas, these activist social scientists and teachers directed the brunt of their "ammunition" against what the anthropologist Ruth Benedict called the "race myth."[11] In other words, they believed that by teaching a particular scientific definition of human race, they would help people understand that race, as an idea, was more a historical and social construction, or myth, than a meaningful way to explain human diversity. Anthropologists wanted Americans to learn that it was the concept of culture, or learned customs in a specific social and historical context, that explained the extraordinary diversity of human life. The anthropologist Margaret Mead played a vital role in popularizing this kind of "intercultural" tolerance education, explaining:

> Intercultural education . . . deals with developing the background, understanding, and skills necessary to understand, in oneself and others, those aspects of behavior which are to be referred to as culture, that is, to the shared learned behavior of a specific society or part of society. It stems directly from popularization of the findings of

anthropologists and psychologists that there are no socially relevant differences among human groups that can be attributed to race, and that the most extreme contrasts in socially relevant capacities can be directly traced to culture.[12]

American teachers seized hold of this new anthropological antiprejudice pedagogy as a powerful weapon in the war against fascism and introduced scientific texts on racial egalitarianism into their classrooms. As a high school teacher in New York City proposed, "Now that the daily headlines have invaded the American classroom with reports of national rivalry and race hatred, we should not barricade ourselves behind routine dictionary work but launch a counterattack for the coming victory of democracy."[13] Mayme Louise Sloat, a science teacher in St. Louis, reiterated, "Science disproves racial superiority and shows that biological differences are slight as compared with cultural differences."[14] Educators in New Jersey agreed, adding, "[Teachers] must meet the poison of race hatred with the inoculation of tolerance. . . . They must arm each child invincibly with the Truth."[15]

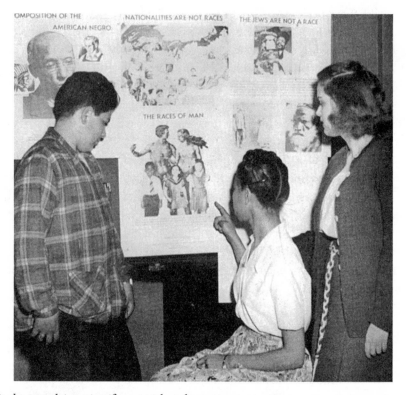

Students studying scientific materials on human race.

In popular new intercultural education textbooks, social scientists suggested classroom practices to help teachers emphasize culture and downplay race. "[Teachers] can select art, music, and literature that will enlarge the children's experience and acquaint them with the cultural contributions of people of various races," read a typical textbook.[16] In this way, teachers taught that each "race" had a special and distinct art, music, and literature. Drawing on more than two decades of antiprejudice education that highlighted the special "cultural gifts" of racial minorities, teachers emphasized the culture concept as a direct rebuttal to racist misperceptions.[17]

By 1954 the rhetorical conflation of race with culture in American schools was complete. This construction of race-as-culture has persisted, with minor alterations, in educational discourse up to the present day, most notably in programs designed to teach multiculturalism.[18] It continues to haunt antiracist initiatives in American schools by inscribing difference as natural while obscuring the social relations of production and the enduring power of racism in a capitalist society.

This book is designed to highlight a period when ideas about race were formed and transformed and to investigate schools as institutions with a special capacity for making race. Studying racialization is a way to call attention to the ideological processes that attach specific meanings to random phenotypic markers, such as skin color or hair texture. These markers are not significant biological distinctions but are used by politically dominant groups who want to naturalize their privileged social positions. In this context, scholars cannot study racial groups like "blacks" and "whites," now widely understood to be historically contingent labels, but rather the racialized identities of minority groups in a continuous state of flux. This approach foregrounds American schools as a race-making institution that perpetuates unequal distribution of wealth, social status, and cultural capital among racialized groups. It also emphasizes the distinct and influential role of teachers in the social construction of race in America.[19]

As the largest state institution dedicated to knowledge production and social reproduction, public schools have influenced how Americans understand not only specific definitions of human race, but also the muted rules of racial etiquette. This study investigates how classroom teachers defined certain racial knowledge and behavior as part of the knowledge set of an "educated" citizen. Even when teachers discussed human race in implicit contexts, the way they approached the subject of race and the meanings they associated with racial difference had the power to shape racial ideologies in America because of teachers' status as authority figures responsible for transmitting a body of state-sanctioned knowledge. No matter what students believed to be the "truth" about race, they learned at a young age what teachers expected them to know about human diversity. It is not that students readily absorbed the lessons on race presented in schools—in fact the opposite seems to be true. Rather, they learned to recognize, and if necessary, to mimic the lessons on race they were taught in school, if only to cash in on the cultural capital of performing as educated American citizens. As an administrator in New York City reflected at the conclusion of a successful "race unit" in 1942:

> The questionnaire administered at the end of the term revealed that the boys improved tremendously in their *verbal* responses concerning Negroes, Italians, Puerto Ricans, and Jews—the groups about which they were asked to state opinions. No member of the Committee would rashly state that the verbal responses necessarily indicated *actual* change in attitude. It is likely that the students merely indicated the answers that they knew the faculty expected them to give.[20]

During World War II American schools demanded the ideal of "tolerance" as a marker of the educated citizen. Teachers reprimanded students for using derogatory racial epithets like nigger, wop, dago, and hunky, and pressured students to demonstrate "good manners" when encountering racial others. Educated American citizens, teachers insisted, did not share the ignorant racialist worldview of fascists and other enemies of democracy. Some teachers put this into idealist terms, suggesting, "Today we must inculcate an enlightened internationalism which teaches that 'Humanity is First.'"[21] Others took a more urgent view of the situation such as the two educators from Oregon who proclaimed, "When the war is over self-respecting Anglo-Saxon nations cannot re-assume their pre-war air of white supremacy and re-assert their right to dominate lands inhabited by people of other races."[22] Inspired by a horrific world war and informed by transnational dialogues on race, democracy, and social justice, American anthropologists and teachers together changed the way that educated Americans spoke about race.

A historical analysis of the social construction of race in schools helps explain how and why World War II had such a powerful influence on race relations and racial ideologies.[23] Leading historians interpret the social justice activism that emerged during the war as a defining feature of a long civil rights movement that originated in the Great Depression and continued into the 1980s.[24] While these studies recognize the important role that public education played in the black freedom struggle, they tend to focus on the drive to equalize public school facilities for black children, improve the salaries and working conditions of black teachers, teach tolerance, and fully desegregate public education.[25] What is missing from this history is how teachers, scientists, and educational reformers worked to transform schools into "arsenals of democracy" that would help undermine racism in the next generation. By insisting that educated Americans know the basic scientific facts of racial difference and by demanding that democratic citizens embody the ideal of racial tolerance, anthropological efforts to reconstruct the race concept helped to cultivate a social climate that recognized the moral righteousness of the black freedom struggle as it exploded onto the national scene after the *Brown* ruling in 1954. The anthropologists, educational administrators, and teachers described in this book, many of them women, were early civil rights warriors who took great risks and tremendous leaps of faith to promote lessons on scientific racial equality to young children, years before the height of the popular civil rights movement. Recovering these stories fleshes out critical details in the history of the civil rights movement, and in particular reveals the important lessons of racial egalitarianism promoted amid a brutal, racialized world war.

Over the first half of the twentieth century, the dominant educational discourse on race changed abruptly as teachers went from teaching about race as nation, to race as color, and finally to race as culture in the years before, during, and after World War II. *Color in the Classroom* is organized to elucidate the ways that activist anthropologists influenced everyday classroom practice. As Chapter 1 demonstrates, between 1900and 1938 American teachers employed the race concept most often to describe European nationals such as Irish, Italians, British, Poles, Greeks, and Russians. Mass immigration and industrialization transformed the purpose and intent of public education during this period. The first explicit discussions on human race took place within Americanization programs designed to assimilate the children of European immigrants in public schools. Teachers tended to conflate race with nation, assuming that people of different national backgrounds shared a racial heritage that determined their potential for intelligence, morality, and health—and ultimately for active citizenship in a democracy. Teachers discussed how the peculiar racial traits of Irish or Italians, for example, determined the best strategies for Americanizing young students. World War I compelled teachers to shift their discussion of "foreigners" living in the United States; when discussing current events in Europe, teachers now had to consider "foreigners" living abroad. Tolerance education blossomed through the interwar period alongside a growing concern with international relations and the rise of fascism. Notably, during this era most of the classroom practice designed to foster tolerance was restricted to *white* racial minorities. Nonwhite minorities remained largely invisible in mainstream teaching journals through the start of World War II. As efforts to encourage tolerance expanded in the late 1930s alongside the rise of fascism, teachers attempted to cultivate understanding for white racial minorities by detailing the wonders of their material culture and historical achievements with the help of a curriculum known as intercultural education.

The onset of war motivated a new group of reformers to turn their attention to the question of how Americans learned racial prejudice. In 1939 the nation's leading scientific expert on race, Franz Boas, interrogated the relationship between public schools and racial equality, academic freedom, and democracy. Boas was provoked when the Chamber of Commerce of the State of New York hired a prominent eugenicist to write a widely publicized report that denounced urban New Yorkers as racially unfit for academic education in the public schools. State legislators cited this report as scientific proof that people from eastern and southern Europe were intellectually inferior to Caucasians, and slashed funding for a public educational system already decimated by ten years of economic depression. As Chapter 2 shows, Boas argued that schools must be fortified as sites of academic freedom and racial tolerance. He believed that public schools must preserve the ideal of academic freedom so that teachers and students would be able to evaluate the evidence marshaled by eugenicists, among others. Boas felt confident that if teachers openly examined scientific data they would find that race, while real, did not determine intelligence or behavior. Boas's insights on the connections between academic freedom, public education, democracy, and racial equality formed the theoretical basis for the race education reform initiative that followed. Summing up a lifetime of research and activism, Boas wanted teachers and students to understand that the anthropological concept of culture offered the best potential for explaining human diversity, not the biological concept of race.

From the ranks of anthropology and other social sciences, liberal intellectuals heeded Boas's cry to reform race education in the nation's primary and secondary schools. Chapter 3 evaluates the reforms proposed by two of Boas's most well-known and influential students, Ruth Benedict and Margaret Mead. They imagined schools as institutions capable of undermining racism and promoting a more just and equitable American democracy, but pursued this goal through very different strategies. Benedict, more critical than Mead, challenged the concepts of race and culture as they were used in schools and wrote scientific texts designed to reeducate Americans on the scientific truth about human difference. While she supported intercultural education, Benedict openly criticized the curriculum's potential to ignore social class inequalities and downplay the function of power within race relations. Benedict was particularly infuriated by the essentialist definition of culture promoted by intercultural education and worked diligently to reform existing race and culture concepts.

In contrast, Mead supported the kind of quaint cultural celebrations that Benedict despised. She joined intercultural educators in devising lesson plans that celebrated ethnic and racial difference in terms of cultural variations on white, middle-class norms. Mead argued that the most effective way to undermine racism in schools was through racial integration in the classroom, not explicit discussions of it. To this end, she helped found and run an experimental racially integrated school in New York City and worked through nonprofit organizations to train teachers to conduct "neighborhood home festivals," where participants would share cultural traditions such as food, song, and folk dance. While Benedict's pedagogy was more theoretically rigorous and had greater potential to undermine racism, Mead's pedagogy was more appealing and ultimately more accessible to teachers. The chapter concludes by looking at why Benedict's definition of race and Mead's definition of culture had such lasting influence on dominant racial discourse in American schools.

Following this consideration of the anthropological movement to reform race education, the next chapter returns to classrooms to analyze the impact of this initiative. Chapter 4, "Race as Color, 1939–1945," follows teachers' dramatically altered conception of human race during the war years. This transformation was brought about by anthropological activism, along with the rising visibility of an African American movement for social justice and deteriorating race relations between white and black Americans. Reflecting Boasian definitions of human race, teachers altered their language to assert that all people of European descent were members of the same "Caucasian" or white race. This had the effect of recasting previously racialized white minorities as members of the dominant racial majority while hardening the racial distinction between "white" people and those who were "colored." With this revised conception of race-as-color, it no longer made sense for teachers to direct tolerance education at European minorities who were no longer "racial" minorities. Instead they began targeting wartime tolerance education at the problem of how to "tolerate" blacks and Asians, and to a lesser extent American Indians and Mexican Americans. Not only were European immigrant groups no longer the subject of tolerance education, according to anthropologists they were no longer racial minorities at all.

While tolerance education remained popular in the immediate postwar years, it expired quickly in the emerging cold war, as Chapter 5 illustrates. During this period, teachers became reluctant to utter the word "race" in the classroom. Not only did they risk losing their jobs if they taught racial equality during the cold war, but they imagined that by not mentioning race in the classroom they were living up to a new and more desirable colorblind ideal. In many ways the logical extension of the anthropological claim that individuals of all races are truly equal, the colorblind ideal asked people to downplay the significance of race in order to diffuse the impact of racism. Inside of schools, teachers believed that the best way to mitigate racism was not to teach scientific lessons on the meaning of race or otherwise dwell on the subject of racial difference, but instead to support the desegregation of American schools, workplaces, and public spaces. Teachers emphasized the importance of good manners in racially mixed company and encouraged students to internalize these lessons in order to perform as properly educated citizens. To perform the colorblind ideal, educators began referring to African Americans, Asian Americans, American Indians, and Latinos as "cultural" minorities, not "racial" minorities, a rhetorical move that obscured the enduring significance of race in America and blinded both teachers and students to the existence of structural racism. Because teachers refused to openly discuss race, racial difference, and racial minorities in the postwar era, the dominant educational discourse on race stagnated in American schools.

Brown v. Board of Education in 1954 marked the culmination of a deliberately colorblind racial discourse in American schools. This landmark Supreme Court case signaled the ascendancy of a new antiprejudice pedagogy advocating the idea that attending schools in racially integrated settings would diminish racism and promote educational equality. There was no need, educators reasoned, to make the message of racial equality explicit. Indeed, teachers after 1948 hardly mentioned the word "race" in their writing, sometimes simply referring to people of African and Asian descent as cultural anomalies on the American landscape. As passionate debates on tolerance pedagogy receded in the postwar era, the idea of culture as a surrogate for race endured.

This study reveals that the social construction of race in schools is not merely a reflection of larger cultural phenomena or the result of "natural" social processes, but the product of individual social scientists, professional educators, and teachers with the power to influence how schools mark particular ideas about race as defining characteristics of an educated citizenry. Reflecting on the manifestation of culture as a proxy for race in contemporary educational theory and practice, the conclusion suggests that the project of race education reform as laid out by anthropologists in the 1930s continues to have the power to fight racism through American schools.

1

Race as Nation, 1900–1938

I think one of the worthiest things the history teacher can do is emphasize the good that has come from other races than our own.
—History Teacher, 1909

How then, ebony Narcissa Larkins and blond Helma Pekkarrinnen, are
your junior high school teachers to lead you gently but firmly and
kindly toward peace and harmony and even brotherly love within the
four walls of your classroom?
—English Teacher, 1933

Writing in the first issue of *The History Teacher's Magazine* in 1909, Dr. William
Fairley, a teacher at Commercial High School in Brooklyn, described his progressive efforts to relate the study of ancient history to the modern lives of the
students before him. He presented human history as a prolonged struggle from
the earliest days of brute savagery to the enlightened state of contemporary
American society. He elaborated, "The great development of civilization
among the peoples we are to study, of course implies long preparatory ages of
slow and bitter struggle upward from savagery." According to Fairley, while
many groups had progressed from the lowest developmental stage of savagery
to the highest stage of civilization, others remained mired in an unseemly state
of savagery and were not worthy of academic study in American high schools.
"Why do we begin west of the Indian peninsula, and ignore the Hindoos, the
Chinese, and Japanese?" he asked rhetorically. "Because these peoples are out of
the great stream of development. The progressive life of to-day's world owes little
to them, if anything."[1]

Drawing on dominant racial paradigms of the day, teachers like Fairley
believed that certain races, such as Anglo-Saxons, were biologically endowed
with the intelligence and resourcefulness to evolve to higher levels of civilization,
while others lacked these inherent capabilities and thus remained hopelessly

savage. Racialist models of human history like this one led many turn-of-the-century Americans to view millions of recent immigrants as inherently unfit for citizenship in a democracy. Public schools became a key site to re-form certain immigrants for potential citizenship. Americanizing white racial minorities would define the dominant discourse on race in public schools from 1900 to 1938.

Fairley, for example, insisted that teachers could apply the "obvious test of color" to determine which immigrants had the potential for citizenship. Only those immigrants who happened to be "white" passed this test, even though Fairley—like most of his contemporaries—viewed these white immigrant children as belonging to different racial subgroups.[2] To help assimilate these students and make them more tolerable to their "native" white classmates, Fairley recommended lessons on the "good that had come from other races than our own" such as fine art, musical accomplishments, scientific discoveries, and great literature from European nations.[3]

Many American teachers from 1900 to 1938 heeded the advice of teachers like Fairley and applied the test of color to determine which minorities were worth Americanizing. Racial discourse in American schools during this period, therefore, was almost entirely limited to those racial minorities who happened to be "white." Within this subset of potential citizens, teachers used the concept of race to differentiate people from various European countries. While color distinguished between white and nonwhite groups in a way that had very clear racial implications, the most salient application of the race concept in American schools was to describe and interpret various peoples of European descent. In this way, certain minority groups benefited from their color-status as white even as they were denigrated for their supposed racial shortcomings. The way teachers constructed race-as-nation was therefore somewhat different from other racial paradigms of the day. For instance, American teachers did not distinguish between racial or color variations *within* European nations the way the federal government did on immigration and naturalization documents, or the way that certain minority groups themselves, such as Italian Americans, did.[4]

Tracing how teachers constructed a dominant discourse on race-as-nation through everyday practice, this chapter argues that two distinct but interrelated phenomena influenced the social production of race in schools: Americanization and transnational dialogue. Both shaped how teachers viewed their work as professional educators and how they understood the function of public education in a modern democracy. Even within the transformative social and political contexts of World War I, immigration restriction, the Great Depression, and the rise of Nazism, teachers remained for the most part fixated on the subject of white racialized minorities and their so-called "cultural gifts."

Foreigners at Home

Public education expanded over the course of the early twentieth century in part because so many citizens believed in the special ability of schools to Americanize the millions of European immigrants and their children who arrived between the 1880s and the passage of immigration restriction in 1924. Not only could schools teach these "foreign" children reading, writing, and arithmetic, but they could also teach the English language and a work ethic that would prepare better workers. As an editor of the *Washington Post* opined in 1914, "It would be poor national economy to turn healthy white immigrants back from our ports simply because they could not read or write."[5]

Americanization programs, intended to embrace European immigrants and ease their transition into mainstream society, were considered progressive, liberal, and even kind. Nevertheless, teachers struggled with the tension between preserving certain worthwhile elements of immigrants' heritage—such as language or artwork—and eliminating these markers of difference altogether.

Teaching journals illustrate the different ways that teachers struggled to make sense of these competing mandates to assimilate foreign children. In 1913 a teacher at Washington Irving High School in New York City published "The Foreigner in Our Schools: Some Aspects of the Problem in New York." In this article, Helen Cohen offered a compassionate portrayal of European immigrant students even as she classified these children as a "problem" for teachers. Cohen reported that white children of foreign parentage had a higher literacy rate than white children of native parentage, and then used this statistic to emphasize the potential strengths of European immigrants in America. According to her, Americanization programs should help students "conserve the best of his own heritage for the benefit of the country which he is to make his home." She continued: "The conservation of all that is worthy in the old life is undertaken as a foundation on which to base the structure of the new."[6]

Cohen's perspective on Americanization programs mirrored the progressive efforts of social reformers and settlement house workers who believed that the fastest way to assimilate immigrants was to appreciate, not denigrate, peculiar Old World traits.[7] In 1913 this route to Americanization was officially sanctioned by the U.S. Commissioner of Education, who instructed teachers to "respect [immigrants'] ideals and preserve and strengthen all of the best of their Old World life they bring with them."[8] This strategy contradicted years of Americanization efforts dedicated to eliminating these undesirable markers of foreignness. Motivated by fear and inspired by potential radicalism and discontent among newly arrived workers, other educators emphasized strict obedience to the law as the groundwork of true citizenship.[9] As Theodore Roosevelt wrote of immigrants a decade earlier, "We must Americanize them in every way, in speech, in political ideals and principles, and in their way of looking at the relations between Church and State."[10] Even politicians like Roosevelt, who imagined European immigrants could be assimilated into mainstream American society, never imagined they would do so while retaining aspects of their Old World language or customs.[11] For a brief window of time before World War I, however, some educators began to question this strict disciplinary approach to Americanization and instead encouraged educators to use positive examples of immigrant lifeways to encourage voluntary assimilation among immigrant students.[12]

In a sympathetic classroom like Cohen's in New York City, students had the opportunity to learn English, civics, and practical steps for acquiring meaningful citizenship in America. As Cohen explained:

> The foreigner is warned against the dangers of unreliable banks, of unlicensed employers who underpay their help, and of unscrupulous business methods; and, on the other hand, he is taught about the right sort of banks and employment agencies, about the prevailing rates of wages and of the need of a certain amount of business training before going into business.[13]

Cohen led students through exercises in reading comprehension, vocabulary, colloquial conversation, and American-style pronunciation and intonation. Students wrote an essay on the subject, "What the Foreign Child Can Contribute to the English Work in American Schools." Cohen was so pleased with the student responses that she quoted them at length in her article. These responses reflected her attempt to balance preservation of certain elements of immigrant life against the larger goal of expanding and improving American "civilization." For example, one student wrote:

> The purpose of the study of English, as of every other branch, is the progress of civilization, and civilization will attain its culmination only when the perfect things, the traditions, the ideas, and the customs of every corner of the world are combined to form what might be called super-perfection.[14]

The *History Teacher's Magazine* detailed other progressive Americanization strategies, such as citywide "citizenship receptions" for newly naturalized immigrants and handbills distributed by schoolchildren and Boy Scouts advertising English classes for adults.[15] Not all teachers imagined that select traditions, ideas, and customs could be culled from each immigrant group and combined in order to reach "super-perfection" of American civilization, however.

After the United States joined World War I, educators and politicians designed new ways for schools to contribute to the war effort. One impact of the war was the immediate contraction of the range of acceptable "foreign" expression in American classrooms.[16] As a school administrator in New Jersey complained, "The influx of foreigners, with their divergent personal ideals and antagonistic racial traits, imposes upon the schools an infinitely difficult problem."[17]

Administrators and school boards instructed teachers to demand "100% Americanism" in an attempt to inculcate patriotism and loyalty in a nation with a large immigrant population.[18] Public schools became sites of skirmishes between competing groups vying for control of wartime education.[19] Local groups like the Chamber of Commerce and Rotary Clubs fought with branches of the National Education Association and newly formed groups like the National Board for Historical Service to determine course content on the war.

Politicians pressured American teachers to assimilate "foreigners" living in the United States as a primary duty of wartime education. Evidence of this pressure was soon visible in teaching journals. Writing after the U.S. entry into the war, an administrator in the Detroit Public Schools reflected on the serious problems of foreign "races" in his rapidly growing city:

> High wages, coupled with the promise of constant labor, have brought a tremendous number of foreigners to the city. These have rapidly colonized among previous arrivals of their race and have changed nothing but their habits of work. Ignorant of the English language, of American customs and ideals, they have helped to swell the so-called "hyphenated" class.[20]

Like the earlier article from New York City, this one detailed the important role of public schools in assimilating European immigrants, describing the courses offered in American "geography, history, federal, state, county, and city government and a study of the Constitution."[21] The tone of this article, however, posed Americanization more as a punitive, disciplinary policy than a kind-hearted movement to assimilate outsiders to American norms. It also reconfigured Americanization campaigns in schools in terms of their function in a time of war. According to the author, "It took the present world-conflict to bring forcibly home to thinking Americans the danger within the country" posed by foreign colonies on American soil. The solution was to "weld the many peoples of any community into one body politic and create throughout the nation the unity and power that come from common ideals, a common language, and a uniform interpretation of citizenship."[22]

Even after Armistice in 1918, teachers continued to promote 100% Americanism. In 1920, Ella Thorngate, an English teacher in Omaha, joined her colleague from Detroit in demanding sure and swift assimilation of problematic foreigners. "The answer is given in the word 'Americanization'; that is, the use of *one language* and the *same ideals*."[23] According to this teacher, the problem with immigrants was that they were handicapped by ignorance of American law and customs. She portrayed these handicaps as potentially dangerous and as directly tied to racial identity:

> Unless these handicaps are removed he becomes a menace to society and the state. By removing these handicaps, protecting and helping him, and finally by encouraging the development of latent racial and personal talents, he becomes a useful and valuable citizen.[24]

Teachers wanted to balance concerns about the potential menace of immigrants in America with the broader role of teachers and education to protect, develop, and encourage young students. Like many Americans in the early twentieth century, Thorngate assumed the children of European immigrants possessed both talents and deficits associated with their racial background. She proposed a form of classroom instruction where teachers could identify and use these racial traits to effectively assimilate immigrant students.

Teachers' frequent use of the race concept in their discussion of European immigrants during World War I and the immediate interwar period coincided with a period of heightened racism and xenophobia. The landmark film *Birth of a Nation* brought Thomas Dixon's racist tract *The Clansman* to the broader American public in 1915. Around the same time the Ku Klux Klan organized a major revival directed not only at African Americans in the South, but at "hyphenated Americans" of every kind. Meanwhile, Americans interpreted World War I as a direct consequence of the particular racial character of the Germans.[25]

The Ascendancy of Cultural Gifts

Popular racialist fantasies culminated in immigration restriction in 1924 that employed eugenics science to limit the percentages of immigrants from each country. These laws effectively cut off immigration from eastern and southern Europe, geographic locations that many Americans associated with inferior racial populations, while reserving the greatest proportion of immigration slots for people from western Europe.[26] Americanization programs lost much of their urgency and softened their strict disciplinary approach in the public schools once the danger of unchecked immigration from eastern and southern Europe passed. The idea of cultural gifts gained currency as teachers asserted that the best way to assimilate foreigners was to respect carefully selected aspects of immigrant heritage. In American schools, the cultural gifts movement blossomed in a curriculum that would become known as intercultural education.[27]

Intercultural education would come to have an especially powerful effect on racial discourse in American schools during World War II because it was the largest and most well-known educational curriculum designed to promote racial tolerance and intergroup harmony. Developed in the 1920s and 1930s, intercultural education would come to shape tolerance education in American schools through the 1940s and 1950s, carrying with it outdated and oversimplified conceptions of culture that were crafted by educators who lacked an adequate foundation in social science models of race and culture.

Intercultural education is attributed to Rachel Davis DuBois, a liberal white Quaker who invented the curriculum as a high school teacher in New Jersey in 1924. Importantly, DuBois was not trained in anthropology; she promoted what is best understood as a popular definition of culture, which was theoretically distinct from the scientific definition of culture offered by anthropologists like Franz Boas. Boas defined culture as a society's complex response to given environmental, historical, social, and political circumstances that made meaning in individuals' everyday lives. A group of people living together in a given geographic location could share a culture—or way of viewing the world—that was constantly changing and adapting to new circumstances. DuBois simplified culture to signify the visible elements of a minority group that stood in contrast to American norms. If people ate food that seemed strange, wore unusual clothing or hairstyles, or performed odd dances and dissonant songs, DuBois explained these affectations as cultural differences between minority groups and the dominant white Protestant majority in America.

Intercultural educators attempted to resignify these negative attributes in positive terms, often highlighting these traits as distinct "gifts" to American culture. Notably, DuBois assumed that all members of a given minority group (alternatively defined as national, ethnic, religious, or racial) shared a culture no matter their geographic location or socioeconomic background. Cultural integrationists like DuBois imagined that American culture would be redefined and ultimately improved by absorbing the best traits of immigrant heritage. Culture in this sense was seen as fluid—a process of becoming.[28] Conversely, in DuBois's attempt to identify immigrant attributes worth preserving, intercultural education had the unintended consequence of reifying culture in static and essentialist terms. This construction of cultural difference attempted to substitute positive stereotypes for negative ones, and failed to challenge or even address the social, political, and economic inequalities that perpetuated the "cultural" distinctiveness of many racial, ethnic, and religious minorities in the United States.

Sympathetic educational reformers like DuBois believed it was better to help immigrant groups help themselves than to force immigrants to assimilate to white Protestant norms. This represented an important theoretical development and, along with new laws that restricted immigration, helped shift the tide from the disciplinary "100% Americanization" campaigns of early twentieth-century schools to more subtle programs of assimilation like intercultural education. Many reformers encouraged immigrant groups to celebrate their unique heritage through folk dancing, traditional arts, and even citywide folk festivals. Not only did such celebrations improve the damaged self-esteem of immigrants and their children, thus making them more amenable to assimilation, but it also helped soften the virulent racism against immigrant groups visible in immigration restriction, the eugenics movement, the rebirth of the Ku Klux Klan, and other racist populist movements in the 1920s.[29]

By the late 1920s the cultural gifts movement had begun to alter Americanization campaigns in the public schools. To take one example, in 1927 Hazel Poole published "Americanizing the Teacher of English" in the *English Journal*, asking colleagues to recognize the value of "rich and varied backgrounds of these children with 'no backgrounds.'"[30] According to Poole, Americanization programs were successful, but she faulted them for their "synthetic" production of new American citizens. She challenged Americanization programs that forced children to give up their charming traditional lifeways, and instead wanted to help students learn to assimilate at their own pace. She proposed a new "organic" Americanization program, which would ease immigrants into a voluntary process of assimilation. In another example, a teacher educator from Ohio State University reflected, "it would seem that true Americanization can never be intelligently carried out until we have first seriously investigated what the foreigner brought with him, and the effect he has had on our political and social history."[31]

Teachers' essays reveal the challenges that celebrating cultural gifts could create in the classroom. For example, Poole described how her class read "articles about the occupations and achievements of various races in this country."[32] As was typical of lessons on Americanization, the teacher used the word "race" to distinguish between different European nationalities. Asking a Greek student to report on the achievements of the Greeks, Poole was surprised when the student was reluctant to participate. Instead of basking in the glory of his group's achievements as she expected, she recounted that he was "sullen" and replied: "I'd rather report on something else. I don't want to stand up there and talk about the Greeks." Upon reflection, Poole decided that it was humiliating "to hear yourself talking, in a half-strange tongue, about yourself or your race before these people, as if you were a curious kind of sideshow at the circus."[33]

Poole's criticism foreshadowed an important critique of tolerance education that emerged in the 1940s, when educators and academics challenged intercultural education for singling out second- and third-generation immigrants and forcing them to identify with a folk culture they knew nothing about.

Well-meaning teachers like Poole asked their students to perform an objectified version of a particular "racial" identity based on achievements in the arts or sciences that students themselves may not have valued at all. Unlike many teachers, Poole adjusted her classroom practice accordingly and devised new ways to speak of minority races in positive terms. She reported that her most successful activity was an "International Number" of the school paper, where her students wrote essays describing their experiences growing up in another country. The teacher was delighted with the results, and described to readers:

> An Italian boy pictured the three-day feast of St. Gennaro as he had seen it in Italy. A Canadian girl described the celebration of Empire Day, and a pupil of Czechoslovakian descent told how Easter Monday was kept in her parents' village. Others drew on their parents' experience for their accounts of St. Patrick's Day in Ireland, St. John's Day in Sweden, and the picturesque procession of floats used to celebrate a Swiss national holiday.[34]

As this example suggests, efforts to promote the cultural gifts of white racialized minorities tended to create generic and even stereotypical conceptions of minority groups. Teachers emphasized America as a "Melting Pot" of European immigrants and asked students to make posters and dolls that celebrated the folkways of each nation. Teachers such as Hazel Poole envisioned an American society that changed and expanded to include the new "gifts" brought by recent immigrants. Importantly, she repeatedly used the term "race" to delineate between various European immigrant groups, but she did not use the term "culture" even when describing aspects of immigrant life that people would later come to understand as cultural. Instead, she painstakingly, although somewhat vaguely, tried to convey an interest in her students' "background," or "this Europe of theirs as they and their parents knew it" or even "things which are familiar to him."

Foreigners Abroad

As the urgency of assimilating European immigrants faded, teachers became more concerned with foreign people living abroad. Teaching about world history and international affairs changed the way teachers presented the concepts of race and culture in the classroom. Working to portray foreign nations and their inhabitants in a more sympathetic light, teachers began to downplay what they at first identified as racial deficits of foreign peoples and instead highlighted the "gifts" these nations had contributed to Western civilization. Because the

Students creating an exhibit on the "Melting Pot" that included posters and dolls.
Courtesy New York City Municipal Archives.

motivation for teaching about foreigners came from international events, teachers tended to devise lessons that considered people of different nations in turn. This overlapped with and amplified a racial discourse that tended to associate race with nation.

During World War I, intellectuals and politicians bemoaned the ignorance of the American public concerning world affairs. They feared that this lack of knowledge would make Americans look provincial and uneducated, and so they worked to foster a more cosmopolitan and sophisticated outlook for future citizens through education in world geography, history, and literature. As early as 1917, a high school teacher from San Diego fretted, "The almost pathetic provincialism of the average American is very generally reflected in the boys and girls of our secondary schools."[35] In 1917 the National Education Association proposed a new program of study in world history to further "international spirit" among American students.[36] Over the course of the war, this view was refined as educators imagined new ways to use the study of world history to promote a stronger American patriotism that specifically valued "Anglo-Saxon" heritage. As New York City Superintendent Dr. William L. Ettinger clarified for teachers, "The present titanic war has made our Anglo-Saxon civilization conscious of its ideals as contrasted with a Teutonic swashbuckler 'Kultur,' which threatened to impose upon us our allies a sordid militarism."[37] Teachers were to teach American students more about world history, but the point was to emphasize the superiority of "Anglo-Saxon" traditions.

History teachers responded quickly with lesson plans on European countries and ethnic groups, as well as studies of more exotic locales ranging from Asia to the West Indies.[38] Lesson plans in history are particularly revealing for the way they presented European national groups as distinct races with their own inherent mental traits. A typical passage describing a history lesson on Central Europe in 1917 read:

> Finally we have various peoples of non-Aryan origin—Hungarians and Roumanians [sic]. These races show their nomadic, Asiatic origin in their individualism, their quickness to adapt themselves to outsde [sic] civilization together with their inability to create for themselves. They have had many able men as leaders whom they have alternately lauded and crucified. Extremely likeable and extremely unreliable—they are in a way the spoilt children of Europe.[39]

Teachers interpreted foreign nations in terms of the racial traits of their inhabitants—such as the inability to create for themselves or being unreliable—that simultaneously explained and determined the nation's supposed inferiority.

Such blatantly demeaning portrayals of other nations would change abruptly after World War I. The declaration of International Good-Will Day in 1923 prompted a new rash of articles with variations on the theme "the peoples of the world have become our neighbors."[40] English teachers took the lead in this initiative, in part because they articulated a special ability to meet the demands for "international-mindedness," usually by reading and discussing stories and poems from other lands.[41] As one teacher reasoned, English teachers were suited for this special task because of "the peculiar service of literature—to make us *know* the heart of humanity, and knowing, to keep us from hate."[42] Similarly, in an article in the *Elementary English Review* entitled "International Friendship through Children's Books" the author cautioned, "Some books like narrow, pinched experiences may be the source of blind prejudice and intolerance." Many articles featured bibliographies dedicated to "giving children right kind of prejudice," or in other words, training them in the desirable and undesirable attributes of foreigners.[43]

Many teachers conceived of international education as a natural expansion of the peace movement.[44] In 1925 a children's librarian from the Brooklyn Public Library made a dramatic appeal for the teaching of "international friendship" as a key process in securing world peace:

Peace is no inert and spineless angel who will let us fool ourselves with safety devices into thinking the world "safe for democracy." We must first teach our children to be friends with the stranger, both within our gates and across the seas. Until the spirit of friendliness has united all the children of mankind national antagonisms and hatreds will continue to dominate governments.[45]

Two teachers writing from Gary, Indiana, and Chicago, Illinois, agreed and designed a bibliography of children's books on Latin American countries in 1938, explaining, "In an effort to make children world-conscious through an appreciative understanding of our neighbors, the foremost authors and illustrators of children's literature have devoted their art to portraying foreign countries and people in so fascinating a manner that international barriers may be broken down and long-cherished prejudice dissolved."[46]

Teachers viewed international understanding as an essential component of Americanization in the 1920s and 1930s. Educators wanted to bring all students—not just the children of immigrants—up to speed with what they considered a set of ideals that defined the educated American citizen, including a working knowledge of international affairs. Class work required only a subtle shift from focusing on foreign students *inside* the classroom to focusing on foreign students *outside* the classroom. This was an especially easy transition for teachers who embraced liberal theories of cultural pluralism and who had previous experience promoting the unique gifts of minority groups in America.[47] In many cases the classroom exercises remained the same, as teachers focused on one or more countries and noted their accomplishments in arts, literature, and science. Furthermore, just as teachers crafted earlier programs of Americanization in response to anxiety concerning American security and unity, these revised programs of international study were a direct response to escalating fears of another war.

Along with English teachers, social studies teachers agreed that teaching "international attitudes and understandings" was a necessary component of "education for citizenship" in the United States in the 1920s and 1930s.[48] According to Howard E. Wilson at the University High School in Chicago, "International intercourse and cooperation have become an integral part of our civilization, and any generation which manages civilization with any degree of efficiency must manage international relations efficiently."[49] Social studies teachers like Alice Gibbons in Rochester, New York, supervised international-relations clubs to promote the celebration of foreign peoples and nations. Gibbons described how students learned about people of different "racial extractions" during a holiday festival:

Eleven students of eleven different racial extractions explained how Christmas was celebrated in the lands of their ancestors. Each student spoke first in the language the group he represented and then translated his speech into English. They represented the French, German, Greek, Dutch, Japanese, Polish, Ukrainian, Arabian, Italian, Hebrew, and English peoples.[50]

For most teachers, this pedagogy translated into a simplistic celebration of foreign people in terms of material culture and historical accomplishments while at the same time assuming the innate, racial distinctions between people of different national backgrounds. This particular understanding of race, nation, and cultural differences would be forged with the help of intercultural education.

The Growth of Intercultural Education

Intercultural education would become the most important and widely used antiprejudice curriculum in American schools through World War II. The growing popularity of the cultural gifts movement through the 1920s and into the 1930s enabled Rachel Davis DuBois to gain financial and intellectual support for her new curriculum in the early 1930s. DuBois left her teaching position in 1929 to begin graduate work at Teachers College at Columbia University, where she worked with high schools in and around Philadelphia to test the effectiveness of intercultural education on student prejudice.[51] Facing a dearth of materials on the contributions of minority groups to American life, she wrote and assembled her own materials and sought the help of organizations in New York City including the China Institute, the Japan Institute, the Block Publishing Company, the National Association for the Advancement of Colored People (NAACP), and the Urban League.[52] During the 1932–1933 school year she initiated intercultural programs in Washington, DC; Boston; and Englewood, NJ.[53] By the spring of 1933 DuBois was teaching a course on intercultural education at Boston University, and in 1934 she drew on her expansive networks of academic and social support for her work to found the Service Bureau for Intercultural Education.[54]

In the summer of 1934 DuBois proudly displayed what was then ten years of dedicated work. Before 1934 the name "intercultural education" had not yet been coined, and the lesson plans DuBois put on display for her colleagues at Teachers College were part of an exhibit on "Teaching Materials in the Field of International Relations."[55] Shown as part of the World Interdependence Exhibit, these lessons suggest that DuBois imagined tolerance education as part of an international peace movement. The point was not simply to reduce prejudice for minorities at home, but to help Americans learn to understand and appreciate human diversity on a global scale. The *New York Times* reported that the new

Service Bureau for Intercultural Education would "give assistance to elementary and secondary school teachers by arranging assembly and classroom activities which will present a sympathetic viewpoint of the various culture groups of the world." The Service Bureau had already prepared booklets on several "culture groups" including: "the Italian, British, German, Jewish, Negro, Mexican and South American, Far Eastern (Japanese, Chinese, and Korean), Near Eastern (Indian, Persian, Turkish and Armenian), Slavic and Scandinavian."[56]

Through the Service Bureau, DuBois created dozens of lesson plans and sent them out to schools nationwide. By 1939, the General Education Board (GEB), which funded the project, reported that 140 lesson plans were available, each focusing on a different minority group and a particular area of contribution—such as art, literature, science, or music. Between November 1939 and March 1940, 3,116 pieces of literature, consisting of lesson plans as well as radio scripts from the popular radio program *Americans All—Immigrants All* had been mailed to teachers and administrators. Most of these schools were in the northeast, Midwest urban areas, and California, although some materials were sent to all but three states and to international destinations including China and Canada.[57]

Like most classroom teachers, intercultural educators like DuBois viewed race in terms of nation. However, DuBois expanded the curriculum to include nonwhite minorities including Chinese, Indians, Japanese, and even African Americans. According to intercultural educators, all of these minority groups suffered from racial deficits, and therefore lessons directly challenged misconceptions such as: "the Indian people are inherently incapable of governing themselves"; "that Japanese pictures are bizarre and meaningless, primitive and unimportant"; "that the Chinese have not the intelligence to think deeply about life, that the Chinese have little moral sense"; "that all Jews are mercenary"; "that Indian religions are all heathenish"; "that Orientals have no sense of honor."[58] References to the "inherent" capabilities of minorities, their natural "intelligence," "honor," and "morality" and words like "heathen" and "primitive" demonstrate that intercultural education was designed to challenge deeply racist assumptions.

Facing ingrained prejudice that assumed a wide variety of ethnic, racial, and religious groups were biologically inferior, DuBois provided teachers with an unlikely weapon: cultural gifts. Service Bureau lesson plans typically included a brief history of a particular minority group and then described outstanding examples of fine art, literature, or scientific discoveries intended to discredit derogatory stereotypes. DuBois took a given and presumably widespread instance of racial prejudice, such as the belief that the Chinese were uncivilized and amoral, and countered it with examples designed to demonstrate the exact opposite, such as early examples of ironwork, stone bridges, porcelain, paper, various food products, and even "two thousand seven hundred and five volumes on Chinese philosophy" assembled in the year 190 BC.[59] These positive examples were presented as each group's unique culture. Where race signified inherent, biological, and clearly negative traits of a given group of people, culture came to signify the exact opposite in terms of outstanding examples from the arts and sciences.

Blatantly evolutionist and scientifically inaccurate examples of the race concept infused many prewar intercultural lesson plans, such as the unit on Italian art and history that tried to counteract the notion that Italians belonged to an inferior "savage" race. The material teachers were supposed to use to counteract this stereotype read:

> In the first place while retaining some of the follies and stupidities of the savage, the Italians appear to have kept not a little of his virtues . . . The savage is of necessity simple in his methods of satisfying his natural wants; however improvident or greedy he may be, he cannot indulge to any great extent in the luxuries of the table, for instance, for he knows too little of cooking and has access to too few and not sufficiently varied supplies of food. He is capable of following not merely brute instinct and preferring to live with his herd, but of showing real devotion in furthering to the best of his knowledge and ability, the interests of his community.[60]

This text continued to explain the rise of Roman civilization as intelligent "borrowing" from other "races" including the Etruscans and the Greeks. This excerpt elevated Italians slightly above the level of brute savage, but failed to challenge the assumption that Italians were inherently distinct from "native" white Americans. Thus, even as intercultural educators worked to counteract negative stereotypes, some of their materials reinforced essentialist racialist misconceptions.

While intercultural educators in the interwar period struggled with, or more commonly, avoided articulating a clear definition of race, they were more confident with their understanding of culture. DuBois believed a positive view of minority group culture could counteract existing Americanization programs that demanded complete assimilation to white middle-class norms. In 1936 DuBois criticized these disciplinary curricula, writing, "It was assumed that an individual could with ease drop those customs, traditions and even language which are basic to personality, much as one might change a dress." In contrast, she explained, "Changes come slowly. . . . Differences in culture persist."[61] She offered what she viewed as a more humane process to ease immigrants and minorities into American culture, one that, importantly, included expanding American culture to adopt carefully selected aspects of minority life. While her expansive model of assimilation was liberal for the time, her more concrete definition of culture was static and limited to material expressions. Thus traditions such as festivals or religious celebrations, customs like eating with chopsticks or making lace, and language became the defining elements not only of a given culture group, but more importantly, of the individuals associated with this group. Although the definition of culture forged by DuBois and other intercultural educators in the early 1930s may have been problematic, it would come to have a powerful influence on the dominant educational discourse on race over the course of the next decade.

The Growing Popularity of the Culture Concept

In the early 1930s American teachers began to use the word "culture" to describe a society's way of life in terms of artwork, literature, history, food, clothing, and special holidays and traditions. However, because each nationality group was understood as racially distinct, the concepts of race and culture overlapped from their earliest usage in teaching journals. For instance, in 1932 a teacher at Theodore Roosevelt High School in Des Moines, Iowa, described how her class came to study the specific cultures of various foreign races. Her English students began by considering the unique "contributions—literary, social, and political—by England to us." Her class soon discovered, however, "the fact that other peoples also had contributed greatly to our advancement and culture."[62] Next the teacher invited students to conduct a study of a foreign country of their choice. She noted in passing that the students selected topics based on their "literary, language, vocational, travel, and racial interests." In this case, a few students elected to study the countries they or their parents originated from, for example, "three chose Scotland because their ancestors came from there."[63] Thus, "race" continued to differentiate among national groups in Europe in this teacher's mind. Promoting the theme of international goodwill, the students composed and mailed letters to children in other nations. She reported, "We have had enthusiastic replies from Lausanne, Paris, Düsseldorf, Cologne, London, Glasgow, Wales, Edinburgh, Australia, Egypt, Czecho-Slovakia, and Spain." Next, the students composed a book on their chosen country that reflected "a study of the people, with emphasis on their cultural life."[64] Indeed, the teacher's description of her students' work reflected a growing awareness of the culture concept and its potential to challenge prejudice:

> As they read, occasions arose for the discussion of the factors which mold a people and the differences which develop because of these factors; the realization that differences do not necessarily indicate inferiority came as a natural conclusion.[65]

The introduction of the culture concept into educational discourse on human diversity did not immediately disrupt existing racialist notions. For instance, a 1931 essay, "Racial Elements in American History Textbooks," carefully delineated the "racial" characteristics of various European nations. Responding to the alarmist claim that American history textbooks were "Pro-British" in a way that denigrated the United States, this Iowa City teacher examined ten high school textbooks to examine their treatment of the following "racial" groups: English, Germans, Scotch-Irish, Italians, and Poles. Thyra Carter discovered that "the non-English groups" were not treated fairly by American history textbooks, which tended to ignore the contributions these minority groups had made to "the upbuilding of the American nation."[66] Carter elaborated, "By this statement I do not wish to be understood to mean that a writer in his chronicle should detract from the achievements of the English racial stock, but I merely wish to express the belief that textbook writers of the future, narrating the complete and true story of the development of the United States, will take into more consideration all racial elements going to make up the warp and woof of the American people and nation."[67]

American educators became interested in whether or not current educational practices helped or hindered a richer, more sympathetic study of minority groups. Writing two years later, a college professor at the North Dakota Teachers College asked rhetorically, "Do We Teach Racial Intolerance?" Her answer was an emphatic yes. Emily Baker described her experience sitting in on a fifth grade history class as they studied the Huns. Baker recoiled in horror as a teacher elicited the following comments from her students:

> The Huns have thick lips and flat noses.
> They lived in small, dirty houses.
> They all ate out of one dish on the floor.
> They ate with their fingers, too.
> They were cruel to other people.[68]

Rising from her seat in the back of the classroom, Baker asked the class how many students were related to the Huns. She reported, "As was to be expected, not one acknowledged relationship to such a race." From there, Baker astonished the class with the simple declaration, "I am," and then traced the route of the Huns across Europe and explained their descendants are to be found across Europe and Scandinavia. Her point was to demonstrate that the "race" of Huns was intermingled with "the land of [the students'] forebears," drawing a hereditary link between these students and the group they denigrated as inferior.[69] In cases where it was less feasible to highlight a biological connection between students and the minority group they were studying, Baker proposed presenting a group's positive attributes. For example, she bemoaned the fact that so many teachers presented the Spanish colonists in America as "cruel" and instead wanted teachers to emphasize that "the Spanish missions from which radiated to the brothers of the Incas the enlightening influences of Spanish culture and good will."[70]

These examples illuminate how and why teachers began to emphasize so-called cultural traits in the classroom. Teachers drew directly on the cultural gifts movement that was expanding though schools, settlement houses, and parent education magazines in order to promote a more fashionable pedagogy.[71] In order to encourage an appreciation of these different cultural groups, teachers asked students to dress up in the folk costumes of their ancestral lands for special events. These images come from the annual report of the New York City Board of Education in 1938–1939. The caption under the photo of the child identified as "the Sheik" read: "As part of the teaching of democracy children are some-times asked to wear to school the costumes of their native land. This young man is proud of his ancestry."[72] By fostering appreciation for minority groups teachers also believed they created stronger feelings of self-worth in minority students, all of which was suppose to aid the "teaching of democracy."

Students dressed in folk costumes to represent the "Children of Many Lands." Courtesy New York City Municipal Archives.

A New York City school celebrating the heritage of its diverse student body. This student was dressed as "the Sheik." Courtesy New York City Municipal Archives.

Articles from the 1930s show that teachers shaped tolerance education as a dichotomy between negative, undesirable racial traits and positive, laudatory cultural traits. In the process, race and culture were woven together because they referred to the same ideological constructs. If certain minority groups were stigmatized for their racial deficits, then these same groups could be uplifted by celebrating their cultural gifts. Inside the classroom, cultural achievements became an antidote for racial shortcomings. Confusion over race and culture permeated the educational literature from this period, so that at times it is difficult to understand what teachers meant by either concept. For example an English teacher from Des Moines, Iowa, reasoned: "We must gather together the experiences of the races and the contributions of the peoples, the common backgrounds and the cultures which have marked the progress of the race, and weave them into a foundation for the instruction of the young in international and interracial understanding and co-operation."[73]

Teachers' bewilderment concerning the distinctions between race and culture would only deepen in the early 1940s as activist scientists challenged the basis for scientific racism and asserted the importance of cultural relativism. As early as 1935 articles in *The Social Studies* reference the work of Franz Boas and other anthropologists, showing that social studies teachers were beginning to make connections between anthropology and tolerance education. For example, a social studies teacher in New York City used the anthropological definitions of race and culture, citing specifically Boas's work to challenge "ethnocentrism" among American students. Noting that many people relied on theories of racial difference to assert their superiority over others, he argued that students must be presented with "facts" on race and culture as scientists understood them. This author explained that once men were forced to acknowledge that racial differences were not a viable explanation for group differences "we find men taking customary recourse to a general depreciation of each other's cultures."[74] This article is significant not only because it marked the first time an educator cited anthropological theories to challenge intolerance, but also because it revealed the confusion this pedagogical approach could foster. It was far too easy, this teacher explained, for prejudiced people to translate their disdain for another group's racial heritage to an equally powerful disdain for their cultural heritage.

Even as they attempted to cultivate respect for racial minorities, teachers first had to account for the fact that students understood minority groups as culturally as well as racially inferior. Introducing a lesson on cultural gifts, another teacher observed: "Students confessed to amazing misconceptions concerning other races that were cleared by wide reading. Mexico suggested sleepy people, Indians, treachery, and countless revolutions." Still, teachers hoped that by introducing a sympathetic perspective on the lives of these racial minorities, they would begin to undermine harsh stereotypes. Through "wide reading" on Mexicans and Indians, the same teacher observed that her students "learned to recognize that a foreign civilization was not necessarily inferior because it was different."[75] These were early lessons on cultural relativism, to be sure. They just happened to cast culture as a foil to race.

African Americans: A Nationless Race

Lessons on "interracial" understanding from 1900 to 1938 largely targeted white minority groups such as Germans, Poles, and Irish. In part this was because teachers understood lessons on foreigners as a practical response to World War I, which focused attention on Europe and to some extent Central and South America. It also reflected, however, the extent of white supremacy and racism in the United States that fostered a climate where teachers could openly teach acceptance of white ethnic groups, but not yet promote acceptance of American Indians, Asian Americans, Latinos, or African Americans. Some historians have interpreted this silence on what we would today consider to be "racial" minorities as evidence that liberals in the 1930s were not attuned to the problem of racial discrimination in America.[76]

Teaching journals, however, show that teachers were not at all silent about the subject of racial minorities; it is just that their concern rarely ventured outside of a specific group of racial minorities understood to be "white." This distinction reiterates the tremendous significance of color at this time, which bestowed on certain racialized groups preferential treatment and access to important resources like quality education, better health care, and safer and higher-paying employment. In the case of schooling, being white also bestowed special attention on white racialized minorities, who were thought to posses the innate traits for democratic citizenship even if they were supposedly racially inferior. This process marked "nonwhite" students as individuals who did not possess the inherent capacities for participatory democratic citizenship.

As sites of citizenship training, public schools had a conflicted role to play in the education of African American and other nonwhite students. In the South, this problem had been "solved" by the creation of rigidly segregated public schools for nonwhites (a category that was defined differently in different states). Not only did African American schools receive only a fraction of the funding that white schools did, but in many cases black schools were run out of one-room schoolhouses with poorly trained teachers for only a few months a year. Very few African Americans in the South had access to a public high school, and what little secondary education existed was typically a "manual" or "training" school designed to prepare African American students for a limited range of jobs, typically domestic or manual labor.[77]

Public education for blacks was not much better in the North. Over one million African Americans migrated out of the South during World War I to urban and industrial centers in the Northeast and Midwest, swelling existing black populations in urban and suburban communities.[78] Nearly every American town and city outside of the deep South maintained segregated and inferior public schools for blacks through the 1930s. In one of the few battles African American social activists won relating to public education, predominantly black schools would often (but not always) be staffed by black faculty and administrators.[79] The near total isolation of black students in black schools with black teachers, combined with the popular assumption by whites that African Americans were not eligible for full citizenship, meant that in the white dominated educational press, there was very little mention of African Americans at all.

As teachers began to consider more carefully this question of "interracial" relations and racial tolerance, the subject of African Americans began to creep into the dominant educational discourse on race in the 1930s. Among white-dominated teaching journals, the *Elementary English Review* and *Social Education* devoted the most attention to the subject of African American education in

United States, although only three or four articles each. While *Social Education* tended to deal more explicitly with the "Southern race question" in terms of social and economic issues, the *Elementary English Review* focused instead on the best ways to instruct black children. Neither of these teaching journals treated African Americans in the same way that they treated white racialized minorities. African Americans could not be conflated with a single nation—instead they were positioned in between, but distinct from, both Americans and Africans. Lacking a national heritage, teachers steered away from speaking and teaching about blacks in terms of culture, even as this trend accelerated for other racial minorities and despite the fact that black educators taught lessons on black achievements through the study of Negro History.[80]

Indeed, most of the white educational discourse on African Americans was prescriptive, that is, it identified problems with black children and suggested solutions. For example, Pittsburgh children's librarian Eugenia Brunot published "The Negro Child and His Reading" in the summer of 1932 to advise white teachers on how to teach black children. She explained that poor reading habits were caused by limited social and economic experiences including unstable families, poverty, overcrowded conditions, and frequent changes in guardianship among "Negroes." Brunot suggested that teachers could observe black students alongside Irish and Italian children in order to consider the specific "racial inheritance" and "peculiar culture" that defined their distinct classroom experiences.

Brunot then detailed the racial and cultural traits that influenced the literacy skills of black children at the public library where she worked. Describing how black students selected books to read, she recounted, "Gold and jewels in abundance must sparkle, satin robes must trail through the pages, giants must be very tall and terrible and the fire-breathing dragon must slay his fair quota of minor heroes before (after desperate struggles) his seven horrible heads are hacked off by the intrepid youngest son." According to the author, "Negro boys and girls are particularly fond" of fairy tales and stories of the "grotesque," and that "being no devotee of Webster," a black child reads "slowly and generally chooses books decidedly below his school grade."[81] Even as the author insisted that economic and social factors explained the literacy skills of black students, she made sweeping generalizations about how and why black students picked certain books to read. The fact that Brunot viewed her own work as benevolent enabled her to cast "Negro" children in stereotypical, essentialist, and derogatory terms.

White teachers writing on the subject of African American education, while frequently sympathetic, could display acute and often appalling racism. For example, Frances Bacon, a children's librarian from Baltimore, composed what was intended to be a funny appraisal of a white woman's experience teaching in an inner city library entitled "Epaminondas at the Library." The title referred to a popular children's book of the era, much like *Little Black Sambo*, that depicted

African Americans as unintelligent, lazy, and generally uncivilized. The author related her dismay at encountering a "seething mass" of colored children on her first day working at a new library. She found she could barely understand the children's spoken English—both syntax and pronunciation—and struggled to answer their questions at the front desk. "How should I ever be able to help them when I couldn't even understand their questions?" she fretted. Bacon shared her discovery with readers: "It takes training and much imagination. I am advised to listen for the rhythms and sounds and translate into the proper words. This is very helpful, for colored children love rhythmic words and will change them to suit their own ears."[82]

Like her colleague writing three years earlier from Pittsburgh, this librarian recounted that black children loved fairy tales as they were fascinated with the "swashbuckling and macabre." She also puzzled over the racial traits that distinguished black children from youngsters of other races. Noting that black children were "naturally noisy" she explained, "The keen intellectual curiosity of, for instance, the Jewish child, that makes him work so hard on scientific problems, is not found to any marked degree in the colored child."[83] Likewise, she tried to understand these differences in a broader social context. She related her dismay at how dirty the "Negro" children were and how they damaged the books whenever they looked at them. "After walking about the neighborhood and realizing the conditions of poverty and crowding, however, I was more tolerant." Yet, Bacon's tolerance had its limits. As she admitted, "It is an uphill job to teach cleanliness and good care of something as perishable as a book to these Elizabelles and Jeffersons when they have no place to keep their possessions, no privacy, no tradition of 'clean hands for reading' and so very many little brothers and sisters."[84] Whatever sympathy this author felt for children coming from these "conditions of poverty and overcrowding" faded quickly as she recounted their families' inability to maintain clean, private, or responsible homes.

Demeaning generalizations about African Americans were not uncommon in the articles written by "tolerant" whites in the mid-1930s as white teachers began to question how to teach black students, or even less commonly, how to teach about blacks to white students. On the rare occasions when white students were introduced to the subject of the "Negro," this was done uncritically. To take one example, an English teacher producing a special "Pageant of America" in 1934 included a scene featuring a slave plantation in the antebellum South. Describing the play to readers of the *Elementary English Review*, she boasted, "The whole scene is refined, showing the best of the colored race, yet at the same time dwelling upon their superstitions, their mannerisms, and their mode of life. This scene gives the pageant much mirth."[85] In this way, white teachers simultaneously highlighted what they believed was the "best of the colored race" while depicting African American life in such a way as to add "mirth" to the lesson.

Notably, the only article in a mainstream teaching journal that asked teachers to celebrate the culture of African Americans was written in 1933 by a self-identified "Negro" author. Wilhelmina Crosson of the Hancock School in Boston promoted the theme of African American contributions to American culture in her article "The Negro in Children's Literature." Crosson explained that she did not enjoy attending school as a child because "We read stories of every race's contribution to the development of literature but our own, and of every race's part in the laying of the bricks in its history but our own."[86] Therefore, Crosson promoted African and African American literature, which she believed would help "the Caucasian race see that the African is not merely a black savage, incapable of leadership and judgment."[87] Not only did "Negro" literature promise to defuse white racialist thinking, but Crosson assured readers that it would "make the Negro child strive to lift his race to higher levels."[88] Crosson's interest in "race pride" and her sophisticated analysis of the benefits of African American literature for all students suggest this teacher drew on the expanding literature and activism from black intellectuals like Carter G. Woodson, W. E. B. Du Bois, and Charles S. Johnson.[89] Few white teachers seemed to have been reading the same work.

While English teachers and librarians considered how to teach to and about black children, social studies teachers reflected on American race relations in terms of questions of political economy. Although typically denigrating in their descriptions of what one teacher described as "Southern Remus darkies," social studies teachers writing in the midst of the Great Depression tended to focus on economic inequalities and a lack of equal opportunities, writing:

> The conviction is spreading, also, that our major problems are not those of race relationship but rather are to be found in the region's poverty, in its health problems, in its poor educational facilities, in the low skill of its laboring millions. Their solution, of necessity, elevates black as well as white. This promises, also, to raise the color line from a horizontal to a vertical position and thus open the door of opportunity to all of both races while it preserves the integrity of each.[90]

An article written by a teacher in North Carolina agreed with the economic roots of the problem:

> Neither the biologist nor the psychologist has given us any reason to believe that these Southern people, either white or black, are fundamentally any better or any worse human stock than is to be found elsewhere in the nation. However, in the midst of a natural environment that could afford the basis for a rich and abundant civilization

they present a picture of poverty, frustration, and deficiency that is almost unbelievable.[91]

While social studies teachers tended to address political and economic concerns more explicitly than English teachers, they were nevertheless unequivocal in their desire to "preserve the integrity" of the black and white races by supporting rigid racial segregation. Like English teachers, social studies teachers in the years leading up to World War II found little cause to celebrate or even consider the culture of American blacks. As racial minorities without a nation, African Americans were also without culture in the mainstream, white-dominated educational discourse on race.

Nazism and Racial Prejudice

By 1937 American teachers were aware of the growing menace of Nazism and its racial doctrines. As early as 1934, social studies teachers criticized the racialist policies of Nazi Germany in teaching journals.[92] The mounting violence in Europe and Asia in the late 1930s was beginning to influence tolerance education in American schools in 1936, 1937, and 1938. Teachers now targeted "racial prejudice" as a specific problem for educators, and they further suggested that tolerance education would counteract the evils of Nazi racism. While teachers had taught about national groups in an attempt to speed the assimilation of recent immigrants and to inculcate a more cosmopolitan outlook among all students, now, for the first time, they expressed concern about the problem of *racial prejudice*. They specifically connected tolerance education to racial discrimination, and later violence, against Jews in Germany. Rising international tensions drew teachers into urgent deliberations on how to promote friendly relations, peace, and goodwill and especially how to combat the growing menace of irrational prejudice against racial minorities. As a result teachers were willing to experiment with different strategies in the classroom.

In 1936 the *English Journal* criticized what it viewed as meager programs of tolerance education in a roundtable entitled, "The English Teacher in Relation to the International Scene."[93] Here the author proclaimed: "We must cease our romantic vaporings on loving our foreign neighbors, with no definite, constructive policy to chart the intermediate steps." Francis Shoemaker argued that the key to an effective pedagogy of international relations was to have students recognize "that races are, after all, mere temporary geographic accidents." Like many English teachers, this one insisted that by reading literature "on the contributions of other cultures" students would become less racially prejudiced through imagined encounters with foreign peoples. He elaborated, "His vicarious experiences will tend to individualize members of these other groups so that all Italians will not remain 'dagos,' all Germans 'huns,' and all Englishmen proverbial cockneys or 'by-jovers.'[94] This kind of tolerance education underscored a more egalitarian understanding of race as well as knowledge of the cultural contributions of racial minorities.

Over the next two years the *English Journal* continued to emphasize the importance of racial tolerance and international goodwill. Writing from a high school in Stambaugh, Michigan, one teacher described her classroom efforts to foster a "peace-inoculating experience." One of the most important features of this teacher's work was her use of an attitude test to gauge her students' racial prejudice before and after her lesson. Attitude tests like this one would become a defining feature of tolerance education during World War II as teachers struggled to defend the effectiveness of their antiprejudice initiatives. In this case the teacher listed twenty-five nationality and occupation groups, and then had the students record their immediate reactions to each one as "pleasant, unpleasant, or indifferent." She then led the class in a discussion of why they might harbor prejudice against certain groups of people. Concluding that students simply did not know the people they disliked, the teacher presented minority groups in terms of their literature and special "contributions to civilization." The students composed essays and presented talks on the group they had studied, practices the teacher understood as "formulas for peace."[95] Lessons like this would become a model for tolerance education once the war broke out. This teacher carefully contextualized the lesson as an educational response to international events, referenced the scientific approach to tolerance pedagogy, and directed a unit that differed little in content from the international relations education or many Americanization efforts of previous decades by highlighting minority groups' "contribution to civilization."

In May of 1938 the *English Journal* reported an entire course dedicated to tolerance education under way in the Santa Barbara High School in California. This course, Builders Together, stated as its goal:

> To build understanding of and sympathy with the various peoples who have contributed to the cultural growth of America; to learn what those contributions have been and to understand the backgrounds that enabled these peoples to contribute . . . to build by the aid of all these elements a creative Americanism.[96]

In this course, the teacher organized a student-led census of the high school to determine the "chief heritages" of the community. The students then interviewed and collected artifacts from among Santa Barbara's Mexican, Scandinavian, and Italian families in order to discover how each group's "racial gifts could be used to build an even better Santa Barbara." Like other teachers of the late 1930s, this teacher used the term "culture" to describe the lifeways of each immigrant group, but because she considered each group to be a distinct race, she sometimes referred to a group's special attributes as "racial gifts." In conclusion, the teacher noted, "wholesome pride in race and in world-citizenship came to many," underscoring the connection between racial tolerance and international affairs.[97]

In 1937, social studies teachers joined the effort to fortify the nation against the impending war by teaching racial tolerance and understanding. As one teacher from Brooklyn bemoaned, "We teach the futility of war, yet we seem to be approaching chaos with recklessness equal to that of the year 1914. We teach tolerance, yet race hatred has shown its consequences in more than one place."[98] Like his colleagues in English, this teacher understood tolerance education as a prescription for world peace. He wanted tolerance education to include open, critical engagements with the key issues that were responsible for animosity between people and nations. Yet, even as the author composed his lesson plan, he acknowledged that any teacher who conducted critical discussions of social and economic bases for war would most likely be labeled an "indoctrinator" and removed from his position.

As international tension escalated, social studies teachers staked out a meaningful role for American public schools. "Should the teacher be a propagandist for peace or a prophet of the inevitable war?" asked a teacher from Two Rivers, Wisconsin.[99] The head of the social studies department in Muncie, Indiana, reminded teachers, "If the school is to meet its obligation of training for citizenship, it cannot fail to give attention to the problems of world community."[100] Teachers from across the country including Abington, Pennsylvania, and South Bend, Indiana, debated how to make civics and history "functional" in terms of the international conflict.[101]

Even as teachers expanded their horizons—articles on "The Moslem World" and American Indian history both appeared in 1938—others argued that the goal of American education was to promote the American Way of Life, not waste time celebrating foreign cultures.[102] A teacher from LeRoy High School in New York wrote bitterly, "if the millions of American dollars spent annually for education have any justification at all, it is certainly this: to further acknowledge, an understanding, and an appreciation of American thought and culture."[103] In a sense, these seemingly contradictory positions would be somewhat resolved during the war itself. American teachers would teach about foreign people and racial minorities in a way that seemed to highlight their proximity to white American norms, a pedagogy that promised to reduce racial prejudice as it fortified national unity.

In December 1937 Rachel Davis DuBois, who now served as director of the Progressive Education Association's Commission on Intercultural Education, published in New York City's teaching journal, *High Points*. DuBois described her three-pronged approach to reducing racial prejudice: the emotional, the intellectual, and the situational approach, which essentially boiled down to changing the way students felt, thought, and acted toward minorities. In one of the most extensive descriptions of tolerance education yet published she explained how intercultural education reduced racial prejudice at Benjamin Franklin High School, a school located at a tense intersection of Italian, Puerto Rican, and black communities in East Harlem. She offered vivid portrayals of homeroom activities, special assemblies, teas, and meetings required to stage an effective antiprejudice campaign. This was no special lesson or even a single course on tolerance education, but instead an opportunity to transform classroom practice through an integrated approach that included teachers, students, parents, and the larger community. Pondering the results, which she measured with an attitude test given before and after her program, DuBois quoted the written comments of students as evidence of success:

> I had been taught, as all French are, by my grandmother to hate the Germans but when the program was given, I found out that they are the same as we are. (9B boy)

> I have learned to call all people my neighbors. I have learned to love their ways of living and to respect them more for what they have done. (8B girl)

> I have changed my attitude toward the Mexicans and now regard them as one of us. My attitude was changed when the program was brought to our assembly. (high school junior)[104]

These quotes reflected DuBois's cherished intercultural pedagogy; by teaching that all people were inherently the same, students would come to love and respect a once-despised minority. As she told New York City teachers in 1937, all schools should be conscious of the need "for developing more appreciative attitudes among our culture groups." Her curriculum focused heavily on the "culture groups" found in a given school, and then introduced a series of lectures, discussions, and activities to highlight each culture group's contributions in terms of music, folk art, dance, athletics, and cuisine. These lessons taught students "how very unique and rich American culture and life is because of its gifts from many lands and races."[105] DuBois, like other educators in the late 1930s, failed to distinguish between the concepts of race and culture and referred to the minority groups she studied including Jews, "Negroes," Italians, Mexicans, and Germans in terms of their distinct racial and cultural traits.

In 1938, DuBois delivered intercultural education to a national audience in the *English Journal*, launching a popular curriculum of tolerance education that would expand over the course of World War II.[106] Teachers throughout the United States raised their voices to protest racial discrimination and promote tolerance education. In the contest between democracy and fascism, racial tolerance would be the "keystone of democracy," and teachers would deliver this powerful tool into the waiting hands of American public school children. Writing from Evander Childs High School in New York City, one educator prophesied, "Just as the glory of the rainbow consists in the harmonious blending of all its colors, so must the glory of these United States emanate from the union, material and spiritual, of all our many peoples, races, and creeds."[107] United in their outrage against Nazi racial prejudice and their unwavering devotion to democracy, American teachers launched a war against racial prejudice to be waged in their classrooms.

‖ 2 ‖

Franz Boas

Reforming "Race" in American Schools

I have always thought of a scientist as a man who works apart from other people, in the laboratory, where he learns about the forces of nature. Why should he bother with such things as government, tolerance, and democracy?

—Student, 1939

Thousands of college and school teachers throughout the country have joined together in a campaign of education for democracy. We have pledged ourselves to protect and extend intellectual freedom, to strengthen our appreciation of the long and glorious heritage of American democracy, to combat propaganda for racial or religious discrimination or intolerance, to make our schools fortresses of democracy.

—Franz Boas, 1939

In July of 1939, the *New York Times* informed Americans that racist Nazi propaganda had been located *inside* of the cherished institution of public schools, charging: "Schools Rebuked on Racial Errors! Professor Boas Charges Many Use Textbooks That Support Nazi Doctrine!" By this time, educated New Yorkers recognized the anthropologist Franz Boas as the nation's leading scientific expert on race. Influenced by his background as a German-born Jew, Boas dedicated his professional life to challenging dominant scientific models of racial understanding.[1] Featured on the cover of *Time* magazine in 1936 for his heroic efforts to defend minority groups against pseudoscientific claims of racial superiority, Boas was renowned for his long and distinguished career as a curator at the American Museum of Natural History and as a professor at Columbia University.[2] Thanks to the *New York Times*, the nation now learned that this distinguished anthropologist had discovered a majority of American schoolbooks "misuse the concept of 'race' in one way or another," while an astounding 20 percent "teach what amounts to Nazi doctrines about superior and inferior races." The *Times* quoted Boas, who explained: "The myth of the 100 percent

'Aryan' and similar nonsense has reached such proportions even in our own country that the fight against race prejudice is now a major problem for educators." In response, Boas declared "a broad educational campaign" would be conducted by more than fifty of the nation's leading educators and scientists "against unscientific teaching of race problems in American schools."[3]

Franz Boas launched the first coordinated effort to change the way American schools taught about the concept of race. Citing the potentially devastating consequences of pseudoscientific Nazi racial doctrines, he introduced anthropologically accurate, egalitarian, and ultimately democratic ideas about human diversity to American teachers through lectures, pamphlets, radio shows, and other venues. He wanted all Americans to learn that culture, which he understood as a complex set of historical, environmental, and social conditions, had greater influence on an individual's way of life than did the biological concept of race. Boas's race education reform initiative, and in particular the culture concept it promoted, would forever change the way American schools taught about human race. This chapter explores the different strategies Boas used to convince teachers, educators, and the broader public that schools in a democratic nation must teach a specific scientific conception of human race.[4]

Boas focused on schools because he recognized public education as a key site of cultural production in American society, and in particular, an important symbolic location for constructing popular conceptions of race. Speaking to reporters, Boas asked how scientists could expect laymen to resist racialist propaganda, "when all through his school days he is impregnated with false and dangerous doctrines, disseminated by teachers usually through ignorance or carelessness and sometimes even deliberately?"[5] Boas recognized that the way teachers taught about human race would have an especially powerful influence on the ways Americans understood race.

In addition, Boas believed public education played a critical role in securing the idealized, but as yet unrealized, aspiration of freedom inherent in a democratic society. He reasoned that public schools must be preserved as sites of academic freedom where teachers and students could explore the myths and realities of scientific knowledge about human diversity. Under such conditions he was confident that teachers and students would discover, as he had, that individuals of each of the three main races were potentially equal.[6] Given the escalating violence against Jews in the name of race purity and mounting challenges to academic freedom in Europe and the United States in the 1930s, Boas became convinced that public schools and universities were among the most important—and most threatened—weapons in the American arsenal of democracy.

Boas produced several pamphlets that identified specific problems with the way American schools taught about human diversity that offered guidance and suggestions for how schools could correct these critical shortcomings. He also composed press releases, public speeches, rallies, lectures, exhibits, and radio shows relating to questions of race education. Boas's antiracist activism was covered in the mainstream and African American presses at the start of the war. The *Chicago Defender* was more than happy to reproduce Boas's increasingly bold insistence on the equality of the black and white races. According to one reporter at this black newspaper, "Dr. Boas' contention should enlighten not only narrow-minded white folk, but should shed equal light to those Negroes who have no faith in the ability of our race to assimilate to this culture, and who have refused to acquaint themselves with Africa's glorious past."[7]

Published texts illuminate the main anthropological critiques of the way American schools used the term "race." Anthropologists implored teachers to understand that there was no scientific proof of any correlation between race and intelligence. For these scholars this was the most glaring and potentially treacherous component of racialist ideology found in schools. Not only did this idea threaten to indoctrinate young students with prejudicial beliefs, but more importantly it threatened the quality and degree of education offered to minority students. Boas's writings posited an alternative model of the race concept that he wanted teachers to teach. In simplified language and surprisingly clear detail, Boas spelled out for teachers the "truth" about race as he understood it. Anthropologists envisioned this educational reform as a direct assault on "racism," a new term at the time, which they defined as the attempt of individuals of one group to dominate another group based on false racial theories.[8] Specifically, they wanted Americans to view human diversity not as fixed, inherited "racial" differences, but as learned, and therefore malleable, "cultural" differences. Boasian anthropologists emphasized that this "scientific" definition of race represented an apolitical and verifiable truth, which they directly contrasted to false racial propaganda of the Third Reich. As Boas explained to reporters in 1939, "we scientists have the moral obligation to educate the American people against all false and scientific doctrines, such as the racial nonsense of the Nazis."[9] As a scientific truth their lessons had special salience in the nation's expansive system of public education, and so Boas launched an initiative to bring egalitarian lessons on human race to American classrooms.

For Boas, academic freedom, racial tolerance, and public education converged in 1939, when the New York business community employed eugenics and appealed to growing anti-Semitism to reduce the state budget for public education. Racial tension in New York City public schools had been growing for years, with reports of incidents against teachers and students, especially Jews.[10] Jewish teachers found swastikas on their blackboards and anti-Semitic literature in their mailboxes, while Jewish students faced ridicule and even violence from their classmates. This hostility toward religious minorities spilled over to Catholic immigrants and their children, and Catholic teachers reported harassment by students.[11] At an open Board of Education meeting in January 1939, angry citizens denounced Jewish teachers and then booed and hissed when teachers stood up to defend themselves. A member of the Board of Education criticized these blatantly anti-Semitic actions the next day, saying, "My heart bleeds to think that we have products of our schools who could so forget themselves to act the way they did at the meeting."[12] The New York City Board of Education stepped up the "Tolerance Drive" it had initiated just months earlier in an attempt to stem these disturbing racial confrontations in local schools.[13]

Mounting suspicion that intellectuals harbored communist sympathies further exacerbated racial tensions in New York City. Journalists baited educators into admitting controversial viewpoints by soliciting information on "liberal" courses in the guise of prospective students. George S. Counts, one of Boas's most famous colleagues at Teachers College, Columbia University, received such a letter and then warned public school teachers that the same thing could happen to them.[14] Boas himself was forced into early retirement from teaching in large part due to his outspoken and controversial political views.[15] Meanwhile, state and federal committees investigated public school teachers from kindergarten through college for any sign of communist sympathies.[16] Across the country Martin Dies's Committee to Investigate Un-American Activities formalized inquiries into teachers' political affiliations, while the Rapp Coudert Committee examined the same question in New York State.[17] Many of the teachers targeted by these inquiries also happened to be Jewish. Organizations in New York such as the League to Protect Our Schools from Communism attempted to persuade citizens that "Communism IS JEWISH."[18]

Amid the mayhem caused by visible anti-Semitism and the deliberate suppression of free speech, New York educators had to contend with a series of rapid attacks launched by the state's most powerful business associations. The Chamber of Commerce of the State of New York launched an attack against the public schools that would result in a crippling $10,000,000 budget reduction after it released a report by the eugenicist Harry H. Laughlin entitled *Immigration and Conquest*. Widely distributed and discussed, this polemical, ostentatiously "scientific" study reproduced the worst fallacies of eugenicist science from an earlier generation. *Immigration and Conquest*, as the name implies, criticized U.S. immigration and naturalization policies, which the Chamber of Commerce felt were far too lax despite the restrictive immigration laws imposed by the Johnson-Reed Act in 1924. It recommended: "The United States Congress should, by statute, declare definitely that the immigration policy of the United States consists basically in recruiting to the American population only such immigrants as are assimilable, in numbers and quality, to the predominating native white stocks of the United States."

Anti-Semitic flyer distributed in New York City schools, reproduced in the *New York Teacher*.

Not only must all American immigrants be white—defined as an individual "all of whose ancestors were members of the white or Caucasian race"—but the report further recommended that "each individual immigrant should be required to possess family-stock qualities which are substantially superior—in physical stamina, in intellectual capacity and in integrity of moral purpose—to the current breeding stocks of the American people."[19] Besides limiting immigration to highly selective levels, the report also suggested repealing social and financial assistance to immigrants and their descendants during times of financial crisis, and even suggested deporting all immigrants currently on the dole. The report reflected business leaders' discontent with rising taxes necessary to support the New Deal, a concern that would soon spill over into questions of public education.[20]

Within weeks of releasing *Immigration and Conquest* the Chamber of Commerce released a second report aimed directly at public schools. It proposed limiting public education to basic literacy and completely abolishing free high schools, charging: "As we see it the great purpose for which the schools were founded was to preserve and strengthen the State by making better and abler citizens. Other benefits derived from it are secondary."[21] Joining forces with the Citizens Budget Commission and the Real Estate Board, the Chamber of Commerce pressed state legislatures to cut state aid to public education by $31 million, or 25% of the state's annual appropriation for education. Supporters promised middle-class citizens that they would see an immediate reduction in their taxes, and the New York state legislature passed a measure that cut $10 million from the school budget.[22]

College professors and many public school teachers in New York City followed these events closely, Boas foremost among them. Not until the legislature passed the $10-million budget cut, however, did a majority of public school teachers realize the scope and intensity of the threat they faced. They were already working for reduced salaries in overcrowded schools with limited supplies.[23] Defending themselves against red-baiting and racial discrimination, most did not even see the budget cut coming until it was too late. Teachers' response, although belated, was swift and effective. The many teachers' organizations in the city united to protest that the budget cut was the first step in a concerted effort to "undermine and destroy the American system of free public education." Inside the schools, teachers organized "leaflets, pamphlets, broadcasts, movies, bulletins, petitions, public rallies, and upstate forums" to defend the schools.[24]

The Teachers Union led a "Save Our Schools" campaign that demanded a return of full state aid and a deficiency appropriation to compensate for the budget reduction. Tensions came to a head in Albany on February 12, 1940, when state budget makers held an open hearing on the fiscal budget.[25] Newspapers across the state gave front-page coverage to the clash between representatives from business and education in "an oratorical free for all" that lasted all day and into the night. The *New York Times* described the five hundred featured speakers as "an inexhaustible volcano of verbosity." Since most of the participants came from New York City, the contest began that morning in Grand Central Station as competing groups vied for seats on available trains and struggled to keep their constituents together. The more powerful groups chartered trains, including a "Save Our Schools Express" by the Teachers Union and a "Taxpayers' Special" by the Taxpayers Federation. Upon arriving in Albany, protestors clambered out of the station and marched up a steep hill to the capitol building, waving placards and chanting. Reporters described the scene as festive, with a "slightly Mardi Gras air" as protestors held their signs aloft: "Save the Schools," "Slash the Gas Tax," "Remove the Noose of High Taxes from Our Neck." Protestors had to check their placards at the door at the giant Armory building set aside for the hearing. For twelve hours, participants listened to arguments for and against tax cuts, but the speech by James Marshall, president of the New York City Board of Education, evoked the most vocal response when he announced, "Our schools and our democracy will be saved despite taxpayer opposition!" Even the forty state troopers on site could not stop the "torrent of cheers and boos" erupting from the audience.[26]

New York City teachers won the battle, and the school budget was restored the following year. While teachers were organizing protests and soliciting support, Franz Boas defended local public schools through academic networks. Boas was immediately wary of *Immigration and Conquest*, emerging as it did

Teachers protesting against school budget cuts in Albany, New York. United Federation of Teachers Photographs Collection, Part 1: Photographic Prints, Courtesy of Tamiment Library, New York University.

from the Chamber of Commerce and affiliated with the prestigious Carnegie Institute. He feared the public would be swayed by the authoritative presentation of what claimed to be scientific materials on race as a marker for potential citizenship. Boas launched an immediate counterattack, first by organizing a response by the American Committee for Democracy and Intellectual Freedom (ACDIF) of which he was chairman.[27] Together with professors and presidents of New York City colleges and universities, the ACDIF announced that the report "deserves the outspoken condemnation of all true Americans." In a press release, reproduced in full by the *New York Times*, Boas asserted:

> We view with alarm the rapid spread in our own country of the hysterical cry that the alien or the Jew or the Catholic or some other scapegoat is responsible for all the ills of society. The report of the Chamber of Commerce seeks to lend scientific support to such demagogy. We would not be true citizens of a democracy if we did not enter our vigorous protest against any such abuse of science.[28]

Dissatisfied with newspaper coverage alone, Boas published a pamphlet, *Science Condemns Racism*, that challenged Laughlin's conclusions point-by-point. The pamphlet proclaimed, "When the sponsorship of the Chamber of Commerce of the State of New York is given to a restatement of such false racial doctrines, men of science must answer." Leading scientists, educators, historians, and major scientific associations, including the American Anthropological Association, endorsed Boas's response.[29]

Within weeks of finalizing *Science Condemns Racism*, Boas was forced to contend with a second report by the Chamber of Commerce that challenged state funding for kindergartens, high schools, and city colleges. "Religion and health, in that order, are the two most important subjects that can be taught to American youth," the report claimed. "It seems to us," the report continued, "that there is a definite line which must be recognized and that is the line between the amount of education it requires to kill illiteracy and the amount of education we give beyond that point." Complaining that the state spent too much money educating children beyond the basics, business leaders insisted they were "entirely out of sympathy with the idea that the State must support youngsters and keep them occupied in school until they reach a certain age."[30]

Boas recognized the underlying racial and class implications of this report. Business leaders wanted to reduce education to basic instruction in health and morality, attributes it suggested were missing in the current public school population. In New York City, most public school students were the sons and daughters of the very immigrants the Chamber of Commerce had rebuked in its first report. By attacking the inherent capabilities of immigrants and their descendants in one report, and suggesting strict limitations on their education in a second report, the Chamber of Commerce and their allies aimed directly at the city's working-class, racially stigmatized population.

Business leaders' coordinated strike on New York public schools at this time suggests that educational retrenchment during the Great Depression at times proceeded along racial lines, even though the students under attack happened to be "white." Beginning in the early 1930s there was a movement to cut "fads and frills" from public education and reduce teachers' salaries—necessary steps given the unprecedented fiscal crisis and the fact that tax bases were so decimated. Public schools simply did not have the funds to operate that they once did, and by 1932 nearly all American public schools had begun to reduce teachers' salaries and diminish educational programming.[31] Faced with difficult choices between further reducing teachers' salaries or cutting special programs, many schools began eliminating the nontraditional courses that had been added over the past three decades of progressive reform. For example, in 1933 *Harper's* magazine observed, "Art, home economics, manual training, physical education, trade and vocational classes, and even foreign languages are all being eliminated or curtailed."[32]

The example from New York stands out for two reasons. First, the attack by the business community came relatively late in the depression, when other school districts had already weathered public calls for budget reductions and the economy was on a moderate, if uncertain, recovery. Second, the example of business activism in New York highlights the racialist logic and rhetoric of school financing in this era. The connection between the two Chamber of Commerce reports was no accident, and the business community clearly intended to emphasize the undesirable racial make-up of the metropolis before stripping public education down to what it deemed were the essentials. The Chamber of Commerce identified the predominantly ethnic, working-class population in terms of racial shortcomings that undermined their potential for citizenship *and* for education. What is especially notable is that, while business associations elsewhere wanted to limit public education to the basics tenets of reading, writing, and arithmetic, the architects of New York school budget cuts wanted to preserve health and moral education. By retaining these two elements of the "fads and frills" that were elsewhere being cut, business leaders strategically emphasized the inherent shortcomings associated with ethnic, urban communities. The racialized nature of this attack explains its emergence five to seven years after the nationwide movement. The New York Chamber of Commerce believed they had discovered a potent new strategy to undermine popular faith in free education—the racial inferiority of urban students, who drew the largest portion of state funding.

Boas organized and led a counterattack against New York business elites fearing this powerful threat to the ideal of American democracy. Writing to Ruth Benedict in October 1939, Boas noted that local concerns were now taking precedence over international ones, and expressed dismay that his physical health limited his efforts:

> I am more interested in our own civil liberties and, as you know, I am in that fight. Just now we are attacking the Chamber [of Commerce] of the State of New York, who want to see our free high schools chopped off, religion introduced, etc. I wish I had more strength, but I cannot undertake any work that requires physical strength. My heart simply won't stand for it.[33]

Boas responded to the second report of the Chamber of Commerce in the *New York Times* with an open letter coauthored with local teachers from the New York State Federation of Teachers Unions, the Association of First Assistants in New York City High Schools, the High School Teachers Association of New York, and the Kindergarten-6B Teachers Association:

> We must condemn the conception of democracy revealed in the report. When it says the purpose for which our schools were founded "was to preserve and strengthen the State by making better, abler citizens." This concept is fascist, not democratic. It implies that citizens exist for the sake of the State, whereas in a democracy the State exists for the benefit of its citizens.[34]

Attempting to reach a wider audience, Boas's ACDIF produced a series of radio shows in 1939 that summarized and critiqued the battle between public schools and the New York Chamber of Commerce. In one show, "This Is Democracy," a family debates whether or not education should be free to all citizens or if education beyond literacy should be paid for by individual families, as the Chamber of Commerce suggested. After listening to an appeal for tax cuts by the Chamber of Commerce, the wife is starting to believe that perhaps it would be better to reduce funding for public education. But her husband cuts her off, saying, "He wants to cut our schools so that a child may learn enough to be a slave, to work machines, and nothing else, unless the kid had brains to pick a wealthy pair of parents." The wife replies that they have already saved enough for their daughter's college education, and the tax cuts would be a welcome break for their family. The husband responds, "That's not the point. If only the rich can go to school to learn the mysteries of science, of government and art, then only the rich will taste the power that's within the kernel of knowledge, so only the rich will rule. Within a single generation we would have an aristocracy upon our shores as arrogant and sterile as the best in Europe."[35] In this radio show and in others, some of which Boas himself appeared on, the ACDIF attempted to spread its message to a general audience.

The Chamber of Commerce attacks on education pushed Boas to experiment with new and more vigorous forms of social activism. At the same time, his prominence as an anthropologist drew the popular support that New York public schools desperately needed to rebuke these powerful business associations. It would have been difficult for teachers to challenge Laughlin's report on their own. They needed a scientist, and not just any scientist but the nation's most respected race expert to evaluate and reject the scientific knowledge cited in *Immigration and Conquest*. Boas's activism on behalf of New York public schools was supported in the national press, including a flattering story in the *New Republic* that portrayed Boas as an honest man of science working to undermine the nefarious and fascist political maneuvering of the New York Chamber of Commerce.[36] Reaching out to teachers directly, Boas published articles on the relationship between academic freedom, tolerance, and public education in the *New York Teacher*, the monthly teaching journal of the New York City Teachers Union.[37]

Propelled by a groundswell of public support, in the spring of 1940 Boas organized a rally to defend New Yorkers against what he called a "determined assault on the free democratic basis of our system of education."[38] Speaking at Carnegie Hall to a large audience of teachers and administrators from New York City public schools as well as allies from academia, social work, churches, and synagogues, Boas recounted a long list of recent attacks against public education, including severe budget cuts, formal investigations into teacher's political views, inquiries into school textbooks, and the proposal of formal religious education in the public schools. Boas passionately denounced these events and the business leaders who orchestrated them. Facing a sea of supporters, Boas saw them as "giving expression tonight to our determination to defend our schools against the attacks of those who wish to abuse them for the purpose of raising a docile, submissive nation willing to follow a group of self-appointed masters."[39] In his speech he explained that free public education was essential to the functioning of a democratic society. Education for democracy required not only ample funding, but more importantly an open intellectual climate that promoted the free exchange of ideas. He continued, "Certainly the kind of culture that we cherish can flower only in a country in which perfect freedom is given to the intellectual and spiritual life of every citizen, where free discussion of free minds will allow every one to contribute his share to the well-being of society."[40]

CITIZENS RALLY

to answer the attack on PUBLIC EDUCATION

•

SPEAKERS

Hon. Newbold Morris
PRESIDENT OF THE CITY COUNCIL

Dean Ned H. Dearborn
VICE-PRESIDENT AMERICAN FEDERATION OF TEACHERS

Rev. H. Norman Sibley
UNIVERSITY HEIGHTS PRESBYTERIAN CHURCH

Prof. Franz Boaz
NATIONAL CHAIRMAN, AMERICAN COMMITTEE
FOR DEMOCRACY AND INTELLECTUAL FREEDOM

AND OTHER PROMINENT SPEAKERS

Prof. Walter Rautenstrauch, *Chairman*
COLUMBIA UNIVERSITY

CARNEGIE HALL
APRIL 13, 1940
8:15 P. M.

SPONSORED BY THE AMERICAN COMMITTEE
FOR DEMOCRACY AND INTELLECTUAL FREEDOM
519 WEST 121st STREET, NEW YORK CITY

Tickets 25c., 35c. and 50c. on Sale at the American Committee office

Flyer advertising an educational rally at Carnegie Hall featuring Franz Boas. United Federation of Teachers Records, Box 1, Folder 13a. Courtesy of Tamiment Library, New York University.

In the ongoing battle to secure New York City schools from budget cuts and attacks on academic freedom, Boas wrote an introduction to another pamphlet designed to rally support in 1941. *Winter Soldiers: A Story of a Conspiracy against the Schools* was published as a joint effort by the Committee in Defense of Public Education, the Teachers Union, and the College Teachers Union of New York City. Written in a colloquial style to appeal to the average American, the text tried to convince New Yorkers that business attacks on public schools were an immediate threat to American democracy.

Boas argued that American security is based on confidence in "the good sense of our people." In order for all Americans to have confidence in their neighbors, he continued, we must ensure that all citizens receive the best education possible. Boas argued that this can only happen "if the teacher himself is free to think, if he is not prevented from presenting facts impartially." In conclusion, Boas described how schoolchildren demonstrated "a complete disregard of race" that epitomized a true democracy. The rest of the pamphlet contained short descriptions and vivid illustrations to persuade the public of the need for academic freedom and security for teachers, and expanded social services for schoolchildren. To promote expanded services for students, *Winter Soldiers* portrayed New York City schools as racially restricted, overcrowded, and generally unhealthy and inadequate institutions. One section explained that 81 cents per day per child could meet the nutritional and educational needs of each child, and yet this money was lacking while another section detailed discrimination against black students in the schools.

Winter Soldiers illustrates how Boas's academic authority buttressed the response by public school teachers in New York City, lending the rigor of scientific certainty to the effort and the extended network of academics and intellectuals to which Boas had access. Ultimately Boas's activism would help turn the tide of popular support and force the legislature to reverse the budget cuts. Even after legislators restored the school funds, Boas remained infuriated with the Chamber of Commerce, which he denounced before the National Federation of Constitutional Liberties in 1941:

> If I were to summarize the recommendations of the Chamber of Commerce of the State of New York I might say that they demand as aims: the teaching of humility so that the poor may accept with gratitude what is given to them, health that they may work effectively for their employer, ignorance that they may not ask questions.[41]

He concluded with a passionate appeal, "Therefore we consider it one of our most important duties to protect the schools and to extend their influence."[42]

Reforming Race Education

Concurrent with his involvement in educational politics, Boas began to question how Americans acquired racial prejudice and wondered what role the schools could play in reducing this prejudice. In 1939 he designed the first scientific study to analyze how American textbooks used and defined the concept of race.[43] With funding from the American Jewish Committee (AJC), Boas discovered that most textbooks presented the race concept in terms that had been rejected by mainstream scientists for ten, twenty, even thirty years. Partially, this gap between scientific theories and textbook content reflected a typical time lag between knowledge production in the academy and textbook publishing for the K-12 market. Furthermore, in nonscientific disciplines such as history the authors were more likely to reflect popular conceptions of race, those familiar to themselves and their readers, than current theories in biology or anthropology. However, the disturbing version of race presented by the vast majority of American textbooks in 1939 had to do with the longstanding, intimate relationship between educators and eugenicists in American schools.

Eugenics wavered on the fringes of scientific respectability for the first half of the twentieth century. Eugenicists claimed to study the science of race, and used scientific classification systems to describe and interpret differences in intelligence, biology, and physiology among people of various so-called races. In fact, the organizational impetus for many early eugenicists came from the rising influence of Boas's theories on racial egalitarianism within the discipline of anthropology.[44] While the professed "scientific" views of eugenicists changed significantly from 1900 through 1950, these scholars remained committed to the immutability of race as a category for explaining human difference and believed that social problems like feeblemindedness, alcoholism, crime, and disease could be abolished through strict breeding programs and attention to the distinct qualities of each racial "stock."

National organizations like the American Eugenics Society were deeply concerned with promoting their theories of "racial betterment" through American schools. They organized national conferences dedicated to improving eugenics education in the public schools and even designed essay contests to recruit high school and college students to the movement.[45] Some teaching journals, notably the *American Biology Teacher*, regularly featured articles that promoted the teaching of eugenics in high school biology courses.[46] As late as 1950, articles in the *American Biology Teacher* lamented the fact that modern societies kept alive "those who cannot do so for themselves," including people with mental and physical disabilities. As one author cautioned, "We house, clothe, and feed them, and very often we allow them to reproduce." Such acts of "emotion" and "pity," warned the author, threatened the very survival of the human race.[47]

Consequently, in the late 1930s, when Boas and other mainstream scientists were turning their attention to race education in the public schools for the first time, they encountered a curriculum and various components of educational policy that had been under the influence of politically engaged eugenicists for more than twenty years.[48] For this reason, American textbooks tended to portray race as a fixed marker of identity that determined an individual's physical health, mental well-being, and overall capacity for functioning as a modern citizen in a democratic society.

Boas suspected that American textbooks taught scientifically inaccurate models of human race from a modern anthropological perspective. To prove this, Boas recruited twenty-five students from Columbia University to examine how the term "race" was used in 166 high school textbooks in geography, history, civics, and biology, as well as a smaller sample of college textbooks in sociology and economics.[49] The results were alarming, and indicated that 66 percent of books misused the term "race" by using it where "nationality" would have been more appropriate. For instance, a history textbook entitled *Our World* stated, "Some races of people are more inclined to do certain things than other races. The French are noted for artistic goods."[50] While such conceptual errors were extensive, they were nothing compared to the shocking finding that 20% of the textbooks surveyed contained teachings of racial superiority. Boas found 32 that contained claims of racial superiority of the white race. For example, a 1933 history book declared: "Civilization has been developed and history has been made chiefly by the white race."[51]

Scientifically inaccurate statements like these were ubiquitous in American popular culture in 1939. Boas specifically chose to examine textbooks in anticipation of the public outrage such findings would inspire. It was one thing to discover that American novels, films, or newspapers spoke erroneously about human race, but to learn that public schools were teaching obsolete scientific knowledge would outrage the American public, which was highly aware that Nazi Germany was teaching false racial doctrines in fascist, government-controlled schools. Boas hoped Americans would be compelled to insist on more scientifically accurate portrayals of human difference in their schools in order to position the United States as clearly anti-fascist and pro-democratic.

At the same time as the Chamber of Commerce of the State of New York was publishing its eugenicist text *Immigration and Conquest*, Boas broadcast his findings about the flaws of textbooks through press conferences, radio shows, and the pamphlet *Can You Name Them?* These public outreach efforts had two fundamental goals: to emphasize the scientific definition of the term "race," and to highlight the social and political significance of limiting educational practice to the scientific meaning of this term. The materials published under Boas's ACDIF focused on what race was not: it was not an accurate way to describe variations among human beings, it did not determine behavior or innate abilities, and it did not predict the achievements of a group of people. Summarizing this position, "There is nothing to justify the belief that any type of man, any one of the large divisions of mankind, is condemned by nature to an inferior status. Until now many have not had the opportunity to participate in those cultural achievements on which we pride ourselves."[52] In the nature versus nurture debate, Boas and his colleagues downplayed biology as an explanatory factor and suggested that "opportunities" had much more to do with determining an individual's success in the modern world.

Can You Name Them? was endorsed by the American Psychological Association, the American Historical Association, the American Sociological Society, the American Federation of Teachers, and the Progressive Education Association, as well as leaders from renowned Jewish, Catholic, and Protestant organizations and the nation's leading textbook publishers.[53] Displayed prominently on the inside cover of the brochure, these endorsements illustrated the broad range of support for Boas's reform initiative. Together, leaders in science, education, publishing, and religion agreed, "A concerted effort should be made to revise all textbooks so that they will conform to the scientific truth on the subject of 'race.'"[54]

Boas ensured that *Can You Name Them?* would attract media attention by mailing the pamphlet to major newspapers across the country. Besides the *New York Times*, stories appeared in the black press including the *Chicago Defender*,[55] as well as prominent papers including *Hartford Courant, Davenport Democrat, Des Moines Tribune, St. Paul Dispatch, Richmond-Times Dispatch, Sacramento Union, Long Beach Press Telegram, Cincinnati Post,* and *Bismarck Tribune*. Boas wanted to persuade readers to reform the way that public schools taught about human race. The title referred to a series of portraits portrayed on the front and back cover of the pamphlet that featured six photographs of middle-aged men of European descent. All were distinguished looking, with styled hair and professional attire. Under each portrait was a simple question asking the readers to guess the subject's nationality, "French? German? Australian? American?"[56] While correct answers were included on page seven of the text, it was clear that Boas intended readers to struggle to identify nationalities on the basis of external appearances.

From this initial challenge, Boas delivered a clear and concise challenge to popular notions of race. The first page highlighted both popular misconceptions about race and the scientific points that refuted them, asserting, "The false dogma of inherited 'racial' differences has often been used to justify political domination. In recent times it has led to merciless persecution of minorities."

In contrast, Boas informed readers, "Serious anthropologists, psychologists, and sociologists have emphasized over and over again that no proof has ever been given to show that the mental characteristics of a 'race' can be deduced from its descent."[57]

The pamphlet then recounted the findings of Boas's impartial textbook study with the harrowing discovery that not only were American schools years behind on the latest scientific developments, but that outdated theories on racial difference posed an immediate threat to the nation's social welfare. According to modern scientists, it was "absurd to speak of the population of any modern nation as a 'race.'" Boas emphasized the significance of environment on physical form, health, and even "mental life" such as artistic achievements. "Nobody has ever proved that the achievements of a people depend upon their innate, hereditary abilities."[58] Boas concluded by revealing the inaccuracy of intelligence tests like the ones conducted during World War I that supposedly demonstrated the mental inferiority of blacks. He argued that IQ scores resulted from individuals' personal and educational experiences, not their "innate qualities."[59] Boas explained that scientific lessons on racial difference were necessary in public schools because, "today the term 'race' has taken on a high emotional intensity and is almost unavoidably associated with an exaggerated nationalism and with claims of 'racial' superiority."[60]

Can You Name Them? outlined Boas's strategy to reform the way American public schools used the concept of race. First, Boas located the problem that needed to be corrected: the misuse of the term "race" in educational materials. He then explained in laymen's terms the inherent dangers of teaching unscientific models of racial difference. Finally, and most significantly, Boas offered a concrete solution to the problem: informing teachers, and by extension students, of the proper, scientific definition of human race. Boas specifically targeted prominent misconceptions, such as the correlation of race with intelligence and behavior, and refuted them with scientific evidence he had amassed over the course of his professional career.

Publishing a pamphlet was but one tactic in a larger strategy to reform race education. He designed a series of radio shows that reproduced the central messages of his pamphlets though engaging dialogues and skits that were broadcast on WNYC.[61] The 1939 World's Fair in New York City offered Boas another venue to garner support to reform race education in American schools. Working through the ACDIF, Boas constructed an exhibit at the Fair's popular Hall of Science and Education that displayed anthropological books and charts to refute scientific claims of racial superiority.[62] The American Anthropological Association's new decree against racism was prominently displayed, reading: "Anthropology provides no scientific basis for discrimination against any people on the ground of racial inferiority, religious affiliation, or linguistic heritage."[63] The exhibit became the model for 239 exhibits installed in libraries and book stores all over the country.[64] Not only did the display challenge the eugenicist claims of the Chamber of Commerce's recent report, it also contradicted the material presented by the American Eugenics Society at the Fair, which promised Americans they could improve themselves and the nation by paying strict attention to the genetic qualities of potential mates.[65]

In a poignant challenge to eugenicists, Boas organized a public session in the Hall of Science and Education in October of 1939 entitled "The Genetic Basis for Democracy."[66] Outside of the "Negro Week" celebration in 1940, Boas's panel was the sole antiracist initiative officially condoned by Fair organizers and performed on Fair grounds.[67] According to introductory remarks by the geneticist and vice presidential candidate Henry A. Wallace, the goal of the panel was to confront a new threat: racism. Boas and his supporters believed that "false racial theories" explained acts of violence and domination over people targeted as racial minorities.[68] According to these activists, the genetic basis of democracy was that all people, regardless of so-called race, were valid, necessary, and equal citizens in a democratic society.[69]

Speaking to a large audience of teachers and community activists from New York City, Boas outlined his model of genetic democracy. In typical academic style, Boas lectured, "Behavior of peoples is evidently primarily determined by cultural environment as expressed in all social and economic conditions. Thus science teaches emphatically that we must value men and women according to their individual worth, not according to the biological group to which we assign them."[70] Other speakers included Wallace on the subject of genetics, Professor Hadley Cantril on race propaganda, and William A. Hamm, Assistant Superintendent of Schools in New York City, on the subject of tolerance education.[71]

The fact that Boas invited a school superintendent to speak alongside a panel of scientific experts indicates his conscious strategy to use education to counteract propaganda and promote racial tolerance in America. Hamm spoke passionately about the efforts of New York City schools to promote tolerance for ethnic, racial, and religious minorities in the classroom. He described initiatives that coincided with the city's school tolerance drive, including special assembly programs highlighting "the influence of various racial groups upon America," student elections of minority leaders in schools dominated by majority groups, home room classes that emphasized "the contributions of various racial groups," as well as tolerance programming in history, art, and drama classes. Finally, Hamm recounted the special role that science classes played in fighting racism, claiming, "Our pupils are familiar with the extent to which science knows no boundary, knows no race, no creed."[72] Overall, Hamm painted a vivid portrait of the extensive efforts undertaken in New York City schools to counteract racism.

The audience, however, was far from convinced. Of the seven people who asked questions at the end of the lecture, three were educators in New York City.

All were critical of New York City's stance on racial equality in the schools. Dr. Rosenthal from the Rand School lambasted the Board of Education for sending prejudiced white teachers to Harlem, complaining, "Among the school teachers of the city of New York there is a feeling that if you are appointed to Harlem it is one of the greatest punishments. Now people with that point of view who go to Harlem to teach certainly cannot have a favorable relationship to the children."[73] Other teachers questioned whether a program designed to foster "tolerance" went far enough in the fight against racism. Mr. Subarsky reported that a fourth grader in one of his classes defined tolerance as "when you put up with certain people but you don't like to have them around anyhow."[74]

For the most part, the panel of scientific and educational experts deftly dodged the barrage of critical questions from New York City educators. Hamm explained that the Board of Education carefully selected principals to work with a given school population, but that the selection of teachers was out of their control. Subarsky's critique of tolerance as an educational ideal was simply ignored. The speakers stood on firmer ground defending the position of scientists in the war on racism. For example, Boas willingly defended his right as a scientist to produce antiracist propaganda, responding, "When we believe that we have definite proof against the current opinion which is so vicious and so dangerous for the well-being of the whole people—when we have these definite opinions and convictions it is our duty to make those public in the most energetic and efficient way we can. . . . If that is considered propaganda, I can't help it."[75]

The fact that Boas was willing to admit his antiracist education campaign was a form of propaganda at this time demonstrates the depth of his commitment to race education reform. By World War II liberal intellectuals like Boas were generally terrified of the concept of propaganda, which they viewed as a form of intellectual manipulation by the state and therefore inherently antidemocratic. Boas's defense of his antiracist activism as potential "propaganda" illustrates liberals' struggle to balance national education campaigns against more malicious, state-sponsored propaganda utilized by fascist leaders.[76]

Confident that dispelling racial ignorance was his ethical duty as a scientist, Boas willingly defended himself against critics who questioned his motives. Through popular media, Boas asserted his core beliefs in intellectual freedom, racial egalitarianism, and education as necessary ideals to protect American democracy. Sometimes he connected these themes in a single paper or presentation, as in pamphlets like *Can You Name Them?* and *Science Condemns Racism*. Other times, they were tied together in a lecture series or the radio show he produced on WNYC. On this show, broadcast during the summer and fall of 1939, Boas and other academics addressed New Yorkers on the subjects of science, literature, education, and race. Boas made transcripts of the lectures available to schools, reporting that there were "many teachers asking for them."[77]

A defining component of Boas's race education reform strategy was his willingness to work directly with teachers in addressing the problem of racial prejudice in American schools. Boas designed coursework on racial egalitarianism and intellectual freedom for the nation's leading schools of education, including Teachers College at Columbia University, but he also met with high school teachers to design practical and informative lesson plans on the subject of race.[78] He published in teachers' journals, including two essays in the *New York Teacher* and an entire lesson plan on race in the *Teaching Biologist*.[79] Additionally, Boas met with administrators from New York City's Board of Education, where he offered to develop "alertness courses for teachers on the race question."[80] While some of his strategies would never be realized, other components of his antiracist campaign would forever transform the way American schools taught the concept of race.

Just as Boas was making progress reforming the scientific teaching of race in American schools, his major funding source, the American Jewish Committee (AJC), withdrew its support. The AJC was a powerful, politically moderate organization led by Jewish men of largely German descent who favored a strong assimilationist policy for American Jews. By 1934, the AJC was fighting to stem a rising tide of anti-Semitism not only in Nazi Germany, but in its own schools and neighborhoods in New York City. According to annual reports, the AJC was hesitant to directly challenge anti-Semitism because leaders feared that a rebuttal by a Jewish organization would only anger anti-Semites and attract unwanted attention to Jewish political activism. Instead the organization carefully developed *indirect* challenges to anti-Semitism through scientific studies, newspapers, radio shows, magazines, and even public schools to challenge claims of Aryan racial superiority.[81]

Funding a prominent anthropologist working to challenge Nazi racial propaganda was at first an ideal way for the AJC to conduct this kind of indirect activism. Beginning in 1934 the AJC funded Boas and his American Committee for Democracy and Intellectual Freedom. By the outbreak of war in 1939, however, the AJC became concerned that Boas's antiracist activism was extending beyond the bounds of neutral scientific inquiry. In September of 1939, Boas outlined a request for funds in a letter to Harry Schneiderman, assistant secretary of the AJC. But, the following month, the organization decided to sever all ties with Boas, his scholarly research, and his political activism, on which it had already spent over $30,000.[82] Internal memos, correspondence, and reports from the AJC suggest the organization soured on Boas's antiracist activism as it took on more critical and outspoken qualities.[83] Citing anthropological definitions that positioned Jews as racially Caucasian, leaders at the AJC insisted on school programming that emphasized the location of Jews within the American racial and cultural mainstream. For this reason, they did not want to advocate for the rights of those scientifically differentiated as racially distinct "Negroes" or "Mongolians." The AJC was also not willing to risk being associated with the ACDIF as it became scrutinized for harboring communist sympathies.[84]

Until his death in 1942, Boas insisted that Americans must revise the way that public schools taught about race and remain committed to educating all students on an equal basis. Although his commitment to these causes never wavered, poor health and limited funding circumscribed the extent of his influence in reforming race education. On a bitterly cold day in December 1942, Boas was addressing a gathering of colleagues at Columbia University on a new strategy to fight racism when he collapsed, abruptly ending a lifetime of research and activism in the name of racial egalitarianism.[85]

While Boas died before he could see his educational reform effort enacted on a large scale, he had convinced two of his star students, Ruth Benedict and Margaret Mead, of the value of race education reform. They turned their full attention on American schools during World War II and began the difficult process of reconstructing racial discourse on a national level.

‖ 3 ‖

Ruth Benedict and Margaret Mead

Teaching Teachers Race and Culture

> No subject you study in school today is more fraught with conse-
> quences than this subject of race. We shall examine it from every angle.
> —Ruth Benedict, 1942

> If educational leaders . . . were able to enlist young people in the task of
> creating new patterns of living congruent with the aims of a democratic
> society, this readiness for any new path might be used in building a
> more democratic state rather than a less democratic one.
> —Margaret Mead, 1940

Speaking to James Baldwin in 1970 in their collaborative effort *A Rap on Race*,
anthropologist Margaret Mead reflected on her civil rights activism of the 1940s. "I
was speaking in those days about three things we had to do," she explained. "Appreciate cultural differences, respect political and religious differences, and ignore race."

Baldwin replied, thoughtfully, "Ignore race. That certainly seemed perfectly
sound and true."

"Yes, but it isn't anymore. You see, it really isn't true. This was wrong, because . . . ,"
stammered Mead.

"Because race can't be ignored," finished Baldwin.[1]

By 1970 it was clear that the ideal of a colorblind society had been hopelessly
optimistic, if not downright destructive to social justice in the United States.[2]
But in the 1940s social activists like Mead firmly believed the most effective way
to eradicate racism was to stop focusing so much attention on the subject of race.
The colorblind ideal was a logical and appealing extension of the scientific critique of racism. It allowed activists to acknowledge that the race concept had no
ability to explain social relations, while providing what appeared to be a simple
solution to the enduring problem of racial discrimination. Instead of trying to
teach scientific theories on racial egalitarianism, proponents of the colorblind
ideal asked Americans to disregard the significance of race as part of a larger
project of gradual racial integration.

Among anthropologists active in educational reform, Mead was the leading proponent of racially integrated, colorblind tolerance education, putting her at odds with her mentor Franz Boas, and by extension Ruth Benedict's strategy of teaching Americans scientific theories of racial egalitarianism. Mead's colorblind approach to tolerance education resonated with leading intercultural educators including Rachel Davis DuBois. In her conversation with Baldwin, Mead praised one of DuBois's most popular pedagogical techniques, the community festival. According to Mead, at DuBois's community festivals "a mixed group of people sit around telling about things that happened and singing songs."[3] Mead was impressed by the way community festivals created space for interracial dialogue on a subject that had nothing to do with racial differences. She noted in 1945, "These are excellent devices to initiate intergroup relationships among people who are frightened and suspicious of one another," adding, "It cannot be emphasized too strongly that methods which evoke strong or painful emotion are not necessary in groups of this type."[4]

In contrast, Ruth Benedict was skeptical of intercultural education, especially programs like DuBois's community festivals. Benedict ridiculed this kind of pedagogy for its relentless insistence on "cultural gifts" and declared that programs like these were detrimental to American race relations. Benedict offered a form of tolerance education that drew on the scientific concepts of race and culture to challenge essentialist perceptions of human difference and foster a more humane understanding of human diversity. Of special importance, Benedict also asked educators to learn more about the social factors like racial discrimination and social class privileges that shaped the opportunities for members of minority groups.

This chapter investigates the different models of tolerance pedagogy developed by Ruth Benedict and Margaret Mead over the course of World War II. As leading academic authorities on education, they influenced the development of tolerance curricula by publishing articles in teaching journals and textbooks, lecturing to educators, and serving on educational committees. The chapter considers the different strategies Benedict and Mead employed to reform race education in America and evaluates the consequences of their efforts to reconstruct racial discourse in American schools.[5] Despite their varying approaches in the early 1940s, Benedict and Mead both ended up supporting a "colorblind" society in the early postwar era, an ideal that would gain momentum in the wake of World War II.

Ruth Fulton Benedict

After graduating from Vassar College in 1909, Ruth Fulton Benedict spent time traveling in Europe and working as a teacher and social worker before deciding to pursue graduate work in 1919, first at the New School for Social Research and later at Columbia University, where she would earn her Ph.D. in anthropology under Boas. Benedict joined Boas at Columbia in 1921, where she continued to work until her death in 1948.[6] Her status in the field was secured with the publication of *Patterns of Culture* in 1934.[7] According to Margaret Mead, this text helped Americans understand culture in anthropological terms as "the systematic body of learned behavior which is transmitted from parents to children."[8] In *Patterns of Culture*, Benedict argued that every cultural group could be understood in terms of a "personality writ large."[9] Comparing three societies—Zuni, Dobu, and Kwakiutl—Benedict discovered that each society developed its own ideal personality such as the serene, peaceful, moderate Zuni as contrasted with the paranoid and suspicious Dobuans or the megalomaniac, egotistic Kwakiutl. Because she viewed these personality patterns as the products of unique historical circumstances, she asserted that each society selected from among infinite choices those attributes it considered desirable, and then reproduced and enhanced these qualities over time by rewarding desirable behavior and condemning deviations from the norm.[10]

Patterns of Culture essentially popularized what Boas had been arguing for years, that historical and environmental factors were far more important for understanding human diversity than inherent physical or racial traits. Benedict was able to articulate this idea in a way that reached beyond intellectual circles to convince many educated, mainstream Americans that culture was far more pertinent than biology in explaining human diversity. Eventually, Benedict employed this definition of culture to analyze structural sources of social inequality in America.[11]

Benedict was initially skeptical when Boas began devoting scholarly attention to international politics in the 1930s. As he focused on the menace of Nazism in 1934, a puzzled Benedict complained to Mead, "He has given up science for good works . . . such a waste!"[12] However, as reports of abuses against Jews in the name of racial superiority filtered in from Europe, Benedict became one of the era's most politically engaged anthropologists. As early as 1937, she joined educational committees dedicated to reducing prejudice in the United States. Boas convinced Benedict to spend her sabbatical in 1939 writing a book for popular audiences designed to challenge racialist thinking. *Race: Science and Politics* translated Boas's scientific definition of race and its political implications into layman's terms, producing a fascinating account of the scientific approach to race and the political manifestation of racism.[13] Through her work with Boas in the 1930s, Benedict became interested in the question of how American public schools could combat the escalating problem of racial prejudice. She quickly became involved in aspects of educational practice that Boas never addressed, particularly regarding the curriculum of intercultural education.

Benedict crafted a stinging critique of intercultural education in an effort to promote a more sophisticated, anthropological view of the culture concept in schools. She hoped that this more rigorous understanding of culture would encourage educators to fight social inequalities in terms of limited access to resources. By participating on influential educational committees and publishing in prominent educational journals, she attempted to reformulate the goals and strategies of intercultural education to account for a vision of "culture" that valued real instead of superficial diversity and focused attention on the plights of Jews and blacks. Second, Benedict influenced the way teachers understood the race concept when she revised her book *Race: Science and Politics* into a pamphlet, *The Races of Mankind*. The 1943 pamphlet, which defined race in simple but anthropologically accurate terms with the help of straightforward text and cartoon illustrations, became an international sensation in American schools with lasting implications for the dominant educational discourse on race.

Like Boas, Benedict became increasingly active in liberal reform movements during the Depression and in the late 1930s.[14] In 1937, she was drawn into New York City educational politics when she joined the Commission on Intercultural Education (CIE) of the Progressive Education Association.[15] Benedict supported the CIE's goals of reducing prejudice and promoting better race relations among American youth. On the surface, she found nothing to disagree with in the CIE's efforts to identify and promote the positive attributes of minority groups. However, as she became familiar with intercultural education and its pedagogy, she realized the curriculum cultivated a static definition of culture that undermined its ability to challenge racialist discourse.

Within months of joining the CIE, Benedict derailed director Rachel Davis DuBois's planned publication of an intercultural education book series on various ethnic groups.[16] Benedict's opposition was not simply that these books promoted "immigrant cultural conservation," but more significantly that they employed a nonscientific concept of culture that threatened to undermine antiracist education.[17] This problematic conception of culture was evident in two books published by DuBois and Emma Schweppe before Benedict terminated the series. For example, in *The Germans in American Life*, DuBois and Schweppe contended that tensions and misunderstandings between "nationality, cultural, and racial groups" in America were caused by proponents of the "Melting Pot" theory who expected immigrants to "drop their customs, traditions, and even language, which are basic to personality, much as one might change a dress." The authors observed that the acculturation process was slow, not immediate, and that the persistence of differences among groups caused members of the dominant group to develop "attitudes of superiority." Therefore, they asserted that American students should develop a "sympathetic understanding" of minority groups while minorities continued the process of acculturation.[18]

To foster this sense of sympathy, DuBois and Schweppe presented a concise and decidedly compassionate analysis of Germans in one book and Jews in another. Besides a brief history of each group in Europe and America, the books recognized each group's achievements in the fields of education, science, art, journalism, literature, drama, and music. For educators, these achievements in various fields represented a group's "culture." DuBois and Schweppe intended this positive view of culture to boost minority children's self-esteem while fostering empathy for minorities among white, Protestant, middle-class students. The authors demonstrated familiarity with Ruth Benedict's famous *Patterns of Culture*, describing Germans and Jews in terms of the "patterns of life" they brought to America and attempting to understand each group in terms of its dominant "personality."[19]

Benedict, nevertheless, strongly disagreed with how intercultural educators translated anthropological theories into practice. Specifically, she disagreed with DuBois and Schweppe's definition of culture as a list of fixed attributes. While interculturalists worked to convince Americans to appreciate select elements of minority "culture," Benedict viewed schoolchildren as active members of a broader, more encompassing American culture. To dredge up and celebrate the specific markers of racial or ethnic "culture" was not just pointless, according to Benedict, but actually harmful to race relations. From her scientific vantage point, culture was not the cute or quaint folkways from the old country, but the active ways that people living together in a community made sense of their lives. From 1937 through her death in 1948 Benedict fought to make intercultural education conform to an anthropological concept of culture, one that she believed offered educators a powerful theoretical tool to undermine racial prejudice in American youth.

In 1941 Benedict publicized her critique of intercultural education through lectures and publications in educational journals and textbooks. She was particularly concerned with the way that intercultural education masked social class inequality in America, or what she called "special privilege."[20] Her article, "Privileged Classes: An Anthropological Problem," in the progressive educational journal *Frontiers of Democracy* directly responded to the recent presidential election, which Benedict believed demonstrated "the lines between America's underprivileged and special privileged were drawn more tightly than ever before."[21] In this essay, she argued that the "special privileges" afforded to the wealthy "sets up a tension which is fatal to the humane satisfactions in the privileged as well as in the under-privileged."[22] By comparing the way that various "primitive" cultural groups reproduced social inequality by refusing to allow commoners to compete with the elite for power, wealth, and status, Benedict suggested that Americans reexamine the way that "special privilege" in America restricted fair competition for education and jobs for racial minorities.

Academics and liberal activists in the 1930s were drawn to questions of social-class inequality generated by the Great Depression. Especially at Teachers College and Columbia University, scholars like George Counts and William Kilpatrick wanted teachers to unmask the inequalities of a capitalist system as the first step in reforming the social order. When this movement dovetailed with the anthropological critique of race, scientists like Boas and Benedict worked to make the connections between social-class exploitation and racism explicit, not only for teachers but for many of their colleagues in academia. As experts on race and on cultural production, Boas and Benedict worked to separate issues of racial and class discrimination for the purposes of analysis, and then to bring these concepts back together to generate a more nuanced and sophisticated critique of inequality in American schools.

Benedict's "Privileged Classes" reflected her faith in the potential of public education to serve as an equalizing mechanism in a democracy. Because she believed that tolerance education must make this agenda of social equality more explicit, Benedict criticized existing programs of intercultural education for their reluctance to directly confront social class inequality. She did not aim to abolish the program but wanted to refine it by downplaying its insistence on "cultural gifts."[23] Benedict wanted to create a pedagogy of inquiry that examined questions of equality of opportunity in education, employment, and health care, problems she understood in terms of class privileges. While educators remained focused on the unique traits of white ethnic groups like Greeks and Poles, Benedict criticized American social inequality in terms of socioeconomic class, race relations, anti-Semitism, and discrimination against women.

Benedict admonished educational initiatives that singled students out for their ethnic or racial heritage and then forced them to enact traditional or stereotypical "cultural" roles. She found this especially inappropriate for second- and third-generation students who were already assimilated to American culture and did not require interference by reformers. Belittling DuBois's version of intercultural education, she explained to an audience at Bryn Mawr College in February 1941:

> One leader in this field I used to call the woman who believed that race problems could be solved by teaching children that Japanese were adept at arranging flowers. So in our schools we put on assembly programs where the Negro children sing their spirituals and the Balkan children dress in their native costume—and wonder why they don't like it. But in America, aliens want more than anything else to be American.[24]

Due to strict immigration legislation passed in the 1920s, the vast majority of American schoolchildren in 1941 had been born in America.[25] They grew up in American towns and cities, learned English in school and on the streets, and participated in the full range of activities that produced what Benedict understood as their culture, even if they lived in minority enclaves. While she recognized that these children might face hardships and discrimination, she could not conceive of emphasizing old-world folk traditions as a way to alleviate discrimination. At another lecture, she explained the wrong-headedness of this technique:

> Many people in America who have tried to improve our race relations here have acted as if America were like Europe. They have provided opportunities for immigrants to show off their costumes and songs on school programs, they have emphasized folk-handicrafts, they have had children tell folktales from their own lore in the old country. But this does not fit the American situation. New Americans are not perpetuating their traditional customs down the generations. Even if in special cases a group lives to itself for two generations, it wants its place as Americans by the third. And usually the pace is much faster. Primarily new Americans want to be accepted as Americans, they want to be asked to participate in American life as Americans.[26]

Benedict saw a nation where the children of immigrants and racial minorities wanted to fit in, not stand out. According to educators, these differences were examples of "culture," which they thought could be used to promote minority self-esteem and temper majority discrimination. In contrast, Benedict believed the best antiracist strategy was exposing and removing barriers to equal opportunity. Benedict asserted that American immigrants, particularly children, wanted desperately to fit into American culture, writing, "Each new generation is ashamed of its hang-overs."[27] For Benedict, the solution to racial prejudice was clear: "working shoulder to shoulder" with minorities of all backgrounds for better city administration, housing, and public schools.[28]

Beyond these challenges to the way intercultural educators employed the culture concept, Benedict disagreed with the curriculum's strategy of targeting minority students for reform. Instead of focusing on minority children "across the tracks" she wanted educators to reform middle- and upper-class white Protestant children "on the hill."[29] Benedict tried to convince teachers: "Bringing a group of Italian-American boys from another school for two hours to perform for a middle-class suburban school will not be likely to influence adult attitudes toward Italian employees or toward a housing project in the Italian district."[30] Unlike intercultural educators, Benedict wanted to discuss the implications of intercultural education for future citizens in terms of political issues like housing covenants and employment discrimination. For this reason, she wanted teachers

to focus on "human worth" and integrate intercultural education throughout
subject matter and extracurricular activities so that "they will not be part of what
are so often intolerably named the 'tolerance' courses."[31]

In her most potent challenge to intercultural education, Benedict suggested
that Jews and blacks faced a more powerful strain of discrimination than white
ethnics in the United States. Benedict summarized her vision for intercultural
education in terms of equal opportunities and civil liberties for a more inclusive
group of American citizens:

> The central plank in realizing this [intercultural education] program
> must be that of opportunity for the development of every talent.
> Opportunity must be without discrimination based on race, birth,
> sex, income, or creed. There will always be inequalities of achieve-
> ment because people differ in energy, intelligence, and ability to lead.
> But inequalities are not socially disruptive in societies where special
> privilege is lacking—special privilege before the law, special privilege
> in educational opportunity, special privilege in positions of prestige.
> All those things which we in our society remove from the category of
> special privilege we call civil liberties, that is, rights which are valid
> only when they are guaranteed to everybody, and our intercultural
> program will therefore be concerned with civil liberties as an integral
> part of its program.[32]

Benedict believed that civil liberties should define intercultural education
and that celebrations of cultural gifts detracted from the curriculum's potential
to promote social justice. Furthermore, she worried about the nature of the cultural attributes teachers elected to highlight. In most programs, Benedict noted,
teachers reduced the world's rich cultural diversity into bland, homogenous variations on American norms, designed so that children "will discover that after all
human beings are a lot alike." Instead, Benedict pleaded with educators, "we
must admit human differences, admit them to the hilt and not deny them. Differences are the most precious thing in life. They give it all the variety and richness
it has; they make possible the achievements of civilization."[33] Benedict wanted
teachers to undermine myths of racial superiority and promote civil liberties for
minorities, not waste time trying to convince students that all people were inherently the same. Better to acknowledge the differences between people, even if
they were disagreeable. Schools attempted to do the impossible, Benedict
claimed, when they tried to "make everybody love everybody."[34]

In 1942 Benedict shifted tactics from critiquing programs of intercultural
education to directly attacking what she understood to be the foundations of
racial prejudice among teachers and students. Like Boas, Benedict believed that

racial prejudice stemmed from a lack of accurate information about human racial differences. She became convinced that the unscientific way that teachers and textbooks spoke about race in the classroom was a serious problem. For this reason she agreed to publish a teaching aid entitled "Race and Cultural Relations: America's Answer to the Myth of a Master Race," a sixty-page text on the scientific definition of human race. The last twenty pages were written by an educator who offered specific suggestions for how to incorporate Benedict's ideas on race into the classroom.[35]

Published as a joint venture by the National Association of Secondary School Principals, the National Council for the Social Studies, and the National Education Association, "Race and Cultural Relations" allowed Benedict to articulate a critique of the race concept that was intended for teachers, and by extension, children and adolescents. Benedict argued that teachers must teach modern and scientific definitions of human race, given the racialized nature of World War II and the related problem of race relations in America. She then delineated the scientific definition of human race including the significance of skin color, eye color and form, hair color and form, shape of the nose, cephalic index, and blood groups. A third section introduced teachers to the relatively new concept of "racism," which was explained as a form of power used to dominate people based on false claims about human biological differences. The final two sections of Benedict's text offered "a short history of racism" that explained the interplay between race and class conflicts, and the relationship between racial and religious conflicts.

As was her style, Benedict ended with a dramatic challenge to teachers to take responsibility for the shortcomings of American democracy. She asked them to move beyond the naive expectation that tolerance education alone could end racism in America, writing, "The program that will finally banish racism is called today 'making democracy work.'" She continued, "It involves using the nation's full manpower for the common benefit, raising housing standards and conditions of labor above the needlessly low standards which prevail in many sections of the country today, encouraging the practice of social responsibility in industry, raising health standards, providing equal educational advantages for all, extending civil liberties and other measures of this nature."[36]

Just because Benedict wanted teachers to understand racism as a dilemma that would require more than tolerance education to fix did not mean she was unwilling to be associated with practical matters of developing classroom content. The lesson plans in the second half of "Race and Cultural Relations" included specific discussion questions, suggested readings and films, and offered classroom activities to improve knowledge of minority achievements and foster familiarity with minority individuals. While some of the suggested activities were provocative, such as the discussion question "Should intermarriage

between the races be allowed?" others were consistent with intercultural education such as ethnic pageants, interviews with minority group leaders, and field
trips to visit minority people where they lived and worked. The intended audience for the lesson plans was clearly white, and the text directed teachers toward
a special concern with American Indians, Chinese Americans, and African
Americans—or nonwhite racial minorities.[37]

There is little evidence that "Race and Cultural Relations" was read by very
many teachers in 1942, although clearly it helped Benedict refine her public presentation of scientific materials on race. She brought her message to a much
larger audience the following year when she published *The Races of Mankind*, an
easy to read, illustrated pamphlet produced for school use. Benedict wrote *The
Races of Mankind* with the help of another female Boas student and Columbia
professor, Gene Weltfish. Originally published in the fall of 1943 by the nonprofit educational group the Public Affairs Committee, the pamphlet sold for ten
cents to schools, civic groups, churches, and synagogues.[38] The book was mod-
estly successful until 1944, when it became the focal point of a nationwide political controversy.[39] Congressional leaders learned that 55,000 copies of *The Races
of Mankind* had been purchased for distribution to American soldiers. Congress
initiated a panel to "expose the motive behind this book," which one con-
gressman scoffed, "described Northern Negroes as the equals in intelligence of
Southern white men."[40] Anthropologists at Columbia University defended the
publication as a "general refutation of Nazi race theories."[41] However, the Congressional subcommittee headed by Representative Durham from North Carolina asserted the book contained statements ranging "all the way from half-truths
through innuendos to downright inaccuracies."[42] The controversy reverberated
through newspaper headlines and radio talk shows, pushing publication from a
substantial 250,000 in 1944 to over 750,000 in 1945 as Americans "sent in their
dimes" to read the pamphlet for themselves.[43]

Although southern politicians were outraged by Benedict and Weltfish's
claim that IQ scores had more to do with the "luck" of educational opportunity
than innate ability, this was but a sidebar in the pamphlet's main narrative.
Written in a casual, conversational tone, the introduction highlighted the need
for American unity in the face of Nazi aggression. Speaking to Americans who
may have felt uncomfortable with a frank discussion of race relations, the authors
framed the discussion in patriotic terms: "Today, when what we all want more
than anything else is to win this war, most Americans are confident that, whatever our origins, we shall be able to pull together to a final victory."[44] Readers
were invited to join "most Americans" in this civic duty through a dialogue
about the meaning and significance of racial difference. Striking a pleasant
tone, Benedict and Weltfish introduced claims that were controversial—if not
threatening—to popular notions about racial difference.

The Races of Mankind by Ruth Benedict and Gene Weltfish, 1943.

The authors established themselves as soldiers on the "Race Front." To address the troubled state of race relations worldwide, Benedict and Weltfish asserted the scientific objectivity of "facts that have been learned and verified" about race.[45] The pamphlet explained physical differences among humans, including height, blood, and skin color, and defined the Boasian model of racial classification as it was understood in 1943. The distributions of the three "primary races," Caucasian, Mongoloid, and Negroid, were plotted on a map, while the authors explained ethnic groups of varying colors and hues as the result of intermarriage among the original three races. The authors were at pains to assert: "Aryans, Jews, Italians are *not* races." "Aryan" was defined as a word that "has no meaning," while Jews represented a religious group and Italians a nationality.[46] The goal of this section was to establish unassailable scientific truths about racial difference, as well as to deconstruct the fallacies of racialist thinking prevalent in the early 1940s. The text included numerous cartoon drawings to illustrate central claims.

Benedict and Weltfish devoted an entire section to explaining the long history of "race mixing" among the three main races: "Wherever they went, some of them settled down and left children." Although it avoided the unpleasant facts of colonization and exploitation over the past four centuries, it definitively stated, "as far as we know, there are no immutable laws of nature that make racial intermixture harmful," openly addressing an aspect of race relations so controversial it was rarely spoken about in public, especially in publications produced for students.[47] Although they refrained from challenging American laws and customs that restricted "interracial" marriages, Benedict and Weltfish offered scientific evidence that "race mixing" was harmless.

Ultimately, *The Races of Mankind* attempted to convince the public of the scientific theory that differences between individuals of any group, whether racial, national, or religious, were due to variations in social environment and historical circumstances and not biologically determined.[48] Thus, the rich diversity of human life on earth was to be understood as the result of cultural

THERE IS NO JEWISH "RACE." In China there are Jews that look just like Chinese. In Abyssinia there are Jews that look like Abyssinians. In Turkey there are Jews that look like Turks. In England and in Germany there are many blond Jews. Jews follow a religion, just as Mohammedans and Christians follow their religions.

This cartoon drawing from *The Races of Mankind* explained that people of various races, nationalities, and ethnicities can be Jewish.

or learned phenomena, not racial or inherited characteristics. While the text successfully deconstructed certain elements of racialist thinking, such as the so-called danger of "race-mixing," it was nonetheless a product of its time. As such, the authors unintentionally reified elements of racialist thinking that they viewed as harmless. For example, while they insisted the only anthropological races were Mongoloid, Negroid, and Caucasian, they sometimes referred to people as Mediterranean or Nordic, a rhetorical move that would have been confusing for readers used to viewing these as racially distinct groups. In one passage, Benedict and Weltfish insisted that Hitler's view of ideal Germans as "Aryans" was incorrect, and that the "anthropological term" was "Nordic."[49]

Another perplexing element of *The Races of Mankind* is the way Benedict and Weltfish used the colors white, black, and yellow interchangeably with anthropological racial classifications. Referencing popular slang of the day, the authors employed color as shorthand for race. Later translations of *The Races of Mankind* made the color for race paradigm even more explicit. For example the 1948 children's book *In Henry's Backyard* portrayed human diversity in terms of boldly

PEOPLE ARE GENTLE OR WARLIKE DEPENDING ON THEIR TRAINING. There is no such thing as a "born fighter." It is just as natural to be cooperative and gentle as it is to be bossy and over-bearing. Race doesn't decide the matter. It's the way you're brought up.

This illustration from *The Races of Mankind* explained that traits like aggression are formed through culture, not race.

colored illustrations of yellow, black, and white men standing next to each other while captions insisted the three men were inherently the same.

With *The Races of Mankind*, Benedict and Weltfish established themselves as rational, unbiased scholars whose scientific authority allowed them to openly challenge popular misconceptions about race. Despite the fact that they went to

The bright ones, as well as the strong ones, . . .

. . . come in all colors.

Illustrations from *In Henry's Backyard* depicted the three "races of mankind" in starkly contrasting white, black, and yellow colors.

considerable lengths to present the material as noncontroversial, it was ultimately public controversy that attracted readers. The public response to the pamphlet sheds light on the state of race relations in America in 1944. The *New York Times* cover story "Army Drops Race Equality Book" lent support to Benedict and Weltfish by portraying congressional leaders as old-fashioned and out-of-touch southerners.[50] Despite grumbling about the portrayal of black and white IQ tests, the pamphlet was well received in New York City and across much of the nation. The New York City Board of Education encouraged teachers to read and implement the text as part of their ongoing tolerance drive, and the Detroit public schools distributed the pamphlet and poster series to every school.[51]

While these texts accurately reflected the anthropological definition of human race, they nevertheless promoted stereotypical and oversimplified examples of racial diversity. *In Henry's Backyard*, the children's book adapted from *The Races of Mankind*, followed the story of a white man wearing a bow tie as he met his neighbors, the brown Mexican wearing a sombrero, the yellow Chinese wearing a peasant hat, and the brown Arab wearing a turban. Despite Benedict's concern with the tendency of intercultural education to conflate race with culture, in this case each racial minority was depicted in stereotypical "folk" dress and not as assimilated Americans.

Following the astonishing success of *The Races of Mankind*, the American Council on Education (ACE) invited Benedict to survey "the treatment accorded religious and racial matters in basic teaching materials used in our public schools and colleges."[52] This study, financed by the National Conference of Christians and Jews (NCCJ), was designed to promote balanced treatment of minorities in textbooks, reduce prejudice and tensions between minority and majority groups, and focus attention on the ethical questions of discrimination against minorities in America. ACE researchers met at Harvard Graduate School of Education, where they surveyed the text and photographs of 267 public school textbooks, 21 college texts in psychology and sociology, 25 manuals for college orientation courses, and 100 popular children's books found in school libraries.[53] The final report, carefully crafted to portray a "positive and constructive" tone,[54] found that "with very few exceptions the textbooks and courses of study are free of intentional bias toward any population."[55] However, the report also demonstrated that "there are frequent value judgments and implications, unconsciously or carelessly expressed, which tend to perpetuate antagonisms now current in American life."[56] Beyond insisting that textbooks should remove stereotypical or harmful depictions of minorities, the report suggested that school curricula and textbooks present more realistic impressions of the range of diversity within each minority group. Furthermore, the report wanted school materials to incorporate basic anthropological, sociological, and psychological theories on the

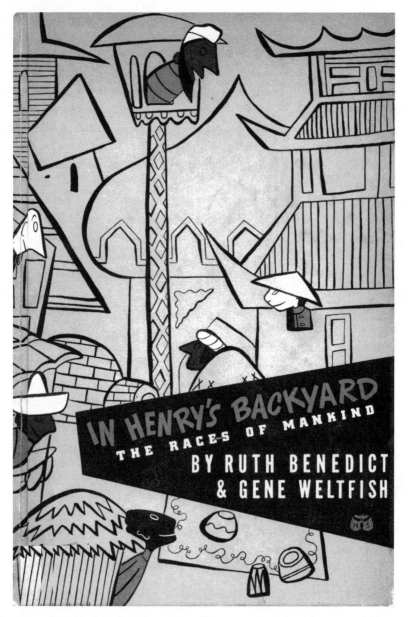

The cover of *In Henry's Backyard*, a version of *The Races of Mankind* for young children.

nature of prejudice and the role of personality on social relations. In a favorable review of the ACE survey, the *New York Times* reminded readers, "The textbooks used in the classroom are the tools through which democracy can be strengthened."[57] As with Boas's survey nearly a decade earlier, publishers promised to revise textbooks to reflect the suggestions made by Benedict and other ACE Committee members.[58]

Working with the ACE's Committee on the Study of Teaching Materials in Intergroup Relations motivated Benedict to move beyond a critique of the race concept in American schools to a broader analysis of American cultural patterns. After 1944 she became more concerned with the way minority groups were portrayed in dominant American culture, such as textbooks and teaching materials, and less concerned with the way these books presented the race concept. Benedict recognized overt racial discrimination as a potentially devastating flaw in American democracy and national culture, and took direct action to remedy this problem. The conclusion of World War II and the subsequent increase in scholarly attention on the subject of American race relations encouraged Benedict to embrace the colorblind ideal. In her final published essays on tolerance education, Benedict no longer asked teachers to present scientific material on race and culture, and instead encouraged them to promote racially integrated schools.

In June 1946 Benedict contributed the essay "Racism Is Vulnerable" to the intercultural education issue of the popular *English Journal*, a publication of the National Council of Teachers of English. According to Benedict, anthropological texts that exposed the fallacies of racism, such as her own *The Races of Mankind*, were examples of "negative" race education.[59] While this was a useful approach to reducing prejudice, Benedict suggested that the postwar world also required a "positive" approach to fighting racism in the schools where students would get to know people of different races through intimate daily contact. She reflected, "It is hard to be simple enough about such a terrible social curse as racism and to recognize that the only positive approach to a world free of racism lies in seeing people as individuals."[60] Grasping that racial integration was not always a viable strategy, she encouraged English teachers to use literature to try to re-create personal knowledge of people from different races. She suggested teachers discuss the good and bad attributes of literary characters, even if this seemed to emphasize unflattering traits of a character who happened to be a racial minority.

According to Benedict, the best way to breakdown racism in the classroom was through thoughtful analyses of people based on their individual merits. She explained to readers, "Racism brands the nice little Jewish boy in the class as a 'kike' and his individuality makes no difference. Americans will never be rid of race prejudice until we are able to drop our group labels, which ignore all that really matters, and learn to judge each person as he really is—mean or kindly, reliable or irresponsible, sane or fanatical."[61] Benedict recommended that English teachers draw on poems, plays, and novels featuring minority protagonists to help students learn to evaluate people based on the values and culture that shaped each character's life. This empathetic or positive approach to intercultural education was Benedict's prescription for better race relations in the postwar world. Thus, Ruth Benedict, the leading academic in race education reform during the war, moved away from promoting scientific lessons on race by 1946. Nevertheless, she continued to emphasize culture as a complex system of shifting values in a continuing effort to convince educators of the anthropological meaning of this term.

In 1948, just months before her death, Benedict completed the shift toward the promotion of a colorblind ideal. In "Can Cultural Patterns Be Directed?" published in *Intercultural Education News*, she questioned how America's unique cultural patterns could be "rationally directed" to improve democracy and individual freedom. She claimed Americans needed to strengthen federal and state laws to protect minority rights in voting, education, and employment. Benedict emphasized the need for federal funding of public education, as well as government oversight to deter racial discrimination in educational politics and practice. Most importantly, Benedict urged teachers to draw on the fundamental American love of "fair play" to improve race relations:

> We tend to interpret anti-racism as meaning that everyone should love everyone else regardless of bad behavior, admit them to colleges regardless of poor records, and employ them regardless of absenteeism. This is a mistake. It is fair play, not universal love and permissiveness, that is needed—fair play which will recognize a man on his merits. With a cultural pattern such as ours, sportsmanship and the spirit of fair play are ethical qualities that are basic to the success of a program of intercultural education.[62]

Benedict envisioned a society free from racial prejudice, but also free from racial preferences that seemed to value people only because of the color of their skin. Guiding intercultural educators to consider minority civil rights, Benedict outlined a strategy that would tackle racial discrimination and support federal funding of American public schools. She believed teachers could play a prominent role by critically evaluating and then mobilizing American cultural patterns so that certain attributes, like the inherent belief in "fair play," could be redirected to generate widespread support for minority civil rights. Teaching the scientific definition of race was conspicuously absent from her argument. Instead, Benedict emphasized the value of the anthropological concept of culture, by which she meant American national culture—not individual minority cultures—to promote social equality in America.

One significant result of Benedict's work was that teachers came to speak of white racial minorities as members of the dominant Caucasian race, a shift that focused antiprejudice education on people of African or Asian descent. Benedict accomplished Boas's goal of raising political awareness of the race concept. As a public intellectual, Benedict followed the shifting tides of postwar liberal thinking to adopt the notion of a colorblind ideal. Instead of focusing on race, Benedict wanted teachers to employ a critical anthropological conception of culture to mobilize direct action against social injustice, especially racial discrimination. Benedict believed teachers could employ American cultural patterns to direct their students toward an understanding of the importance of individual worth and equal opportunities. Inspired by what was, in hindsight, an overly optimistic view of postwar race relations in America, Benedict believed the time had come to consider all people on their individual merit in an essentially colorblind world. Her student, friend, and colleague Margaret Mead came to a similar conclusion at the same time—only Mead lived long enough to regret it.

Margaret Mead

In 1922, a young Margaret Mead took a course with Franz Boas and his teaching assistant Ruth Benedict during her senior year at Barnard College and was convinced to switch fields from psychology to anthropology. She also decided to pursue a doctorate degree under Boas at Columbia University and quickly signed up for fieldwork in the South Pacific to study the trendy subject of "adolescence" among the Samoan. She published her research as *Coming of Age in Samoa* in 1928, a national bestseller that described in tantalizing detail the uninhibited sexual relations of Samoan teenagers and skyrocketed the young scholar to lasting fame. Mead contrasted Samoan expressions of free love to the strict sexual mores of Americans, ultimately suggesting that sexuality was socially constructed and that behavior deemed immoral in one society could be condoned, if not encouraged, in another. In the Boasian tradition, Mead's work encouraged Americans to consider what aspects of their own culture were socially constructed as opposed to natural or inevitable.[63] From the start of her career through the early 1950s, Mead found the subject of American public education to lie at the intersection of her diverse professional interests.

Mead's background in psychology and her expertise on adolescence pushed her into American educational debates long before 1939, when Boas identified the topic as a salient problem for anthropologists. In 1926 Mead accepted her first professional job as assistant curator of ethnology at the American Museum of Natural History (AMNH). The AMNH was dedicated to disseminating scientific knowledge to the public, including knowledge about human beings produced by anthropologists.[64] Mead used her association with the museum to publish an article in *School and Society* the following year that challenged the use of intelligence tests in American public schools.[65] In the 1920s, educational reformers dedicated to improving the "efficiency" of public education promoted

IQ tests as an accurate way to determine which curricula was best for students: a precollegiate academic curriculum or vocational education that prepared students for skilled trade, domestic, and factory work. In the United States, these tests justified promoting industrial education for all black students in the South as well as many racial and ethnic minority students in the North.[66] In her article, Mead demonstrated that IQ scores for Italian American students were directly correlated to the amount of English spoken at home. Disputing the way educators used these tests to track students into nonacademic curricula, Mead asserted that IQ tests were "not a just evaluation of the child's innate capacities."[67] If IQ scores did not reflect "innate capacities," as social efficiency experts argued, but instead reflected social variables like the amount of English spoken in the home, then Mead had identified a major defect in contemporary educational theory and practice. While she avoided a direct critique of educational policy, her early scholarship laid the foundation for later professional involvement in problems of social justice and public education.

Early in her career at the AMNH, Mead encouraged educators to teach anthropology at schools of education. In 1927, she suggested that future teachers could learn more "constructive" thinking skills through the study of non-Western cultures. She explained, "Anthropology is a special technique for enabling people to step outside their own civilizations and view them objectively."[68] Mead designed a lecture series for teachers on primitive cultures at the AMNH in 1930 and 1931, gave talks for teachers at the museum on Wednesday afternoons, and invited New York City public school teachers to attend for free. In the lecture series, Mead explained how different culture groups across time and space have crafted alternative ways of adapting to physical and social environments. In one lecture she contrasted the rich artwork and elaborate social structure of the northwest coast Indians to the "poor" culture of California Indians. She explained that economic conditions, including the abundant food supply in the northwest, allowed this culture group to devote more time to leisure activities like art and religion while the harsh conditions of the California desert meant that people who lived there spent most of their time securing basic necessities like food and shelter. Mead hoped these lessons would demonstrate for teachers the "flexibility of human nature" and emphasize the social, environmental, and historical factors that shaped each group's culture and civilization.[69] Her lessons attempted to illustrate that different cultures were just that—different, and that they should not be viewed as better or worse. Even more importantly, Mead wanted teachers to recognize that social factors, not biological ones, determined the varied cultural expressions of human beings. Many of these same themes could be found in her 1930 book written for a popular audience, *Growing Up in New Guinea: A Comparative Study of Primitive Education,* a comparison of educational institutions in New Guinea and public education in the United States.[70]

Mead's ongoing interest in education, her prestigious position at the AMNH, and her continued association with Boas and Benedict at Columbia University primed her to enter one of the most contentious educational debates of the 1930s. Like most liberal social scientists interested in the period's problems of public education, she supported "progressive" education. Mead envisioned her lecture series as a resource for progressive teachers committed to experimental education and relating schoolwork to the "immediate problems" of the real world, rather than standardizing the curriculum and rigidly separating subject matter.[71]

In 1932 Mead's colleagues at Columbia University's Teachers College took over the nation's most prominent organization dedicated to progressive education, the Progressive Education Association (PEA), ousting the private school teachers and principals who had been running it. The Columbia faculty, led by George Counts and William H. Kilpatrick, wanted to change progressive education's goals and direction to stand more aggressively against what they saw as the evils of unrestrained capitalism. In the midst of the Great Depression, these "social meliorists" found powerful support for their claims that education must be used to transform the values undergirding the capitalist economy.[72]

The progressive education movement inspired the historian Charles A. Beard to organize a committee within the American Historical Association (AHA) to investigate the teaching of social studies in public schools. His report, published in 1934, identified laissez-faire capitalism and individualism as dangerous and destructive forces within American society. He called for teachers to embrace politics and promote social criticism through the public schools. "Today," the report declared, "because of . . . the timidity and weakness of the profession and the power of vested interests and privileged groups, the teacher seldom dares to introduce his pupils to the truth about American society and the forces that drive it onward."[73] The report was so bombastic that it drew vehement criticism from both conservatives and liberals. For liberals like John Dewey, the point of progressive education was to teach critical thinking through an open intellectual climate. Dewey and others specifically opposed promoting a "pre-determined social ideal" on children, or anything that sounded remotely like "indoctrination."[74]

Mead was quickly drawn into the heated PEA debate, where she identified with Dewey's liberal critique. In the summer of 1934 she first met the intellectuals associated with the PEA at a retreat at Dartmouth College. Lawrence Kelso Frank, with financial support of the Rockefeller Foundation, organized the retreat to investigate "everything then known about teaching adolescents." The interdisciplinary group of the nation's most outstanding scholars assembled, in Mead's words, to pull together "all that we knew about human development as we would want to teach it in the schools."[75] Following the retreat, Frank organized the same social scientists into the Commission on the Secondary School

Curriculum (CSSC). One of their most urgent tasks in 1935 was to respond to the report by Beard that called for a radical restructuring of the social order, a goal Mead and her colleagues in the CSSC did not share. The debate was so volatile and the lines drawn between "liberal" and "radical" intellectuals so contentious that Mead originally agreed to participate on the CSSC only if she could do so anonymously.[76]

The CSSC asked Mead to develop a statement on the problem of teaching social studies. Chairman V.T. Thayer urged her to address this matter, writing, "As you know the teaching of the social studies has been oversimplified and at the present time we are in the hands of the indoctrinators."[77] Mead and other moderate liberals sought a more subtle method of reform by promoting an intellectual climate of inquiry and debate. It was through her involvement in this project that Mead first expressed her belief that schools should be used to change social attitudes, not social structures. As she elaborated at the PEA conference in New York City, "Changing the mechanics of the social order can only be done though the schools after at least part of the society is ready for the change." Educators were not equipped to disrupt established patterns of political economic behavior, she continued, "But changing the climate of opinion in which young people are reared, a change which will inevitably have profound reverberations in the social order, is well within the power of educational leaders."[78]

Mead refined and developed this critique in her report to the CSSC. She directed teachers and administrators to alter student attitudes by first studying the "total personality" of adolescents in their school, which shared a given culture defined by a set of ideal traits. In a single-spaced, thirty-six-page report she offered detailed instructions on how to do an anthropological study of a single school. She instructed educators to investigate seemingly mundane topics that defined school culture:

> What is the attitude of the school towards athletics? Are students fighting for more athletics or praying for less, or is this an individual matter? Is the student's health continually watched until the student fights for ill-health, a bad digestion, a faulty posture, etc., as if for individual liberty? For girls, what are the penalties to prevent, athletics during menstruation? Is the information that a girl is menstruating known to her whole gym class, beyond its borders, is it in any way accessible information to the boys—through being excused from gym, not dressing, etc?[79]

By evaluating adolescent culture closely, Mead believed educators could identify the best ways to alter undesirable attitudes. Her experience with the PEA

Commission helped her formulate this strategy, which would be developed, tested, and revised over the next two decades.

In April of 1940, after fieldwork in the South Seas and having a child, Mead joined the intellectual debates on education swirling around her in New York City with an article on antiprejudice education in the PEA journal *Frontiers of Democracy*. Echoing the themes she developed at the PEA conference in 1934, Mead criticized scientists for expecting "facts" about race to dissuade Americans of prejudicial beliefs. She carefully summarized the scientific case for racial egalitarianism, emphasizing "culture, a common character structure which results in a similar response to similar conditions" as responsible for shaping the patterns of life of different minority groups in America.[80] Nonetheless, she reflected, "in the face of all this documentation, all this research and exposition, the belief in race differences remains a part of the ordinary attitudinal equipment of the man in the street."[81]

The problem, according to Mead, was that "opponents of race prejudice" misunderstood the scientific argument for racial equality. While anthropologists asserted, "There is no physical inherited basis for the observed differences in achievement level between groups," well-meaning "propagandists" translated this statement as "there ARE no differences." This made no sense, explained Mead, to the man on the street whose personal experience dictated that "Negroes" and women were less skilled and successful than white men. These differences, of course, were due to the way that blacks and women were raised— usually with less education than white men—and to their employment opportunities and expectations, again, far below that of white men. Mead declared, "If the propagandist would shift his ground and deal more realistically with the problem of changing social attitudes, he might have much more effect."[82]

As this suggests, by 1940 Mead had created an alternative model of antiprejudice education different from either Boas's or Benedict's. While Mead valued and promoted scientifically accurate understandings of human difference, she was more interested in changing attitudes that she believed were formed through personal experience. Recruited to help with the war effort, from 1942 to 1945 Mead worked as the executive secretary of the Committee on Food Habits (CFH) of the National Research Council, where she attempted to influence American attitudes on a large scale. Initially belittled by her male colleagues for accepting a position as a "kitchen anthropologist," Mead stepped in and organized the CFH into a powerful and successful organization that would eventually evolve into the Committee on Living Habits, then the National and World Federations of Mental Health, and finally the United Nations Educational, Scientific, and Cultural Organization.[83]

From her position on the CFH, Mead directed a team of fieldworkers to address different economic, political, and nutritional problems related to food supply and production during the war. She wrote pamphlets instructing American housewives how to make food purchases and described how nutritious meals could be made out of unusual, but abundant, ingredients. An important component of her work at the CFH was the promotion of block associations "so that people on this side of the street can find out how people on that side of the street are dealing with what they can find to shop for and cook and eat."[84] Soon, Mead began to envision the potential of block association gatherings to bring together people from different social, economic, and ethnic backgrounds in order to break down prejudice and promote unity, a national imperative during World War II. She made a compelling argument for this tactic in the article "Food Can Be a Bridge between Different Groups," published in 1945 as part of the widely circulated series *Learning to Live in One World*. Mead encouraged neighborhood associations to throw potluck parties where everyone contributed a favorite family dish, something that was supposed to reflect their special cultural heritage.

By bringing Americans from different backgrounds together to share a meal, Mead devised a strategy not only to promote healthy eating, but also to break down prejudice and misunderstanding. She described how foodways were socially constructed and culturally relative, offering examples of different religious and cultural sanctions on what was considered edible. According to Mead it was only natural that the foodways of another group seemed strange, or even offensive, as one group may violate the dietary laws of another. "After all," Mead wrote, "people's bodies are built up from the food they eat, and if garlic is felt to be odd then the people who eat garlic are likely to seem odd also. But if the foods which other peoples eat seem attractive, eating their foods may be one of the surest ways of getting acquainted with them."[85]

While Mead was promoting block parties to help Americans "get acquainted" with one another, she helped intercultural educators devise a new strategy for combating racial prejudice in the schools known as the "neighborhood home festival." In 1943, Mead joined Rachel Davis DuBois's Intercultural Education Workshop just as racial tensions in America erupted into riots in Detroit, Los Angeles, New York, and Beaumont, Texas.[86] The festivals were designed to bring people of different backgrounds together in a friendly, nonthreatening climate where they could share food, stories, and songs. DuBois and Mead believed people would have the kind of intimate experiences with others that would help transform deeply ingrained attitudes. Mead believed this method of promoting real-life experiences between people was far more effective than teaching scientific facts about race. From 1943 through the end of the war, Mead played an important role as an advisor on programming for DuBois's Intercultural Education Workshop. She reported that neighborhood home festivals were "a real social invention for bringing people together in an atmosphere of friendly understanding, as a first step in getting them working together on common problems."[87]

In 1945 DuBois and Mead supervised neighborhood home festivals in New York City public schools 169, 173, 132, and 24 in Washington Heights and Harlem and trained teachers through intercultural education workshops in Princeton, Baltimore, Philadelphia, Pittsburgh, Coatesville, and Tarentum, Pennsylvania.[88] While Mead's role was primarily as an advisor, she did participate in at least one teacher-training workshop at Wellesley College.[89] The neighborhood home festival, alternatively called the "group conversation method" or "parrandas," defined Rachel Davis DuBois's intercultural education strategy well into the postwar years, even after Mead resigned from the project in 1947.[90] Like Mead, DuBois believed that the best way to improve race relations was by creating experiences between people that would act as a catalyst to dissipate individual prejudice. DuBois reported in 1945, "We know of no way to overcome these feelings of distrust on the part of the whites and of discouragement of the part of Negroes except to continue to provide for more face-to-face contacts . . . which by their very nature produce feelings of understanding and generate confidence and trust and hope for the future." Echoing Mead, DuBois continued: "the main aim of the Workshop is not to take specific social action, but to develop the kind of attitudes which could be counted on to take such action in a democracy."[91]

Under Mead's influence food became an important strategy for bringing people together for "face-to-face" encounters. Newsletters and textbooks describe the apparent success of special teas, dinners, and even entire festivals dedicated to sharing special food items like bread. Notably, these festivals asked participants to perform identifiably "cultural" traits, which organizers like Mead insisted all people possessed. Beyond selecting and preparing a dish related to one's ethnic, racial, or religious heritage, participants usually progressed from the communal act of eating to exchange crafts, dances, poetry, and songs. A teacher from Kalamazoo described how her school reached out to local Hungarian-Americans by hosting a dinner: "We shared delicious Hungarian food—we sang together, our Hungarian friends matching every song with folks songs [*sic*] from the plains of Hungary."[92]

Holding up particular material aspects of "culture" for scrutiny was exactly the tolerance pedagogy Benedict objected to. In contrast, Mead supported intercultural programming and helped design new ways for educators to talk about and share an idealized sense of minority group culture. Mead and DuBois expected festivals to induce strong emotional and even cathartic experiences in participants. A newsletter recounts the poignant example of a bread festival held in Princeton, New Jersey, where an "elderly Viennese woman" gushed, "you gave me courage to go on." The organizer reported how the participant's comments affected everyone at the event: "With deft and graceful gestures, she showed us how her mother had cut the bread, rescuing every crumb that fell with the cutting."[93] Descriptions of festivals offered precise strategies to elicit emotional responses in participants, such as holding hands and singing songs in a circle. In her account of how to conduct a spring festival, DuBois suggested, "Perhaps each person takes a spring of blossom or pussy-willow from a vase in the room and holds it aloft as all join in singing."[94]

By nurturing these emotional reactions, DuBois and Mead believed they had created a pedagogical method to combat racial prejudice by subtly influencing people's attitudes toward others. In her promotional brochure, "Build Together Americans," DuBois insisted: "when working in the area of racial and cultural conflicts one should remember that people seldom change their attitudes about other groups of people merely by being presented with facts. People do not act according to what they know, but according to how they *feel* about what they know."[95]

Mead agreed with these statements, although she preferred to qualify them by insisting that emotional experiences should be combined with intellectual training, especially the ability to judge interracial situations "objectively." Nevertheless, Mead's work in intercultural and interracial education during the 1940s continued to emphasize the importance of emotion over intellect and experience over knowledge. The most useful part of intercultural education workshops for teachers, she explained in 1945, was not the content of the coursework, but the opportunity for teachers to live with other teachers of different racial, ethnic, and religious backgrounds in integrated dormitories.[96]

Mead's faith in the power of personal experience to alter attitudes and thereby reduce racial prejudice encouraged her to found and help run an experimental intercultural school in Manhattan in 1945. At the Downtown Community School, Mead wanted the racial, ethnic, and religious diversity of the student body to reflect the demographics of New York City, and so the school offered scholarships to offset the cost of $400 tuition and fees. She believed the integrated student body would, by itself, foster understanding and tolerance among students and for this reason did not promote lessons on the scientific definition of race or racial discrimination in American society.[97] "Don't mention differences unless they are relevant," she scolded a reporter from the *Chicago Defender* in 1946. "It is not important to mention the race of someone who has lost his hat. Use it only when the issue is so important that you have to make the designation."[98]

In matters of classroom instruction, Mead did not find it useful to dwell on a student's racial identity. Decades later, she attributed the failure of the Downtown Community School to the fact that teachers and administrators worked so hard to ignore race in the classroom.[99] However, during the war Mead pressed

Americans to embrace a colorblind model of intercultural education to reduce tensions and promote unity in local politics, schools, youth groups, and churches. She presented intercultural education as a necessary form of social activism, and asked Americans to join her in this important endeavor. Writing in the Young Women's Christian Association newsletter she elaborated, "It is not that we have chosen this hour for action, but rather that the hour has chosen us."[100]

The end of World War II precipitated a dramatic shift in race relations in the United States and quickly altered the context of tolerance education. In 1947, Mead politely resigned from Rachel Davis DuBois's Workshop for Cultural Democracy, as the Intercultural Education Workshop was now known, although she remained associated with the organization as a special consultant.[101] Mead focused instead on her work at the American Museum of Natural History and at the Institute for Intercultural Studies, which she had founded during the war with the help of other prominent social scientists. She became more interested in global interdependence and the study of "complex" cultures, including the United States. At this time, she transitioned from a scholarly interest in American race relations to the broader subject of global human relations, a project Mead pursued for the remainder of her career through the Institute for Intercultural Studies. Mead became a well-known public intellectual, lecturing on a national and international circuit as well as publishing in the popular press and speaking on radio, and later, television shows.[102] Although she remained interested in the subject of "The School in American Culture," she distanced herself from her wartime efforts at teaching racial tolerance.[103]

Even though Mead cited her busy committee schedule as the main reason for her departure from DuBois's Workshop for Cultural Democracy in 1947, there are hints that she was dissatisfied with intercultural education for other reasons. Unlike Benedict, Mead did not offer a formal critique of intercultural education, but an essay she wrote in 1955 suggests her growing discomfort with the way tolerance education ignored cultural differences and relied on a vague discussion of relationships between different "groups" of Americans. Instead, Mead argued that the intercultural education should use an anthropological lens in order to emphasize "that there are no socially relevant differences among human groups that can be attributed to race, and that the most extreme contrasts in socially relevant capacities can be directly traced to culture."[104]

By the mid-1950s, intercultural education had drawn serious criticism from scholars on the left and right. Some critics complained that intercultural education promoted a dangerous form of cultural relativism that failed to hold individuals or nations responsible for ethically unjust deeds. Others charged that intercultural education fostered ethnic and racial nationalism through its relentless emphasis on minority group attributes. Mead discounted both of these critiques, insisting that cultural relativity left room for judging the ethical behavior of a given act within a specific cultural context, and then explaining that the problem of fostering ethnic nationalism was unlikely since second- and third-generation immigrants were more likely than "native" Americans to strongly disapprove of cultural expressions that deviated from a standard, national American culture.[105] Mead argued that intercultural education must remain flexible enough to respond to the needs of local communities, such as reducing prejudice against specific groups, establishing a sense of "common humanity," or helping individuals deal with their own "multicultural inheritance."[106]

In comparison to Boas and Benedict's tolerance pedagogy, which was based on imparting scientific facts about race and promoting an analysis of American culture that revealed social inequalities, Mead's approach to tolerance education was more politically moderate and focused on reforming individual prejudice through an appreciation of cultural diversity. Two factors influenced Mead's more cautious approach to fighting racial prejudice in American public schools. First, her theoretical emphasis on adolescence and childrearing encouraged her to interpret everyday lived experiences as the building blocks of individual personality and group culture. Because Mead understood attitudes such as racial prejudice as the direct result of experiences during the formative years of childhood, she believed that schools could best fight racial prejudice by constructing alternative experiences to cultivate more desirable attitudes like racial tolerance. Given her understanding of the human psyche, simply providing students with scientific facts about race would have little impact on these basic "personality" traits. Second, Mead's position at the AMNH and her fieldwork from 1936 to 1939 distanced her from the racialized political debates that consumed Franz Boas, and to a lesser extent, Ruth Benedict on the eve of war. Unlike Boas and Benedict, Mead never felt compelled to refute Nazi racial doctrines or to promote a more scientifically accurate definition of the race concept in American society.

In her final essay on intercultural education, Mead suggested that the curriculum should "learn to ignore race, respect religious and political differences, and appreciate or discount cultural differences." Praising the curriculum for generating the kinds of experiences necessary to break down prejudices, she explained, "The aim of such racial experience is to increase trust, reduce any tendency to lump people together because they belong to a specific stock, and to disassociate race from culture and religion."[107] For Mead, the defining goal of tolerance education was to separate the race and culture concepts, an intellectual feat that could be only be accomplished through lived experience. Unfortunately, as it was practiced, intercultural education demonstrated a stubborn tendency to conflate the race and culture concepts in a way that diminished the potential of anthropological theory to help Americans think critically about human diversity.

New Lessons on Race and Culture

Margaret Mead and Ruth Benedict's outreach in American public schools in the 1930s and 1940s represents some of the earliest and most significant anthropological social justice activism in American history. These two women developed creative, and very distinct, models of tolerance education that drew on their Boasian training to challenge essentialist notions of racial difference and promote cultural relativity. Boas targeted educational reform as a strategic way to promote the scientific facts of race through textbooks and other materials to disseminate the very knowledge required to modify prejudicial views. Benedict followed Boas's initiative by publishing popular texts on the scientific definitions of race and culture. While she shifted her emphasis in the postwar years to embrace a "positive" approach to antiracist education that included an emphasis on attitudes, she hoped to "direct" these attitudes to specific problems of social injustice like equal opportunities in health care, education, and employment.

Mead was less convinced that scientific facts alone could function as a useful weapon against racial bigotry. Mead asserted that lived experience was far more powerful than school knowledge in shaping and reforming racial prejudice. Therefore, she promoted an antiprejudice pedagogy that emphasized social interactions designed to foster goodwill, empathy, and tolerance. Mead's strategy promoted a concept of culture in American schools that was somewhat antithetical to her own scientific definition of the term. She saw no harm in asking Americans to perform idealized cultural traits like eating ethnic foods and singing folk songs. She elected not to emphasize the political dangers of racism, as Boas and Benedict had done, or to reflect on the unjust barriers to equal opportunity and minority civil rights in America.

While both Benedict and Mead shared a conception of "culture" as an overarching personality, their educational activism produced competing definitions of this term. Benedict directly challenged the way educators used culture to construct diversity in terms of quaint, stereotypical cultural traits. She believed all Americans shared the same culture, especially the younger generation, and that efforts to celebrate old-world traits were not only artificial but dangerous as they erased the markers of true cultural diversity that made the study of human diversity so theoretically engaging. Especially during the war, Benedict struggled to make educators understand culture in terms of more scientifically accurate terms as a set of patterns that all Americans shared and reproduced. In contrast, Mead embraced a more static definition of culture designed to promote positive interpersonal relations in mixed company. Through her wartime work on foodways and nutrition, Mead came to imagine that breaking bread together could foster the kind of experiences that would reduce individual racial prejudice. If these experiences relied on a nonscientific definition of culture as quaint folk-ways, that was a risk Mead was apparently willing to take.

Benedict and Mead's different versions of tolerance education generated mul-tiple and conflicting definitions of the race and culture concepts for educators. Benedict produced explicit instructions for defining race according to scientific principles. As the next two chapters in this book illustrate, teachers took rather quickly to this educational imperative and modified the way they spoke about race in the classroom to conform to Boasian models of human race. Mead's rela-tive silence on the subject of race, in contrast, had a less discernable impact on teachers. It seems likely, however, that Mead taught teachers how to silence dis-cussions of race in the classroom, a practice that emerged as part of the domi-nant educational discourse on race after 1947. In other words, teachers learned what race was from Benedict and how not to speak about it from Mead.

In tracing the influence of Boas, Benedict, and Mead on American educa-tional politics and practice, it is important to consider that while all three were active during the period surrounding World War II, their main periods of influ-ence were distinct. Boas had the greatest influence in the years leading up to American involvement in the war, when a tense and highly racialized political climate threw educational issues into stark relief against questions of democ-racy, academic freedom, and racial tolerance. Whatever uncertainties Ameri-cans may have felt about the value of free education in the 1930s were quickly resolved with American entry into the war. As schools became sites for prein-duction training, few questioned their function or purpose in a modern democ-racy. At the same time, Americans expected public schools to promote absolute loyalty and national unity, especially as growing racial unrest seemed to threaten the Allied war effort. These factors influenced Benedict's reform efforts, espe-cially by creating a welcoming context for the publication of her popular book on the meaning of race. Patriotism during wartime engendered a tolerance ped-agogy so intent on promoting unity that teachers insisted all Americans were inherently the same. Benedict struggled to make teachers understand that while all Americans shared a national culture, differences between individuals should be assessed and treated fairly.

Finally, Mead joined the intellectual debate on tolerance education just as the war came to a dramatic end. She was skeptical of her colleagues' efforts to pro-mote factual knowledge as a strategy to undermine racism. Instead, she envi-sioned a form of tolerance education that could create empirical knowledge of people of different races and backgrounds. Her previous attempt to reform American class relations through schooling in the 1930s made her suspicious of drastic reforms imposed by outsiders. She viewed intercultural education, espe-cially activities such as the neighborhood home festival, as a more realistic way for educators to influence social change. This was the only democratic way for educators to change the social order, by laying the foundation for new ideas among the nation's youth, not by indoctrinating them with ideas outside of their interest and understanding.

Boas, Benedict, and Mead were three of the twentieth century's most famous anthropologists, a fact they capitalized on as social justice activists committed to reforming American democracy. Training their sights on public education, these anthropologists developed not only a new and potent site of antiracist activism, but a revision of racial discourse in American schools that would help redefine the racial knowledge and etiquette of the "educated" citizen. In this way, the anthropological movement to reform the race concept in American schools helped lay both strategic and ideological foundations for the growth and expansion of civil rights activism.

|| 4 ||

Race as Color, 1939–1945

Indeed, the normal community in the United States is made up of people with many different cultural experiences. Of our one hundred and twenty-five millions, some thirty millions are only one generation removed from Europe, and many more millions are from the black and yellow races.

—Intercultural Educator, 1938

Well, I believe that the members of this class are as grievously uninformed about our Negro population as I am. I have questions I'd like to have answered. For instance, what is the difference between Negro and white blood?

—Teacher, 1945

They are just like us, only their skin is colored.

—Student, 1944

Writing in the popular *English Journal* at the start of World War II, a high school teacher reported, "There are in my city a number of racial groups gathered into neighborhoods, as one finds them everywhere: Syrians, Italians, French, and a large number of Germans and Jews, as well as three distinct communities of Negroes drifted up from the South." Noting that Terre Haute, Indiana, was "as typically American as any section of the country, more American than most," Margaret Gillum was troubled when Carl, one the more popular boys in the class, made "a sneering remark about 'Hunkies.'" When the teacher reprimanded the young man for his outburst, he shot back, "Well, they're all dirty foreigners!"[1]

Reflecting on her personal experience of watching "queerly attired foreigners making their entrance into the new world" in New York City as a child, Gillum knew she had to do something to make her students understand that their "attitude of antagonism and unfriendliness toward the newcomers" had a direct impact on American democracy. The next day Gillum walked into her classroom and started her tolerance lesson by repeating Carl's comment from the day before and then demanding, "What do we call Italians?" "Dagoes," called back the students. "And the Germans," asked Gillum. "Dutchmen," answered the class. "The Irish," pressed the teacher. "Oh, Pat or Mike," retorted the students, amicably.[2]

Now that she had the students' attention, Gillum asked which of their parents, grandparents, and great grandparents had been born abroad. Eventually, all the students in the class admitted to having "foreign" heritage. "I've been wondering, too," Gillum pondered out loud, "how really different from us these people are, in spite of their foreign clothes, their foreign customs, and their foreign speech. Don't they have the same feelings we have? Let's see for ourselves. I'm going to read to you."[3]

Explaining that she had chosen the author T. A. Dally to make her case for the "dago," Gillum read poetry with an exaggerated Italian accent. Poems like "Da Besta Frand" were supposed to help students understand what it would feel like if they suddenly found themselves in a vast foreign city where they did not speak the language, had no money, and did not know anyone. Gillum selected other European authors to read to the class, proudly explaining: "We had learned that intolerance and ridicule frequently emanate from ignorance and that knowledge often leads to tolerance and friendliness."[4] At this point the students became interested in learning all they could about "foreigners" in America. Gillum elaborated, "The many suggestions from the children, now interested in another angle of the foreign problem, recalled to our minds the gifts of science, of art, of music, of literature, even from those countries whose political policies we condemn or whose sons and daughters we call wops and dagoes and hunkies."[5]

Margaret Gillum's lesson on racial tolerance in 1941 is notable because it focused exclusively on racial minorities who also happened to be white. This particular conception of race would change as a host of previously racialized European minorities finally acquired the full material, social, and political benefits of whiteness over the course of the war.[6] Some minority groups, like Poles and Italians, were finally and permanently recategorized as members of the dominant racial majority. In this sense the concept of whiteness was simplified as racial distinctions within whiteness simply evaporated. And yet, as the distinctions between color and race dissolved, the demarcation between white and colored solidified with a new sense of scientific certainty. Inside schools this process unfolded in distinct ways as teachers grappled with an existing educational discourse on race inscribed in textbooks, curriculum materials, and everyday practice.

Between 1939 and 1945 American teachers reconstructed the dominant education discourse on race as they consolidated a host of racialized white minorities into a singular and monolithic Caucasian race. Informed by massive wartime social transformations, teachers began equating race with color in a way that collapsed the racial divisions within whiteness. Motivated by a national educational movement to promote tolerance and inspired by new anthropological materials on the scientific meaning of race, teachers altered their understanding of *who* was a racial minority while leaving the implications of *what* this racial distinction meant relatively unchanged. Even as teachers identified people of African and Asian descent—and only those people—as "racial" minorities, they continued to believe that race determined traits like intelligence, morality, and way of life. Together, anthropologists and intercultural educators in the early 1940s reinforced the idea that racial difference could best be understood as cultural difference.

Beginning in 1943, anthropological materials on human race become a regular feature of tolerance education in the United States. Even if teachers did not personally use these scientific pamphlets, posters, comic books, and children's books, they came to understand the significance of teaching about race in scientifically accurate terms. As this chapter illustrates, teachers' expanding knowledge of the race and culture concepts, combined with the social upheaval of war, ushered in a paradigmatic shift in the social construction of race in American schools.

Teaching racial egalitarianism in order to promote tolerance represented a valuable educational contribution to the war effort. "There is nothing more un-American than a teacher who favors one child because she is a nice, clean little Anglo-Saxon and scorns another whose skin is dark or whose religion does not conform with her own," scolded one teaching journal.[7] Many students agreed, such as a class from New Jersey tired of hearing words like "nigger," "wop," "Pollack," and "kraut eater" on a daily basis. As one student insisted to his principal, "We're Americans and we think you and the teachers ought to do something about it."[8] Teachers believed that lessons on racial tolerance were not only socially desirable and scientifically accurate, but that these lessons were also morally just. As an administrator from New York proposed, "Let us teach our teachers and children to denounce bigotry by our inculcation of moral and spiritual values, which values of themselves involve a respect of scientific truth."[9] Encouraged by politicians, school administrators, social scientists, and professional associations, teachers taught special units with names like "Education and Race Prejudice," "Tolerance and Democracy," and "This Hate Business," and attended "Franz Boas Workshops."[10] Reporting on widespread efforts by American teachers to combat Nazi racism and secure American unity with the help of scientific knowledge, *Science Teacher* magazine in 1943 declared, "Scientists and science teachers are descending from their ivory towers to pitch in and help win this war. The spirit of Franz Boas lives."[11]

Over the course of World War II teachers modified their language to reflect Boasian theories of race by insisting that all "white" people belonged to the same

"Caucasian" race, a fact that meant only people of African and Asian descent were "racial" minorities. As their understanding of who was a racial minority changed, so too did the subjects of lessons on racial tolerance. Teachers stopped teaching tolerance for white racial minorities and began teaching tolerance for African Americans, Asian Americans, and other "colored" minorities. "Plays, round-tables discussions, and stories about Negroes are taking a great place in school programs," observed an African American teacher from Chicago in 1944.[12] Teachers compared the Nazi persecution of Jews to American mistreatment of racial minorities, so that by the end of the war a teacher from Bellingham, Washington, reflected: "The main part of the unit was concerned with the study of flagrant examples of race persecution in the contemporary scene: Nazi treatment of Jewish people, the position of the Negro in American life after three-quarters of a century of freedom, and the origin and growth of 'The Yellow Peril' idea on the Pacific Coast."[13] Thus even as educators were motivated to fight racial prejudice in response to Nazi racism, it was the social and cultural transformations on the American home front that served as a catalyst for change in the dominant educational discourse on race.

Escalating racial tensions in the United States fed a growing demand for anti-prejudice programming in public schools. Educators offered a new and revised intercultural curriculum designed to improve minority student self-esteem while dampening unwanted expressions of racial prejudice by majority white students. Intercultural textbooks promoted a modern, scientifically grounded tolerance pedagogy that drew on social science expertise from anthropology, sociology, and psychology. Supporters of "intercultural" and "intergroup" education declared that teachers had a patriotic duty to fight racial prejudice in the classroom and offered teachers the tools to do so in the form of pamphlets, textbooks, posters, and articles in teaching journals.[14]

At the outbreak of war, teachers understood tolerance education as a new and better form of Americanization that would cultivate the democratic ideal of tolerance while forging a unified, patriotic citizenry.[15] As one teacher insisted, "The most vital problem of our country today and one, therefore, especially important to our schools is the promotion of the doctrine of tolerance as a means of knitting our nation into one closely integrated unit."[16] Teachers writing in journals from 1939 through the end of 1941, therefore, emphasized the ways that tolerance education healed social relations in local communities and improved interactions between minority and majority students in their schools.

American entry into war in December of 1941 transformed both the rationale and the objectives of tolerance education, adding to the already formidable project of nation-building the daunting task of showcasing the moral superiority of democracy on a global stage while tending to violent outbursts of racial conflict on the home front. Suddenly teaching racial tolerance had far more pressing goals than restoring minority student self-esteem or improving relations between minority and majority groups in a given school. Noting that the world "focuses its attention on America to see if this great nation is going to give leadership in democracy over all the world," an Ohio educator declared, "We can hardly expect others to be enthusiastic about our brand of democracy if we cannot handle problems of race, religion, and color successfully after 150 years of unparalleled opportunity to do it."[17] Teachers like this one believed that only by modeling successful race relations at home would the future of democracy around the world be secure, no easy task with the eruption of race riots, hate strikes, and an increasingly visible and demanding African American movement for social justice.[18]

Teachers hoped that their ambitious lessons would serve as proof that Americans were trying actively to diminish white supremacy, while inculcating the ideal of racial tolerance so painfully absent in the average "educated" citizen. While it is difficult to ascertain whether or not tolerance education had any discernable impact on students' racial prejudice, what is clear is that this new tolerance pedagogy reconstructed the dominant discourse on race in American schools in an extremely short time. This chapter details this transformation through the varied experiences and perspectives of American teachers.

Wartime Expansion of Tolerance Education

Eager to intervene in the spread of Nazi propaganda and combat the prolonged effects of the Great Depression, the New York City Board of Education announced the nation's first educational "tolerance drive" to counteract widespread "intolerance, racial bias, and misunderstandings in the classroom" in January of 1938. The Board of Education contended that tolerance education would help minority students withstand "feelings of inferiority" intensified by the international crisis. The *New York Times* reported favorably on the initiative, noting: "The tense atmosphere created in the world at large is reflected in the classroom. The pupils, reading the newspapers and hearing it discussed at home, are aware of the ill feeling between the Jew and the German, the Chinese and Japanese and other nationalistic groups." Interviewed for the article, Rachel Davis DuBois cited "numerous instances of unhappy, thwarted, frustrated pupils who became problem cases because of racial or religious prejudice shown them by their classmates."[19] Emphasizing that tolerance programming was a natural part of the Americanization process of public schools, interculturalists promised to teach "various incidents chosen from American history" that were "selected as demonstrating that intolerance is basically un-American."[20]

Reformers targeted minority students as potential "problem cases" and hoped to counteract this trend by fostering "appreciable attitudes" toward minority groups by demonstrating how "Jewish, Italian, Japanese, German, Irish or other groups had helped enrich the American culture."[21] Drawing from theoretical developments in psychology and sociology, reformers interpreted the behavioral problems and poor academic performance of minority students as the result of psychological damage they suffered as outsiders to dominant American norms. This damage manifested itself as poor self-esteem, and reformers argued that intercultural education could reverse this trend by making students proud of their heritage.[22] In 1939 New York City's Service Bureau for Intercultural Education claimed to provide tolerance education to all 1,200,000 students and 40,000 teachers in the nation's largest public school system.[23]

"Tolerance" became a national buzzword as religious leaders, educators, and politicians stressed it as essential for democracy. New York City was a driving force in this movement with debates over the meaning of tolerance, tolerance rallies, and the national distribution of 10 million "badge of tolerance" buttons by the National Conference of Christians and Jews.[24] Politicians nationwide asserted that tolerance was a desirable ideal, agreeing with President Franklin D. Roosevelt's proclamation: "we should renew our fealty to the principles of tolerance and equality forever embodied in our Declaration of Independence."[25] Wartime demands for greater tolerance were spearheaded by the United States Office of War Information (OWI) created by Roosevelt in 1942 to explain the war to the American people in a way that would reinforce national unity. Officials at the OWI were determined to portray "the conflict as a battle for democracy and tolerance against fascism and intolerance."[26]

In particular, politicians and educators wanted Americans to "tolerate" the cultural anomalies of America's diverse minority groups in the name of patriotic duty. This represented an important refinement to tolerance education pedagogy. Whereas intercultural educators in the 1930s imagined that their curriculum would facilitate assimilation without explicitly forcing students to conform to white, middle-class norms, the war prompted educators to articulate a more specific plan of forging a united, homogeneous citizenry.[27] Speaking to 150 teachers at an intercultural education conference in the spring of 1939, the Dean of New York University's School of Education explained, "Democracy assumes differences and heterogeneity of culture."[28] The role of wartime tolerance education became, in a sense, to define which traits of minority groups were acceptable and which traits would have to be modified to fit American standards. Furthermore, proponents of tolerance expected that minority groups would repay this gesture of goodwill with complete and unquestioned loyalty to the United States. Sometimes this point was made explicitly, as when a politician combined his "plea" for racial and religious tolerance over the radio with a stern reminder to the "heterogeneous people making up this county" that they owed their allegiance to America.[29]

Intercultural education quickly became the nation's premier form of tolerance education, though modified from the original curriculum in significant ways. While early interculturalists like Rachel Davis DuBois envisioned a tolerance education that valued minority cultures and specifically challenged the old "melting pot" ideal, politicians like Commissioner Studebaker viewed intercultural education as an instrument to further the assimilation of ethnic and racial minorities to a fixed white, Anglo-Saxon, Protestant ideal. Strengthening democratic ideals and practices reinforced a common culture because, as Studebaker articulated, "every school is a melting pot refining human alloys with the ores of a common language and of common experiences."[30] Professional educators picked up on this revised function of tolerance education and published new textbooks and special journal issues designed to help teachers integrate new social science theories on prejudice into the new intercultural theme "One Land, One Language, One People."[31] As one popular textbook instructed teachers: "If seeking to develop the culture traits which all Americans should have in common is the positive aspect of education for democracy, eliminating those patterns of thought and action which are contrary to democratic principles is its equally important negative aspect."[32] By working to "develop" certain cultural traits and "eliminate" others, educators believed American schools could promote a more refined program of Americanization.

Wartime tolerance education was fraught with inherent contradictions, as teachers were supposed to simultaneously inculcate open-mindedness while encouraging conformity to white, middle-class norms. This tension erupted at the 1941 annual convention of the National Council of Teachers of English (NCTE) in Atlanta, where organizers urged teachers to "direct Americanism efforts toward assimilating all foreign-born groups into a unified nation."[33] The prominent African American teacher and writer Sterling Brown described the scene that unfolded when NCTE members arrived for the conference in this southern city, which insisted on strict racial segregation by barring "colored" members from all "social" events such as teas and dinners, and by roping off black teachers within special "colored" sections at paper sessions. NCTE leadership, white men who hailed from outside of the South, were perplexed but ultimately complied with the hotel's Jim Crow policies. Black teachers and college professors were unwilling to abide by these blatantly racist practices and employed a variety of protest strategies, from deliberately integrating roped off seating sections to canceling scheduled appearances. Brown recalls how the keynote speaker regaled the audience with stories about "darkys" and an "old nigger," while noted interculturalists from New York City looked on with passive interest. The special panel on "Intercultural Relationships" was disrupted when the

Spelman-Morehouse Glee Club, scheduled to sing as part of the session on "Negro Contributions," canceled their appearance in protest. Meanwhile, the African American panelist Dr. Sidney Reedy of Lincoln University (Missouri) declined to speak at the intercultural luncheon where he was the main speaker, noting that he would be have been excluded from the very luncheon he was invited to address as an expert in the field of racial tolerance. Since he could not deliver his speech in person, the Intercultural Committee asked Dr. Reedy to send in a phonograph of his speech, since "his voice could be allowed in the Hotel Biltmore dining room" even if his body could not. Dr. Reedy readily complied, and sent over a "spirited and incisive" speech that scolded, "the Committee on Intercultural Relations is even now dying, having lived briefly in vain." As Brown noted with pleasure, "the record was considered too hot to be played."[34]

Despite potentially glaring internal tensions and inherent contradictions, intercultural education surged under the political mandates of war and drew tremendous attention to a previously marginal curriculum. In 1939 the entire city of Springfield, Massachusetts, became a laboratory for intercultural education under the guidance of Superintendent John Garund.[35] By 1945 reformers had secured funding for two new organizations dedicated to intercultural education: the Project in Intergroup Education in Cooperating Schools at the University of Chicago and the College Study in Intergroup Relations at Wayne State University in Detroit.[36] Meanwhile the Bureau for Intercultural Education opened a West Coast office in San Francisco and ran a workshop for future teachers at Stanford University's School of Education.[37] A list of intercultural workshops planned for the summer of 1945 included teacher-training workshops at universities in California, Colorado, Wisconsin, Vermont, Massachusetts, Illinois, Minnesota, Oregon, and New York.[38] The National Association for the Advancement of Colored People (NAACP) hired an educator to travel the country and promote intercultural education in hundreds of schools.[39] By the end of the war, the National Education Association claimed that nearly every school district in the United States had implemented some form of intercultural education.[40] Of course, each school—not to mention individual teachers—enjoyed a great deal of latitude in terms of deciding how much "tolerance" education was appropriate, and surely not all teachers complied with tolerance decrees. For instance, archival materials from the city of Boston suggest that despite strong administrative and governmental support in Massachusetts, Boston teachers declined to teach lessons on the subject of tolerating racial minorities such as Jews and African Americans.[41] What is significant, however, is that wartime tolerance education had become a national fad and was politically solvent enough to be promoted by school districts and educational organizations nationwide.

Apart from teachers in Boston, American teachers insisted that they had a special role to play by fostering tolerance, democracy, and international goodwill in American classrooms. "Now that the daily headlines have invaded the American classroom with reports of national rivalry and race hatred, we should not barricade ourselves behind routine dictionary work but launch a counterattack for the coming victory of democracy," insisted an enthusiastic New York City teacher.[42] Rachel Davis DuBois shared this sentiment, asking: "Is it enough then for teachers, faced with this serious situation, to prepare the attitudes of their students with vague talk of hope for internationalism? Aware of the racial and cultural conflicts in this country and the close ties between ourselves and the Old World, can teachers quietly sit back with a 'come what will' attitude?"[43] For many teachers the answer was no. Viewing prejudice as a condition that stemmed from a lack of factual knowledge and emotional sympathy for minority groups, teachers believed they could undermine racial prejudice through creative lessons that were informative and engaging. Typically, these lessons on racial tolerance were intended to promote world-friendship with European minority groups.

For instance, in 1941 a Missouri teacher created a unit called "Developing World-Friendship through a Study of Immigrants." Distributing storybooks about foreign lands, the teacher hoped to "introduce the readers to the children of other places and help them to make friends with these people and to understand them." According to the teacher, her students became naturally interested in the subject of "strangers within our gates" and so the class tackled the subject of American immigrants. "Each child was reminded that his own ancestry, however remote, was inevitably foreign," the author announced, as she recounted her class's exhaustive study of European immigrants. At the end of the lesson, when the teacher asked "What can we do to help," the students knew "they must be friendly with the young aliens; must banish prejudices."[44]

First-hand accounts of classroom practice suggest that teachers and students viewed European minority groups as racially, biologically different from "old stock" white Americans. Identifying racial prejudice against these minorities, teachers attempted to promote goodwill by emphasizing laudable group traits such as artistic or scientific achievements. Although well-intentioned, celebrations of cultural gifts were sometimes superficial, such as the teacher who emphasized, "color from Italy, stamina and restraint from the Scandinavian countries, artistry from France, steady nerve and purposefulness from Britain—we could encircle the globe saying 'thank you' to one nation after another for what each has brought us."[45]

Likewise, William Suchy of Cicero, Illinois, chastised "the small minority of old-stock Americans" who directed his school's curriculum for ignoring the seven thousand students of Czech, Polish, Irish, German, Dutch, Scandinavian, and Italian background.[46] By teaching students how and why their ancestors immigrated to the United States, with a special emphasis on the contributions each group had made to American civilization, Suchy believed he improved student morale. For Suchy, the "immigrant problem" was understood as a disconnect between home and school life. He explained, "Those who retained cultural ties with the home were considered backward, reticent, or 'foreign' in the school."[47] In contrast, by painting a sympathetic picture of American immigrants Suchy found he could improve minority student self-esteem and social relations between these students and their peers.

Other teachers sought out prejudicial beliefs and then designed course content to counteract harmful stereotypes. J. M. Klotsche in Milwaukee conducted his own informal survey of high school students to ascertain "international attitudes." When Klotsche casually asked students, "What is your first reaction when you hear the word 'Japan'?" the students answered with a list of angry racial slurs: "Queer people, primitive, war-like race of slanty eyed people, blood thirsty, sly, people sitting on floors, cheap goods, a backward nation with lots of fights."[48] When asked the same question about the people of other nations, students described Russians as "bearded, illiterate men, a stupid peasant race and governed by a blood thirsty group. . . . Mexicans were classified as lazy, Germans as crooks, Chinese as opium eaters, and Italians as robbers."

Klotsche responded by promoting "factual information completely divorced from sentimentalism, superstition, and emotionalism."[49] Armed with these facts, he argued students would learn to appreciate foreigners on their own terms, and avoid "quaint, queer, or strange" characterizations of other people. While student comments suggest they viewed both Japanese and Russians as distinct "races," Klotsche neither confirmed nor contradicted this characterization. Furthermore, while Klotsche made a compelling case for the appreciation of foreign lifeways, he never used the term "culture" to explain these differences. Instead, he spoke of the "customs," "manners," and "habits" of each group. This kind of informal usage of the race and culture concepts was poised to change.

Teachers across the country from Detroit, Michigan, to Webster Groves, Missouri, and from Redwood City, California, to Askov, Minnesota, described similar programs of intercultural education at the start of World War II.[50] These teachers instituted tolerance education for white ethnic minorities, occasionally referred to as racial groups, and then directed lessons on each group's cultural gifts. Teachers focused on race relations in their local communities and not necessarily racial prejudice on a national or international scale. As the superintendent of schools in Askov, Minnesota, explained, "We are informed by sociologists that the disproportionately high crime rate among children of foreign-born parents is due largely to the conflict of culture in the immigrant home."[51] Interpreted as a "culture-conflict," educators believed that they could mediate this chasm by promoting the old-world heritage of students' parents. They hoped this would improve parental authority, familial relations, and the social fabric of their communities.

Lessons on race, therefore, included a celebration of European folkways through classroom activities like singing, eating, reading stories, writing letters, and putting on plays. For instance, Jeanora Don Wingate, a fifth-grade teacher in New Rochelle, New York, designed a unit she called an "Around the World Museum" that focused exclusively on European nations. Noting that "twelve foreign nationalities were represented among the thirty-two children in the class," the teacher decided to devote half an hour each day to "intercultural discussion." Students participated eagerly, bringing in objects that represented their heritage such as "a beautifully hand-embroidered nightgown of Grecian design and a Hungarian peasant costume." The celebration of European nations continued over the course of the semester with a special Christmas celebration in December and an art show in the spring featuring student posters on each country. As a grand finale, the class decided to host an "international luncheon" for the entire school. The class served the following menu:

> Tomato juice—American
> Smorgasbord—Swedish
> Meat pie—English
> Spaghetti—Italian

Students dressed in European folk costumes served European food and sang European songs as part of one school's "Around the World Museum."

Spring salad—Portuguese and Spanish
Stewed fruits—German
Oatmeal cookies—Scotch
Cocoa—Holland[52]

Wingate describes how, "The lunchroom was attractively decorated with the posters, and children in their native costumes served the class." In between each course, the students serenaded the room with an international selection of songs:

"Tic-e-tic-e-toc"—Italy
"My Spanish Guitar"—Spain
"Oh, Dear, What Can the Matter Be?"—England
"Auld Lang Syne"—Scotland
"Jolly Winter"—Sweden[53]

Dressing up in "peasant costumes," eating "foreign" food, and singing European folk songs was supposed to help students develop empathy for minorities, at this point still minorities who happened to be white. Teachers envisioned tolerance education as a way to promote patriotism and national unity. Wingate wrote, "The luncheon ended with the children's rising to sing 'God Bless America,' led by a colored boy."[54] Similarly, in Illinois, William Suchy's high school students ended with a patriotic review:

Boys and girls of Polish descent did Mexican dances. Czech mothers craned their necks to see their daughters jigging with the colleens. And a little Italian grandmother moved to the front to see a familiar figure step up and turn among the smiling Gretels. A patriotic grand finale combined all the dancers around an American flag review. To the thousands of parents who attended, the conclusion had a special meaning.[55]

While a "colored boy" might have a special role in a classroom performance and girls of Czech descent might jig with the "colleens," teachers rarely emphasized the special cultural heritage of African Americans or Mexican Americans. As Jeanora Don Wingate explained in the conclusion of her article, "This activity, while teaching European culture, also developed tolerance."[56]

The outbreak of World War II encouraged some teachers to include non-white minorities including African Americans, Asians and Asian Americans, and Mexican Americans in classroom discussions of racial tolerance. Teachers justified these lessons in terms of the war, such as the New York teacher who explained: "Reports of Axis infiltrations in the republic south of us have made us anxious about the defense of the Western Hemisphere and our neighbor's loyal cooperation for the purpose."[57] Teaching racial tolerance and goodwill for South Americans, therefore, could serve a strategic defensive function by securing "loyal cooperation" in the defense of the United States and was promoted through efforts at Pan-Americanism.[58] In Hartford, Connecticut, an English teacher introduced novels about "the American Negro," "the Chinese," and various European immigrant groups in order to strengthen American democracy by fighting racial prejudice.[59] Teachers were particularly concerned that the sparks of American racial prejudice could be fanned into disastrous race wars by Axis propaganda, which a New York Times reporter described as "Trojan Horse" tactics designed to sabotage American democracy.[60] Therefore, teachers like the one in Hartford taught students about the "diverse gifts of temperament, character, and culture that are being woven together to form the rich pattern of America."[61] Like other lessons from the early war years, this one implied that each minority group possessed its own unique "gifts" that corresponded to static forms of behavior, morality, and material culture.[62] The large majority of lessons described in the mainstream press and white-dominated teaching journals, however, neglected to include nonwhites in their celebration of America's diversity at this time. In the words of one New York City teacher in 1941, "In short, all of American life, civilization, culture is based on a firm belief in the value of using and combining the different qualities and abilities of the many European stocks that make up the U.S."[63]

In contrast to the dozens of articles that described international education or education for goodwill in terms of these European minority groups, there were only a handful of articles that touched on the subject of African Americans before 1943. These came from southern white schools in places like Moultrie, Georgia; Louise, Mississippi; Chattanooga, Tennessee; and Marshfield, Missouri.[64] In one example, a Mississippi teacher instituted a formal study of "Negroes" after one of his male high school students punched a young African American woman in the face for no reason as she was walking down the sidewalk. Citing this behavior as both unmanly and uncivilized, the teacher successfully petitioned the state of Mississippi to institute a formal plan to emphasize Negro contributions in white schools. Much like tolerance education in the North, southern white students studied "Negro" literature, music, food, and historical achievements. Two white teachers in Missouri described how their students eagerly collected stories of black achievements in sports, religion, government, entertainment, and science from books and magazines and then created a class bibliography of "Negro life." Next students wrote letters to black schools, requesting information and scheduling visits to places of work and study. According to the authors:

Some students had toured southeastern Missouri and were eager to tell of the share-cropping system and its effect on general living conditions of the Negro. One girl visited in Oklahoma at the time the study was being made, and she came to class bubbling with news of the cotton-pickers. Another group attended a young people's convention in Memphis, Tennessee, and visited a cotton gin where Negroes were at work.[65]

Despite this enthusiasm for studying black lifeways, this white class engaged in an objective analysis of the materials they gathered. At the end of the article the authors wrote, "After having finished the study, each student was able to conclude for himself whether or not the Negro had been a help or hindrance to American life. . . . Some students were so convinced one way or the other that they asked to debate the subject."[66] Tolerance education directed at reducing white racism against blacks was crafted as a different pedagogy than tolerance education directed at reducing racism against European ethnics. While both sought to understand minority groups in terms of achievements in the arts, literature, sciences, and sports, tolerance education did not demand appreciation of "Negroes," nor did white schools celebrate the cultural gifts of blacks to American civilization. Such lessons in the South functioned to buttress white supremacy by dampening unacceptable expressions of racial hostility while leaving structural inequality intact.[67]

Only very rarely did major white-dominated teaching journals publish articles that emphasized black cultural contributions before 1943. Even so, these were viewed as contributions to the black race, not as gifts to world or to American civilization. Thus, Myrtle Crawford from the Second Ward High School, a segregated black high school in Charlotte, North Carolina, described her school's performance of a "Negro Pageant" before an audience of over five thousand people.[68] The pageant featured 150 students dressed as famous black historical figures dating all the way to ancient Egypt. The students filed on stage and mounted the bleachers as the narrator introduced each character and their special contribution to the race. As the glee club sang black spirituals, the students slowly formed a giant pyramid symbolizing the outstanding achievements of the black race. Projects like this were popular in black southern schools during the war, although the white press for the most part declined to report on them.[69] Remarkably, once African Americans became the subject of mainstream white tolerance education after American entry into World War II, white students in the North would participate in similar programs of tolerance education including singing "Negro" spirituals, studying black history, and even dressing up and performing as African Americans.

American Entry into the War

The Japanese attack on Pearl Harbor significantly altered the context for tolerance education in America. The strike generated such profound anger that many
American high school and college students, as well as their teachers, immediately left school to enroll in the armed services.[70] Sudden demands for wartime
production created hundreds of thousands of new jobs, and impoverished blacks
and whites living in rural communities followed jobs into industrial centers.
Very quickly, then, the need for tolerance came to have new meaning as all of
these people adjusted to living and working together, often crowding and over-
whelming previously small and homogeneous school districts.[71]

One result of these social, economic, and political transformations was that
American teachers began to implement tolerance education not as a response to
local prejudice, but instead to stabilize national race relations and defeat the
worldwide spread of fascism. At the National Education Association's annual
conference in 1944, teachers were told "it is just as important . . . to get rid of
intolerance in this country as it is to crush the Nazi armies or sink the Japanese
fleet."[72] Headlines like "Supreme Duty of All Teachers Is to Clear Children's
Minds of Bias" and "Teachers Urge Americanism in Racial Strife" ran in newspapers including the *New York Times, Washington Post, Atlanta Constitution, Chicago Daily Tribune, Christian Science Monitor, New York Amsterdam News,
Afro-American, Atlanta Daily World, Pittsburg Courier,* and the *Chicago Defender.*[73]
Teaching associations made fighting racial prejudice a central function of wartime education and insisted that everyone from principals to kindergarten students had a vital role to play. As leaders of the National Council for the Social
Studies announced in their official "Statement of Wartime Policy":

> Total war mobilizes civilians as well as armed forces. It mobilizes chil-
> dren and youth as well as adults. It mobilizes the minds and hearts as
> well as the physical strength of all the population. This is a war involving
> every citizen—a people's war.[74]

Teachers from across the country echoed the rallying cry, "The schools are
the battleground on which the issue of racial tolerance is now being fought."[75]
Journals like *American Unity* offered pamphlets on racial tolerance as "Ammunition" in the educational war on racial discrimination such as: *Sense and Nonsense
about Race, Let's Not Forget We're All Foreigners, What about Our Japanese-
Americans, Together We Win, Intolerance Is a Crime against Democracy,* and *The
Races of Mankind.*[76]

Participation in World War II cast American racial injustice in stark and
unflattering relief. The United States waged a war against Nazi Germany with a

Jim Crow army, set up its own concentration camps for racially stigmatized citizens, and restricted the best defense jobs and available housing to whites. Teachers were the professionals best positioned to reach vast numbers of young Americans in order to mediate this racialized hatred thereby securing national unity and improving American democracy.[77]

In their efforts to combat prejudice, teachers struggled to balance the American ideal of democracy with blatant policies of exclusion and discrimination against nonwhite citizens in classes jammed with students who felt passionately one way or another about minority civil rights. Over the course of 1942 and 1943 tolerance education shifted and reformed around two new themes. First, teachers focused on teaching goodwill for "Negroes," "Mexicans," and "Orientals" as these minority groups experienced the brunt of the "racialized rage" in America.[78] Second, teachers became sensitive to teaching carefully delineated "scientific" lessons on human diversity in terms of race and culture, a rhetorical strategy that strengthened the social science claims of tolerance pedagogy while simultaneously shielding teachers from charges of political indoctrination.

In the wake of Pearl Harbor, teachers renewed their dedication to intercultural education even as they shifted from teaching about the eastern and southern European countries that reflected the diversity of their homerooms to exploring the Japanese, Chinese, and Russian people featured in daily headlines. Because promoting racial tolerance and cultural appreciation were central to these efforts, teachers began to develop more complex models of both the race and culture concepts. For instance, at an emergency meeting held over the Christmas holiday of 1941, leaders of the National Council of Teachers of English (NCTE) agonized over how to define their new role as educators in a warring nation. Finally, they devised a list of wartime goals for English teachers, writing:

> In the teaching of English we are in a position to promote national unity:
>
> 1. through the democratic integration of diverse cultural groups.
>
> 2. through recognition of the unique contribution of each to our national culture.
>
> 3. through emphasis upon the contribution which America has made to each of them.[79]

Not only did the NCTE emphasize the significance of *culture* to wartime tolerance education, but they insisted that cultural appreciation was a dialectical process where minority students, understood to be racially and culturally distinct, learned to value America. In the subsequent issue, editors of the *English Journal* took this idea one step further, contending, "If we are to build a new world—a democratic world—we must have an exhaustive knowledge of world cultures." Lest readers misconstrue this knowledge as nothing but mindless appreciation for foreigners, the author, a teacher from Jenkintown, Pennsylvania, elaborated, "We must understand what we are fighting to change."[80] Teachers advocated studying enemy cultures so that they could be altered more efficiently at the conclusion of the war.

Inspired by the world war, teachers emphasized public schools as the best institution to forge diverse American citizens into a single, unified nation. For some, this required "exhaustive" knowledge of foreign cultures, especially since the United States was burdened with so many "foreigners" living within its borders. "Shall We Teach Them to Hate?" queried one elementary school teacher, wondering what to teach about the Germans and Japanese now that they were national enemies. She answered in the negative, arguing that not only would such hatred later undermine prospects for world peace, but that "it's easier to hate Germans and Japanese who are geographically close to us than those who are overseas." Driving home the significance of this point, she added, "Hatred thus becomes a divisive force which fights against us."[81] For American teachers in 1942 there was no greater risk than fracturing the American nation.

Teachers responded to demands for strengthening American unity with creative lessons on Americanization and "The American Dream."[82] One teacher in Atlanta, Georgia, devised a unit called "Americanism: Qualities That Make up the Term." In this class, Paul Farmer reported recycling material from past lessons on Americanization, such as the history of great presidents and excerpts from the Western literary canon. But this time, he added the popular song "Ballad for Americans," which his students enjoyed so much they demanded to hear it again and again. The song began as Paul Robeson, an African American singer, asked, "Are you an American." His response, sung in a "rich baritone voice," boasted: "I'm just an Irish, Negro, Jewish, Italian, French and English, Spanish, Russian, Chinese, Polish, Scotch, Hungarian, Litvak, Swedish, Finnish, Canadian, Greek and Turk and Czech and double-Czech American."[83] According to Rachel Davis DuBois, the song was an expression of "The American Dream" set to music.[84]

Teachers were particularly interested in the people and cultures of warring nations. There was little good to be said about the Japanese, although *Common Ground* awarded first place in its annual essay contest to a Japanese American student for her poignant story of internment in the Santa Anita concentration camp.[85] The Chinese, in contrast, offered teachers the opportunity to present an "Oriental" country and culture in the warmest terms. Minnie Rugg, a teacher at the Barratt Junior High School in Philadelphia, described how to conduct a proper "Chinese unit" in an English class. Her class read the Chinese fable *Shen of the Sea,* whose cover featured "tiny silhouetted folk dressed in the traditional manner and flaunting tantalizing pigtails." This story provided the perfect opening to appreciate these "four hundred and fifty million allies." To begin, Rugg invited her students to air their prejudices about the Chinese. The students obliged, describing "the Chinese as opium smokers, 'sneaks,' 'murderers,' and laundrymen from whom one . . . ran for fear of being kidnapped."[86] Rugg then organized a semester-long study of Chinese history and culture, emphasizing the special gifts this nation brought to the world. Her class learned, for example, how:

> Old peace-loving China whom the world had forgotten for centuries had given us many gifts too—printing, tea, porcelain, silk, gunpowder put to the pacific use of firecrackers, the science of terracing, proverbs to guide the way of men, and a great reverence for learning.[87]

Rugg's lessons emphasized the naturally peaceful, or "pacific," temperament of the Chinese and highlighted similarities between Chinese folklore and American traditions. Thus, the Chinese belief in ghosts was compared to American superstitions about black cats, Friday the thirteenth, and broken mirrors. Like other intercultural educators, Rugg followed a study of Chinese culture and history with more "emotional" exercises including Chinese American pen pals and lectures by Chinese American community leaders. A display on the bulletin board, "Our Chinese Friends," featured articles, essays, maps, and other items collected by the students. The class ate at a Chinese restaurant, organized a series of skits about China, and raised money for the United China Relief Fund Drive. Attempting to convince others of the importance of such a comprehensive unit, Rugg concluded her essay: "If we are to convince the peoples of the Far East of the sincerity of our war and postwar aims we shall have to do more than engage in abstract declarations. We shall have to develop an understanding of our interdependence and an appreciation for their history, their culture, and their potentialities."[88] Lessons like this one shifted the primary purpose of tolerance education from forging American unity to demonstrating the common bonds of humanity that united people of all nations.

Following the lead of intercultural educators, teachers tried to combine a factual study of "foreign" contributions to Western civilization with a personal appreciation of each nation through activities like letter exchanges, guest lecturers, sampling foreign food, and meeting upstanding Americans of foreign descent. These activities concentrated on elements understood now as *cultural*—not only the unique "gifts" to American civilization but also foodways, traditional dress, songs, stories and folklore, and superstitions. These lessons did not examine the history, politics, or economy of foreign nations. Because they focused so intently on traditional or folk culture, they taught very little about the

A teacher in New York City reads a book about the Chinese to her young students in order to promote tolerance. Courtesy New York City Municipal Archives.

lives of contemporary Chinese people. Furthermore, teachers frequently invited students to list demeaning stereotypes of each minority group, which the teacher then countered with positive stereotypes. Working without a scientific definition of either race or culture, Rugg described Chinese culture in static and highly racialized terms.

As tolerance education expanded alongside American entry into the war, so too did student resistance to lessons on goodwill and friendly relations. Even teachers sometimes resisted teaching tolerance, complaining that it was pointless to teach complex lessons on intercultural relations to "our average boys and girls who have no special intellectual equipment."[89] An educator in New Jersey described how one teacher urged his young students to buy defense stamps to get money for bullets to kill the "dirty Japs," making the project of tolerance education all the more difficult.[90] The English teacher Marie Syrkin in New York City reported that her cynical students rebelled against the citywide campaign to teach tolerance, democracy, and international friendship. When she instructed the students to write an essay with the title, "The Meaning of Tolerance," her students responded resentfully, writing: "Why must we be tolerant? This is a free country. We have the right to be intolerant."[91] Syrkin's students liked to express this intolerance, often in class, and typically for each other. The students of

Greek and Italian background gave her particular trouble that year. Racial conflict between schoolchildren was not uncommon in America during the war, with accounts of drawn-out, violent conflict between Italian American and African American students in Newark and Philadelphia, Jewish and Italian students in Brooklyn, and Polish and African American students in Buffalo and Chicago.[92] Sensational media coverage of "race riots" in the public schools served to reinforce popular and educational support for stronger tolerance programming.

Widespread support for tolerance education did not alter the fact that teachers were working in racially charged, sometimes intimidating classrooms. A social studies teacher in Bellingham, Washington, reported that student outbursts were "quite common" during lessons on tolerance, such as the time one of her students announced: "I believe that all these examples of abuse and mistreatment of one race by another are true, but I still hate the Japs!"[93] In Muncie, Illinois, a social studies teacher bemoaned that even after a lesson on racial prejudice, one of her white students retorted, "I don't like Negroes, I never did like Negroes, and I never will like Negroes."[94] A Chicago-wide study of "the Negro" ran up against similar problems when, after a lengthy unit on

Media coverage of student "race riots" in schools generated popular support for tolerance education. Courtesy of the Historical Society of Pennsylvania, Leonard Covello Photographs.

African American contributions, students told their teacher, "It would not be nice having Negroes with white people, I would not feel safe, they would spoil the neighborhood."[95]

A minor skirmish between black and white students in one New York City school prompted white students to demand that black students be removed or at the very least segregated within the school, complaining, "Most of the white students try to foster a more human understanding between their brothers of the different race. There must be a 100 percent cooperation or racial segregation."[96] Typically these outbursts came either during or immediately after a lesson on racial tolerance. As this teacher reflected, "Their fine talk about Jim Crow in the South had apparently not registered."[97] Racial animosity flowed both ways, and at times black students became infuriated by the comments made by white students or teachers. After suffering through a long discussion of why blacks should "hold out for better jobs and not be menials all their lives" a black student in Newark, New Jersey, called out:

> I don't like to talk about this subject. It gets me mad clean through. I can't stand it when some white friends of the Negro people say, "You must be patient. It may take a hundred years to clean up this mess." I won't wait that long. I'll be dead by then and what good will it do me? What satisfaction will I get from it? I believe in direct action. Fight back. Don't take it lying down. That is the only way the Negro people will get anywhere.[98]

In another instance, a black student listened incredulously as his white classmates discussed the need for fair trials for Nazi war criminals. Finally the young man stood up and demanded, "Why are you so worried about fair trials for Nazis? How about lynching in the U.S.A.?"[99] Similarly, another teacher complained of a black girl in her class who refused to buy war stamps and would not help with classroom salvage campaigns. When pressed, the student finally admitted that her brother had been telling her horrible stories about the racial segregation and discrimination he suffered as a soldier in the U.S. Army.[100]

In New Jersey, a lesson on Japanese Americans came to a dramatic end when a white boy rose from the back of the classroom and yelled: "The only solution is to get a tommy-gun and kill them off. The rest is nonsense. There is no room for idealism in this war."[101] Similarly, in Dover, Delaware, white parents and community leaders threatened to shut down the high school when they learned that intercultural education now included racially integrated sports and drama programs. "Why, you are practically saying Negroes and whites are to be equal," charged an angry school board member after a teacher explained the curriculum. "That's exactly what we're saying," retorted the teacher. When the administration refused to call off what the principal described as "our best English unit ever," the school board responded by requiring parental letters of permission to study intercultural education. "That will fix that," chortled a school board member, and according to the principal, it did.[102]

As these varied examples suggest, teaching racial tolerance during World War II was a project fraught with complications that varied according to when, where, and even in which classroom a teacher happened to be teaching. By inviting students to discuss race relations, teachers risked provoking white students into angry tirades or unintentionally offending minority students, not to mention drawing the wrath of the wider community. While some teachers simply refused to teach tolerance given these circumstances, others developed even more sophisticated lessons on racial equality. Teachers like Pearl Fisher from New York City argued that to be truly effective, antiprejudice education must expose American racism and instruct children in democratic strategies to secure social justice for racial minorities. "America professes democracy and practices caste," Fisher charged in her article, which was a reprint of a speech she had given a few weeks earlier at a meeting of the New York Association of Teachers of English.[103] "Tolerance is not enough. It is at best a patronizing snobbery," she continued, arguing that unless America quickly resolved its "color" problem the people of Latin America and Asia would never learn to trust the United States or its system of democratic government.[104] In order to show the world the best democracy had to offer, Fisher suggested direct action, such as analyzing the Red Cross policy of discrimination in blood banks and "blasting the myth of a super-race or a master-race or a superior white race."[105]

While some teachers organized letter writing campaigns to train their students in the tools of democratic protest, others worried that teaching racial equality would confuse children into "tolerating" the enemy. New York City English teacher Clara Molendyk anguished over how to teach boys and girls the "right" kind of tolerance. Writing with Captain Edwards of the U.S. Army, Molendyk called for teaching "intelligent tolerance of the minority groups who work with us in the preservation of democracy" while advocating "intelligent hatred" toward the cruelty and injustice of enemy nations.[106] Molendyk wanted teachers to distinguish the culture of enemy nations from their despicable fascist regimes. Thus she suggested students study "'enemy' music, 'enemy' art, 'enemy' language and literature," in positive terms, but only if they could balance this with "intelligent hatred" of political oppression and social injustice.[107]

Very quickly, then, teachers stopped teaching tolerance for white racialized minorities and began directing tolerance education at nonwhite minorities, especially African Americans. As an article in *Social Education* testified:

The sudden outbreak of race conflict in cities of the United States during the present war period is symptomatic of basic, underlying tensions which have been heightened by the crisis of war. The existence of these tensions in Negro-white relations is indicative of fundamental changes in the nature of race adjustment.[108]

Teachers claimed that American citizens must be taught to perform as racially tolerant human beings—or risk the worldwide collapse of democracy. Not only did teachers now see race as color, they also began to contemplate the global implications of faltering race relations. An article in *Social Education* entitled "The American Negro—A World Problem" tried to make teachers see that the war had revolutionized race relations, not just in the United States, but around the world. Writing from Chicago, Horace Cayton warned:

The nature of the war itself has given rise among non-white and oppressed people to aspirations for complete liberation. India, China, and parts of Africa have been stimulated by the fact that for months, Japan, a yellow nation, successfully fought off three white nations. Probably the beginning of hope for the overthrow of white supremacy as a world doctrine and practice began in 1905 when Japan whipped Russia. This feeling has found recent expression in the expectation which all non-white people have obtained from the principles articulated in the Atlantic Charter.[109]

Frightened by the global implications of white supremacy, teachers refined tolerance education to address race relations in terms of color. "Nazi leaders have bragged that because of this friction which breeds dislike and distrust, it would be easy for them to create chaos here," warned a social studies teacher from Pennsylvania. For this teacher the only way to effectively mitigate white racial prejudice was to encourage a critical analysis of American racism. Through education, teachers could "eliminate these tensions and strains which result from the past and present treatment of many minority groups, such as the sharecroppers, the Negroes, the relocated Japanese-American citizens, and others."[110] The antidote to these tensions, now specifically understood as white prejudice against nonwhite citizens, was "tolerance and understanding between groups." Whereas earlier intercultural education emphasized teaching about minority groups in terms of factual information devoid of sentimental feelings, Richard McFeely proposed a curriculum that used students' feelings about minorities to cultivate particular actions. He explained:

Information about these racial, economic, and cultural groups, and the tensions which exist between them, necessary as it is, is not enough. We must use already existing methods and devise new techniques to dramatize and emotionalize these facts with a view to developing better attitudes in students which will in turn lead them to better actions.[111]

However, a new trend was visible in McFeely's classroom as he advocated proper etiquette as an important component of tolerance education. This logic suggested that minority students should take responsibility for mitigating white racism by conforming to standards of behavior, dress, and work habits of the dominant society. As McFeely explained:

Social studies teachers can also help their pupils develop good manners of speech, of dress, and of conduct, and thereby do much toward overcoming intolerances. Ill-mannered acts, though small, often become irksome enough to create prejudices.[112]

In McFeely's course, minority students were held responsible for "creating prejudices" in whites. Increasingly, teachers came to agree that minority students should and could alleviate white racism by simply avoiding "ill-mannered acts." This would emerge as distinct tolerance pedagogy in the postwar era that stood in stark contrast to the more critical lessons of antiracist educators committed to minority civil rights.

Articles like McFeely's celebrated the unique cultural gifts of racial minorities while refusing to acknowledge any part of minority life that potentially clashed with white, middle-class norms. Such lessons objectified the culture concept to refer only to interesting things that other people did in terms of material culture and folklife. At the same time, teachers demanded compliance with white hegemonic norms. For this reason promoting good manners through "friendly relations" and being a "good neighbor" were consistent themes through 1943, even as more critical scientific and intercultural lesson plans began to emerge.[113] For many teachers an emphasis on intercultural friendships was the only practical way to teach tolerance to very young children. In some cases, a similar approach was advocated by black educators, who feared that "Bad Manners Can Ruin Us." Writing in the *Pittsburg Courier*, two educational administrators warned readers of this black newspaper: "Segregation cannot be beaten down by bad manners, walking over everybody else's feet in a bus, outpushing and outshoving everybody and creating unnecessary scenes. Such tactics do not frighten our enemies, but they do alienate our friends. This is no time to be LOUD and WRONG."[114]

Teaching Anthropological Definitions of
Race and Culture

For those teachers who did not enlist in the armed services or leave the teaching profession for better-paid industrial work, fighting racial prejudice in the classroom became a strategic function of wartime education. It was a way to modernize the curriculum and make schools relevant to the war effort without special training, new textbooks, or expensive materials. Viewing tolerance education as a critical contribution to the war effort, teachers sought out new and more effective kinds of "ammunition."

For many teachers, scientific data on human race was the most powerful ammunition in the educational arsenal against prejudice. In 1941, the educational movement to teach tolerance collided with the anthropological movement to reform the race concept in American schools. Beginning in 1943, nearly every article on tolerance education cited the anthropological definition of race and used the culture concept to create more sophisticated, scientifically informed tolerance pedagogy.

The first examples of anthropological lessons on racial equality come from New York City, ground zero for both intercultural education and anthropological activism. Articles in *High Points* magazine, *The American Biology Teacher*, and an intercultural textbook described classroom lessons on biological racial equality as early as 1939. According to a teacher at Evander Childs High School, "When we discuss the origin and development of man it is also simple to show that we are all related, if we go back far enough, and that regardless of difference of color, race, or religious belief we are all brothers and sisters under the skin."[115]

Across town, teachers from DeWitt Clinton High School (DCHS) and Benjamin Franklin High School (BFHS) both offered "race units" to teach the anthropological definition of race. Both units began with a special test designed to illustrate the scientific principle of racial egalitarianism. At BFHS, the biology teacher Maurice Bleifeld borrowed an example from the anthropologist Franz Boas's pamphlet on racial equality, *Can You Name Them?* Displaying photographs of well-dressed European men he asked students to identify each man's country of origin.[116] The purpose of this test was to show that there was no accurate way to identify nationality based on external appearances. At DCHS, the biology teacher Alfred Kishner incorporated an "attitude test" designed to measure prejudice. The point of this test was to emphasize that all groups were potentially equal in individual variations of mental ability, honesty, work ethic, and cleanliness.[117]

Despite some confusion concerning the scientific meaning of race, the two race units were ultimately comprehensive and suggested the potential equality of individuals from any racial group. Both challenged Nazi race theory and the claim of a superior "Aryan" race, and both grappled with potentially difficult questions concerning the social equality of blacks. Designed to be six to twelve weeks long, each race unit devoted significant time to the question of "Negro" racial equality. Overall, these two units are notable for their creative activities designed to challenge racial stereotypes with scientific data. Yet, this strategy led both teachers into activities that potentially reified harmful biological understandings of racial difference.

Striving to undermine the precise forms of racial prejudice they located among their students, both New York City teachers asked students to compare and contrast the physical appearance and "racial traits" of blacks with that of apes.[118] According to these teachers, a common misconception among whites was that blacks were closer to apes than to Caucasians on the scale of human evolution. Kishner listed "Ape, Caucasian, Mongolian and Negro" on the blackboard. Asking the students to recall their last visit to the Bronx Zoo, Kishner listed the physical attributes of apes on the board including "length of arms, and legs, lips, body hair, hair texture, nose, prognathism." The students then offered a "comparative anatomical description" for Caucasians, Mongolians, and Negroes. Kishner reported, "Boys infer that Negroes are furthest removed from the Ape in as many respects as the Caucasians." Reflecting, perhaps, on the incongruity of an exercise that lingered so long on the significance of physical characteristics, Kishner added, "And in any case, physical characteristics have nothing to do with one's conduct or behavior."[119]

The teachers at BFHS developed a nearly identical classroom activity, also intended to counteract white racism against blacks. "The students were especially interested in obtaining information concerning Negroes," they recalled at one point. The authors continued:

> Racial superiority is sometimes claimed on the basis of physical appearance. Thus the Negro is often supposed to be inferior to other racial groups in the scale of evolution because of alleged resemblance to the apes. He has wide nostrils, comparatively long arms, and dark skin.[120]

This casual observation was followed by a confusing list of "truths" that apparently counteract this falsehood, such as the fact that apes have thin lips, thus the thick lips of "Negroes" demonstrate distance, not proximity to this species. Classroom activities like these suggest the kinds of complications that arose as teachers attempted to translate scientific data on race into classroom practice. These early, haphazard lessons on racial equality stand in stark contrast to the steady stream of articles that referenced scientific definitions of race that emerged two years later.

Beginning in 1943 lessons on the anthropological definition of race became a regular feature in nearly every article on tolerance education. This change coincided with the publication of *The Races of Mankind* by Ruth Benedict and Gene Weltfish.[121] Teachers latched on to *The Races of Mankind*'s egalitarian message and its easy to read, illustrated text. In reviews in teaching journals, educators praised the text as the perfect blend of scientific authority and light-hearted social critique. *Social Education* bragged, "*The Races of Mankind* . . . is a very readable little booklet for school pupils. Its purpose is to show the meaning of the term 'race,' and to fight the idea that one race is innately superior to another. The explanations are clear and forceful, and are amusingly illustrated by cartoons."[122]

The text emphasized the anthropological concept of culture, or learned habits and worldview, as the best explanation for human diversity. Importantly, in *The Races of Mankind* pamphlet, books, movie, and poster series Benedict and Weltfish moved back and forth between using the scientific names for the three races of mankind and the more colloquial terms: white, yellow, and black. Together with the illustrations, anthropological texts on race therefore collapsed race and color in a way that would prove to be particularly confusing for teachers.

The Races of Mankind was an educational sensation. Entire school districts including New York City used the text, while national teaching journals lauded its message and even reproduced images and text from the pamphlet.[123] In Detroit, the English teacher Marion Edman reported her school system secured the "unique and splendid" traveling poster exhibit of *The Races of Mankind*, while copies of the pamphlet were distributed free of charge to every teacher in Detroit's public schools. "This exhibit doubtlessly will clear up, both for teachers and pupils, many of the common misconceptions concerning race differences," Edman predicted.[124] The editors of *American Unity* agreed, explaining that the text "is simply written, sensible and explodes the race myth so completely that it makes a fool out of Hitler and his 'aryan' nonsense," and offering readers a free copy of the ten-cent brochure.[125] Teachers complained there were not more scientific texts like *The Races of Mankind* available. Teachers from Washington wrote, "We wished many times in the course of the work that there had been available more material like Ruth Benedict and Gene Weltfish's Public Affairs Pamphlet, *The Races of Mankind*, which is within the range of the understanding of junior high school students."[126] A national survey of tolerance education in 1946 confirmed the widespread usage of the text in American classrooms, reporting: "Almost all the special units in intergroup education described included study of the facts of race and the fallacies of racism using such materials as *The Races of Mankind* by Gene Weltfish and Ruth Benedict."[127] The text was so popular it was reproduced for school use in the form of a traveling poster series, a comic book, a color children's book, and an animated color filmstrip.[128]

The *Social Studies* announced to readers in 1944 that "Race Can Work toward Democracy." Norman Humphrey in Detroit described common misconceptions about race and countered these with "irrefutable conclusions" to the contrary. "*Race*, as generally used, is a catch-word applied indiscriminately and categorically to ethnic groups, with little regard for the bases of their oneness," Humphrey explained, criticizing teachers who believed that European nationality groups were racial minorities.[129] He elaborated:

> In contrast with such catch-phrase thinking, scientists have marshaled together a convincing array of facts regarding race and cultural groups, and have drawn irrefutable conclusions from them. This is succinctly shown by Drs. Ruth Benedict and Gene Weltfish in their pamphlet "The Races of Mankind."[130]

What Humphrey wanted teachers to understand was that white ethnic groups were not racial minorities, but that blacks *were* racial minorities.

Even if they did not lay hands on these anthropological materials, teachers became aware of the vital importance of using the word "race" in more carefully bounded terms. Not only did teachers begin to emphasize the significance of using scientifically accurate information about minority groups, but they also shifted their understanding of who was a "racial" minority to reflect the tripartite division of human races offered by anthropologists.

A New Discourse on Race

Teaching journals from science, English, and social studies illustrate that American teachers made racial tolerance a key function of wartime education and that the anthropological definition of race was central to this effort. In 1943 two administrators from Eugene, Oregon, published the article "Education for Racial Equality" in the journal *Social Studies*. Mildred Williams and W. L. Van Loan insisted that students learn not only the cultural contributions of America's many races, but that differences in *culture* and not *race* explained human diversity:

> Boys and girls must have an opportunity to learn the facts about the nature of our population, the reasons why people of various races and nationalities have come to the United States to live, that differences among races and national groups are due to differences in environment and cultural background and not to differences in innate ability, and that all racial and national groups have made worthwhile contributions to our culture.[131]

The authors of this unit distinguished carefully between "races" and "nationalities." The explanation for this distinction becomes clear as the authors attempt to dislodge racial prejudice not against European "nationalities," but instead against racial minorities, in this case: "Negroes," "Indians," "Orientals," and "Jews."

This narrowing of the race concept marked a paradigmatic shift in educational discourse on race, and one that would solidify quickly in revised goals for tolerance education in America. By 1943 teachers began to fret that unless America could demonstrate a successful model of participatory democracy for the rest of the world then democracy itself was at risk. Williams and Van Loan warned:

> When the war is over self-respecting Anglo-Saxon nations cannot reassume their pre-war air of white supremacy and re-assert their right to dominate lands inhabited by people of other races. Neither can the people of the United States ignore their own racial problems.[132]

Citing "all of the reliable, scientific information that is available" these educators designed a special curriculum of tolerance education for middle school students that included rigorous testing with "attitude tests" to make sure the students internalized the message of racial egalitarianism and displayed the "ability to apply principles to concrete situations."[133] Although this unit dwelled on the special "cultural" contributions of each race, it combined cultural gifts with an analysis of the scientific meaning of race as Caucasian, Mongoloid, and Negroid, or in more colloquial terms: white, yellow, and black. According to scientists, minority students of European descent were no longer "racial" minorities at all. For instance, a photograph from a New York City shows students making posters for a display labeled, "What Democracy Means." The posters visible on the wall with titles like "Brotherhood," "Americans All," and "Teamwork" depict friendly relations between blacks and whites.

The anthropological definition of human race blossomed in American schools, emphasizing both the egalitarianism of the three "races of mankind" as well as cultural relativity. As one social studies teacher reflected, "every student should acquire some appreciable knowledge of the elementary principles of anthropology basic to the intelligent understanding of democracy within our country as well as within the world ... different customs, dress, food, economic organization, arts, opinions, and religion do not imply inferiority."[134] Detailing what she called the "Scientific Aspects of the Race Problem" for readers of the *American Biology Teacher*, Sister Mary Henry of River Forest, Illinois, offered a thorough review of recent anthropological findings on human race. "The cool, objective findings of science invariably have a way of

Students creating posters on racial tolerance for an exhibit entitled "What Democracy Means." Courtesy New York City Municipal Archives.

tempering our enthusiasms and lessening our prejudices," she concluded with apparent satisfaction.

Occasionally, teachers' experiments with lessons on anthropological theories of race led to critical investigations of social equality. Faced with continuing racial tension in their neighborhood, one class of New York City students decided that "promoting unity between the Negro and white people of the neighborhood was the most valuable thing we could do." These students described a palpable "friction over the fiction that Negro and white blood was different." To find out the truth about black and white blood for themselves, these students decided to take samples from their classmates and study the results under a microscope.

Discovering that "Negro" and "white" blood was the same, just as scientists had promised, the students decided to challenge the American Red Cross's policy of segregating blood donations on the basis of race. They wrote a story for the school newspaper, made copies of the slides of "Negro" and "white" blood for the science teachers in their school, and created a poster for the national Youthbuilders organization. Delighted with the poster, Youthbuilders reproduced it for schools nationwide. In the poster, a fallen soldier reaches out for help as two arms, one black and one white, offer the desperately needed blood transfusion. "IT'S ALL THE SAME TO HIM," states the caption, "AND TO SCIENCE TOO."[135]

Junior high school students created this poster challenging the Red Cross policy of maintaining segregated blood banks during World War II.

Fearful of reproducing fascist ideology, teachers refined their language to reflect new scientific definitions of human racial egalitarianism. Three biology teachers in New Jersey reported that they adjusted their curriculum to analyze "the errors in the theories of racial superiority as propounded by the Axis biologists." Their revised lesson in biology now included "the contributions of oppressed groups, like the negroes [*sic*], to the culture of the United States."[136] Similarly, a science teacher in St. Louis insisted, "Science disproves racial superiority and shows that biological differences are slight as compared with cultural differences."[137] Some teachers explained anthropological knowledge about human diversity in extended "heredity units" that insisted: "National groups do differ from each other in *cultural* characteristics (language, food preferences, social customs, etc.), but these are predominantly environmental, i.e., acquired *after* birth. There is no evidence that the cultural traits that distinguish national groups are hereditary in a genetic sense."[138]

Although science, English, and social studies classes were favorite places to teach about the scientific definition of human race and the cultural contributions of minority groups, even elementary school teachers found ways to incorporate these materials into their classroom work. Students at Jordan Junior High School in Minneapolis had the opportunity to put on the musical play "Meet Your Relatives," which presented the central idea of *The Races of Mankind* set to the catchy western swing song, "Pistol Packin' Mama."[139] Dressed as scientists in white lab coats, the school drama club belted out:

> All the people in the world
> Are from one Family tree
> It starts with Eve and Adam
> Right down to you and me.
> In the ancient Bible
> The tale is told to you
> And now scientifically
> It's proven to be true—
> So . . .
> Lay that pistol down, Babe
> Lay that pistol down
> Pistol packin' mama
> Lay that pistol down.[140]

The scientific definition of race, while trendy, created a practical dilemma when translated for tolerance education. "Race" as defined by anthropologists reified the biological division between whites and nonwhites even as it asserted that race was a meaningless concept. Teachers struggled to mediate this apparent paradox. The Detroit teacher Norman Humphrey, for instance, insisted that white Americans should not be prejudiced because they themselves were racially mixed: "The Caucasoid American can less justifiably 'look down his nose' at the mulatto if he knows that his own genealogy contains Negroid Moors, and Mongoloid Tartars and Cherokees."[141] Humphrey's awkward charge, although well-meaning, did little to help teachers analyze or fight endemic racism in American society. In his attempt to design a lesson plan, Humphrey fell back on describing "facts about known Negro achievements" that he hoped would counteract stereotypes about blacks. Thus, even though teachers adopted a new and more scientifically accurate definition of human race, they struggled to teach racial tolerance and in many cases simply continued the decades-old practice of discussing the cultural gifts of minority groups.

As a result, more teachers began describing their lessons on "Negro" cultural achievements after 1943. In Ashland, Ohio, a high school English teacher decided to put on a play as part of his unit on "the Negro." His white students studied black achievements in the arts, science, and sports. As Hamill Hartman told readers of the *English Journal*: "Came the day. Came the payoff. The black paint was applied, the mammy dresses were donned. The entire high school was assembled and waiting."[142] Although Hartman was trying to teach white students to empathize with blacks and better understand unjust racial discrimination against African Americans, the play served as much to confirm stereotypes about blacks as it did to challenge them. Hartman's description of his play illustrates the inherent tensions of his pedagogy:

> The narrator begins: 'This is the story of the Negro, the black man, the "nigger" . . .' The chorus pleads, 'Let My People Go.' The scene reveals a Negro slave about to be auctioned off to the highest bidder; a lashing in a cotton field, the acting upon a decision to 'Steal Away.'[143]

The play then followed "Negroes" forward in time, highlighting their achievements and describing the many barriers to black success such as blatant employment discrimination. Yet the lesson served to confirm as many stereotypes as it set out to deconstruct. By dressing in "mammy rags" and literally applying blackface, the students had little opportunity to learn about the lived experiences and concerns of contemporary black Americans. Performing a strange twist on traditional blackface minstrel shows, these students distanced themselves from the very people they were supposed to be empathizing with.[144]

Hartman, nevertheless, was pleased with his show. "Being a living, breathing interpreter of the Negro ground into them an emotional understanding of, a 'feeling' insight into, this particular 'inhumanity of man to man,'" he explained. Hartman described how his students had taken away the desired message at the end of the unit, quoting student comments such as: "I learned that Negroes are just as good as we are"; "I think it gave a different feeling toward Negroes to a lot of people"; "I think Negroes should have the same privileges as the whites and I think more so that they should after the play."[145]

By the end of the war, white students were more likely to study Negro History, consider ideals of "fair play," and even sing Negro spirituals in an attempt to reduce racism against blacks. Working in an integrated classroom, the English teacher Marjorie Watts from Bloomfield, New Jersey, decided to institute an "indirect" program of tolerance education, the goal of which was to cultivate empathy for racial minorities among white students, instead of simply instructing them to be more tolerant or making them memorize facts about Negro achievements. The teacher began by passing out sheet music of Negro spirituals. Standing at the front of the classroom, Watts called out, "Think how you feel when you flunk a test," and the students flipped through their songs to select and sing "Nobody Knows the Trouble I've Had."[146] The class sang not only black spirituals, but also cowboy ballads and American Indian chants. This activity, the teacher believed, served the dual function of getting students to "appreciate" music by minority groups while also engaging her racially mixed classroom in a shared activity. Reflecting on her success, the teacher observed, "Henry and Dollee, of the black faces, sang entranced. In this world of music they were both at home and accepted into the larger group."[147]

Next, the class discussed why the cowboy ballads were so much more glamorous than the Indian songs and Negro spirituals. At this point, the teacher introduced texts to help students learn more about the history and culture of "Negroes" and American Indians. From this reading, the students concluded that the American government had not treated either minority group fairly. They drew up a list of "standards of fair play" that would help Americans in their relations with individuals from minority groups. Finally, the teacher had the class read two of the most popular anthropological texts on racism, Benedict and Weltfish's *The Races of Mankind* and Hortense Powdermaker's *Probing Our Prejudices*, which "left the class wide-eyed by tearing down scientifically the myth of white superiority."[148] In conclusion, the teacher fell back on the favored activity of "discovering the contributions of various races and nationalities to the enrichment of life in America, as well as the rest of the world."[149] Reflecting on the palpable success of this lesson in racial tolerance, the teacher explained, "Henry and Dollee did not stand out as Negroes but as individuals with their own peculiar gifts."[150]

Even as teachers incorporated more scientifically accurate information about race into the classroom, they solidified tolerance education's already formidable tendency to present racial minorities in terms of static cultural traits. While they celebrated the unique attributes of a racial minority's "culture," they insisted that these cultural anomalies were really just fascinating variations on American norms. Teachers began to speak in term of "racial cultures." One professor of education in Minnesota reflected, "Participation in a global war and plans for wide popular fellowship in the world of tomorrow has precipitated whole new studies of ethnic and racial cultures."[151] Teachers were more likely to carefully distinguish between racial, nationality (sometimes now called ethnic), and religious groups. Thus a teacher could observe casually, "The types of conflict between races is more acute than the conflict among nationality groups."[152]

Culture in educational discourse was tied to race in classroom practice despite the fact that anthropologists emphasized these as discrete analytical tools.

Teachers hoped that a celebration of a racial minority's "culture" would help white students learn to accept and even appreciate America's most despised minorities. One Chicago teacher proposed, "Maybe white children will become more tolerant when they study the achievements of the Negro."[153] Teachers taught about minority traits that were supposed to illustrate similarities between racial minorities and the dominant white majority. One teacher believed "Negro History" helped white students learn to better understand and tolerate blacks when one of her students declared, "They are just like us, only their skin is colored." Another student was less certain, but was at least willing to acknowledge a shared humanity between whites and blacks: "They are human just like the rest of us but I just haven't been with them enough to get used to their dark skin."[154]

Through their professional journals, educators reiterated the special function of tolerance education as the war drew to a close. "The future is no one's responsibility if it is not ours," noted one teacher, who wrote that "a future of happiness" required a world "in which the rights of all will be recognized."[155] Writing from a more pessimistic perspective, another teacher delineated the "price" of continued racial prejudice in dire terms, listing: "denial of democratic traditions, death of reason, insecurity for all, no world peace possible." To avert this imminent catastrophe, Edward Dale asked colleagues to teach the scientific definition of race and to emphasize the themes of "fair play" and "friendliness."[156] Other teachers echoed these urgent calls to end racial prejudices, including the entire social studies department at Long Island City High School in New York, who had been measuring student prejudice against minority groups with regularly administered "attitude tests" for years. The faculty was dismayed to discover an *increase* in levels of student prejudice toward racial minorities despite the fact the school had been conducting rigorous tolerance education throughout the war.[157]

By 1945 racial tensions in American schools were at the breaking point. In the northern cities of Gary, Indiana, and New York City, the National Association for the Advancement of Colored People reported "school strikes," where white students walked out of class to protest the growing numbers of black students at their school.[158] A relatively minor fight between black and white students at Benjamin Franklin High School in New York City was exaggerated in the press as a "race riot" involving hundreds of students attacking one another with weapons. Meanwhile, teaching journals described troubling incidents of violence, harassment, and discrimination against minorities—Jews, "Orientals," and "Negroes"—in schools nationwide. Fearing repercussions, teachers published articles anonymously. A female principal in an undisclosed northeastern industrial city described how her normally quiet school broke into mob violence after she invited a black male student to lead the school's elite color guard. Angry that a "colored boy" was giving orders and holding a gun over a group of white classmates, the school disintegrated into chaos after rumors spread that black boys had been pushing white girls around and asking them out on dates. The principal's measured response was met with open hostility by the local white community, who sent a policeman to arrest the young color guard captain and then waited for his release from school that afternoon.

"Well," said the policeman who appeared in the principal's office that afternoon, "They've got your big nigger locked up."

"What for?" the principal asked incredulously.

"Riotin' and incitin' to riot," the officer explained.

The principal pleaded with readers of *American Unity* to understand: "Suddenly I knew that riots and lynching were not far-away things of which one reads in the papers; they were lurking on my very doorstep. A few stories about girls being mistreated and I could shout into the high heavens without a hearing."[159]

Motivated by racial violence in their schools and racism in their communities, teachers produced increasingly sophisticated lessons on scientific racial equality. Describing the influx of African Americans into St. Louis during the war, Mayme Louise Sloat explained that many had been forced to live in overcrowded conditions in segregated sections of the city. Eager to challenge this racial injustice, Sloat developed a "Unit on Heredity." The "objectives" of this unit illustrate how teachers used the anthropological definition of race as a key component of tolerance education. These objectives also demonstrate a greater sensitivity to cultural factors that influenced minority life. This unit on tolerance education focused squarely on the subject of antiblack prejudice.

Objectives:

1. To develop a scientific concept of the true meaning of "race."

2. To develop some understanding of the scientific method, particularly as it applies to delusion of race superiority.

3. To develop an understanding of causes of prejudices and their effect on the individual.

4. To attempt to cultivate an attitude of tolerance.

5. To develop an awareness of the inadequacy of Negro facilities and the costs to both Negroes and whites.

6. To become acquainted with great scientists, both Negroes and whites, and appreciate their contributions to humanity.[160]

Sloat devoted a great deal of time to explaining differences among the three races "White or Caucasoid; Black or Negroid; Yellow Brown or Mongoloid," citing *The Races of Mankind*. But what is even more interesting are the activities developed to supplement the scientific data on race, such as, "Keeping a memo-book with signature of prominent business and professional peoples of the different races. Taking the pulse beat of several relatives or friends, and of a Negro or Chinese you know. Interviewing a Negro nurse and asking her to give data on temperatures of a group of Negro children."[161] These activities were supposed to prove that people of all races shared physical traits such as body temperature, and emphasized that "prominent business and professional peoples" included representatives from different racial groups. The lessons described here also encouraged interaction between white students and racial minorities. At the end of the unit, the teacher suggested a series of pointed discussion questions for the class, such as "What is the attitude of your community toward people other than those of white racial stock?" In another example, students were asked to list in two columns "1. All the reasons you know to show racial superiority, 2. All the reasons know to show no racial superiority."[162]

Sloat wanted students to understand that differences in culture, particularly opportunities in education, healthcare, and employment, shaped many of the visible characteristics of racial minorities in her city. The author carefully limited her discussion of "racial" minorities to the anthropological groups of Negroids and Mongoloids, and also took seriously the anthropological critique of culture by pointing to limited educational and employment opportunities, as opposed to the celebration of minority cultural "gifts."

Indirect Tolerance Education

By the end of the war anthropologists had established themselves as major contributors to tolerance pedagogy, even breaching the resistant journals of science teacher associations, which published fewer articles on racial tolerance than journals in English or social studies. For example, 1945 was the first year that an explicit discussion of racial prejudice appeared in *Science Teacher*. Ashley Montagu, a well-known anthropologist and an avid antiracist, published an article, "Eugenics, Genetics, and Race," that explained why the race concept was invalid and why teachers should use cultural factors to understand human diversity.[163] Teachers in all disciplines demonstrated a greater familiarity with anthropology by the end of the war. "Comparison of races and nationalities the world over shows that human nature is all pretty much the same, regardless of language or color," reported an English teacher from Wauwatosa, Wisconsin, accurately summarizing the position of anthropologists like Montagu. She continued, "And occasionally the American ego suffers through the discovery that foreign people think *we* are queer."[164] Indeed, anthropologists had been trying to help teachers and students see that through the lens of cultural relativism, no particular way of life was more rational or better than another. From this perspective, even aspects of American culture could be viewed as "queer," a lesson that intercultural educators hoped would alleviate racial prejudice.

By 1945 tolerance education had achieved national acclaim and experienced a surge of financial and political support by educational associations, colleges and universities, nonprofit groups, and government offices including the U.S. Department of Education and even First Lady Eleanor Roosevelt.[165] Detroit boasted that 210 out of its 220 public schools had established substantial intercultural education programs.[166] That fall, *Common Ground* listed a few of the most recent intercultural education workshops, including those run by the Bureau for Intercultural Education at Teachers College at Columbia University, Goddard College in Vermont, the College of Education of the University of Minnesota, and the School of Education at Stanford University. These were in addition to intercultural education conferences sponsored by the National Conference of Christians and Jews at Vassar College, the University of Denver, Eau Claire State Teachers College in Wisconsin, Harvard University, Milwaukee State Teachers College, the University of Oregon, Syracuse University, the University of Wisconsin, and the University of Chicago. In the South, Fisk University made intercultural education a focal point of its first annual Race Relations Institute in 1944. Other programs, such as the intercultural education workshop at Reed College in Portland, Oregon, were joint projects between local religious, secular, and government organizations. In large and diverse school districts, such as that of Dade County, Florida, Boards of Education appointed teachers to study intercultural education at national workshops with the expectation that these teachers would then implement the curriculum back home. Commissioners of Education in New York and Massachusetts sent surveys to every public school in their respective state, demanding a written description of current tolerance programming. Superintendents in Detroit, Cincinnati, and Los Angeles encouraged their schools to institute and expand intercultural learning as soon as possible.[167]

Even as institutional support for tolerance education expanded nationwide, many teachers disagreed with the curriculum and tried to undermine its implementation. When two black teachers in Detroit tried to convince the predominantly white faculty at their school to institute a formal tolerance curriculum, they met resistance, despite the fact that district administrators strongly supported intercultural education. A few white teachers admired intercultural education, but others balked, arguing that a "slower, more evolutionary program" was needed and that teachers should hold out for more accurate "scientific research on racial problems" before they attempted to solve race relations on their own.[168] In the pages of the *American Biology Teacher*, many educators continued to grapple with the immense social responsibility of refuting false claims of racial superiority and the seemingly equally important task of teaching scientifically informed theories of eugenics. While some of the articles managed to strike a balance between these contradictory lines of reasoning, others explicitly argued that biology teachers had a professional responsibility to teach the "fact" that "human beings are genetically and biologically *un*equal." According to an article by the eugenicist Oscar Riddle at Cold Spring Harbor laboratories in New York, "the [human inequalities] to which I refer are serious and largely unacknowledged inequalities which may prove more dangerous to Democracy than to other forms of government."[169]

Within cities with strong intercultural education programming, like New York City, teachers who disliked tolerance education began to organize and push back against these required courses. In New York City in 1945, various Catholic organizations coordinated a letter writing campaign to protest in-service courses on intercultural education offered by the Board of Education. In particular they objected to a course entitled "Promoting National Welfare through Intercultural Cooperation," featuring a lecture by the anthropologist Gene Weltfish. Letters poured into the administrative offices of the New York City Board of Education demanding that it immediately end this course and others like it. Some letters complained that the course portrayed Catholics as a monolithic cultural group that glossed over important ethnic and regional diversity. Others argued that the content of the course was inherently "communistic."[170] One letter by a member of the Teachers Alliance explained, "We believe that the persons scheduled to speak on this course are all of one definite type point of view, namely the radical one. . . . This course, if sponsored, would probably be the cause of more inter-racial friction than it could possibly accomplish good."[171]

Not everyone, it appears, was pleased with the growth of lessons on racial tolerance, and the growing criticism of intercultural education forced supporters to make substantial changes to the curriculum. By 1945 teaching journals reflect a mounting interest in what teachers described as "indirect" tolerance education. Instead of formal intercultural instruction, proponents of indirect lessons believed they could weave racial tolerance into regular subjects, or, alternatively, that the regular subjects already taught tolerance implicitly and that no changes to the curriculum were necessary.

In Lansdowne, Pennsylvania, administrators bragged that by distributing textbooks and pamphlets to teachers on the subject of racial tolerance, they had successfully instituted an "indirect" form of tolerance education. Superintendent Carmon Ross believed that the best tolerance program was to enrich the curriculum generally instead of creating special units on the subject of racial tolerance, explaining: "There may be extracted from every such subject or activity worthwhile outcomes to create in the minds of our growing young citizens desirable appreciations of the good traits, characteristics, and cultural contributions of other peoples to the life of America."[172] This school district envisioned intercultural education as a form of "democracy in action" that did not require special intercultural lectures, assemblies, or classroom activities. In a special report on the intercultural programming in the state of New York, various school administrators reported that the best way to tackle racial prejudice in the classroom was to avoid the topic of tolerance altogether. As the superintendent of Beacon, New York, public schools wrote:

> In the Beacon public schools there always have been many pupils of various nationalities, creeds and colors. At all times it has been the intent of those in charge of the schools to call attention to these differences as little as possible. This policy, we believe, so far as our own local setup is concerned, has produced a maximum understanding among the pupils of our schools without ever calling to their attention the basic fact that problems are being faced.[173]

This revised approach to tolerance education, calling "attention to these differences as little as possible," emerged as a more cautious and politically expedient method once the threat of war was receding. Examples of indirect approaches to tolerance programming included interfaith Christmas-Chanukah celebrations, international clubs, a classroom unit called "A Class Becomes a Town," and school assemblies with names like "The Story of America."[174]

Race relations experts cautioned that armistice would mean tense confrontations as soldiers returned to civilian life and sought new jobs, improved housing, and a better life. "During and after World War I, there was a discouraging increase in intolerance and intergroup conflict, and during World War II mounting tensions have been evident," cautioned one intercultural educator. "There is every reason to believe that the difficult period of adjustment that lies ahead will see a further increase of dissension and conflict."[175] The growing militancy of black civil rights activists through organizations like the NAACP and the Urban League forced white Americans to acknowledge the severe injustices imposed on "black" and other racial minorities through legal and extralegal discrimination. The war brought the international implications of racism home to many educated Americans, who consequently threw their support behind moderate programs for better interracial understanding and improved human relations. Many saw intercultural education as a way to reduce white racism by focusing attention on individual prejudices instead of dramatic structural or political inequality.[176]

Teachers willingly experimented with intercultural education and other forms of antiprejudice programming, but few were completely satisfied with the results of their work. The more teachers taught tolerance in American schools, the more alternatives they created to the original curriculum of intercultural education. Many came to prefer understated lessons that expanded the traditional canon to include minority literature and historical contributions, while others wanted to expose individual prejudice and social injustice. Finally, some educators focused on the scientific definition of race and the national and international implications of racism in terms of democracy and world peace. Together these competing visions of tolerance education would vie for prominence in the postwar era.

|| 5 ||

Race as Culture, 1946–1954

Before minorities can claim their rightful places in such a social studies textbook, however, the prevalent conception of American culture as the culture of the old American Anglo-Saxon group will have to be radically revised.

—Teacher, 1946

[Teachers] can select art, music, and literature that will enlarge the children's experience and acquaint them with the cultural contributions of people of various races.

—Intercultural Educator, 1949

Surveying the terrible casualties of modern warfare, the destruction by atomic bomb of Hiroshima and Nagasaki, and the Holocaust, many Americans felt that the expansion of training in racial tolerance in the school had come too late or that the task at hand was too daunting. From across the nation a chorus of teachers bemoaned what they saw as devastating educational shortcomings. As a teacher from Portland reflected, "If, for the past twenty-five years, American education had stressed world geography, world economics, world culture, world order, we might very well have adopted a strong and enlightened foreign policy that would have headed off World War II! Truly a tragic 'might-have-been'!"[1]

Lamenting their failure to avert the world war and the murder of millions of innocent people, American educators redoubled their resolve and crafted an ambitious agenda to secure world peace. Teaching journals in 1946 and 1947 are filled with visionary articles by educational leaders, social scientists, professors of education, and classroom teachers promising to fortify global democracy through intensive tolerance education. Now understood in terms of its potential for world peace and international security, teachers made racial tolerance a defining feature of their classroom practice. Perfecting the strategy they had experimented with during the war, teachers asserted the importance of teaching a "scientific" analysis of human race to promote tolerance. Nearly every article cited anthropological facts to explain the relative equality of all human beings and to emphasize teachers' political neutrality and professional authority.

And yet, this inspired classroom work quickly came to a screeching halt. After 1948, there was a rapid decline in lessons on racial tolerance as teachers literally silenced discussions of race in the classroom. Instead, teachers preferred to use the word "culture" to identify and describe those people they understood to be "racial" minorities. They did this to emphasize that differences between the white majority and nonwhite minorities were not biological, or racial, but instead learned. However, by insisting that all racial minorities were culturally distinct, teachers crafted a discourse that depicted racial minorities as somehow inherently different from the white majority. Constructing this difference as cultural rather than racial was an improvement in educational discourse on race, to be sure. At the same time early twentieth-century assumptions about racial immutability were carried over into the new and more fashionable language of cultural diversity. As open discussions of race became increasingly rare during the emerging cold war, teachers solidified this conception of race-as-culture as the dominant educational discourse on race. By 1948, the rhetorical conflation of race with culture in American classrooms was complete.

Teachers disciplined students to internalize the social standards of "the group," a thinly veiled reference to white, middle-class norms. In revised, yet subtle Americanization programs children were taught that tolerance was a two-way process. First, each individual had to demonstrate the characteristics that made him or her pleasant and agreeable to others. Second, educated citizens were to refrain from making harmful generalizations about other individuals based on factors like racial or religious background. Teachers pressured students to imagine what traits made them likable to others, and to internalize the surveillance of teachers and classmates as they interacted with racial others. Any audible expression of a racial stereotype or epithet was unanimously declared a sign of bad manners, marking the speaker as profoundly uneducated and calling into question his or her status as a "real" American. American citizenship, particularly the status of an "educated" person, was thus tied directly to an individual's ability to perform the desired attributes of a tolerant *and* tolerable human being.[2]

Paradoxically, teachers stopped teaching about racial equality just as the African American civil rights movement erupted in national politics.[3] Many American teachers had been swept up in a growing civil rights agenda that centered around basic rights for African Americans—especially fair employment, an end to the poll tax, and antilynching laws—during World War II.[4] Yet, they retreated from teaching lessons on race and social injustice just as religious groups and civil rights organizations began more aggressive campaigns for political action. By the time this growing civil rights activism culminated in the 1954 *Brown v.*

Board of Education ruling, American teachers were unable or unwilling to speak about race in the classroom, much less teach explicit lessons on racial equality and civil rights, imperiled by a political climate in which they could be accused of harboring communist sympathies.

This chapter explains this paradox by examining the convergence of factors that curtailed teachers' ability to develop antiracist pedagogy in American schools after 1947. It recognizes the importance of McCarthyism, which specifically targeted public school teachers as potential communist "indoctrinators."[5] It also explains how anthropological models of tolerance pedagogy quickly lost ground to psychological models that emphasized prejudice as an individual problem, a sickness that could be corrected through therapy.[6] Teachers actively chose and were encouraged by professional educators to shift the focus of tolerance education away from racial minorities and to instead promote a "colorblind" pedagogy. Strikingly enough, on the rare occasions when teachers spoke of racial minorities, it was in positive terms and relied on a celebration of their supposed culture to demonstrate sympathy and support for beleaguered minorities.

Expanding Tolerance Education in Postwar America

Disheartened by the wave of intolerance that swept the country as it dismantled its warfare state, teachers continued to adapt the curriculum as part of a national movement to reduce racial prejudice and secure peace.[7] Tolerance posters were distributed to more than 5,000 secondary schools in 125 American cities during this period, reminding Americans, "We fought together . . . let's work together!" and "If you hear anyone condemn a fellow American because of race or religion, tell 'em off!"[8] National politicians, educators, and youth leaders publicly advocated tolerance. Dwight Eisenhower, then army chief of staff of the War Department, instructed New York City teachers, "For your own part, you should teach your students to abstain from prejudgment of other nations and races and to strive for as full a knowledge as possible of America and the rest of the world without hatred and without prejudice."[9] Tolerance education was specifically constructed, as it always had been, as a process to discipline the educated American.

A surge of textbooks and journal articles redefined and reasserted the relevancy of intercultural education as a curriculum capable of promoting tolerance and stabilizing international relations.[10] In textbooks with titles like *Democratic Human Relations*, teacher educators cautioned, "The aftermath of the war offers simultaneously high opportunity and grave danger. The opportunity is that now is the psychological time to harness tensed emotions into a great forward movement for democracy. The danger is that the frustrations and fears of humanity will eventuate in violence and scapegoating."[11]

Intercultural education, now called intergroup education or education for human relations, secured a new purpose for schools during the war, one that brought national acclaim to the undervalued work of American teachers.[12] Interculturalists insisted their curriculum was more relevant and necessary than ever in peacetime. They promised tolerance education could produce educated citizens with the self-discipline to resist prejudice. "In the face of the intergroup tensions that disturb the peace of our schools, communities, and country, what shall we regard as the necessary qualities of a good citizen for public education?" queried one textbook. "How shall he act when faced with a problem involving racial or religious prejudice? How can we educate our children for participation as good citizens in the typical mixed community? For national participation? For world-wide participation?"[13] Intercultural education offered teachers, parents, and community activists a curriculum for producing "good citizens" by inculcating values like tolerance and self-esteem, understood to promote social stability between racial minorities and the dominant white majority. While the goal of intercultural education was essentially unchanged, the meaning of "racial" minorities had narrowed—in part thanks to the social scientists who shaped the curriculum—to refer to African Americans, Asian Americans, Mexican Americans, and Native Americans.

In 1946 and 1947 teachers from all subject areas regularly claimed that teaching students the scientific, anthropological definition of race helped reduce racial prejudice. In his presidential address to the National Council for the Social Studies, I. James Quillen assured his audience, "The social studies teacher can contribute to the development of international understanding and world citizenship by . . . introducing more content from anthropology to show the extent to which human behavior is culturally determined."[14] Likewise, Superintendent Dr. William H. Lemmel of the Baltimore Public Schools told the *Washington Post*, "By disseminating facts of history, anthropology, psychology, and biology, children will learn that there is no point to any racial superiority claim, for brown, white, yellow and red people have all made their contributions to man's advancement."[15] Joseph Gallant, an English teacher in New York City, casually remarked that, "In biology, for example, many classes take organized units in racial anthropology." These were not simple lessons in science, they were intended to have a larger purpose. According to Gallant, "The objectives of such units are, among other things, to explode the myths about race and thus to intensify the democratic acceptance or to neutralize prejudiced rejection of various racial and cultural groups in America."[16]

The *English Journal* published a special issue on intercultural education in 1946 that was designed to help English teachers integrate a critical scientific perspective on race, culture, and prejudice into their classroom practice.[17] Ruth Benedict contributed the article "Racism Is Vulnerable," tracing the history of racism as an ideology that emerged toward the end of colonialism as a justification for slavery and domination of native people and lands. Challenging the assumption that racism was a natural and enduring feature of human history, she explained, "The Indians of the New World, the Negroes of Africa, the Malays and Melanesians of the Pacific were killed or enslaved because they stood in the way of progress; but these massacres and conquests were not 'race' wars . . . It was not until 1859 that the theory of the master-race was formulated."[18] Benedict wanted English teachers to recognize race as a social and historical construct, or a "myth," and demanded that they impart the scientific truth about human racial differences to their young students.

The special issue also included essays by well-known psychologists, philosophers, and educators who reiterated the significance of using science to undermine racism in English classes. Essays by teachers and students described "scientific" lessons on race in schools nationwide. Marjorie B. Smiley reported that based on her national survey on tolerance education, "Almost all the special units on intergroup education described included study of the facts of race and the fallacies of racism using such materials as *The Races of Mankind* by Gene Weltfish and Ruth Benedict, and Hortense Powdermaker's *Probing Our Prejudices*."[19] According to Smiley, students then applied this scientific knowledge to political questions in their daily lives, such as "What Is Democracy?" and "What America Means to Me" and "What Shall We Do about Our Japanese-Americans?" Using race as a carefully delineated concept, teachers and students in this context understood racial minorities to be people of African or Asian descent, including Native Americans. Teachers asked students to read literature by and about minority groups, including works by Pearl Buck, Richard Wright, and Langston Hughes.

While teachers who introduced lessons on the scientific definition of human race often used this material to analyze controversial political issues like racial equality, the very "scientific" nature of this material lent itself nicely to protecting teachers from charges of indoctrination. Teachers strategically cited the scientific definition of human race to make their lesson plans simultaneously more authoritative and less political, as science was understood to be a neutral and objective discipline. Especially for teachers whose lessons dealt with volatile subjects like racial discrimination, citing a body of scientific scholarship helped deflect criticism. It was easier, perhaps, to teach a lesson on the equal intelligence of black and white Americans if a teacher observed: "Anthropologists have worked for years on problems of race and have scientifically proved that there is no connection between racial characteristics and intelligence."[20]

While this was "scientifically" true, the fact remained that many Americans still objected to lessons that dwelled on the intellectual equality of blacks— lessons that typically led into a consideration of social and political inequality in the United States. Nevertheless, teachers continued to assert the pedagogical merit of teaching scientific lessons on race. In another example, the National Council for the Social Studies (NCSS) included the scientific analysis of race as the *first* step in teaching "democratic human relations." This race unit suggested discussion questions such as:

> What is meant by the term "race"? How did races develop? What physical characteristics may be inherited? How may blood be classified? How may you account for the differences in the intelligence test results? What country is doing the most to prevent racial discrimination? What is racism? When and where did it originate? Why did it originate? What is the difference between race and nationality? Race and religion?[21]

Lessons that included the scientific study of race sometimes led to critical discussions of racial equality and American democracy. "The delusion that our country already has achieved true democracy must be shattered," wrote the head of one English department, who advocated critical lessons on "American ideals and American practices in housing, in education, in employment, [and] in political rights."[22] Similarly, Dana Niswender, a high school English teacher in New York City, reminded his colleagues of the importance of ferreting out racial stereotypes in textbooks in the typically urgent prose of the day. "As a convinced and crusading believer in the democratic principle of the brotherhood of man, I am acutely conscious of the implicit use of racial stereotypes in the various communications media," Niswender reported.[23] Niswender recommended the movie *Brotherhood of Man*, which was based on Ruth Benedict and Gene Weltfish's popular pamphlet *The Races of Mankind*. Likewise, a teacher from Boston printed his simple "Unit on Prejudice" in the *English Journal*, reminding teachers that "The cure for prejudice is scientific investigation, straight thinking, and proper education."[24] Teachers at Garfield Intermediate School in Detroit invited an anthropologist to lecture the students on the meaning of race.[25] A teacher from Bellingham, Washington, noted, "The children learned, in a limited fashion of course, that, as Ruth Benedict points out in *Race: Science and Politics*, the history of race persecution is to be found not in the history of racial conflict, but in the history of persecution."[26] Because these teachers employed anthropological texts on race, they portrayed racial minorities as people of African and Asian descent, an interpretation that cast all people of European descent as members of the white racial majority in the United States.

Journals like *American Unity, Journal of the NEA, English Journal, Social Education,* and the *Science Teacher* encouraged teachers to include a scientific perspective on race relations in their teaching. The *Journal of the NEA* printed what they called "A Primer on Race" whose five illustrated boxes offered teachers a simple overview of what were held to be scientific truths:

1. In the beginning God created man, of one blood, spread over earth.
2. A nation is not a race, a religion is not a race, a language is not a race, a culture is not a race (There is no primitive race) . . . NO habits, customs, ideals or forms of government are inherently typical of any racial group.
3. There are three great groups of races, Caucasic, Mongoloid, and Negroid.
4. There is no truly superior nor inferior race.
5. What can I do? If you are an employer, a teacher, a veteran, etc.[27]

American Unity insisted that "Tolerance Can Be Taught" and provided "Ammunition" in the war on racism in the form of books, pamphlets, posters, cartoons, and movies that emphasized a scientific, rational approach to the problems of race relations and democracy.[28] Organizations like the Race Relations Institute at Fisk University, the National Conference of Christians and Jews, the American Jewish Congress, the American Jewish Committee, the Workers Education Bureau of America, the Chicago Urban League, the American Federation of Labor, the Council against Intolerance, and the American Council Institute of Pacific Relations produced texts to educate the public about race and unjust discrimination. In teaching journals these texts were advertised, reviewed, and promoted for teachers. In addition to Benedict and Weltfish's *The Races of Mankind,* teachers were advised to employ texts like *Hate Challenges America, Labor Fights Bigotry, Minorities, Race Riots Aren't Necessary, Sense and Nonsense about Race, The Myth That Threatens America, Together We Win, Tolerance on Trial, Jews in American Life, The Japanese in Our Midst,* and *Labor Fights Bigotry.*[29] In the American battle against racial discrimination, social activists believed that scientific knowledge about race, prejudice, minority groups, and discrimination was required to uproot deeply entrenched racism.

Teachers, therefore, had the support of national teaching organizations and often their local school districts to teach lessons on racial tolerance because politicians and educators viewed teaching the scientific facts on race as a vital component of a larger project to inculcate tolerance and democracy in the postwar era. Even science teachers, historically the least likely to publish journal articles on racial equality, finally risked speaking out in their national organ, *Science Teacher.* "Because of his training in objectivity, the scientist can perform an outstanding service in the promotion of friendly understanding," offered a cautious professor at Massachusetts Institute of Technology.[30] Morris Meister, president of the National Science Teacher's Association (NSTA), put the problem more urgently. Arguing that science teachers must organize to defend "the spirit of science and the democratic faith with which it is entwined," Meister lamented that science teachers had consistently failed to bring their discipline to bear on issues of worldwide importance. "By comparison with teachers of the social studies, of English, or of mathematics, we have been inarticulate," Meister scolded. Meister wanted science teachers to organize nationally and contribute to the educational effort to challenge racial prejudice, for example by teaching "how race theories are to be corrected."[31]

Even as teachers articulated more critical lessons on racial equality and social justice, many of their lessons preserved aspects of the older, more conventional tolerance education, especially the teaching of cultural contributions by each race. "Knowledge of the contributions made to American and world civilization by people of all races, religions, and nationalities is considered by many teachers to be an essential phase of intercultural education," reported Smiley on the basis of her national survey.[32] Similarly, a junior high school teacher in Detroit developed a unit designed to promote better understanding between "Negroes" and whites in local schools. The goal of this unit was "to stimulate the desire to know more about cultural groups other than one's own, and to develop mutual respect and friendship."[33] The director of social studies in the Cleveland public schools developed an intercultural curriculum that emphasized, "every race and nationality has brought its culture to Cleveland."[34] In Baltimore, the superintendent explained that, "By helping students to understand religious customs and ritual and their basic significance, they will be able to substitute respect for others' religion in place of prejudice."[35] As these examples suggests, teaching about racial groups in terms of "customs," "ritual," and "culture" led teachers to describe racial minorities as cohesive "cultural groups."

At the same time, some teachers adamantly challenged the cultural-contributions approach to tolerance education. Smiley noted that some teachers were "fearful that studies of cultural contributions of minorities and talks by representatives of these groups may counteract the basic principle of democracy by implying that individuals are to be accorded recognition on the basis of the record of the group in which they happen to be born." Others believed any focus on minority group "song, dress, food, and the like" were inherently superficial and fostered "sentimentality" rather than "true understanding."[36] Charles Glicksberg, a teacher from Newark, observed that lessons that went out of their way to celebrate "the Negro" or point out his supposed intelligence, civility, and cultural accomplishments were inherently racist. Glicksberg faulted teachers who celebrated black achievements in the classroom, claiming "the hesitation with which the step was taken, the apprehension, even the cheers and self-righteousness, smack dangerously of prejudice in reverse." The problem, according to this teacher, was that "The Negroes are still being singled out as a group different, peculiar, apart."[37] The director of social studies in Cleveland agreed, writing: "It is an indication of subconscious race prejudice to treat the Negro 'problem' as separate and distinct from other minority problems. Such separation may be considered 'Jim-Crowism' in the curriculum."[38] Teachers were supposed to teach racial tolerance, but singling out a particular minority group for special treatment would potentially reproduce a racist social order. This dilemma remained unresolved for most teachers, who, for the time being, continued to teach concurrent lessons on the scientific definition of human race *and* the cultural contributions of racial minorities.

Lessons on Racial Etiquette

The dozens of articles on teaching racial tolerance found in teaching journals during the immediate postwar years illustrate that many teachers struggled with the question of how to bridge the gap between factual knowledge, such as an understanding of the scientific definition of race, and "true understanding," or the expectation that students would internalize lessons on tolerance and act accordingly. Almost all teachers agreed that simply learning facts was not enough; developing lessons that went beyond facts, however, was challenging and often veered into uncharted or worse, ineffective pedagogy. Drama and literature were viewed as two strategies to help students empathize at a more personal and emotional level with minorities who suffered discrimination.[39] Other teachers believed lessons in personal etiquette, or good manners, would improve social relations in the classroom. For example, one teacher insisted he or she had managed to bridge the gap between "knowledge and practice" through a unit for twelfth graders entitled "Achieving Intercultural Friendship through Tact." In this lesson, the students discussed the case of a recent graduate of their school who quit her job as a secretary after learning her boss was Jewish. The students assessed the problem and then devised a list of "Do's and Don'ts of Tactful Procedure" to help each other remember the proper way to act in such a situation.[40] Likewise, teachers were reminded that "To teach equality of opportunity regardless of race, creed, or color, teachers themselves must be free of hampering prejudices. Examples set by teachers speak louder than their words."[41]

One of the most pronounced changes in postwar intercultural education was the new effort to teach tolerance in terms of learning to perform good manners.[42] Elisabeth Lasch-Quinn notes the detrimental impact of race experts and their insistence on racial etiquette in the 1960s–1990s, however, it appears there was a historical precedent for this movement in public schools as early as the late 1940s. Some teachers viewed good manners as an effective strategy to help students transform classroom lessons into meaningful lived experiences. Others conceived of etiquette as a strategy to offset resistance to tolerance education by students or their families. By the postwar era, teachers had been experimenting with intercultural education for years—some even for a decade or longer. In particular, they struggled to translate social science theories on race and racial prejudice into effective classroom practice. Given their responsibility to teach lessons on tolerance in what could easily become a racially charged setting, many teachers began focusing explicitly on having good manners as a foundation to developing the "good will" and "friendly relations" so urgently needed, and still so visibly lacking in the American citizenry.

Esther Williams, a social studies teacher in the all-white Oakwood Township High School in Muncie, Illinois, explained: "Surmising that the attitudes of some of the freshmen toward minority groups, particularly Negroes, were socially undesirable, a unit on dealing with racial prejudices was introduced." First, Williams handed out an anonymous attitude test as a way to measure racial prejudice against Negroes. The test consisted of a list of "yes or no" questions, beginning with straightforward statements such as "Negroes as a race are inferior." The test quickly pushed into more challenging territory, asking: "I would be willing that Negroes attend Oakwood Township High School," "I would be willing that Negro students attend the school parties and dances," and finally "I would approve of the marriage of white people with Negroes." Although forty-nine out of seventy students agreed that Negroes as a race were not inferior, only nine students were willing to welcome black students into their high school, and only seven students could conceive of interracial school dances. Not surprisingly, not a single white student admitted to being able to "tolerate" the idea of interracial marriage. After the class considered the way racial prejudice and discrimination impacted the life opportunities of Negro citizens, the teacher remarked, "All the students agreed that each one of them could make an attempt to do the following three things: 1. refrain from name calling, 2. be courteous and friendly to colored people, 3. help to clear up the misconceptions of others concerning the Negro."[43] Notably, lessons like this one on interracial etiquette did not ask students to revise their stance on racial segregation or legalized racial discrimination.

Directing intercultural education in Detroit, Marion Edman published "We'd Better Mind the P's and Cues," an article that instructed teachers how to create "understanding, co-operation, and generally good relationships among diverse groups of people."[44] This required a certain amount of tact on the part of teachers, who needed to model appropriate behavior in the classroom, especially when dealing with students who were racially prejudiced. According to Edman, teachers became easily frustrated when carefully orchestrated tolerance education fell on obstinately deaf ears. One teacher reported that after months of tolerance education, one exasperated student ranted, "No, I don't say what [the teacher] wants me to. It's tough enough to try to dope out what I think myself with out trying to dope out what *she* thinks."[45] A Washington student echoed this sentiment when he was asked to take yet another attitude test to determine the precise degree of racial prejudice he harbored. "In answering the questions do we answer the way we should or do we answer the way we really think?" he demanded bluntly.[46] While these students were perhaps being honest, it was nevertheless exasperating for teachers to think that students actively resisted their efforts. A teacher at South Side High School in Newark, New Jersey, echoed this frustration when he asked, "How can the ingrained habits of a lifetime be completely changed by an occasional hour devoted to the reading and interpretation of intercultural material?" In his experience, "As soon as the students leave the classroom, they revert to form."[47] It was difficult for teachers not to become angry at the very students they were trying so hard to connect with, a fact that compounded their difficulties presenting lessons on tolerance and understanding. The answer, according to interculturalists like Edman, was that "Each individual teacher must find and mind her own peculiar P's and Q's."[48]

Resisting Tolerance Education

By the postwar era tolerance education had become a regular feature of the American educational landscape. While all American teachers would have recognized this newly defined function of schooling, not all of them appreciated it or agreed with popular forms of tolerance education. In particular, while some teachers asserted the importance of teaching scientific texts on race and racial prejudice, others believed these texts were unnecessary and potentially harmful to young students. The expansion of tolerance education meant that teachers crafted more variations on existing intercultural curricula, many of which not only refused to consider the scientific definition of race, but failed to consider racial discrimination at all.

For example, Frances MacIntire from New Canaan, Connecticut, described "What Is an American?" a unit that did not reflect either a scientific approach to tolerance or intercultural pedagogy, although it is evident that MacIntire believed her unit promoted tolerance and understanding. Reflecting on the success of her lesson plan, she observed, "While working out this program we had no thought of tolerance. We were simply Americans, reviewing our history, thankful in these days of world turmoil to be citizens of the United Sates of America."[49] By emphasizing that she had "no thought of tolerance" in terms of a formal curriculum and in contrast acted as "simply Americans" talking about a shared past, this teacher asserted what she believed to be a better and more effective method for molding and uniting young citizens that did not require formal tolerance curricula.

Designing a lesson that intentionally ignored the kinds of scientific and professional educational materials so many other teachers cherished, MacIntire emphasized patriotism and American loyalty as her primary goals. She highlighted the heritage of each student in her class, all of whom were apparently white, and then considered the cultural gifts each group brought to America. MacIntire began the unit by having children list their "ancestral background" and plotting these locations on a map in the front of the classroom. Next, the students interviewed their parents in order to answer the question, "How I happen to be an American," or how each family "happened" to arrive in this country whether three or three hundred years ago. The culmination of this project was a Thanksgiving play featuring Indians, Pilgrims, and "folk" people from Europe. According to MacIntire, "The announcer explained how in the early days many immigrants came from Scotland, Ireland, Spain, France, Holland, Germany, bringing rich gifts in music, art, ideas of democracy, science." She continued, "If the children representing these countries chose to, they could speak, sing, or dance."[50] Apparently, many students did just that, and their parents helped by sewing European peasant costumes and teaching folk dances from their native lands. For the grand finale, MacIntire related:

> As the children entered the stage, they formed a large "V," the apex of which was at the back of the stage. After all the countries were represented, a Boy Scout entered bearing the American flag, flanked by either side by a Girl Scout . . . Everyone on the stage faced the flag, and the people in the audience joined them in the pledge of allegiance and in singing "America the Beautiful."[51]

A lesson in "tolerance" such as this once was ripe with calculated disregard for formal intercultural education and its emphasis on scientific knowledge. Certainly there was no consideration here of social justice for racial minorities. In fact, the very concept of race was distinctly missing from the entire lesson, while an overarching emphasis on cultural gifts from European nations set the tone for understanding American diversity within the limits of whiteness. Lessons like this one delineated the boundaries of acceptable diversity, such as quaint foodways, charming clothing, and traditional dances, while strictly excluding and even obscuring the important differences in the way minority groups lived in America compared to the middle-class, white majority.

Increasing numbers of teachers devised lessons on intercultural education that studiously avoided questions of both race and prejudice. For example, the special 1947 intercultural education issue of the *Elementary English Review*, "Good Neighbors Unlimited," did not offer a single article that discussed the scientific definition of race or the problems of prejudice. Of six articles, the first, from Chicago, promoted lessons on being a "good neighbor" as a way to model the behavior of a "good American."[52] Two articles from Buffalo, New York, and Frostburg, Maryland, offered lesson plans almost identical to MacIntire's, including plays featuring the peasant backgrounds of various European folk groups, although in this case they included "Negroes," whose "folk" culture was represented by spirituals. By tracing their own and one another's "ancestry," as one teacher from Buffalo described it, teachers roused "appreciation for the contributions made by various nations and races."[53] Again, the boundaries of "appreciating" this cultural diversity was made painfully clear in class, which celebrated artificial and sanitized versions of each student's heritage. Other articles emphasized themes like student heritage, national unity, and world peace while carefully avoiding any discussion of race or racial discrimination. The final article, written by a teacher from Great Neck, New York, reiterated the importance of doing such work "indirectly," so as not to draw unwanted attention from students or parents.[54]

In 1947 teachers began to express a preference for teaching tolerance "indirectly," a fact that hastened the curriculum's demise.[55] For example, a majority of white teachers in Atlanta, Georgia, agreed that they observed "undemocratic relations" between majority and minority groups in their communities, but at the same time only a fraction of these teachers advocated teaching "democratic aims" through a direct approach.[56]

Teaching racial tolerance in America in the years following the war was undoubtedly a tricky proposal; as a principal from Delaware stated more eloquently, "in teaching, one is always risking martyrdom."[57] Besides competing tolerance pedagogies and the constant fear of reprisal, many teachers faced hostile, openly racist students and parents. A dedicated English teacher in Huntington, West Virginia, spent an entire semester teaching racial tolerance through reading and performing carefully selected plays. In her article, Virginia Rider recounted how classroom discussions often slipped into confrontations between students who supported racial tolerance and those who did not. At one point, students in her class debated whether or not blacks were really more superstitious and less intelligent than whites. While a few students suggested that "Negro" superstitions reflected a lack of education and that scientists had disproved white intellectual superiority, others responded with hostility and drew on the authority of personal experience to challenge their classmates. A girl named Betty retorted, "I think the educated Negroes are a bigger problem than the ignorant ones."[58] Later in the semester, another student wrote an essay that directly contradicted the lessons his teacher had been pressing on him:

In real life the Jew is unlike David in Israel Zangwill's *The Melting Pot*. The Jews I know are overbearing with a tendency to associate only with other Jews. My opinion, which is based on my contacts with Jews, is that most of them are crude, overbearing, and aggressive. They are courteous only when money is involved and when it is to their advantage to be polite. Most of them are petty, selfish people who think only of themselves.[59]

Understandably, teachers became increasingly frustrated with what many perceived to be a failing curriculum. Alfred Fisk, a philosopher at San Francisco State College who ran intercultural workshops for teachers over the summer session, reported his distress after sitting in on various intercultural activities in San Francisco schools. In one case, Fisk visited a class studying American Indians. He noted the wigwam the children had constructed in the center of the room, photographs of American Indians in "native dress," and beadwork and birch-bark canoes the children made during art period. On the day Fisk was there, the teacher had arranged for an American Indian woman to come speak to her class. The visitor, who had served in the war, walked into the room wearing her "snappy" Cadet Nurse uniform. She told the children of her experiences growing up on her father's sheep farm, her education in California, and her service as a Cadet Nurse during the war. Despite this excellent presentation, Fisk reported the children simply "could not accept her as an American Indian." When she was finished speaking, one child blurted out "You're not a real Indian!" When assured that she was, another child asked bluntly, "Do you eat acorns?"[60] To Fisk, this episode represented the complete failure of the cultural approach to intercultural education. Studying the culture and history of Native Americans in the past, or for that matter the "folk" culture of any group, did very little to help children in their daily relations with minorities who themselves were far removed from these characterizations. Students, of course, despised this approach when it was applied to them. "Why must we always be connected with eating spaghetti? I don't happen to like it myself—and most of my friends eat a normal American diet, not spaghetti!" protested a boy of Italian descent after another intercultural lesson.[61]

For educators like Fisk who wanted to improve tolerance education, the challenge was how to balance a genuine appreciation of minority groups with the ideal of a world where "race" and other markers of difference did not matter. Fisk tried to elaborate on this complicated proposal, wondering "How to acknowledge the Negro's gift to America without admitting a special 'Negroid' status." In response, Fisk promoted the ideal of cultural democracy. When all of the cultural contributions of the many different strands of Americans had been woven together "like Jacob's coat of many colors," then Americans would ultimately be united. Struggling to articulate how this might work in practice, Fisk offered, "In that day the Chinese American will feel Negro spirituals *his* (but he will be an American, not a Chinese American)."[62] While an admirable idea, cultural democracy had yet to be worked out in the classrooms that Fisk and other teachers described in teaching journals in 1947.

The Removal of the Race Concept, 1948

American teachers' support for tolerance education shifted rapidly after 1947. This represents less of a critique of tolerance education than an abrupt abandonment. The shift did not occur overnight; there were still numerous articles on tolerance education in teaching journals in 1948 and some in 1949, 1950, and 1951. But the number of articles rapidly declined, as did the scope of critical lessons on racial equality. Teachers were less likely to teach critical lessons on race and social justice and more likely to ponder the psychological phenomenon of prejudice within each individual. Contact, not content, became the cry as teachers promoted interracial contact between students but shied away from informing students of scientific facts such as the anthropological definition of human race. The scientific definition of race, captured with such precision by scholars like Ruth Benedict, vanished from American classrooms by 1954.

The timing of the decline of tolerance education as well as the specific shifts within educational discourse on race implicate the cold war as the prime culprit in the evisceration of antiracist education. Tolerance education, after all, had emerged as part of a national agenda to prepare American citizens for their obligation to defend democracy against fascism, a battle that necessitated tolerance for diversity. The end of the war only accelerated the urgency for teaching "world mindedness" and how to be a "good neighbor." Soon the problem of how to contain communism trumped other concerns in American classrooms as well as in the nation at large. As the actor John Wayne insisted from his pulpit as president of the Motion Picture Alliance for the Preservation of American Ideals, "Let no one say that a Communist can be tolerated in American society."[63] Communism, many Americans felt, was not something to be "tolerated" under any circumstances.

Thus began the infamous crackdown on civil liberties and political freedoms known broadly as McCarthyism that would come to characterize the domestic side of America's cold war. One of the markers for communism was whether or not an individual supported racial equality. Loyalty boards asked federal and state employees if they entertained individuals of another race at their home, and a positive answer was considered evidence of subversive opinions.[64] Teachers found themselves in particularly vulnerable positions. As public employees they

were forced to sign loyalty oaths and considered suspect by local and state governments.[65] In 1947, New York City teachers were warned "not to allow personal
prejudices to creep into their classroom presentation of controversial subjects."[66]
Teaching tolerance in a way that seemed to emphasize racial egalitarianism was
no longer safeguarded as teaching "scientific" facts. Writing in *Social Education*,
an anonymous teacher in 1953 complained: "This atmosphere of fear and uncer-
tainty has penetrated all strata of the system, not only the teaching ranks, but as
high as the new Board and as low as the staff employees. None are certain, none
are secure." This teacher explained that popular lessons on international relations and the United Nations in her school had to be revised because of these
new concerns, adding: "Now, the UNESCO section of that unit has been thrown
out. Once, free discussion of controversial political issues was permitted, even
encouraged. Now, for the probationary teacher, such a discussion is tantamount
to declining tenure."[67] The following year, another teacher reported, "Many educators and publishers are worried as they see censorship and attack becoming
more widespread each day"[68]

Postwar politics invited political criticism of intercultural education as, at the
same time, it tightly restricted the curriculum's purpose. While not all Catholic
educators were opposed to lessons on racial tolerance, there is compelling

Initially popular after World War II, lessons on the United Nations became risky in the
emerging Cold War. Courtesy New York City Municipal Archives.

evidence that Catholic educators and politicians in Boston and New York City worked to undermine lessons that promoted racial tolerance for Jews and blacks. Both Massachusetts and New York were strongholds of intercultural programming, yet the Catholic-dominated teaching force in Boston appears never to have adopted wartime tolerance programming to any significant degree, even though nearby towns with predominantly Jewish and Protestant teachers had some of the most aggressive forms of tolerance education in the country.[69]

In New York City, Catholic leaders fought tolerance programming that had a great deal of support among the city's liberal Protestant and Jewish teachers through the 1930s and well into the 1940s. Not until the end of the war did Catholic efforts to undermine intercultural education begin to pay off. In the fall of 1945, the New York City Board of Education ran a course entitled "Promoting National Welfare through Intercultural Cooperation" that current teachers could take in order to earn "alertness" credits required for pay increases. This course included a lecture by the anthropologist Gene Weltfish. The Teachers Alliance of New York City, a predominantly Catholic and socially conservative organization, complained to the Board of Education: "We believe that the persons scheduled to speak on this course are all of one definite type point of view, namely the radical one. . . . This course, if sponsored, would probably be the cause of more inter-racial friction than it could possibly accomplish good."[70] Over the next three years, Catholics in New York City organized a letter writing campaign complaining about the content of intercultural programming. Some of these complaints had to do specifically with the way intercultural classes treated Catholics as an "ethnic" group, a characterization they disputed. But largely, the Catholics who participated in these letter writing campaigns were opposed to the effort to teach racial tolerance in general, which they characterized as "indoctrination" and inherently communist.[71]

When the Board of Education failed to answer these charges to their satisfaction, Catholic leaders unleashed a wave of negative criticism in the press with stories such as "City Sponsors Course by Reds for Teachers" that forced the New York City public schools to scale back intercultural offerings, despite the protests of many local teachers associations.[72] The New York City Teachers Union tried to halt the removal of intercultural programming, protesting, "Teaching school kids not to hate each other because of race or religion is now communistic, and must be done away with!"[73] But Catholics made a compelling case, and used the media to insist that teaching racial tolerance was the same as promoting communist ideology. An article in *The Tablet*, the official organ of the Brooklyn diocese, insisted: "The word intercultural has now generally come to be associated with propaganda of the Communist Party line." The article continued: "One lecture on the means of combating prejudice might be expected in such a course—but six? The overemphasis on prejudice is part of the party-line technique which seeks to divide and conquer by stirring up hate among minority groups by making them feel more discriminated against than they actually are."[74] Administrators at the Board of Education eventually folded under the pressure. "We have found," admitted Associate Superintendent Jacob Greenberg, "that some of our intercultural courses apparently are causing disunity rather than unity. We are re-examining all of them."[75] Many in-service intercultural education courses in New York City were scaled back at this time. The *New York Times* reported that educational debates vacillated between those who insisted that "democracy is split asunder when prejudice and bigotry possess our people" and others who charged "there are too many soft-headed liberals . . . who are often duped and become unwitting propagandists for the Communist Party."[76]

While it is clear that teachers were deeply affected by restrictions to academic freedom during the McCarthy era, it is difficult to trace the precise impact of the cold war on the way teachers taught about race and culture in the classroom because so many teachers stopped publishing journal articles on the subject of tolerance education. Teachers or journal editors, or possibly both, began to distance themselves from teaching racial tolerance in general and teaching racial equality in particular after 1947. Whereas in the first four decades of the twentieth century, teachers used the race concept somewhat indiscriminately to describe the challenges of teaching minority children, teachers increasingly recognized the subject of "race" in any context as politically volatile.

Beginning in 1948, there was a noticeable decline in the numbers of articles on teaching racial tolerance as well as in the analytical or critical quality of the articles published. Fewer authors wrote about teaching tolerance and began speaking in vague terms of "brotherhood" and "neighborliness," concepts that did not necessarily refer to *racial* discrimination. For similar reasons, teachers shied away from discussing the scientific concept of race and its implications for undermining prejudice, which had been a necessary component of intercultural education. While some teachers still taught about racial equality and civil rights, most teachers omitted any mention of the scientific concept of race or the social consequences of racial prejudice. Instead, teachers invited students to trace their ancestry, read literature by minority authors, and celebrate the cultural achievements of various minority groups.

For instance, a junior high school teacher in Louisville, Kentucky, described her successful tolerance program in "Brotherhood: Pattern for World Peace." Notably, Mary Hodge Cox reflected that at her white, segregated public school her pupils were "scarcely aware that racial and religious problems exist" due to the fact that this school had "practically no foreigners at all," and "never more than a dozen Jews and fifty Catholics at any one time."[77] To Cox this ignorance was a devastating shortcoming that needed to be corrected. To impress the "tremendous importance of world-wide brotherhood" on her students, Cox explained that she helped her students visualize two worlds: "one a happy, friendly world of the future in which peoples of all races, creeds, and colors will work together in harmony and peace for the good and advancement of all; the other a terrible place of unreasoning prejudices, hatred, strife, and wars that will result eventually in annihilation."[78] The only way to secure the first vision and avoid the second, according to this author, was by cultivating the ideal of tolerance in terms of brotherhood.

Cox's month-long tolerance unit included 650 students working in both English and social studies classes studying the urgent need for "world-wide brotherhood." She explained how the 1947 report of President Truman's Committee on Civil Rights entitled *To Secure These Rights* "hit like a bombshell" in her community.[79] Given this tense climate, the teacher devised a tolerance curriculum including the most popular and least threatening forms of tolerance education. She did not use the word "intercultural" or even "tolerance" education, as she had to present a curriculum that would not challenge the established social order in this southern city.

Like the most popular versions of tolerance education implemented since the war, Cox's program introduced her students to the scientific facts about race through Benedict and Weltfish's animated film *Brotherhood of Man*, traced each student's European lineage, and conducted group reports of the "contributions that have been made to American life and culture by all races, creeds, and colors." Besides these main lessons, students also wrote book reports, radio scripts, plays, poems, and essays, many of which were selected for the grand finale—a special issue of the student newspaper on the theme of "brotherhood." In this way, students at this Louisville school continued the well-established protocol of learning scientific and cultural facts, as well as using dramatic materials to develop empathy for racial minorities. The teacher contextualized her program on "brotherhood" as a way to respond to postwar politics, where allowing students to be racist threatened "annihilation." Walking this line was a perilous duty, indeed, for a southern white teacher. It did, however, reflect a direct concern with racial prejudice, a concern that was fading fast from other American classrooms.

In the North there was a bit more freedom to consider controversial subjects. Writing from Brooklyn, one social studies teacher recommended that teachers secure a copy of *To Secure These Rights*, as his high school had done, and use this document to engage students in a critical discussion of democracy and civil rights. Saul Israel compiled a "factual outline of the report" summarizing its key findings and recommendations, listed fifteen direct quotes from the report as topics for classroom discussion, and finally described a series of potential forums or roundtables on specific topics, such as "How can we protect the right to equality of opportunity?" He cited Benedict and Weltfish's *The*

Races of Mankind among other suggested readings at the end of his article, but did not otherwise highlight the significance of studying the scientific facts of racial equality. Instead, his focus was on civil rights in areas such as education, employment, and the military.[80]

Israel's lesson plan for teaching *To Secure These Rights* was one of the most direct challenges to racism published in a national teaching journal after 1947.[81] A few others touched on racial equality, such as three authors from the northwest who instructed social studies teachers to reflect on the "growth of new ideas of justice in dealing with other races, nationalities, and minority groups— intercultural, intergroup, and interracial education."[82] But these three teachers had nothing more to say on the subject, and their vague directives did not include any specific instructions on how to promote racial equality; they merely suggested teachers "reflect" on some "new ideas." Such carefully couched language illustrates teachers' hesitant approach to racial tolerance. Furthermore, articles like this one did not justify the need for tolerance education, but simply presented tolerance as part of a larger strategy for improving democratic education. In this case, the three authors from public schools in Washington and Oregon entitled their article "What Social Changes Should Be Reflected in the Social Studies Curriculum?" This was not an argument in favor of tolerance education at all, but rather a subdued attempt to "recognize that we are living in a changing world" and promote "an understanding of man in his social activities."[83] The authors cited the growing power of communist Soviet Union, the new role of international cooperation through the United Nations, and the atomic bomb as the three most critical issues of the day for social studies teachers. Similar concerns were echoed in 1949 by New York City Superintendent Dr. William Jansen, who announced "a sustained, long-range campaign to intensify 'teaching for democratic living' on all levels of the city's public school system."[84] Given these concerns, teaching racial equality was no longer a main focus for teachers trying to make their coursework relevant to contemporary issues. As the focus on racial prejudice quietly receded, so too did the priority of teaching the "scientific" facts about human race.

The Rise of the Colorblind Ideal

As the ideological underpinnings of tolerance education shifted in the postwar era, so too did the pedagogical approach to improving social relations through education. An article entitled "New Viewpoints in Teaching Better Intercultural Relations" written by a social studies teacher in Brooklyn, demonstrates the growing emphasis on individual psychology over social group relations. This teacher fully supported intercultural education; however, he critiqued the curriculum for its tiresome focus on "nationalism and political rights" and suggested instead that "the teaching of mental hygiene should be more carefully utilized." Explaining that "those persons with racial, ethnic, and religious prejudice, which constitute discrimination are essentially . . . maladjusted," Ralph Guinness asked teachers to attend to the psychological "integration" of each individual.

This version of intercultural education targeted the individual as the site of reform to reduce racial prejudice in a democratic society and explicitly chose to ignore "political rights" and other social factors, which this author saw as secondary to the process of psychological and moral education.[85] In conclusion, Guinness reflected that too often tolerance education was viewed as a strategy to unite the nation, whereas he envisioned it as a strategy to unite the individual. He stated that tolerance education "should appeal for human unity or moral unity, and not for American unity."[86] To achieve what he called "personal democracy," where a student would act completely without prejudice toward others, Guinness suggested that teachers work to create "socialized cooperative methods of learning" such as integrated classroom activities that encouraged children of different backgrounds to work together on a given topic.[87] There was no need, in this case, to teach students facts about the cultural achievements of each minority group, or the exact way that scientists understood race as a biological and social construct.

Asking students to demonstrate a complete lack of prejudice was a challenging proposition. While Guinness suggested a combination of psychological conditioning and moral education, other teachers attempted to meet the same goal by simply instructing children to act with good manners. In her article "Oral Language and Inter-Group Harmony," Althea Berry from Cincinnati explained that while it was easy for children to have respect for some minority groups, such as the Chinese, it was very difficult for them to have respect for every individual they should happen to meet. Like Guinness, Berry encouraged teachers to cultivate opportunities for students of different backgrounds to meet and work together in informal settings. She explained, "Out of the patterning of right attitudes and kindly daily speech to individuals he meets and works with now will grow respect for the rights, and understanding of the basic attitudes, of people whom he meets at present only through reading and discussion and will meet later chiefly through his country's representatives."[88] Notably, this teacher left unstated the question of whom, exactly, students were being trained to tolerate. A teacher from Atlantic City, New Jersey, suggested that the ideal teacher should model this tolerant behavior for students, writing, "Kindness and consideration for each individual no matter what his background can be implicit in all his teaching."[89] Of special concern to the State Department of Education in New Jersey was the problem of "name-calling."[90]

Sema Herman echoed similar sentiments in her article published a few months later in the *Elementary English Review*. A primary teacher in Chicago, Herman insisted, "The classroom teacher who seeks to develop and establish attitudes of understanding and friendliness toward all people in very young children, will find that the key to all democratic relationships lies in the term 'Neighbors,' a word whose meaning the child has experienced in his own home environment at an early age, and with which the parent is familiar and sympathetic."[91] Herman believed that poetry and singing were two effective means of "enabling the child to express his newly acquired attitudes" because these two forms of expression in particular "illustrate and set patterns for individual and group behavior."[92] As in Berry's article, it is not exactly clear whom the students were being instructed to tolerate. There was passing reference to racial tolerance in one poem, which stated:

> I've never met these neighbors
> And whether they're short or tall,
> Or black, brown, white or yellow
> Doesn't matter much at all.[93]

Such lessons, perhaps, were intended to promote tolerance for everybody—taking broad aim at all of humanity. The concept of race was not something that this teacher wanted to dwell on either by pointing out the contributions of each minority group to America or by teaching the scientific definition of the term. Rather, as this poem explained, skin color was to be understood as a physical variation much like height, and, in the end it "doesn't matter much at all."

The main point for Herman, in fact, was to emphasize the concept of being a "good neighbor" as a defining feature of the American Way. Another poem summarized this theme:

> We're learning to live the American Way,
> By sharing our things with our neighbors each day.
> By helping in work, and sharing at play,
> We're learning to live the American way.[94]

The concept of being a "good neighbor" reflected the more fashionable form of tolerance education in 1948. Its goal was to instill good manners and correct attitudes—a pedagogy that skipped over potentially uncomfortable discussions of minority civil rights and the biological concept of human race, and instead focused on a subject "with which the parent was familiar and sympathetic." Additionally, promoting the ideal of good neighbors seemed to reflect both local and international politics, thus making the program relevant to current social needs while also making tolerance broad enough to avoid arousing suspicion. Finally, the actual concept of tolerance, much like that of race, was less present in this lesson plan. Being a good neighbor retained space for American citizens to be intolerant of those people who were acting as "bad neighbors," such as the Soviet Union, which was at that moment tightening its grip on Eastern Europe and supporting communist revolutions in Asia.

The defining concepts of tolerance education developed in the 1930s and expanded during World War II were slipping out of teachers' vernacular in 1948.[95] Teachers were more comfortable with the language of psychology, which turned classroom discussions toward a more palatable consideration of maladjusted individuals. If intolerance existed because students were poorly trained to interact with minorities—racial and otherwise—then teachers faced the relatively simple task of properly socializing students to interact in more diverse social settings. This could be done by indirect means, the preferred method of tolerance education by most teachers, and conducted in a setting that was unlikely to draw criticism from students or the larger community.

It is perhaps due to these rising tensions that one of the only articles on the subject of racial prejudice published in a national teaching journal in 1949 came from the *Science Teacher*. In the journal's first antiprejudice article, in January of 1949, three high school teachers writing together from Phoenix, Arizona; East St. Louis, Missouri; and Portland, Oregon, offered specific instructions on how to use the scientific method to challenge racial stereotypes, investigate claims of racial superiority, and analyze inequalities among white and nonwhite Americans in the areas of housing, health care, and employment. Years after other lessons were reviewed in professional magazines, the article remarked, "The wartime experience of separating white and Negro donations to the Blood Bank may be examined for the scientific baselessness of the separation."[96]

Beyond this one article, there is little evidence that teachers presented lessons that included critical discussions on racial equality and civil rights in 1949. The journal *Common Ground*, published by the Common Council for American Unity and a major supporter of intercultural education, published its last article that fall. Across the country educators voiced new criticisms of tolerance education. "Who, may I ask, wishes to be tolerated? Do you? Do I?" asked a disillusioned English professor at a teachers college in Maryland.[97] In another article, "Not Out of Books," Rabbi Sanford Rosen of Bakersfield, California, agreed that it was pointless to drill students in material supposedly related to tolerance. Rosen praised teachers that could promote tolerance without ever mentioning the dreaded word: "Miss Gaffney never delivered a lecture on tolerance—she skillfully led her pupils into the paths of brotherhood." In this case, Miss Gaffney organized various opportunities for the boys and girls in her class to get to know each other better, such as wiener roasts, sledding parties, and other amusements. According to the teacher, "At Tony Caruso's, after an exciting two hours of sledding one evening, we feasted on Italian spaghetti and veal cutlets—and learned that Tony's people were kind and good, warmhearted and hospitable. We learned the same about Effie Lee Morris' folks, who, tho their skin was black, were no different..."[98]

These kinds of carefully arranged activities came to define cold war intercultural education, which emphasized social experience over factual knowledge. No special teaching materials were necessary; all teachers had to do was bring students together and encourage them to "get along." Rachel Davis DuBois published a description of one of her favorite new techniques called a "parranda" in the *Journal of the National Education Association*. DuBois recounted how she had invited New Yorkers of various ethnic, racial, and religious backgrounds to participate in a "Bread Festival" where each person took a turn describing a poignant memory that had something to do with bread—a topic carefully selected for its complete lack of political controversy.[99]

In 1949 the NCTE Committee on Intercultural Education admonished readers of the *English Journal* that the world sorely needed better human relations in general, not just in interracial and intercultural areas.[100] The implication was that the prolonged focus on American race relations had drawn away attention from the more substantial problem of global human relations. In fact, this rhetorical shift from intercultural or intergroup relations to human relations was a widespread phenomenon in liberal American organizations including the civil rights movement in the late 1940s. Contextualizing civil rights as a struggle for human rights made it less a specific problem about a single minority group (e.g., the Negro Problem) and asserted the transnational affiliations between social justice for racial minorities in America and anticolonialism in Asia, Africa, and the Middle East. Within schools, however, the new focus on human relations shifted teachers' attention away from racial minorities in America to a more inclusive—and less specific—subject of human relations.

The complexities of teaching tolerance in a political setting where it was no longer welcome and a theoretical context that refused to consider racism can be glimpsed in a provocative essay written by Mabel Finley, an English teacher at the Collinwood High School in Cleveland. Using a textbook on intergroup education, Finley led the class through a series of thematic topics such as "Patterns in Family Life," "Belonging to Groups," and "Experiencing Acceptance and Rejection." Short stories on each subject were carefully selected and read, after which students wrote essays that were used to facilitate class discussion. The students, reported Finley, were especially interested in the theme "Experiencing Acceptance and Rejection."[101] Students evaluated their own experiences with acceptance and rejection in popular school clubs like the Girls' Gym Leaders and the Hi-Y Boys. The students explained to the teacher how people had to be *invited* to join these clubs. The teacher reflected, "It was at this time that I learned that it made a difference whether a girl wore just a wool sweater of about eight-dollar value or an angora one worth twenty-two dollars." Other criteria for acceptance into school clubs emerged, including "sharp" clothes, differences in race and religion, and "homes that offered facilities for parties."[102]

Given students' passionate interest in social acceptance and rejection, which the teacher noted emerged "naturally," the teacher dedicated classroom time to consider these injustices in greater depth. According to the teacher's description, the entire class "opened up" and shared their most intimate personal betrayals with each other. "I still cannot quite account for the mood in the class that led an Italian girl, with tears rolling down her cheeks and in a voice choking with emotion, to tell an experience which had happened about two years before." This girl's recounting of being dumped by a potential suitor when his mother learned of her ethnicity represented what the teacher understood to be a kind of therapeutic breakthrough for the entire class, ultimately transforming her students into more tolerant citizens. In response to this highly emotional classroom experience, the teacher and students together came up with the idea of describing and celebrating cultural contributions by each group to America as the best way to promote greater tolerance and understanding between Americans. As one student wrote in his final essay on Negro contributions to America, "We can encourage all of these various culture groups to share with us the best of their customs and traditions. By accepting what they have to offer we can enrich American culture."[103]

Despite major changes in the theory and practice of tolerance education, therefore, many teachers and students continued to find solace in the technique of celebrating minority groups in terms of their cultural gifts to a larger, national culture, or what some called "cultural democracy." As the subject of racial difference became more implicit to these discussions, culture emerged as the preferred vocabulary to describe racial minorities. Thus, while teachers a few years earlier described lesson plans on the subject of "race and culture problems," teachers in 1949 tended to write about lessons on the subject of "various culture groups." Contrasting the ideal of cultural pluralism to the totalitarian specter of cultural "monism," one teacher elaborated: "Carried to the extreme, the ideal of monism leads to 'genocide'—mass murder of one culture or 'race' by another culture or 'race.' This is done in the belief that the culture can be made 'pure,' or monistic."[104] In these examples, the distinction between the race and culture concepts disappeared completely.

Teachers came to view the problem of prejudice as something divorced from the issue of race. In this context, prejudice against a white girl who could not afford an angora sweater was treated as a significant form of discrimination that merited tolerance education. It is not so much that this was unreasonable—a situation where students were excluded from social clubs may have warranted a response by the teacher—but rather that the teacher in this case opted not to push the lesson on prejudice any further. Race was not hidden or implicit in this pedagogy, but deliberately excluded. Since the program's initial design in the 1920s, nearly every lesson on tolerance education was dedicated to exploring and alleviating *racial* discrimination. Now, however, it was possible and even desirable to teach tolerance without ever bringing up the subject of race. The idea of culture, notably, was preserved essentially unchanged, and continued to refer specifically to those people understood (although rarely identified) as racially distinct.

Teachers in the early 1950s were still concerned with the problem of prejudice, but most refused to directly confront the subject of racial minorities or the problem of racism in the classroom. The use of the word "tolerance" declined or was employed in strategically apolitical terms in teaching journals. For example, the article "Some Lessons about Tolerance from the Past," published in *Social Studies*, discussed tolerance as a religious ideal developed during the sixteenth century, but made no attempt to connect this intellectual history to current social or political issues.[105] The *English Journal*, which published a monthly segment on "Better Human Relations," vacillated from promoting Benedict and Weltfish's *The Races of Mankind* pamphlet, book, and film in January of 1950, to pondering how to help junior high school students "understand each other better" in June that included dating advice such as: "a girl who is 'not too anxious' is more apt to get and keep a boy friend."[106]

It was practical for teachers to obscure the subjects of tolerance education, which explains why an elementary teacher in Cleveland created a tolerance unit entitled "Adjustment of Newcomers to New Places." Despite the fact that the teacher observed "the remarks these children made about books revealed their race prejudices," her attempt to mitigate discrimination deliberately avoided any discussion of race.[107] Instead the teacher developed "sociometric" seating arrangements to help students make new friends, employed a "sociogram" to map out interpersonal relationships, and asked students to answer benign questions such as: "Why I Am Thankful? What Holidays Do You Like Best? What Is the Most Precious Thing to You?"

Much of the unit reiterated the individual's responsibility to be pleasant, likable, and thus easily tolerated. For example, the teacher reviewed with the class: "Characteristics which make people like you, Characteristics which make you happy and pleasant, Characteristics which discourage friendship."[108] The implicit message was that individuals who suffered discrimination brought this injustice on themselves because they failed to perform the correct social attributes. The vast majority of teachers writing in journals avoided any analysis of how and why racism functioned in America, as well as related subjects like institutionalized inequality and civil rights for racial minorities.

Much like Americanization programs in the first quarter of the twentieth century, tolerance education after 1950 pushed an assimilationist agenda that asserted white, middle-class values as normative. An important difference was that cold war Americanization required students to possess an explicit consciousness of tolerance that included an appreciation of other "cultures," sometimes articulated as cultural democracy. National politicians criticized the public schools for failing to emphasize lessons on Americanization strongly enough. As one member of the House Committee on Un-American Activities charged: "We assume that a child knows what Americanism and democracy are, but we never explain what living in a democracy means."[109] Teachers believed that democratic citizenship required a certain amount of racial tolerance in order to avoid the unjust persecution of minorities visible in fascist and communist regimes. The National Council of Social Studies called on teachers to continue to oppose "totalitarianism whether it takes the form of communism, fascism, attack on religious or ethnic minorities, or attack upon freedom of the mind."[110]

Educated American citizens, representing not only their nation but a larger democratic way of life, needed to be able to interact gracefully and competently with people from minority racial, ethnic, or religious groups. Teachers encouraged students to internalize these lessons on tolerance—to act as if their every action was constantly surveyed by "the group."[111] Thus, educated American citizens needed to present well by performing "characteristics which make people like you," and they needed to interact properly by demonstrating a lukewarm but nevertheless required "tolerance" of minorities. Using racial epithets or derogatory stereotypes to refer to minorities was therefore not just uncouth, it was profoundly ignorant of the values of educated American society.

Teachers employed a psychological discourse to discipline student behavior and social interactions, citing their lessons as "therapy" to "integrate the personalities" of damaged youth. In his article "Release: A Human Relations Approach to Writing," the English teacher David Mallery from Philadelphia recounted his method to improve human relations by engendering psychological "release" in the classroom. Discussing the "basic ideas of democracy" with his class, this teacher discovered "ideas and assumptions even more fundamental than the 'freedoms' and 'rights.'" These ideas boiled down to the belief "that the individual is something of special value and dignity in his own right, as an end in himself."[112] Mallery's class wrote essays on the theme "A Moment of Special Awareness of One's Self as an Individual," which the teacher intended to elicit profound and deeply personal responses. Mallery described his most successful student responses, such as the football player who was nervous about playing his first varsity game, and Karen, a young woman who was deeply disappointed when she learned that her friend cheated on a test. Teachers like Mallery used psychology to help students internalize how their actions were viewed by their peers. This self-disciplining through a deliberate internalization of peer criticism was a very different strategy than the training of students in the scientific facts on race and prejudice. This downplayed student agency, self-control, and critical thinking and assumed instead that the key to improving social relations in the United States was through rigid, disciplinary training in social etiquette.

The most challenging aspect of cold war tolerance education was the need to balance an appreciation for cultural diversity with a very narrow range of acceptable minority traits. The result was that teachers continued to highlight the cultural attributes and historical distinctions of various minority groups. However, they were reluctant to emphasize the cultural peculiarities of individual minority students. "No boy's needs can best be met by singling him out for his unfamiliar differences," the Committee on Intercultural Education in the *Elementary English Review* reminded teachers in 1950.[113] But other articles continued to celebrate the more inclusive category of minority group culture, for example "the contribution to ideas and thought made by Irish dramatists, Negro poets, and Jewish novelists."[114] In a sense, this pedagogical approach resolved the dilemma of teachers who could not decide whether it was helpful or harmful to single out minority groups in intercultural education. It allowed teachers to highlight the rich cultural diversity of minority groups while treating every individual as inherently the same.

A journal article from 1951 illustrates that students were internalizing and reproducing the notion that blatant displays of prejudice reflected not only a complete lack of education, but also "bad manners." Alice Spaulding, an English teacher at Brookline High School in Massachusetts, invited students to discuss harmful "type names" in her intercultural unit. "Chink, dago, yid, gook," called out agreeable students. In the classroom discussion that followed, Spaulding reported: "The class decided that the use of such epithets is stupid, unkind, and therefore, bad manners."[115] Lessons like this one that emphasized good manners as markers of the educated citizen often included a celebration of cultural gifts of the minority groups students were supposed to learn to tolerate. In this case, Spaulding had her students study "famous poets of the world" highlighting "what each nation had contributed to the world's welfare." Such lessons identified desirable cultural traits such as poetry and associated them with "nations" in a way that obscured race altogether. Because race was invisible and implicit in this discourse, teachers and students easily conflated the categories of race and culture.

Occasionally, an article would challenge this conformist pedagogy, and it was the *Social Studies* journal in particular that took the lead in critiquing tolerance education. A college professor from Washington, for example, took aim at educators who were unwilling to engage in critical, dynamic views of tolerance as a defining feature of a democracy in her article "Tolerance—Its Function in a Democratic Society." A. C. Keller encouraged teachers to abandon their conception of tolerance as a necessary component of assimilationist education, and instead to see tolerance as "an active stimulation of minority self-expression."[116]

Keller's challenge to fortify tolerance education was ignored by most teachers, who barely dared to publish on tolerance education or intercultural education at all. Instead, teachers like Elsie Butler from Springfield, Missouri, wrote vague articles on the goal of promoting increased understanding and friendliness among students in the classroom. These articles struggled to make sense of why individual students did not fit into the classroom "group," school, or community, but they were careful to avoid any charge that the students in their class or the people in their community might be prejudiced. Thus, in her article "Living Together in the Third Grade" Butler instructed teachers to forge a unified group sentiment in the classroom. The problem, Butler reflected, was that the students in this classroom were so diverse that they failed to bond together into a cohesive group. She explained to readers:

> If you have been used to working with children who are well acquainted and have had a common background, it is hard to imagine how big the problem of developing a "group feeling of oneness" can be. The teacher was sure of one thing—the group needed to carry on many activities together![117]

In this case, the teacher detailed the classroom activities she created so that, essentially, her students would have the opportunity to get to know each other and become friends. She listed seventeen different activities her students were engaged in, from typing on the class typewriter to making puppets to playing with the class pets. Teachers believed that these kinds of activities, in and of themselves, functioned to break down prejudices and promote tolerance and understanding.[118]

Sema Herman reported that two effective ways to make young students feel they belong to the group was to make "a statement of admiration concerning their attractive appearance" and to make provisions "for every pupil to taste the wine of leadership."[119] This would help prepare "forty Johns and Sallys to function as good citizens in a democracy," Herman declared. Creating good citizens, in this case, meant forging pupils into conscientious and helpful members of the group, which teachers might accomplish by making a "citizenship chart" to record the contributions of each child to the class. This recording of individual contributions was seen as a strategic way to undermine prejudice because it allowed each child to fulfill a special role in order to become a valued member of the group. As Herman explained, "Encouraging recognition of fine qualities possessed by the less affluent, the unattractive, the foreign born, the ethnic variant, and finding opportunities for the public use of such in filling a group need, will stimulate good relationships and eliminate exclusion and discrimination."[120] This was a modification of the long-time celebration of cultural gifts. Instead of fitting minority groups into a larger American culture, this strategy now aimed to fit individual students into the unit of the "group." Notably, Herman's list of students who were potentially discriminated against included the poor, the unattractive, foreigners, and ethnic minorities, but not racial minorities. It is unclear from this article whether Herman would have advocated "eliminating exclusion and discrimination" against blacks or not. Given the scrutiny that teachers faced under McCarthyism, this may have been a strategic move on her part, or it may mean that she was simply not concerned with racial equality.

After 1952 American teaching journals published very few articles that could be described as intercultural or tolerance education. No doubt, teachers hesitated to take a public stand on racial egalitarianism at a time when most had to sign a loyalty oath to secure employment, and they witnessed peers hauled in and interrogated by government commissions for their supposedly "subversive" political views.[121] Even students took note of the deliberate silence on controversial topics like race relations. For instance, an article in the *Washington Post* noted that American students "feel limited especially by the invisible taboos that surround discussion of religious sects, of Marxism, and of racial problems."[122] Additionally, by 1952 the political pressures that shaped American educational policy and practice had shifted dramatically. Teachers who wanted to address foreign affairs and current political events in the classroom had to choose their subjects very carefully, and no longer worked in an atmosphere pervaded with the threat of Nazi pseudoscientific racism. For all of these reasons there was little motivation to teach about racial equality, including the scientific definition of race, and there were in fact powerful incentives not to discuss potentially controversial issues.

This does not mean that teaching journals were completely silent on the subject of race relations, which were after all still crucial and highly visible subjects in national and international politics. From *Social Studies* and *Social Education* cautiously emerged a critical perspective that drew on anthropology to challenge racial discrimination, but only at the rate of one or two articles a year. Additionally, some articles paused to consider the development of African American literature or the portrayal of Native Americans in textbooks.[123] These articles painted a sympathetic image of minorities and encouraged teachers to include minorities in the curriculum. For instance, an art teacher in Chicago defended the controversial Uncle Remus stories, which were written by a white author in African American dialect, as "part of the cultural heritage of the American Negro."[124]

Teaching journals from the early 1950s preferred to publish articles that portrayed minority groups in positive terms and reflected a cautious, yet politically astute perspective on the role of educators in addressing social relations. Some of the articles were unduly optimistic in their approach to the subject. One went so far as to argue that harmful stereotypes of American Indians had "passed" and were replaced by an "honest and good" depiction of this minority group. Ethel Newell of Mesa, Arizona, explained to readers of the *Elementary English Review*, "The Indian in new books is the Indian of reality who is psychologically valid for our boys and girls today."[125] Whether or not educational texts portrayed minority groups and individuals as "psychologically valid," it is clear that teachers felt more comfortable speaking about minority literature than they did about minority individuals. There was no room, or so it would seem, to consider the everyday lives of African Americans, Asian Americans, or Native Americans, or their profoundly compromised experiences as minority citizens in a democratic nation.

In 1954, the intercultural educator William Martin published "Gee! I'm Glad We're All Different!" in the *Journal of the NEA*.[126] In the article, he offered a four-step program designed to "modify attitudes," presumably prejudiced ones, by acknowledging the differences that made every American special. By accepting the child as he is, argued Martin, teachers would help the child gain status in the group through fair competition and reward. In this sense, students would come to understand the benefits of diversity in terms of the unique talents each person contributed to the welfare of the group. There was no mention of race or racial minorities in this article, and the presumption that each individual could actually compete in a "fair" market for social status went unquestioned.

Insistently upbeat articles like this one, which failed to assess racism or social inequality in America, represented the final efforts of intercultural educators to promote tolerance education in the cold war era. Already, civil rights activists like those at the NAACP and the Race Relations Institute at Fisk University were revising their strategic use of public schools as agents of social change in America. Instead of teaching students the facts about race and prejudice in an attempt to reduce racism, civil rights activists believed judicial action could bring about faster and more substantial opportunities for racial equality.[127] Charles S. Johnson, the renowned black sociologist and the president of Fisk University, ceased to offer intercultural education workshops at his annual Race Relations Institute in 1952. He explained to the audience of educators and social activists gathered before him, "There has been a growing popular acceptance of *law* as the most expeditious educational device to precipitate changes in race relations as rapidly as they now must be made."[128] Johnson, among other civil rights activists, turned his full attention to the courts to secure equality for black

Americans, including access to white educational institutions and the end of racial segregation. In the process he dismissed intercultural education as an ineffective strategy that had failed to substantially alter white prejudice against blacks. Johnson was inspired in large part by recent Supreme Court victories by the NAACP that laid the groundwork for dismantling racial segregation. According to Johnson, recent Supreme Court cases made it "unmistakable [sic] clear that there has been a re-evaluation of the 14th Amendment, and that the tools have been made available to put an end to all governmentally-imposed racial segregation."[129] Tolerance education, which Johnson had strongly advocated since 1944, was no longer necessary or desirable in the shifting political landscape of the early 1950s. Johnson joined with civil rights activists across the nation in targeting structural inequalities in the American political economy to force the issue of equal opportunity. There was no need to work within a broken system; these activists intended to build an entirely new one. Likewise, in New York City, a newly formed Intergroup Committee on New York Public Schools was formed, not to promote tolerance programming in the classroom, but to address the continued problem of racial segregation and corresponding inequality in New York City's public schools.[130]

All of the factors that explain the demise of tolerance education by 1954 also clarify a related phenomenon in the racial discourse of American schools. By 1954 racial minorities were rarely mentioned in American classrooms. Teaching journals, such as *American Unity*, encouraged teachers to actively ignore racial differences in the classroom in an effort to promote the ideal of a "colorblind" society where such differences did not matter. One photograph depicted a boys' basketball team featuring white, black, and Asian players, while the caption beneath asserted, "Stuyvestant [sic] High School, New York, was so interested in developing a good basket ball team, they forgot to ask the players race or color."[131] Similarly, intercultural textbooks asked teachers to ignore race or color in favor of more immediate concerns, illustrated with photographs such as this one that insisted, "Jim's color is clean."

Photographs on the subject of tolerance typically featured interracial scenes, even if the article never mentioned the subject of race or racial discrimination. In 1953, *American Unity* ran a photo essay under the heading: "Typical classroom scenes that show they're interested in the subject at hand, not in their classmates' skin color, eye shape, or country of origin."[132] The photos depicted interracial classrooms and activities, but the accompanying text suggested that educators simply had to train students to live and work with people from different backgrounds in order to encourage racial integration, and that they could suppress explicit discussions on race.

The colorblind approach to racial tolerance, nonetheless, did complicate classroom instruction for teachers. They had to be careful *not* to highlight the

JIM'S COLOR IS CLEAN

Intercultural textbooks insisted that teachers should ignore "color" and promote integrated learning environments in the postwar era.

racial status of individuals, and they were supposed to discourage explicit discussions of racial diversity in America. In the end, teachers promoted a vague celebration of cultural gifts, a strategy they could use to promote tolerance for racial minorities without drawing attention to the concept of race. In their effort to create warm and welcoming interracial classrooms and activities, teachers emphasized good manners when encountering racial others. This meant that racial slurs were unacceptable in the classroom, and teachers were attentive to any sign that a student had crossed the line between a racially tolerant, educated citizen and an ignorant racist.

Combined with the domestic political pressures of the cold war, an emphasis on the colorblind approach created the curious situation where teachers refused to acknowledge or discuss the everyday lives of racial minorities. In the larger public realm of culture, however, teachers felt more secure and believed it was fair to discuss subjects like "Negro" literature or American Indian stereotypes. This was a form of self-censorship that teachers imparted to their students as an attribute of an educated citizen in a modern, global democracy. Performing as a colorblind citizen in a blatantly racist society required teachers to create an intricate way of teaching race that relied on coded words and a shared understanding

of racial etiquette. Teachers, like most Americans, had come to accept the conflation of race with color. To realize the colorblind ideal, however, teachers in the
postwar era had to equate the concepts of race and culture, which functioned to
effectively silence or at least mystify the race concept. The only way that teachers
could live up to the promise of the colorblind ideal, after all, was if they stopped
talking and teaching about race in the classroom. In the process, they reified race
as color and entrenched a static and essentialist conception of race-as-culture
into American educational discourse.

Conclusion: Race and Educational Equality after *Brown v. Board of Education*

> Whether we like it or not, culturally, biologically, and otherwise every white person is a little bit Negro and every Negro is a little bit white. Our language, our music, our material prosperity and even our food are an amalgam of black and white.
>
> —Martin Luther King Jr.

> I do not believe my teacher education students are unusual in their tendency to suture race to culture and then struggle to disentangle the two.
>
> —Gloria Ladson-Billings

On the brink of a terrifying and highly racialized world war in the late 1930s, activist anthropologists believed they could combat racism and fortify democracy by insisting on a more scientifically informed and reflexive way of thinking, speaking, and teaching about "racial" others in American classrooms. Working with teachers, anthropologists crafted an antiracist pedagogy that combined a study of the biological facts of human race with a social critique of American culture, a strategy that Ruth Benedict, among others, believed would illuminate structural inequalities of American society. In classrooms, teachers drew on decades of experience teaching about racial others in terms of cultural gifts to design antiprejudice lessons that tied racial identity to a cultural attribute, such as lessons on "Negro" literature, American Indian artwork, and Chinese food. Teachers believed that highlighting the positive attributes of racial minorities in terms of their distinctive culture would mitigate racial prejudice by whites and increase the self-esteem of nonwhites. In the process, teachers came to speak of racial minorities as cultural minorities.

This construction of race-as-culture, although directly influenced by anthropologists, did not embody the antiracist pedagogy designed by scholars like

Benedict. Although there is evidence that many teachers taught lessons on the anthropological definition of race from 1944 to 1947, these lessons virtually disappeared with the start of the cold war. Teachers had even less luck translating anthropological definitions of culture in the classroom. Instead of viewing American culture as a cohesive and fluid entity as Benedict asked, teachers assumed the existence of a static, normative, white, middle-class culture and held up all students against this norm. They had difficulty acknowledging that working-class people, racial minorities, and ethnic communities were a defining feature of what Benedict saw in larger terms as American culture.

In the postwar period anthropologists retreated from antiracist activism and educational reform. Meanwhile, psychology replaced anthropology as the social science that offered the most insight on the problem of racial prejudice in America. The rise of psychology as the preferred discipline to address racial prejudice was a social phenomenon in its own right. This intellectual turn was shaped by postwar economic prosperity and cold war politics, and in particular the powerful influence of foundations and governmental agencies who doled out research grants and showed a preference for studies that analyzed individual racial prejudice as a psychological problem.[1] The dominance of psychology in the postwar era was also strongly influenced by Gunnar Myrdal's massive social scientific investigation of American race relations in 1944, *An American Dilemma*.[2]

Psychologists asserted that teaching people "facts" about human equality did little to eradicate racial prejudice. Instead, they believed that only early exposure to diverse people could socialize students to be less prejudiced. Because psychologists believed racial prejudice was created in individuals through interpersonal relations, they identified the individual as the ideal site for reform. Whereas an anthropological study of American culture revealed structural inequalities such as inadequate education, jobs, housing, and health care available to racial minorities, psychologists were more interested in how people thought about and related to one another. They were not concerned, therefore, with how racism was institutionalized in American society, as through the near complete disenfranchisement of African Americans in the South. Instead, they believed that social manifestations of racism would disappear as people became less racist through intergroup therapy in American schools.[3]

Drawing directly from psychologists in the postwar era, American teachers crafted a revised tolerance pedagogy premised on the idea that young children could be socialized to be less racist. Teachers asserted that explicit lessons on the biological meaning of race were unproductive, if not downright harmful to students. Instead of preaching racial tolerance, teachers wanted to demonstrate and inculcate this ideal through racially integrated activities such as art projects, work camps, and classrooms. If such racially integrated settings were unavailable, teachers fell back on exposing students to racial others through songs, art, literature, and other forms of racial minorities' material life. Of course, all of the so-called culture being celebrated in these lessons was presented as the result of group preferences and never as the consequences of sustained economic exploitation and exclusion, political oppression, or endemic poverty that historically defined life for many American "racial" minorities. Although careful not to dwell on the racial identity of any one individual, teachers believed that celebrating racial culture would help inculcate empathy for racial others. In an effort to direct the outcome of tolerance education, teachers insisted that all students exhibit good manners and proper etiquette in interracial settings.

As a result, by midcentury teachers intentionally silenced the subject of race in American classrooms. Instead of teaching about racial others they promoted a colorblind ideal based on the psychological argument that it was better to ignore race and practice racial integration than to dwell on racial inequalities or race relations in America. For liberal activists and intellectuals the silencing of race in everyday discourse represented the pinnacle of the colorblind ideal in schools. It signified that teachers had mastered the complex social science knowledge on racial prejudice while also being savvy enough to conduct "indirect" lessons intended to guide students to ignore race and judge every individual according to his or her potential. Importantly, the colorblind ideal in American schools could only work in a society that refused to acknowledge—or segregate—citizens on the basis of race.

On May 17, 1954, in *Brown v. Board of Education of Topeka,* the United States Supreme Court agreed that segregating American children on the basis of race in public schools violated their constitutional rights according to the 14th Amendment. Signifying the growing authority of social science in American jurisprudence, Supreme Court Justice Earl Warren cited a study by the psychologists Kenneth Clark and Mamie Clark to argue that segregated schools were profoundly harmful to the psyche of black students, who were isolated and excluded from mainstream American life.[4] The timing of *Brown* and the ascendancy of the colorblind ideal in American schools was no accident. In fact, the same psychological theories of racial prejudice that underwrote postwar intercultural education also underwrote the social science used in the *Brown* decision.[5] The Court even cited the work of intercultural educators in its unanimous decision, including an article by the prominent interculturalist Theodore Brameld, in which he advocated developing "on a much wider scale, intercultural education for students in schools; for teachers already on the job; for adults in trade unions, in churches, in business groups, in the home itself."[6]

Both postwar intercultural education and *Brown* were premised on psychological theories of prejudice that identified racism as a problem of individual attitudes or maladjustment.[7] This psychological model of racism focused on how people thought about other people, and diverted scholarly attention from entrenched structural racism and inequality in American society, culture, and political economy. Following a similar logic, in the early 1950s the NAACP abandoned decades of work fighting for the equalization of black schools in the South in terms of better facilities, materials, and teacher salaries—a strategy that had been increasingly successful by 1954. Instead, NAACP activists decided to pursue black equality and fight endemic white racism by removing the legal barriers to quality education, good jobs, adequate health care, and the franchise. Desegregating schools was the first step in what they viewed as a lengthy and strategically crucial battle, but the important factor is that these civil rights activists believed that racial integration was the key to social equality. Significantly, this meant the NAACP and other social justice activists stopped fighting for structural improvements such as better resources for black schools in the South or in predominantly African American schools in other parts of the country in the wake of *Brown*. Instead, they focused on winning access to better-funded, more prestigious white educational institutions.[8]

Neither postwar intercultural education nor the mandated desegregation of schools in the *Brown* ruling turned out to be effective antiracist strategies. Charles Payne explains that this is because *Brown* marked a peculiar moment in the mid-twentieth century when the idea of race and the phenomenon of racism were profoundly "mystified." Intercultural educators, psychologists like Kenneth Clark, and ultimately the Supreme Court Justices agreed that racism was a function of interpersonal relations. This construction of racism ignored how racial inequality was entrenched in American society through harsh and often violent acts of "political disenfranchisement, economic exploitation, racial terrorism, and personal degradation."[9] This rhetorical move separated the social system of racial segregation from the systematic oppression of racial minorities in all aspects of American political and economic life.[10] Furthermore, it failed to account for the material and social privileges that racial segregation offered to the white working class and therefore underestimated the magnitude of white backlash to integrated schools in both the North and the South over the next fifty years.[11]

Advocates for *Brown* believed the time had come to implement a colorblind approach to the problem of race relations in America. Race-blindness was a popular liberal response to the revelations of the scientific definition of race and the horrors of the Holocaust. Ignoring race seemed to exemplify social equality, and the promotion of integrated education in particular carried the colorblind ideal through to its most obvious conclusion in a modern democracy. *Brown* represented a major success in the transnational narrative of American race and democracy, projecting an image of American racial progress to an international audience attuned to the glaring inconsistencies between the American Creed and racial discrimination against African Americans. The liberal credo of colorblind education, therefore, was adopted by the federal government as an important component of foreign policy as a way to put democratic ideals into practice.[12] The combined efforts of social justice advocates, social scientists, and liberal intellectuals helped bring about the ruling in *Brown* that symbolized the institutionalization of the colorblind ideal in the nation's cherished institution of public schools.

Winning the desegregation of American public schools signaled to social justice advocates and many educators that tolerance lessons were no longer necessary or desirable. By 1954, the expansive tolerance education visible across the country during World War II had virtually disappeared. The ruling in *Brown* only confirmed what many educators and intellectuals already believed—that it was more important to cultivate equal opportunity and racial integration than explicit lessons on how and why to "tolerate" racial minorities. With the law now firmly on their side, social justice advocates paid little attention to the content of American curricula and focused on the complicated logistical issues of easing the nation into racially integrated schools. This relationship between integration and curricular content would prove to be durable over the next fifty years as the nation struggled with the persistent failure of *Brown* to meet the educational needs of disadvantaged minority students.

Acknowledging the Failure of the Colorblind Ideal

Although American schools remained racially segregated for ten years after *Brown*, this stalemate came to a head in 1964. With the civil rights movement in full swing, a strong economy, and a rising black middle class, the pressures on the American government to intervene in the embarrassing state of race relations in the American South accelerated. The Civil Rights Act of 1964 took aim at racial segregation in public accommodations and employment, but it also featured Title VI, empowering federal officials to cut off aid to racially segregated school districts. The following year the Voting Rights Act of 1965 and the Elementary and Secondary Education Act granted the federal government more power to ensure blacks had access to the ballot and to integrated public schools. The Elementary and Secondary Education Act, in particular, tied huge sums of federal money for local school districts to specific requirements about the acceptable degree of racial segregation. If school districts did not demonstrate racially integrated schools, they could lose federal funding. Federal and district circuit court judges joined the effort to desegregate schools at the same time. Following this change in jurisprudence, American schools in the 1970s began massive efforts to foster racial integration through programs such as racial balancing, busing, and affirmative action. Such projects were complicated from the beginning by white flight, white and Hispanic resistance to integrated schools, and black resistance to the breakdown of community schools and the inconvenience and hardships of busing children long distances to attend predominantly white (and sometimes hostile) schools.[13]

As it became increasingly obvious that creating racially integrated public schools was going to be a longer and more difficult process than anyone had ever imagined, a new approach to combating racism emerged in school practice in the 1980s. Black educators and students amplified demands for courses in African and African American history, art, and culture. White educators embraced the idea that teaching about racial others would be an effective substitute for attending racially integrated schools. What became known as "multiculturalism" flourished in liberal educational discourse as a new and improved method to reduce racial prejudice and promote better race relations. Faced with the persistent failure of policy makers to create racially integrated learning environments, educators decided to revise the content of schooling in an attempt to find a more effective way to use schools to decrease racial prejudice and promote better race relations.[14]

The continuing struggle to integrate schools in the 1970s and the growing popularity of multiculturalism in the 1980s both acknowledged in different ways the failure of the colorblind ideal that framed the *Brown* decision in 1954. If educators and social activists in 1954 believed the most effective antiracist strategy was to ignore race and quietly remove the barriers to racial integration, by 1980 activists and intellectuals believed that the best way to fight racism was to pay very careful and explicit attention to the subject of race. They wanted schools to identify and quantify each student's race in a given district and make school assignments accordingly. They wanted students in the classroom to learn about the lives and history of racial minorities in terms of their historical accomplishments and cultural achievements. American schools were to become "multicultural," a term that referred specifically to *racial* diversity.

Efforts to desegregate schools peaked in the 1980s and have declined ever since, mostly through legal challenges by whites resisting efforts to desegregate schools in their communities. Gary Orfield and Chungmei Lei of the Civil Rights Project explain that race-conscious school integration plans, although bitterly contested, result in substantial improvement in the quality of education and academic success for minority students. They elaborate: "This does not mean that desegregation solves all problems or that it always works, or that segregated schools do not perform well in rare circumstances, but it does mean that desegregation normally connects minority students with schools which have many potential advantages over segregated ghetto and barrio schools especially if the children are not segregated at the classroom level."[15]

Resegregation in American schools took hold in the early 1990s after three Supreme Court rulings from 1991 to 1995 limited the ability of school districts to implement racial integration.[16] Forced to acknowledge the limits, if not the failure of American schools to create racially integrated learning environments, liberal educators and intellectuals searched for alternative ways to address racial equality through public education. They latched on to curricular programs designed to teach students about diversity in terms of race and ethnicity, such as multicultural education. In the 1990s multiculturalism became institutionalized through ethnic studies programs at American universities and defined as a required component of teacher training in most schools of education. The expansion and rapid adoption of multicultural curricula and policy drew scrutiny and criticism by intellectuals, many of whom found the implementation of multiculturalism to belie the theoretical rigors of the academy.[17]

More recently, multiculturalism has retreated because of what many view as its limited potential to impact student prejudice or race relations in America. Others have been discouraged because the religious right and other politically conservative constituencies have claimed protection as persecuted minority "cultures."[18] Today, the term "multicultural" as it applies to school programming is declining, and critical social justice advocates prefer to use the more specific term "antiracist" or the broader term "antibias" education, which encompasses discrimination based on religion, gender, and sexuality.[19] While academics and liberal educators remain deeply committed to the potential of schools to mitigate racism in America, this is a rarely a function of public schools that draws significant public support.

The Revival of the Colorblind Ideal

The decline of multiculturalism and the failure to racially integrate American schools have contributed to an overall climate of apathy toward antiracist initiatives in public education today. Many Americans feel that aggressive programs to redress educational inequality for racial minorities were a failure, due in part to the fact that multiculturalism and school desegregation placed too much emphasis on the subject of "race."[20] In the wake of the terrorist attacks of September 11, 2001, there were renewed calls to disband multicultural education and its supposedly hazy emphasis on cultural relativity, and instead to assert the moral superiority of Western democracy.[21] The rise of the "colorblind" ideal in terms of a "postracial" United States is once again gaining prominence, despite substantial and durable historical evidence that ignoring race in educational policy and practice is detrimental to social justice in America.[22]

Most recently, the United States Supreme Court delivered what many see as a devastating blow to *Brown* and the promise of racially integrated schools in *Parents Involved in Community Schools v. Seattle School District* (2007). In this ruling, the conservative majority of a bitterly divided Court ruled that efforts by Seattle and Jefferson County, Kentucky, to racially integrate K-12 public schools were unconstitutional because they assigned too much importance to the racial identity of individual students when making school assignments. Writing the majority opinion, Chief Justice John Roberts explained, "Before *Brown*, school-children were told where they could, and could not, go to school based on the color of their skin." Noting that this practice was reprehensible, but long gone, Roberts argued that the practice of assigning students to schools on the basis of skin color was equally wrong when it was done today "even for very different reasons." In conclusion, Roberts proclaimed, "The way to stop discrimination on the basis of race is to stop discriminating on the basis of race."[23]

The Court employed the colorblind ideal to claim that identifying students based on their skin color (race) was inherently undemocratic. This was the same colorblind logic used in the *Brown* ruling, but constructed for an entirely different purpose. Whereas *Brown* paved the way for racially integrated schools in America, *Parents Involved in Community Schools* erects new barriers in the way of the already difficult process of breaking down racial segregation and corresponding inequality in American schools.[24]

No matter how it is constructed, the colorblind ideal masks institutionalized racism in America. It treats racial prejudice as the problem of interpersonal relations, assuming that if people would simply stop being prejudiced the problems of racial inequality in America would evaporate. It does not take social science experts to explain why this is impossible. Especially with sixty years of recent history to draw on, we know that simply removing barriers to racial integration does not result in an equalization of education for minority students.

The Promise of History

A historical analysis of the social construction of race in American schools underscores the relationship between antiracist curriculum and educational policy. World War II was a transformative event because it forced educators and policy makers to seriously consider racism as a paramount threat to democracy and to imagine schools as a location with the potential to expunge dangerous racism. Since 1940, we have seen a consistent relationship between the rise of school content designed to mitigate racism, such as intercultural education, and efforts to racially integrate schools. Both tolerance education and integrated classrooms have been constructed as solutions to the persistent dilemma of racial inequality in America. However, they have also been viewed in terms of a binary. Educators used either racial integration or multicultural curricula to address racism. It would be anathema to use both because they were understood to address racism in completely different ways. Multicultural education asks students to study and discuss people of minority descent in an attempt to develop more intimate knowledge of minority groups. Conversely, integrated classrooms are supposed to work by downplaying the significance of racial difference and instead teach students that all people are the same on the inside. Reiterating group features such as supposed cultural practices, which essentially substitute positive stereotypes for negative ones, would only undermine the potential of students to get to know each other on an individual basis. While efforts to promote multicultural programming and desegregate schools coexist in the minds of educators and social activists, one approach or the other tends to dominate school policy and practice in the United States at a given time.

This trend suggests a pattern that connects racial discourse in American schools to the development of antiracist policy and practice. Historically, when educators have treated race as an explicit topic for analysis and discussion they engendered creative and original ways to counteract racial prejudice through the institution of public schools. In contrast, when educators have adopted a colorblind approach to education, the result has been that teachers are unable to acknowledge or address the continuing problem of racism in American society.

The Supreme Court rulings in Seattle and Louisville that challenge school districts' plans for considering race as a factor in school placement seem not to recognize this history. The conservative majority used a seductive "colorblind" logic to insist on an approach to educational policy that history shows us is ineffective and in fact detrimental to educational equality. In a democratic society where free education serves a special function as an equalizing mechanism in an otherwise deeply unequal social order, the failure of American public schools to address the problem of inferior educational opportunity for a majority of the country's minority citizens is an aberration of justice and a profound failing of democracy.

History, however, also reveals the kinds of reforms that could dramatically improve educational equality. In the 1940s, there was a transformation in how educators spoke and taught about the race concept on an everyday basis. If educational policy and practice are tied to the way educators think and talk about race and human diversity, then this research suggests that we should return to the question of how American educators today think and talk about the slippery concept of race.

The Promise of Anthropology

In 1939 the anthropologist Franz Boas identified racial discourse in the public schools as a serious problem for social scientists and educators, but also as a site of reform with the potential to influence American racism and race relations on a global scale. He launched what could be described as a social movement, although it was largely limited to academic intellectuals, to reform the way that American teachers and students spoke about and understood the race concept in their everyday lives. He insisted they learn that scientifically speaking there was no significant biological difference between individuals of different "races" and that the race concept itself referred only to the relatively insignificant patterning of phenotypic markers. He motivated others, including Ruth Benedict and Margaret Mead, to intervene in educational policy and practice as race experts and to teach Americans scientifically accurate models of human diversity.

For roughly four years, from 1944 through 1947, American teachers had students reading, writing, acting, and even singing lessons on the anthropological definition of human race. There were illustrated black and white pamphlets, full-color children's books, posters, films, comic books, and magazine cutouts that teachers employed to teach the scientific meaning of race. We know from teaching journals that these inexpensive, readily available, and appealing materials were widely and enthusiastically used. The use, however, was cut short by a combination of factors surrounding the cold war, which resulted in suspicion cast on lessons on racial equality, and changes in social science theories on the nature of prejudice.

Nevertheless, the existence and popularity of scientific definitions on race during World War II have important implications for today. First of all, they illustrate that such lessons can be easily integrated into everyday learning in American schools by teachers who are not necessarily trained in anthropology or human genetics. Second, and more importantly, they show that lessons on the biological nature of human difference illuminate the socially constructed nature of race. This book has offered direct evidence that when students in the 1940s studied the biological equality of all people they sometimes developed critical insight into the ways that social inequality was perpetuated through structural racism in American society. For example there were the New York City students who wrote angry letters to the American Red Cross concerning segregated blood banks, the Missouri students who visited African American schools and worksites, and the Delaware students who initiated interracial drama and sports programs.[25] All of these students, in different ways, were learning about how racism functioned not only at the personal level, but much more importantly at social and economic levels by denying equal opportunities to American citizens based on the single and unjust qualification of race.

But, if lessons on the scientific definition of race have the potential to illuminate the socially constructed nature of the race concept, then we are left with the problem that past examples failed to permanently alter racial prejudice in American society more broadly or educational equality for racial minorities in particular. The solution here is evident through a historical lens as well, and was pointed out by the anthropologist Ruth Benedict in the 1940s. American schools cannot construct antiracist pedagogy without a more sophisticated under-standing of how *culture* works. The culture concept cannot be limited to the vis-ible or assumed practices, habits, and material culture that defines particular minority groups, but must include a more robust anthropological analysis of American culture as the active ways that people living together in a community make meaning. This means that it is impossible to understand "Puerto Rican" culture in America without investigating the dynamics between Puerto Ricans, Dominicans, Italians, African Americans, and Jews in a particular neighborhood of New York City, not to mention the rivalries and factions within local New York Puerto Rican communities. Furthermore, it is not that these minority groups can be understood as outside of American culture—anthropologists understand these groups as active participants in American culture. They *are* American culture. An anthropological perspective of American culture reveals the structural inequalities that intentionally restrict access to quality education, safe housing, and rewarding jobs according to race. The way that school district lines are drawn and redrawn, the influence of elected school board members, the pressure of state and federal courts on desegregation plans—all of these are examples of how racial inequality can be inscribed in the structural foundations of American society, and they are all visible through a cultural analysis of schooling.

Teaching scientific definitions of human race in a way that highlights the socially constructed nature of racism should be a defining feature of successful antiracist pedagogy, as examples from the 1940s demonstrate. However, teachers must be vigilant that students do not substitute a racialist conception of human difference with an equally essentialist cultural conception of differ-ence. Introduced by anthropologists to popular audiences in the 1930s, Ameri-cans have become used to explaining difference in the way people chose to live their lives as the expected outcome of cultural difference. In schools, this creates the particularly dangerous situation where teachers accidentally substitute a racialist conception of human difference with an equally essentialist cultural one, as we saw in classrooms in the late 1940s and early 1950s. More recently, Walter Benn Michaels noted a similar phenomenon among his college students. He explained, "Once the students in my American literature classes have taken a course in human genetics, they just stop talking about black and white and Asian races and start talking about black and European and Asian cultures instead."[26] In other words, students continued to view the categories of white, black, and Asian as primary determinants in the lives of individuals. A lesson on human genetics emphasized there was no such thing as black and white and Asian races, but based on their own experience the students understood these groups to be different and distinct. If the difference was not racial, they reasoned, it must be cultural.

Likewise, Gloria Ladson-Billings, one of the nation's leading antiracist educators, criticizes teacher training programs for their failure to teach future teachers a scientifically rigorous conception of culture. She describes how white preservice teachers working with minority students invoke the culture concept "as one of the primary explanations for everything from school failure to problems with behavior management and discipline."[27] According to Ladson-Billings, the problem is that teacher education is constructed entirely around psychology to the exclusion of other social sciences. White, middle-class teachers are unable to see the subtle ways that culture can function to constrain or motivate individual students from different backgrounds. She calls for an active program to train teachers not only in the fundamentals of anthropological theory, but practice as well. She wants teachers who know how to do ethnographic research—who visit their students outside of the classroom in the more familiar settings of home, church, and community life in order to understand the kinds of teaching strategies that would work best in their particular classrooms.

Anthropologists in the 1940s recognized the special potential of their discipline to revitalize and transform American pedagogy in a way that would make schooling more democratic and responsive to the needs of oppressed racial minorities. Their activism in the schools, although brief, was tremendously potent and ultimately changed the way American schools constructed the ideal of the educated citizen. American schools during World War II insisted that teachers speak of racial minorities in scientifically accurate terms and that students learn the limits on acceptable interracial behavior. By 1950, psychology had replaced anthropology as the social science discipline best positioned to solve the problem of racial prejudice. While there have been important efforts by anthropologists to reassert the relevancy of their discipline to educational theory and practice, by and large anthropology remains peripheral to mainstream teacher training and educational reform in America.[28]

The antiracist initiative originally laid out by Boas and Benedict, in which hundreds of thousands of American teachers and students participated, still offers hope for exposing and challenging structural racism in the United States. Hortense Powdermaker, an anthropologist and intercultural educator, once claimed, "It would be naïve to think that prejudices, racial and otherwise, will be wiped out by teaching anthropology to more people."[29] The problem was that educators in the 1940s appropriated anthropology and tried to use it to wipe out racial prejudice. They believed that if they reduced individual prejudice first, structural transformations in social justice would follow. We know now that this approach was ineffective, and that anthropological theories of race and culture have much greater potential to illuminate not only the socially constructed nature of race, but also how white supremacy is deeply embedded in the American political process and civic culture.[30] It is this process of illuminating structural racism, I believe, that has emancipatory and transformative potential for contemporary antiracist activists willing to use the nation's classrooms as battlegrounds for social justice and racial equality.

NOTES

Introduction

1. Alice B. Nirenberg, "Meet Your Relatives," *Common Ground* 2, no. 4 (1944): 17–23, quotes page 17. This play is also mentioned in Violet Edwards, "Note on the 'The Races of Mankind,'" in Ruth Benedict, *Race: Science and Politics* (New York: Viking, 1945): 168, suggesting that Benedict was familiar with the script. A revised version of the play *Meet Your Relatives* was published by the Public Affairs Committee, Inc., in New York City, see: "'Race of Mankind'(Versions of)" in folder, Minorities—General—Publications, Box 50, Philleo Nash Papers, Harry S. Truman Library, Independence, Missouri. Thanks to Tom Guglielmo for sharing this last source.

2. Ruth Benedict and Gene Weltfish, *The Races of Mankind*. Public Affairs Pamphlet No. 85 (New York: Public Affairs Committee, 1943): 5.

3. Marjorie B. Smiley et al., "Intercultural Education in English Classrooms: An Informal Survey," *English Journal* 35, no. 6 (1946): 337–49, quote page 341.

4. Jewel Bell, "My Experiences in Promoting Better Understanding," *American Unity* 5, no. 6 (1947): 21.

5. A complete list of teaching journals analyzed in this project are listed in the bibliography. African American teachers belonged to separate teaching associations including the National Association of Teachers in Colored Schools founded in 1907, which became the American Teachers Association in 1937, as well as state teaching associations in the South. On African American teaching associations, see: Carol F. Karpinski, *A Visible Company of Professionals: African Americans and the National Education Association during the Civil Rights Movement* (New York: Peter Lang, 2008); Adam Fairclough, *A Class of Their Own: Black Teachers in the Segregated South* (Cambridge, MA: Belknap Press of Harvard University Press, 2007); Thelma D. Perry, *History of the American Teachers Association* (Washington, DC: National Education Association, 1975).

6. Nell Irvin Painter, *The History of White People* (New York: W.W. Norton and Co., 2010); Peggy Pascoe, *What Comes Naturally: Miscegenation Law and the Making of Race in America* (New York: Oxford University Press, 2009); Victoria Hattam, *In the Shadow of Race: Jews, Latinos, and Immigrant Politics in the United States* (Chicago: University of Chicago Press, 2007); Bruce Baum, *The Rise and Fall of the Caucasian Race: A Political History of Racial Identity* (New York: New York University Press, 2006); Vernon J. Williams Jr., *The Social Sciences and Theories of Race* (Urbana: University of Illinois Press, 2006); Thomas A. Guglielmo, *White on Arrival: Italians, Race, Color, and Power in Chicago, 1890–1945* (New York: Oxford University Press, 2003); Gary Gerstle, *American Crucible: Race and Nation in the Twentieth Century* (Princeton, NJ: Princeton University Press, 2001); Audrey Smedley,

Race in North America: Origin and Evolution of a Worldview, 2nd ed. (Boulder, CO: West-view Press, 1999); Matthew Frye Jacobson, *Barbarian Virtues: The United States Encounters Foreign Peoples at Home and Abroad, 1876–1917* (New York: Hill and Wang, 2000); Matthew Frye Jacobson, *Whiteness of a Different Color: European Immigrants and the Alchemy of Race* (Cambridge, MA: Harvard University Press, 1998); Thomas F. Gossett, *Race: The History of an Idea in America,* rev. ed. (New York: Oxford University Press, 1997).

7. Smiley, "Intercultural Education in English Classrooms," 241.
8. Charles I. Glicksberg, "Education for Hate," *English Journal* 34, no. 1 (1945): 19–26, quote page 21.
9. Alain Locke, "With Science as His Shield: The Educator Must Bridge Our 'Great Divides,'" *Frontiers of Democracy* 6, no. 53 (1940): 208–10.
10. Dorothy Ross explains how and why the social sciences came to adopt the theoretical premise of the hard sciences, what she calls "scientism." See Dorothy Ross, *The Origins of American Social Science* (Cambridge: Cambridge University Press, 1991): 390–470. See also Leah Gordon, "The Question of Prejudice: Social Science, Prejudice, and the Struggle to Define 'the Race Problem' in Mid-Century America, 1935–1965" Ph.D. diss. University of Pennsylvania, 2008; David Paul Haney, *The Americanization of Social Science: Intellectuals and Public Responsibility in the Postwar United States* (Philadelphia: Temple University Press, 2008); John P. Jackson, *Social Scientists for Social Justice: Making the Case against Segregation* (New York: New York University Press, 2001); Daryl Michael Scott, *Contempt and Pity: Social Policy and the Image of the Damaged Black Psyche* (Chapel Hill: University of North Carolina Press, 1997); Ronald G. Walters, ed., *Scientific Authority and Twentieth Century America* (Baltimore: Johns Hopkins University Press, 1997); Ellen Herman, *The Romance of American Psychology: Political Culture in the Age of Experts* (Los Angeles: University of California Press, 1995).
11. Ruth Benedict, "Ammunition to Slay the Race Myth," *American Unity* 1, no. 2 (1942): 18–23.
12. Margaret Mead, Intercultural Education, 1, Container I76 Margaret Mead Papers and the South Ethnographic Archives (MMP), Manuscript Division, Library of Congress, Washington, D.C.
13. Joseph Bellafiore, "Intercultural Understanding through World Study," *English Journal* 30, no. 8 (1941): 640–44, quote page 640.
14. Mayme Louise Sloat, "Science Teaching Can Develop Intercultural Understanding," *American Unity* 3, no. 9 (1945): 15–19, quote page 16.
15. William L. Fidler, "We Meet a Challenge," *New Jersey Educational Review* 12, no. 8 (1939): 227–28, quote page 227–28, emphasis in the original.
16. Ina Corinne Brown, *Race Relations in a Democracy* (New York: Harper and Brothers Publishers, 1949): 161.
17. Diana Selig, *Americans All: The Cultural Gifts Movement* (Cambridge, MA: Harvard University Press, 2008).
18. Doug Foley, "Questioning 'Cultural' Explanations of Classroom Behaviors," in *Everyday Antiracism: Getting Real about Race in School,* ed. Mica Pollock (New York: The New Press, 2008): 222–25; Vivian Louie, "Moving Beyond Quick 'Cultural' Explanations," in *Everyday Antiracism: Getting Real about Race in School,* ed. Mica Pollock (New York: The New Press, 2008): 257–61; Gloria Ladson-Billings, "It's Not the Culture of Poverty, It's the Poverty of Culture," *Anthropology and Education Quarterly* 37, no. 2 (2006): 104–9; Sarah Jewett, "'If You Don't Identify with Your Ancestry, You're Like a Race without a Land': Constructing Race at a Small Urban Middle School," *Education and Anthropology Quarterly* 37, no. 2 (2006): 144–61; Marvin Lynn, "Race, Culture, and the Education of African Americans," *Educational Theory* 56, no. 1 (2006): 107–19; Mica Pollock, "Everyday Antiracism in Education," in Ellen Gordon Reeves, ed., *The New Press Education Reader: Leading Educators Speak Out* (New York: New Press, 2006): 157–60; Antonia Darder and Rodolfo D. Torres, "Shattering the 'Race' Lens: Toward a Critical Theory of Racism," in *The Critical*

Pedagogy Reader, ed. Antonia Darder, Marta Bartodano, and Rodolfo D. Torres, (New York: RoutledgeFalmer, 2003): 245–61; Amanda Lewis, *Race in the Schoolyard: Negotiating the Color Line in Classrooms and Communities* (New Brunswick, NJ: Rutgers University Press, 2003); Susan Florio-Ruane, *Teacher Education and the Cultural Imagination: Autobiography, Conversation, and Narrative* (Mahwah, NJ: Lawrence Erlbaum Associates, 2000); Daniel A. Yon, *Elusive Culture: Schooling, Race, and Identity in Global Times* (Albany: State University of New York Press, 2000).

19. I am drawing on a rich variety of scholarship on the subject of race and racialization in the United States and as a transnational phenomenon. The scholarship on race and racialization is informed by Michel Foucault's theoretical models of discourse and knowledge production as well as Antonio Gramsci's understanding of hegemony, which explain the ways that knowledge becomes "commonsense," or an accepted part of everyday life that is "a product of history and a part of the historical process." See Antonio Gramsci, *Selections from the Prison Notebooks*, ed. and trans. Quentin Hoare and Geoffrey Nowell Smith (New York: International Publishers, 1971): 325–26, 326n; Michel Foucault, *The History of Sexuality: Volume 1: An Introduction* (New York: Vintage Press, 1990). Also see Paul Gilroy, *Against Race: Imaging Political Culture Beyond the Color Line* (Cambridge, MA: Belknap Press/Harvard University Press, 2000); E. Nathaniel Gates, ed., *Critical Race Theory: Essays on the Social Construction and Reproduction of Race* (New York: Garland Publishing, 1997); Kwame Anthony Appiah and Amy Gutman, *Color Conscious: The Political Morality of Race* (Princeton, NJ: Princeton University Press, 1996); Ian F. Haney Lopez, *White by Law: The Legal Construction of Race* (New York: New York University Press, 1996); Ann Laura Stoler, *Race and the Education of Desire: Foucault's History of Sexuality and the Colonial Order of Things* (Durham: Duke University Press, 1995); Kwame Anthony Appiah, *In My Father's House: Africa in the Philosophy of Culture* (New York: Oxford University Press, 1993).

20. Committee for Racial Cooperation, Benjamin Franklin High School, "Building Concepts of Racial Democracy," in Department of Supervisors and Directors of Instruction of the National Education Association, *Americans All: Studies in Intercultural Education* (Washington, DC: Department of Supervisors and Directors of Instruction of the National Education Association, 1942): 52–69, quote page 69, emphasis in original.

21. Irwin A. Eckhauser, "Education for International Understanding," *Social Studies* 38, no. 7 (1947): 294–95, quotes page 295.

22. Mildred Williams and W. L. Van Loan, "Education for Racial Equality," *Social Studies* 34, no. 7 (1943): 308–11, quote page 308.

23. On the relationship between World War II and race, see Anthony Chen, *The Fifth Freedom: Jobs, Politics, and Civil Rights in the United States, 1941–1972* (Princeton, NJ: Princeton University Press, 2009); John Howard, *Concentration Camps on the Home Front: Japanese Americans in the House of Jim Crow* (Chicago: University of Chicago Press, 2008); Timothy L. Schroer, *Recasting Race after World War II: Germans and African Americans in American-Occupied Germany* (Boulder: University Press of Colorado, 2007); Jason Morgan Ward, "'No Jap Crow': Japanese Americans Encounter the World War II South," *Journal of Southern History* 73, no. 1 (2007): 75–104; Anthony S. Chen, "'The Hitlerian Rule of Quotas': Racial Conservatism and the Politics of Fair Employment Legislation in New York State," *Journal of American History* 92, no. 4 (2006): 1238–264; Thomas A. Guglielmo, "Fighting for Caucasian Rights: Mexicans, Mexican Americans, and the Transnational Struggle for Civil Rights in World War II Texas," *Journal of American History* 92, no. 4 (2006): 1212–237; Kevin Allen Leonard, *The Battle for Los Angeles: Racial Ideology and World War II* (Albuquerque: The University of New Mexico Press, 2006); Laura McEnaney, "Nightmares on Elm Street: Demobilizing in Chicago, 1945–1953," *Journal of American History* 92, no. 4 (2006): 1265–291; Gary Gerstle, "The Crucial Decade: The 1940s and Beyond," *Journal of American History* 92, no. 4 (2006): 1292–299; Jennifer E. Brooks, *Defining the Peace: World War II Veterans, Race, and the Remaking of Southern Political Tradition* (Chapel

Hill: University of North Carolina Press, 2004); Alan M. Osur, *Separate and Unequal: Race Relations in the AAF during World War II* (Honolulu: University Press of the Pacific, 2004); Lauren Rebecca Sklaroff, "Constructing G.I. Joe Louis: Cultural Solutions to the 'Negro Problem' during World War II," *Journal of American History* 89, no. 3 (2002): 958–83; Daniel Kryder, *Divided Arsenal: Race and the American State during World War II* (Cambridge: Cambridge University Press, 2000); Ronald Takaki, *Double Victory: A Multicultural History of America in World War II* (Boston: Little, Brown, 2000); Barbara Dianne Savage, *Broadcasting Freedom: Radio, War, and the Politics of Race, 1938–1948* (Chapel Hill: University of North Carolina Press, 1999); E. Nathaniel Gates, ed., *Race and U.S. Foreign Policy from 1900 through World War II* (New York: Routledge, 1998); John W. Dower, *War without Mercy: Race and Power in the Pacific War* (New York: Pantheon Books, 1986); Philip Gleason, "Americans All: World War II and the Shaping of American Identity," *Review of Politics* 43, no. 4 (1981): 483–518. On the impact of World War II on American schools, see: Charles Dorn, *American Education, Democracy, and the Second World War* (New York: Palgrave Macmillan, 2007); Charles Dorn, "'I Had All Kinds of Kids in My Classes, and It Was Fine': Public Schooling in Richmond, California, during World War II," *History of Education Quarterly* 45, no. 4 (2005): 37–50; Gerard Giordano, *Wartime Schools: How World War II Changed American Education* (New York: Peter Lang, 2004); Robert Shafer, "Multicultural Education in New York City during World War II," *New York History* 77, no. 3 (1996): 301–32; Thomas James, *Exile Within: The Schooling of Japanese Americans, 1942–1945* (Cambridge, MA: Harvard University Press, 1987); Isaac L. Kandel, *The Impact of the War upon American Education* (Chapel Hill: University of North Carolina Press, 1948).

24. Jacquelyn Dowd Hall, "The Long Civil Rights Movement and the Political Uses of the Past," *Journal of American History*, 91, no. 4 (2005): 1233–64. Also see: Glenda Elizabeth Gilmore, *Defying Dixie: The Radical Roots of Civil Rights, 1919–1950* (New York: W. W. Norton, 2008); Thomas Sugrue, *Sweet Land of Liberty: The Forgotten Struggle for Civil Rights in the North* (New York: Random House, 2008); Matthew J. Countryman, *Up South: Civil Rights and Black Power in Philadelphia* (Philadelphia: University of Pennsylvania Press, 2007); Kevin Mumford, *Newark: A History of Race, Rights, and Riots in America* (New York: New York University Press, 2007); Peniel E. Joseph, *Black Power Movement: Rethinking the Black Power–Civil Rights Era* (New York: Routledge, 2006); Jeanne Theoharis and Komozi Woodward, eds., *Groundwork: Local Black Freedom Movements in America* (New York: New York University Press, 2005); Martha Biondi, *To Stand and Fight: The Struggle for Civil Rights in Postwar New York City* (Cambridge, MA: Harvard University Press, 2003); Jeanne Theoharis and Komozi Woodward, eds., *Freedom North: Black Freedom Struggles outside the South, 1940–1980* (New York: Palgrave Macmillan, 2003); Charles W. Eagles, "Toward New Histories of the Civil Rights Era," *Journal of Southern History* 66, no. 4 (2000): 815–48; Penny M. Von Eschen, *Race against Empire: Black Americans and Anticolonialism, 1937–1957* (Ithaca, NY: Cornell University Press, 1997); Charles M. Payne, *I've Got the Light of Freedom: The Organizing Tradition and the Mississippi Freedom Struggle* (Berkeley: University of California Press, 1995); Patricia Sullivan, *Days of Hope: Race and Democracy in the New Deal Era* (Chapel Hill: University of North Carolina Press, 1993).

25. Carol F. Karpinski, *A Visible Company of Professionals: African Americans and the National Education Association during the Civil Rights Movement* (New York: Peter Lang, 2008); Sonya Ramsey, *Reading, Writing, and Segregation: A Century of Black Women Teachers in Nashville* (Urbana: University of Illinois Press, 2008); Adam Fairclough, *A Class of Their Own: Black Teachers in the Segregated South* (Cambridge, MA: Harvard University Press, 2007); Jeanne Theoharis, "'Alabama on Avalon': Rethinking the Watts Uprising and the Character of Black Protest in Los Angeles," in *The Black Power Movement: Rethinking the Civil Rights–Black Power Era*, ed. Peniel E. Joseph (New York: Routledge, 2006): 27–54; Cherry A. McGee Banks, *Improving Multicultural Education: Lessons from the Intergroup Education Movement* (New York: Teachers College Press, 2005); Davison Douglas, *Jim Crow Moves North: The Battle over Northern School Segregation, 1865–1954* (New York:

Oxford University Press, 2005); Lani Guinier, "From Racial Liberalism to Racial Literacy: *Brown v. Board of Education* and the Interest Divergence," *Journal of American History* 91, no. 1 (2004): 92–118; Lauri Johnson, "A Generation of Women Activists: African American Female Educators in Harlem, 1930–1950," *Journal of African American History* 89, no. 3 (2004): 223–40; Charles M. Payne, "'The Whole United States Is Southern!': *Brown v. Board* and the Mystification of Race," *Journal of American History* 91, no. 1 (2004): 83–91; Daryl Michael Scott, "Postwar Pluralism, *Brown v. Board of Education*, and the Origins of Multiculturalism," *Journal of American History* 91, no. 1 (2004):69–91; Jonathan Zimmerman, "*Brown*-ing the American Textbook: History, Psychology, and the Origins of Modern Multiculturalism," *History of Education Quarterly* 44, no. 1 (2004): 46–69; Lauri Johnson, "Multicultural Policy and Social Activism: Redefining Who 'Counts' in Multicultural Education," *Race, Ethnicity and Education* 6, no. 2 (2003): 107–21; Yoon K. Pak, "'If There Is a Better Intercultural Plan in Any School System in America, I Do Not Know Where It Is': The San Diego City Schools Intercultural Education Program, 1946–1949," *Urban Education* 37, no. 5 (2002): 588–609; Yoon K. Pak, *Wherever I Go, I Will Always Be a Loyal American: Seattle's Japanese American Schoolchildren during World War II* (New York: Routledge, 2001); James A. Patterson, Brown v. Board of Education: *A Civil Rights Milestone and Its Troubled Legacy* (Oxford: Oxford University Press, 2001); Vanessa Siddle Walker, "African American Teaching in the South: 1940–1960," *American Educational Research Journal* 38, no. 4 (2001): 751–79; Daniel Perlstein, "American Dilemmas: Education, Social Science, and the Limits of Liberalism," in *The Global Color Line: Racial and Ethnic Inequality and Struggle from a Global Perspective*, ed. Pinar Batur and Joe R. Feagin (Stamford, CT: JAI Press, 1999): 357–79; Jack Dougherty, "'That's When We Were Marching for Jobs': Black Teachers and the Early Civil Rights Movement in Milwaukee," *History of Education Quarterly* 38, no. 2 (1998): 121–41; James A. Banks, ed., *Multicultural Education, Transformative Knowledge, and Action: Historical and Contemporary Perspectives* (New York: Teachers College Press, 1996); Davison Douglas, *Reading, Writing, and Race: The Desegregation of the Charlotte Schools* (Greensboro: University of North Carolina Press, 1995); Michael Fultz, "Teacher Training and African American Education in the South, 1900–1940," *Journal of Negro Education* 64, no. 2 (1995): 196–210; Michael Fultz, "African American Teachers in the South, 1890–1940: Powerlessness and the Ironies of Expectations and Protest," *History of Education Quarterly* 35, no. 4 (1995): 401–22; Michael Fultz, "'The Morning Cometh': African-American Periodicals, Education, and the Black Middle Class, 1900–1930," *Journal of Negro History* 80, no. 3 (1995): 97–112; James D. Anderson, *The Education of Blacks in the South, 1860–1935* (Chapel Hill: The University of North Carolina Press, 1988); Nicholas V. Montalto, *A History of the Intercultural Education Movement, 1924–1941* (New York: Garland Publishing, Inc., 1982); Harvie J. Wilkinson, *From Brown to Bakke: The Supreme Court and School Integration, 1954–1978* (New York: Oxford University Press, 1979); Ronald K. Goodenow, "The Progressive Educators, Race, and Ethnicity in the Depression Years: An Overview," *History of Education Quarterly* 15, no. 4 (1975): 365–94.

Chapter 1

1. William Fairley, "Ancient History in the Secondary School," *History Teacher's Magazine* 1, no. 1 (1909): 7–8, quote page 7.
2. Bruce Baum, *The Rise and Fall of the Caucasian Race: A Political History of Racial Identity* (New York: New York University Press, 2006); Thomas A. Guglielmo, *White on Arrival: Italians, Race, Color, and Power in Chicago, 1890–1945* (New York: Oxford University Press, 2003); Gary Gerstle, *American Crucible: Race and Nation in the Twentieth Century* (Princeton, NJ: Princeton University Press, 2001); Matthew Frye Jacobson, *Whiteness of a Different Color: European Immigrants and the Alchemy of Race* (Cambridge, MA: Harvard University Press, 1998); Audrey Smedley, *Race in North America: Origin and Evolution of a*

Worldview, 2nd ed. (Boulder, CO: Westview Press, 1999); Thomas F. Gossett, *Race: The History of an Idea in America*, rev. ed. (New York: Oxford University Press, 1997); David B. Tyack, *The One Best System: A History of American Urban Education* (Cambridge, MA: Harvard University Press, 1974); Lawrence A. Cremin, *The Transformation of the School: Progressivism in American Education, 1876–1957* (New York: Knopf, 1969 [1961]); David M. Kennedy, *Over Here: The First World War and American Society* (New York: Oxford University Press, 1980): 49–75; John Higham, *Strangers in the Land: Patterns of American Nativism, 1860–1925* (New York: Atheneum, 1963): 200–250.

3. Fairley, "Ancient History in the Secondary School," 8.

4. Guglielmo, *White on Arrival.*

5. "Immigrants and Education," *Washington Post*, January 30, 1914, 6.

6. Helen Louise Cohen, "The Foreigner in Our Schools: Some Aspects of the Problem in New York," *English Journal* 2, no. 10 (1913): 618–29, quote page 629. The same argument that children of immigrants had higher literacy rates than native-born children can be found in "Immigrants and Education," *Washington Post*, January 30, 1914, 6.

7. Kennedy, *Over Here*, 64. Also see Higham, *Strangers in the Land*: 236.

8. *Education of the Immigrant*. U.S. Bureau of Education, Bulletin no. 51 (Washington, DC: GPO, 1913): 6.

9. Higham, *Strangers in the Land*, 237. Also see Julie Reuben, "Beyond Politics: Community Civics and the Redefinition of Citizenship in the Progressive Era," *History of Education Quarterly* 37, no. 4 (1997): 399–420.

10. Theodore Roosevelt, *The Rough Riders* (New York: Collier, 1899): 22–23. For more on Theodore Roosevelt's civic and racial nationalism, see Gerstle, *American Crucible*. See also Leroy G. Dorsey, *We Are All Americans, Pure and Simple: Theodore Roosevelt and the Myth of Americanism* (Tuscaloosa: University of Alabama Press, 2007); Gail Bederman, *Manliness and Civilization: A Cultural History of Gender and Race in the United States, 1880–1917* (Chicago: University of Chicago Press, 1995): 170–215; Thomas Dyer, *Theodore Roosevelt and the Idea of Race* (Baton Rouge: Louisiana State University Press, 1980); George Sinkler, *The Racial Attitudes of American Presidents: From Abraham Lincoln to Theodore Roosevelt* (Garden City, NY: Doubleday, 1971): 308–73.

11. Gerstle, *American Crucible*, 44–80.

12. Gary Gerstle notes that this era witnessed "the first demands for cultural pluralism." Gary Gerstle, "The Protean Character of American Liberalism," *The American Historical Review* 99, no. 4 (1994): 1043–73, quote page 1044.

13. Cohen, "The Foreigner in Our Schools," 619.

14. Cohen, "The Foreigner in Our Schools," 626.

15. See for example, "City School Campaigns for Americanization," *History Teacher's Magazine* 8, no. 3 (1917): 95; "Civic Education for Immigrants," *History Teacher's Magazine* 6, no. 8 (1915): 248; G. Stanley Hall, "Teaching the War," *History Teacher's Magazine* 6, no. 3 (1915): 67–70.

16. To consider a few relevant examples, Jeff Mirel describes the debate between ethnic and civic nationalism in various Americanization campaigns, see Jeffrey E. Mirel, *Patriotic Pluralism: Americanization Education and European Immigrants* (Cambridge, MA: Harvard University Press, 2010): 4–6, 48–100. David M. Kennedy explains the tensions between progressive Americanizers like Jane Addams and more coercive, socially conservative "old-stock" Americans, see *Over Here*, 63–69. Jonathan Zimmerman explores the tensions within and between ethnic and racial minorities on the one hand and school boards, textbook publishers, and patriot organizations like the Daughters of the American Revolution on the other in his book *Whose America? Culture Wars in the Public Schools* (Cambridge, MA: Harvard University Press, 2002): 13–80. See also Jonathan Zimmerman, "Ethnics against Ethnicity: European Immigrants and Foreign-Language Instruction, 1890–1940," *Journal of American History* 88, no. 4 (2002): 1383–1404. James Barrett explores the tensions between labor unions and capitalists, both of whom worked to Americanize workers

in different ways. James R. Barrett, "Americanization from the Bottom Up: Immigration and the Remaking of the Working Class in the United States, 1880–1930," *Journal of American History* 79, no. 3 (1992): 996–1020. James R. Barrett and David R. Roediger consider how generational differences within certain immigrant groups, particularly the Irish, influenced the diverse ways that immigrant communities influenced the assimilation of their own and other ethnic groups in the United States in "The Irish and the 'Americanization' of the 'New Immigrants' in the Streets and Churches of the Urban United States, 1900–1930," *Journal of American Ethnic History* 24, no. 4 (2005): 4–33; William Ross investigates how World War I xenophobia inspired communities to outlaw the use of foreign language instruction in schools, and the courts' responses to this legislation in *Forging New Freedoms: Nativism, Education, and the Constitution, 1917–1927* (Lincoln: University of Nebraska Press, 1994): 26–29, 57–95.

17. M. Snyder, "Schools a Target for Critics," *New York Times*, September 24, 1916, 21.

18. Stephan F. Brumberg, "New York City Schools March Off to War," *Urban Education* 24, no. 4 (1990): 440–76.

19. Kennedy, *Over Here*, 53. Also see Ross, *Forging New Freedoms*, 30–56.

20. Frank Cody, "Americanization Courses in the Public Schools," *English Journal* 7, no. 10 (1918): 615–22, quote page 615.

21. Cody, "Americanization Courses in the Public Schools," 621.

22. Cody, "Americanization Courses in the Public Schools," 620.

23. Ella Thorngate, "Americanization in Omaha," *English Journal* 9, no. 3 (1920): 123–28, quote page 124, italics in original.

24. Thorngate, "Americanization in Omaha," 125.

25. Gossett, *Race*, 339–41. See also Gerstle, "The Protean Character of American Liberalism," 1052–54.

26. Higham, *Strangers in the Land*. Chapter 11 describes the passing of national origin laws in the 1920s and the recession of nativist sentiment after 1924. Philip Gleason elaborates on this discussion in his article "Americans All: World War II and the Shaping of American Identity" *Review of Politics* 43, no. 4 (1981): 483–518. Also see David H. Bennett, *The Party of Fear: From Nativist Movements to the New Right in American History* (Chapel Hill: University of North Carolina Press, 1988).

27. Diana Selig, *Americans All: The Cultural Gifts Movement* (Cambridge, MA: Harvard University Press, 2008); Cherry A. McGee Banks, *Improving Multicultural Education: Lessons From the Intergroup Education Movement* (New York: Teachers College Press, 2005); James A. Banks, ed., *Multicultural Education, Transformative Knowledge, and Action: Historical and Contemporary Perspectives* (New York: Teachers College Press, 1996); Robert Shafer, "Multicultural Education in New York City during World War II," *New York History* 77, no. 3 (1996): 301–32; Michael Olneck, "The Recurring Dream: Symbolism and Ideology in Intercultural and Multicultural Education," *American Journal of Education* 98 (1990): 147–74; Nicholas V. Montalto, *A History of the Intercultural Education Movement, 1924–1941* (New York: Garland, 1982); Ronald K. Goodenow, "The Progressive Educator, Race and Ethnicity in the Depression Years: An Overview," *History of Education Quarterly* 15, no. 4 (1975): 365–94.

28. Montalto, *A History of the Intercultural Education Movement*.

29. Daniel Walkowitz, *City Folk: English Country Dance and the Politics of the Folk in Modern America* (New York: New York University Press, 2010); Victor Greene, "Dealing with Diversity: Milwaukee's Multiethnic Festivals and Urban Identity, 1840–1940," *Journal of Urban History* 31, no. 6 (2005): 820–49; Zimmerman, *Whose America*, 13–80; Zimmerman, "Ethnics against Ethnicity"; Ross, *Forging New Freedoms*, 26–29, 57–95; Barrett, "Americanization from the Bottom Up"; Kennedy, *Over Here*, 63–69; Higham, *Strangers in the Land*; Gleason, "Americans All."

30. Hazel B. Poole, "Americanizing the Teacher of English," *English Journal* 16, no. 9 (1927): 705–10, quote page 706.

31. Carl Wittke, "The Immigrant in American History," *Historical Outlook* 13, no. 6 (1922): 193–95. Also see, Evarts B. Greene, "Suggestions on the Relations of American to European History," *History Teacher's Magazine* 8, no. 7 (1917): 218–19.

32. Poole, "Americanizing the Teacher of English," 706.

33. Poole, "Americanizing the Teacher of English," 706.

34. Poole, "Americanizing the Teacher of English," 708–9.

35. Andrew N. Cleven, "Latin American History in Our Secondary Schools," *History Teacher's Magazine* 8, no. 7 (1917): 219–22, quote page 219.

36. Harriet E. Tuell, "A Study of Nations: An Experiment," *History Teacher's Magazine* 8, no. 8 (1917): 264–75.

37. "Wanted: Teachers, But No Pacifists," *New York Times*, September 29, 1918, 34. Dr. Ettinger in 1919 once again made headlines when he fired New York City teachers whose political views he found potentially "communist," "9 to 3 Patriots Barred by Ettinger," *New York Times*, November 18, 1919, 17.

38. See for example, A. V. Brown, "Gandhi and His Policy," *Historical Outlook* 13, no. 4 (1922): 123–25; C. C. Crawford, "India To-Day," *Historical Outlook* 10, no. 3 (1919): 117–20; K. S. Latourette, "The Study of the Far-East," *Historical Outlook* 10, no. 3 (1919): 131–32; R. J. Kerner, "Historic Role of the Slavs," *History Teacher's Magazine*, 8, no. 8 (1917): 294–95; Harriet E. Tuell, "A Study of Nations . . . An Experiment," *History Teacher's Magazine* 8, no. 8 (1917): 264–75; Waldemar Westergaard, "American Interest in the West Indies," *History Teacher's Magazine* 8, no. 8 (1917): 249–53.

39. Four Committees of Historians in Co-Operation with the National Board for Historical Service, "Timely Suggestions for Secondary School History," *History Teacher's Magazine* 8, no. 8 (1917): 256–61.

40. E. Estelle Downing, "International Good Will through the Teaching of English," *English Journal* 14, no. 9 (1925): 684. See also, Harrison C. Thomas, "The Teacher and International Relations," *Journal of the National Education Association* 24, no. 3 (1935): 91. World Goodwill Day was declared in 1923 at the World Federation of Education Associations. "World Goodwill Day," *Journal of the National Education Association* 25, no. 2 (1936): 54.

41. See for example, Marita Hogan and Margaret Yeschko, "Latin American Countries in Children's Literature," *Elementary English Review* 15, no. 6 (1938): 225–28; Marion Ewing, "China in Children's Books," *Elementary English Review* 11, no. 8 (1934): 203–5; Ruth A. Barnes, "Developing International-Mindedness in Junior High School," *English Journal* 22, no. 6 (1933): 476–81; Alice M. Jordon, "Children's Books as Good-Will Messengers," *Elementary English Review* 6, no. 4 (1929): 104–6.

42. Downing, "International Good Will through the Teaching of English," 679, italics in original.

43. Clara W. Hunt, "International Friendship through Children's Books," *Elementary English Review* 2, no. 1 (1925): 34.

44. Alison S. Fell and Ingrid Sharp, *The Women's Movement in Wartime: International Perspectives, 1914–1919* (New York: Palgrave Macmillan, 2007); Katherine Kish Sklar, "'Some of Us Who Deal with the Social Fabric': Jane Addams Blends Peace and Social Justice, 1907–1919," *Journal of the Gilded Age and Progressive Era* 2, no. 1 (2003): 80–96; Harriet Hyman Alonso, *Peace as a Women's Issue: A History of the U.S. Movement for World Peace and Women's Rights* (Syracuse: Syracuse University Press, 1993); *The Women's Peace Union and the Outlawry of War, 1921–1942* (Knoxville: University of Tennessee Press, 1989); Charles Chatfield, *For Peace and Justice: Pacifism in America, 1914–1941* (Knoxville: University of Tennessee Press, 1971); Also see Alan Brinkley, *Liberalism and Its Discontents* (Cambridge, MA: Harvard University Press, 1998), 107–10.

45. Elizabeth B. Wisdom, "International Friendship in Children's Reading," *Elementary English Review* 2, no. 5 (1925): 157–61, quote page 157.

46. Hogan and Yeschko, "Latin American Countries in Children's Literature," 226.

47. The philosopher Horace M. Kallen coined the term "cultural pluralism" in 1924 to celebrate "variations of racial groups." Horace M. Kallen, "Culture and the Klan" in *Cultural and Democracy in the United States* (New York: Arno, 1970 [1924]), 41–43. See also Zimmerman, *Whose America*, 14–16.

48. See for example, Robert J. Kerner, "The Importance of Eastern European History," *Historical Outlook* 10, no. 8 (1924): 343–47; Jessie Evans, "The Teaching of International Relations through the Social Studies," *Historical Outlook* 14, no. 7 (1923): 251–53; Frances Ahl, "Pageant of Ancient Civilizations," *Historical Outlook* 14, no. 5 (1923): 182–85.

49. Howard E. Wilson, "Development of International Attitudes and Understandings in the Secondary School," *Historical Outlook* 10, no. 2 (1929): 71–75, quote page 71. This article was also given as a speech before the eighth annual meeting of the National Council for the Social Studies, Minneapolis, July 2, 1928. Wilson later received his Ed.D. from Harvard University and became an expert on the subject of international education.

50. Alice N. Gibbons, "An International-Relations Club," *Social Education* 1, no. 6 (1937): 398–400, quote page 400. Also see William T. Stone, "Education in International Affairs," *Social Education* 1, no. 4 (1937): 271–72; "International Understanding—A Symposium," *New Jersey Educational Review* 3, no. 4 (1930): 19–22.

51. Montalto, *A History of the Intercultural Education Movement*, 78.

52. Montalto, *A History of the Intercultural Education Movement*, 88–94. Also see Goodenow, "The Progressive Educators, Race, and Ethnicity in the Depression Years."

53. Montalto, *A History of the Intercultural Education Movement*, 96.

54. The original name of the organization was Service Bureau for Education in Human Relations. The name was changed in 1936. See Montalto, *A History of the Intercultural Education Movement*, 110 and 132.

55. "Teaching Materials in the Field of International Relations, Summer 1934," in Classroom Materials 1928–1936, Box 17, Folder 5. Rachel Davis DuBois Papers (RDD Papers), General/Multiethnic Collection, Immigration History Research Center, University of Minnesota, Minneapolis, MN.

56. "New School Bureau Seeks Racial Amity," *New York Times*, April 8, 1934, N3.

57. Report B and Appendix, Report of the Committee for Evaluation to the General Education Board, page 55. Box 31, Folder 6. RDD Papers. Also see Barbara Dianne Savage, *Broadcasting Freedom: Radio, War, and the Politics of Race, 1938–1948* (Chapel Hill: University of North Carolina Press, 1999).

58. "AH (Art History) 01: The Orient," 1; "Art 02: The Orient," 1; "Eng. 02: The Orient—China," 1; "E.J. 1: Literature," p.1; "Lit. 04: The Orient," 1; "Eng. 03: The Orient," 1; all found in Classroom Materials 1928–1936, Box 17, Folder 5. RDD Papers.

59. "General Science: 01," 1–2, in Classroom Materials 1928–1936, Box 17, Folder 5. RDD Papers.

60. "American History I-1: Ancient History," no date, in Box 17, Folder 5, "Classroom Materials 1928–36," RDD Papers.

61. Rachel Davis DuBois and Emma Schweppe, eds. *The Germans in American Life* (New York: Thomas Nelson and Sons, 1936): 8.

62. Ida T. Jacobs, "A Project toward Goodwill," *English Journal* 21, no. 7 (1932): 565–67, quote page 565.

63. Jacobs, "A Project toward Goodwill," 565–66.

64. Jacobs, "A Project toward Goodwill," 566.

65. Jacobs, "A Project toward Goodwill," 566.

66. Thyra Carter, "Racial Elements in American History Textbooks," *Historical Outlook* 12, no. 4 (1931): 147–50, quote page 151.

67. Carter, "Racial Elements in American History Textbooks."

68. Emily V. Baker, "Do We Teach Racial Intolerance?" *Historical Outlook* 14, no. 2 (1933): 86–89, quote page 86.

69. Baker, "Do We Teach Racial Intolerance?" 86–87.

70. Baker, "Do We Teach Racial Intolerance?" 87.

71. Selig, *Americans All.*

72. Harold G. Campbell, "All the Children: 41st Report of the Superintendent of the Schools of the City of New York." 1938–1939. (New York: Board of Education of New York City, 1939): 23.

73. Ida T. Jacobs, "The Heritage of America," *English Journal* 22, no. 4 (1933): 314–17, quotes page 314.

74. Maurice T. Price, "Our Amateurishness in Promoting International Goodwill, I," *Social Studies* 16, no. 6 (1935): 361–70, quote page 369. Franz Boas is cited two years later in another article in the *Social Studies*, J. F. Santee, "Determinisms—Geographic, Racial, and Cultural," *Social Studies* 18, no. 7 (1937): 318–20. Also see A. K. King, "Enigma of the South," *Social Education* 3, no. 1 (1939): 4–12.

75. Essie Chamberlain, "International-Mindedness through Books," *English Journal* 22, no. 5 (1933): 382–91, quote page 386–87.

76. Alan Brinkley, *Liberalism and Its Discontents*, 99–101; Stuart Svonkin, *Jews against Prejudice: American Jews and the Fight for Civil Liberties* (New York: Columbia University Press, 1997): 62–78; Gerstle, "The Protean Character of American Liberalism"; Walter A. Jackson, *Gunnar Myrdal and America's Conscience: Social Engineering and Racial Liberalism, 1938–1987* (Chapel Hill: University of North Carolina Press, 1990): 279–93; Goodenow, "The Progressive Educators, Race, and Ethnicity in the Depression Years."

77. Sonya Ramsey, *Reading, Writing, and Segregation: A Century of Black Women Teachers in Nashville* (Urbana: University of Illinois Press, 2008); Adam Fairclough, *A Class of Their Own: Black Teachers in the Segregated South* (Cambridge, MA: Harvard University Press, 2007); Adam Fairclough, *Teaching Equality: Black Schools in the Age of Jim Crow* (Athens: University of Georgia Press, 2001); Vanessa Siddle Walker, "African American Teaching in the South: 1940–1960," *American Educational Research Journal* 38, no. 4 (2001): 751–79; Davison Douglas, *Reading, Writing, and Race: The Desegregation of the Charlotte Schools* (Greensboro: University of North Carolina Press, 1995); Adam Fairclough, *Race and Democracy: The Civil Rights Struggle in Louisiana* (Athens: University of Georgia Press, 1995); Michael Fultz, "Teacher Training and African American Education in the South, 1900–1940," *Journal of Negro Education* 64, no. 2 (1995): 196–210; Michael Fultz, "African American Teachers in the South, 1890–1940: Powerlessness and the Ironies of Expectations and Protest," *History of Education Quarterly* 35, no. 4 (1995): 401–22; David S. Cecelski, *Along Freedom Road: Hyde County, North Carolina, and the Fate of Black Schools in the South* (Chapel Hill: University of North Carolina Press, 1994); James D. Anderson, *The Education of Blacks in the South, 1860–1935* (Chapel Hill: The University of North Carolina Press, 1988).

78. Alferdteen Harrison, ed., *Black Exodus: The Great Migration from the American South* (Jackson: University Press of Mississippi, 1991); James R. Grossman, *Land of Hope: Chicago, Black Southerners, and the Great Migration* (Chicago: University of Chicago Press, 1989); Carole Marks, *Farewell—We're Good and Gone* (Bloomington: Indiana University Press, 1989).

79. Thomas Sugrue, *Sweet Land of Liberty: The Forgotten Struggle for Civil Rights in the North* (New York: Random House, 2008), especially chapter six; Jeanne Theoharis, "'Alabama on Avalon': Rethinking the Watts Uprising and the Character of Black Protest in Los Angeles," in *The Black Power Movement: Rethinking the Civil Rights–Black Power Era*, ed. Peniel E. Joseph (New York: Routledge, 2006): 27–54; Davison Douglas, *Jim Crow Moves North: The Battle over Northern School Segregation, 1865–1954* (New York: Oxford University Press, 2005); Lauri Johnson, "A Generation of Women Activists: African American Female Educators in Harlem, 1930–1950," *Journal of African American History* 89, no. 3 (2004): 223–40; Jack Dougherty, "'That's When We Were Marching for Jobs': Black Teachers and the Early Civil Rights Movement in Milwaukee," *History of Education Quarterly*, 38, no. 2 (1998): 121–41.

80. Pero Gaglo Dagbovie, *The Early Black History Movement: Carter G. Woodson and Lorenzo Johnston Greene* (Urbana: University of Illinois Press, 2007); Zimmerman, *Whose America*, 9–134.

81. Eugenia Brunot, "The Negro Child and His Reading: A Public Library Point of View," *Elementary English Review* 9, no. 6 (1932): 159–60. Also see Ann Elizabeth Coolidge, "Origins of Our Negro Folk Story," *Elementary English Review* 9, no. 6 (1932): 161–62.

82. Frances Atchinson Bacon, "Epaminondas at the Library," *Elementary English Review* 12, no. 9 (1935): 257–59, quotes page 257.

83. Bacon, "Epaminondas at the Library," 258.

84. Bacon, "Epaminondas at the Library," 258.

85. "Classroom Practices: Pageant of America," *Elementary English Review* 11, no. 2 (1934): 36–40, quote page 40. Also see an article from New Jersey that described a special boarding school for "Negro" students that taught manual labor and industrial education, W. R. Valentine, "The State Aids Negro Youth," *New Jersey Educational Review* 9, no. 2 (1935): 46–47.

86. Wilhelmina M. Crosson, "The Negro in Children's Literature," *Elementary English Review* 10, no. 10 (1933): 249–55.

87. Crosson, "The Negro in Children's Literature," 250.

88. Crosson, "The Negro in Children's Literature," 250.

89. Wilhelmina Crosson was active in the Association for the Study of Negro Life and History, see "The Eighteenth Annual Celebration of Negro History Week in Retrospect," *Negro History Bulletin* 6, no. 7 (1943): 164–65, 167; Pero Gaglo Dagbovie, "Black Women, Carter G. Woodson, and the Association for the Study of Negro Life and History, 1915–1950," *Journal of African American History* 88, no. 1 (2003): 21–41; Janet Simms-Wood, "Wilhelmina Marguerita Crosson," in *Notable Black American Women*, Jessie Carney Smith and Shirelle Phelps, eds. (Detroit: Gale Research, 1996): 152–56.

90. Chester M. Destler, "Perspective for the Southern Race Question," *Social Education* 1, no. 7 (1937): 478–80, quotes pages 478 and 480.

91. A. K. King, "Enigma of the South," *Social Education* 3, no. 1 (1939): 4–12, quote page 5.

92. Adolph E. Meyer, "Nazi Education in Germany," *Social Studies* 25, no. 2 (1934): 61–63; Karen Monrad Jones, "Jew Street," *Social Studies* 25, no. 1 (1934): 6–10.

93. Francis Shoemaker, "Round Table: The English Teacher in Relation to the International Scene," *English Journal* 25, no. 8 (1936): 673–75, quote page 673. See also, Helen Rand, "To Our International Relations," *English Journal* 25, no. 3 (1936): 215–20; "International Goodwill Education," *English Journal* 25, no. 3 (1936): 247.

94. Shoemaker, "Round Table: The English Teacher in Relation to the International Scene," 673 and 674.

95. Alice L. Pearson, "Disarm the Hearts, for That Is Peace," *English Journal*, 26, no. 5 (1937): 401–3. Also see Nathaniel P. Clough, "Making Nazis in Czechoslovakia," *Social Education* 3, no. 5 (1939): 301–6; John J. DeBoer, "A Program for Peace Education," *English Journal* 25, no. 4 (1936): 286–92.

96. E. Louise Noyes, "Round Table: Builders Together," *English Journal* 27, no. 3 (1938): 258–60, quote page 258.

97. Noyes, "Round Table: Builders Together," 260.

98. Julian Aronson, "Can the Social Sciences Function?" *Social Studies* 28, no. 2 (1937): 58–60, quote page 58.

99. Sherman Gunderson, "Peace and the Schools," *Social Studies* 28, no. 7 (1937): 309–11.

100. Russell T. McNutt, "Educating for World Citizenship," *Social Education* 4, no. 1 (1940): 33–38, quote page 33.

101. Glen W. Maple, "Functional Civics," *Social Studies* 28, no. 7 (1937): 308–9; C. E. Sohl, "The Function of History in an Americanism Program," *Social Studies* 28, no. 3 (1937): 107–9.

102. Frances Norene Ahl, "The Moslem World," *Social Studies* 29, no. 5 (1938): 217–18; Alban W. Hoopes, "The Need for a History of the American Indian," *Social Studies* 29, no. 1 (1938): 26–27.

103. Roger Barber, "American Thought and Culture," *Social Studies* 29, no. 4 (1938): 164–65, quote page 164.

104. Rachel Davis DuBois, "Intercultural Education at Benjamin Franklin High School," *High Points* 19, no. 9 (1937): 23–31, quote page 25.

105. DuBois, "Intercultural Education at Benjamin Franklin High School," 29.

106. Rachel Davis DuBois, "Can We Help to Create an American Renaissance?" *English Journal* 27, no. 9 (1938): 733–40.

107. Hymen Alpern, "Tolerance, the Keystone of American Democracy," *High Points* 20, no. 10 (1938): 41–44, quote page 44.

Chapter 2

1. Vernon J. Williams Jr., *The Social Sciences and Theories of Race* (Urbana: University of Illinois Press, 2006); Lee D. Baker and Thomas C. Patterson, "Race, Racism, and the History of U.S. Anthropology," *Transforming Anthropology* 5, no. 1 and 2 (1994): 1–7; Elazar Barkan, *The Retreat of Scientific Racism: Changing Concepts of Race in Britain and the United States between the World Wars* (Cambridge: Cambridge University Press, 1992). Barkan explains the role of Boas's many students in perpetuating this claim, including Ruth Benedict, Alfred L. Kroeber, Melville J. Herskovits, Robert H. Lowie, and Walter Goldschmidt. See footnote 25, page 76. For a closer analysis of Boas's work, primarily up to 1911, see George W. Stocking, *Race, Culture, and Evolution: Essays in the History of Anthropology*, 2nd ed. (Chicago: University of Chicago Press, 1982). For a critical view of Boas, see Marvin Harris, *The Rise of Anthropological Theory: A History of Theories of Culture* (New York: Thomas Y. Crowell, 1968).

2. "Anthropologist Franz Boas," *Time*, May 11, 1936.

3. "Schools Rebuked on Racial Errors: Prof. Boas Charges Many Use Textbooks That Support Nazi Doctrines," *New York Times*, July 17, 1939, 21.

4. For an analysis of Boas as a public intellectual and educator in the broadest sense, see Regna Darnell, "Franz Boas: Scientist and Public Intellectual," in Jill B. R. Cherneff and Eve Hochwald, eds., *Visionary Observers: Anthropological Inquiry and Education* (Lincoln: University of Nebraska Press, 2006): 1–24. Also see, Lee D. Baker, "Franz Boas Out of the Ivory Tower," *Anthropological Theory* 4, no. 1 (2004): 29–51; Claudia Roth Pierpont, "The Measure of America: How a Rebel Anthropologist Waged a War on Racism," *New Yorker* 80, no. 3 (2004): 48–63; Herbert S. Lewis, "The Passion of Franz Boas," *American Anthropologist* 103, no. 2 (2001): 447–67; Lee D. Baker, "Columbia University's Franz Boas: He Led the Undoing of Scientific Racism," *Journal of Blacks in Higher Education*, no. 22 (Winter 1998/1999): 89–96; Julia E. Liss, "Diasporic Identities: The Science and Politics of Race in the Work of Franz Boas and W.E.B. Du Bois, 1894–1919," *Cultural Anthropology* 13, no. 2 (1998): 127–66; Marshall Hyatt, *Franz Boas Social Activist: The Dynamics of Ethnicity* (New York: Greenwood Press, 1990). For a consideration of how Boasian ideas about culture influenced school desegregation policies, see: Lee D. Baker, "Unraveling the Boasian Discourse: The Racial Politics of 'Culture' in School Desegregation, 1944–1954," *Transforming Anthropology* 7, no. 1 (1998): 15–32.

5. "Schools Rebuked on Racial Errors."

6. While Boas led a powerful attack against racial discrimination in American society, historians note that at times he accepted some of the discriminatory beliefs of his day. For example, Vernon Williams writes: "Boas believed that because of a supposedly defective ancestry that had resulted in purportedly smaller brain sizes and cavities, blacks were a little inferior—on average—to whites in intelligence" (1). At the same time, Williams acknowledges that Boas argued vociferously against blanket discrimination against blacks, believing they should be judged on individual merit, not as members of an inferior race. Importantly, Boas insisted that one reason blacks had such low status in America was not due to innate inferiority, but to enduring prejudice. Vernon J. Williams Jr., *Rethinking Race:*

Franz Boas and His Contemporaries (Lexington: University Press of Kentucky, 1996). Steven Selden, *Inheriting Shame: The Story of Eugenics and Racism in America* (New York: Teachers College Press, 1999), explains how Boas's theories on race directly challenged the scientific theories of eugenicists, 108 and 110. For an overview of how Boas's theories fit into larger intellectual histories of race in America, see Thomas F. Gossett, *Race: The History of an Idea in America*, rev. ed. (New York: Oxford University Press, 1997): 409–30. For a discussion of how anthropological theories on race were disseminated in popular culture see Lee D. Baker, *From Savage to Negro: Anthropology and the Construction of Race, 1896–1954* (Berkeley: University of California Press, 1998).

7. "The Inferiority Myth," *Chicago Defender*, August 23, 1941, 14. Examples of articles on Boas's efforts to fight racial prejudice in Germany and the United States during the war: "U.S. Scientists Ridicule False Nazi Doctrines," *Washington Post*, December 11, 1938, M4; "Natural Scientists Rally to Defense of Democracy," *Christian Science Monitor*, December 12, 1938, 18; "Franz Boas Blasts Pure Race Myth," *Chicago Defender*, April 16, 1939, 24; "Negroes Join Boaz [sic] Tribute," *New York Amsterdam News*, July 22, 1939, 2; Franz Boas, "White Anthropologist Decries Race Prejudice; Pleads for Equal Rights," *Chicago Defender*, August 2, 1941, 4; "Franz Boas," *Washington Post*, December 24, 1942, 8; "Race Theory Debunker Dies at Columbia U.," *Chicago Defender*, January 2, 1943, 13.

8. Ruth Benedict brought the term "racism" to the broader American public in 1940 through the publication of her book *Race: Science and Politics*, which was written for the general public and subsequently reprinted in multiple editions. The first chapter begins, "Racism: the 'ism' of the modern world," and offers a thoughtful and drawn out explanation of racism. Ruth Benedict, *Race: Science and Politics*, rev. ed. (New York: Viking, 1945). The definition of "racism" here is paraphrased from the pamphlet *The Genetic Basis for Democracy* (New York: American Committee for Democracy and Intellectual Freedom, 1939): 2.

9. "Nazi Conception of Science Scored," *New York Times*, December 11, 1938, 50.

10. Anti-Semitism in the New York City schools in the late 1930s and 1940s is documented in Ruth J. Markowitz, *My Daughter, the Teacher: Jewish Teachers in the New York City Schools* (New Brunswick, NJ: Rutgers University Press, 1993). Over the 1920s and 1930s the number of Jewish teachers increased while the number of Irish American teachers decreased in New York City, so that by the mid-1940s a majority of New York City public school teachers were Jewish. Christina Collins, "Ethnically Qualified: A History of New York City Public School Teachers, 1920–1980," Ph.D. diss. University of Pennsylvania, 2006; Ronald Bayor, *Neighbors in Conflict: The Irish, Germans, Jews, and Italians in New York City, 1929–1941*, 2nd ed. (Urbana: University of Illinois Press, 1988).

11. Celia Lewis, "Schools for Tolerance," *New York Teacher* 4, no. 3 (1938): 10–11.

12. "Teachers Warned Bias Is Spreading," *New York Times*, January 8, 1939, 13.

13. "Drive to Teach Tolerance Ideal," *New York Times*, March 5, 1939, D9; Benjamin Fine, "Schools Fight Racial Hatred," *New York Times*, February 12, 1939, 10; Benjamin Fine, "Schools to Open Tolerance Drive," *New York Times*, January 16, 1938, 46. Also see Robert Shafer, "Multicultural Education in New York City during World War II," *New York History* 77, no. 3 (1966): 301–32.

14. William H. Kilpatrick, Jesse H. Newlon, and George S. Counts, "The New Attack on Freedom of Teaching," *Journal of the National Education Association* 24 (1935): 51. Also see "A School Used by Reds," *New York Times*, January 11, 1939, 3. Counts gained notoriety in educational circles for his bold claims in "Dare the School Build a New Social Order," first given as a speech to the Progressive Education Association in 1932, where he called for schools to lead the way in a drastic restructuring of the American political economy. See the introduction by Wayne J. Urban in George S. Counts, *Dare the School Build a New Social Order?* (Carbondale: Southern Illinois University Press, 1978). Patricia A. Graham, *Progressive Education from Arcady to Academe: A History of the Progressive Education Association, 1919–1955* (New York: Teachers College Press, 1967): 64–65.

15. Hyatt, *Franz Boas Social Activist*, 148–49.

16. "The Attack on the City College System of New York City," *Science* 94 (1941): 409.

17. "Subversion of Freedom," *New York Teacher* 6, no. 7 (1941): 12. For a passionate description of this process see Louis Lerman, *Winter Soldiers: A Story of a Conspiracy against the Schools* (New York: Committee for Defense of Public Education, 1941). Franz Boas wrote a short introduction to this pamphlet, which is available in the Tamiment Library and Robert F. Wagner Labor Archives at New York University's Bobst Library, New York, NY. Also see Stephen Leberstein, "Purging the Profs: The Rapp Coudert Committee in New York, 1940–1942," in *New Studies in the Politics and Culture of U.S. Communism* (New York: Monthly Review Press, 1993).

18. An image of this flyer is reproduced in Lewis, "Schools for Tolerance," 11. For an overview of anti-Semitism in schools during this period see Stuart Svonkin, *Jews against Prejudice: American Jews and the Fight for Civil Liberties* (New York: Columbia University Press, 1997): 1–10.

19. Harry H. Laughlin, *Immigration and Conquest* (New York: The Special Committee on Immigration and Naturalization of the Chamber of Commerce of the State of New York, 1939): 90–91. For more on Laughlin and his work with immigration restriction and eugenics see John P. Jackson Jr. and Nadine M. Weidman, "The Origins of Scientific Racism," *Journal of Blacks in Higher Education*, no. 50 (Winter 2005/2006): 66–79; Philip K. Wilson, "Harry Laughlin's Eugenic Crusade to Control the 'Socially Inadequate' in Progressive Era America," *Patterns of Prejudice* 36, no. 1 (2002): 49–67; Gary Gerstle, *American Crucible: Race and Nation in the Twentieth Century* (Princeton, NJ: Princeton University Press, 2001): 105–9; Matthew Frye Jacobson, *Whiteness of a Different Color: European Immigrants and the Alchemy of Race* (Cambridge, MA: Harvard University Press, 1998): 82–97; Gossett, *Race*, 401–2;

20. For an overview on the response of business leaders to FDR's New Deal as it pertained to education, see David Tyack, Robert Lowe, and Elisabeth Hansot, *Public Schools in Hard Times: The Great Depression and Recent Years* (Cambridge, MA: Harvard University Press, 1984): 58–59.

21. As quoted by Franz Boas, "Freedom of Education," testimonial dinner, National Federation Constitutional Liberties, March 12, 1941, 1–2. Franz Boas Professional Papers, American Philosophical Society (APS), Philadelphia, PA.

22. Charles J. Hendley, "A Message," *New York Teacher* 5, no. 3 (1939): 1. Also see: "School Funds Slash Fought," *New York Amsterdam News*, February 15, 1940, 17; "Budget Slash Hurts Harlem," *New York Amsterdam News*, July 29, 1939, 20; "Demand Unity of All Harlem Racial Groups," *New York Amsterdam News*, July 1, 1939, 3; "CIO Demands Restoration of Big Cuts," *New York Amsterdam News*, June 17, 1939, 4; "Don't Let the Schools Down," *New York Amsterdam News*, June 10, 1939, 6.

23. For a review of Depression-era budget cuts to New York City schools, see Diane Ravitch, *The Great School Wars: A History of the New York City Public Schools*, revised ed. (Baltimore: John Hopkins University Press, 2000): 236–40. Interestingly, Ravitch notes that an influx of federal money to New York City public schools made up for many of these initial cutbacks and she therefore characterizes the Depression era as a period of "remarkable improvement in the schools" (239). This stands in contrast to the litany of complaints in the pages of the *New York Teacher* in 1939, where teachers complained about overcrowded classrooms, lack of supplies, and salary reductions. Also see descriptions and illustrations of crowded and unhealthy conditions in New York City schools in Lerman, *Winter Soldiers*.

24. Irving Adler, "Public Education under Fire," *New York Teacher* 5, no. 1 (1939): 7.

25. Warren Moscow, "8000 Invade Albany Today for State Budget Hearing," *New York Times*, February 12, 1940, 1. Also see: "Save Our Schools," special edition *New York Teacher* 6, no. 4 (1941): 1–30; Herman Ruchlis and Samuel C. Greenfield, "School Budget and Tax Dodgers," *New York Teacher* 5, no. 5 (1940): 3–4; "Save Our Schools," special issue *New York Teacher* 5, no. 3 (1939):1–32; Irving Adler, "Public Education under Fire," *New York Teacher* 5, no. 1 (1939): 7–9.

26. Sydney M. Shallett, "Battle of the State Budget Booms Day and Night in Word Barrage," *New York Times*, February 13, 1940: 1, 3.

27. An overview of the history and political activism of the American Committee for Democracy and Intellectual Freedom (ACDIF) can be found in Peter J. Kuznick, *Beyond the Laboratory: Scientists as Political Activists in 1930s America* (Chicago: University of Chicago Press, 1987): 171–226. Kuznick credits the ACDIF for politicizing American scientists "along decidedly progressive lines" (226). Boas served as the national chairman of the ACDIF, which was founded in 1939 with support from the American Jewish Committee. See Barkan, *The Retreat of Scientific Racism*, 284, and Margaret Mead, *An Anthropologist at Work: Writings of Ruth Benedict* (Boston: Houghton Mifflin Co., 1959): 348–49; For more on the Textbook Committee of the ACDIF see Jonathan Zimmerman, *Whose America? Culture Wars in the Public Schools* (Cambridge, MA: Harvard University Press, 2002): 72–73.

28. "Aliens Defended in 'Race' Dispute," *New York Times*, July 23, 1939, 5.

29. American Committee for Democracy and Intellectual Freedom, *Science Condemns Racism: A Reply to the Chamber of Commerce of the State of New York* (New York: American Committee for Democracy and Intellectual Freedom, 1939): 1.

30. "Study of Religion in Schools Is Urged," *New York Times*, August 14, 1939, 14.

31. For a consideration of American education during the Great Depression, see Tyack, Lowe, and Hansot, *Public Schools in Hard Times*, especially 27–41. For an analysis of elites and their varying degrees of support for educational retrenchment see Jeffrey Mirel, "The Politics of Educational Retrenchment in Detroit, 1929–1935," *History of Education Quarterly* 24 no. 3 (1984): 323–58.

32. Avis Carlson, "Deflating the Schools," *Harper's* November, 1933, 713–14, as quoted in Mirel, "The Politics of Educational Retrenchment in Detroit, 1929–1935," 343.

33. Franz Boas quoted in Margaret Mead, *An Anthropologist at Work*, 413.

34. "Report on Schools Scored as 'Fascist,'" *New York Times*, October 3, 1939, 30.

35. American Committee for Democracy and Intellectual Freedom, "This Is Democracy," September 18, 1939, 14. Radio Scripts Collection, 1937–1966 (RSC). Manuscripts, Archive, and Rare Books Division, Schomberg Center for Research in Black Culture, New York Public Library, New York, NY.

36. "Be Careful of the Word 'Race,'" *New Republic*, July 26, 1939, 319.

37. Franz Boas, "Freedom Defined," *New York Teacher* 6, no. 9 (1941): 25; Franz Boas, "Freedom of Thought," *New York Teacher* 6, no. 4 (1941): 21. The New York City Teachers Union later awarded Boas a medal of honor for his activism, see Lauri Johnson, "'Making Democracy Real': Teacher Union and Community Activism to Promote Diversity in the New York City Public Schools, 1935–1950," *Urban Education* 37, no. 5 (2002): 566–87.

38. "Rally Will Protest Blows to Education," *New York Times*, April 7, 1940, 42. Boas also participated in another rally on April 21, 1939, at Carnegie Hall, sponsored by the American Society for Race Tolerance. "Racial Inferiority of Negro Flatly Rejected by Scholars," *New York Amsterdam News*, April 22, 1939, 3.

39. Franz Boas, "Education, Freedom, and Democracy," April 13, 1940, 1, Franz Boas Papers, Professional Papers, APS.

40. Boas, "Education, Freedom, and Democracy," 3.

41. Franz Boas, "Freedom of Education," 2. He repeated a similar line in a radio show, American Committee for Democracy and Intellectual Freedom, "Young America," September 11, 1939, 1. (RSC).

42. Boas, "Freedom of Education," 3.

43. While earlier studies had examined how specific minority groups, for example African Americans, were portrayed in textbooks, Boas's study was the first to analyze the various meanings of the race concept within textbooks. On controversies over the portrayal of racial, ethnic, and religious minorities in textbooks see Zimmerman, *Whose America?* and Jonathan Zimmerman, "*Brown*-ing The American Textbook: History, Psychology, and the

Origins of Modern Multiculturalism," *History of Education Quarterly* 44, no. 1 (2004): 46–69. For examples of academic studies of how African Americans were presented in textbooks, see Carter G. Woodson, "Race Prejudice in School Books," *New York Teacher* 4, no. 6, (1939): 13–14; Lawrence D. Reddick, "Racial Attitudes in American History Textbooks of the South," *Journal of Negro History* 19, no. 3, (1934): 225–65.

44. Selden, *Inheriting Shame*, 13.

45. "Summary of the Discussion at the Conference on Education and Eugenics," March 20, 1937. American Eugenics Society Records (AESR), American Philosophical Society, Philadelphia, PA. Also see: "Notes and Memoranda: Eugenics Prize Essay Contest." *Eugenical News* 14, no. 3 (1939): 45–46.

46. *American Biology Teacher*, the teaching journal of the American Biology Teachers Association first published in 1938, includes articles from a variety of theoretical perspectives on the subject of eugenics in the 1940s and 1950s. Some of these articles were by college professors and well-known eugenicists who favored rather strict interpretations of eugenics theories of racial betterment, while others asserted that all humans belonged to the same "race" and that heredity did not have as much of an influence on individual behavior or intelligence as social environment. To cite just a few examples, see: Harold Nagler, "The Place of Anthropology in the Biology Course," *American Biology Teacher* 12, no. 3 (1950): 65–67; Jesse V. Miller, "Biology—1949 Model," *American Biology Teacher* 11, no. 4 (1949): 101–4; John E. Shoop, "The Development of Proper Emotional Attitudes in Children," *American Biology Teacher* 11, no. 3 (1949): 75–82; Oscar Riddle, "Genetics and Human Behavior," *American Biology Teacher* 10, no. 3 (March 1948): 69–74; E. Laurence Palmer, "Biological Behavior and Society," *American Biology Teacher* 10, no. 2 (1948): 45–49; Theodosius Dobzhansky, "What Is Heredity?" *American Biology Teacher* 7, no. 6 (1945): 127–28; A. J. Carlson, "The Science of Biology and the Future of Man," *American Biology Teacher* 7, no. 4 (1945): 75–78; G. W. Jefferson, "International Biology," *American Biology Teacher* 7, no. 3 (1944): 65–68; C. M. Farmer, "An Experiment in Biology Teaching," *American Biology Teacher* 6, no. 2 (1943): 31–32; Melvin W. Barnes, "The Relation of the Study of Biology to Biological Misconceptions," *American Biology Teacher* 5, no. 5 (1943): 114–16; Frank J. Bruno, "The Influence of Biology on Theories of Human Behavior," *American Biology Teacher* 5, no. 3 (1942): 55–59; John Edwin Coe, "Why Study Biology?" *American Biology Teacher* 2, no. 5 (1940): 113–16; Oscar Riddle, "Epic of Life," *American Biology Teacher* 2, no. 2 (1939): 35–39; Edwin G. Conklin, "Science in the World Crisis," *American Biology Teacher* 1, no. 8 (1939): 171–74, 206.

47. D. F. Miller, "Biology for Survival," *American Biology Teacher* 12, no. 1 (1950): 7–12. Also see "Racial Deterioration Feared by Convention Speakers," *New Jersey Educational Review* 9, no. 3 (1935): 71–72, 86.

48. Clyde Chitty, *Eugenics, Race, and Intelligence in Education* (New York: Continuum, 2007); Ann Gibson Winfield, *Eugenics and Education in America: Institutionalized Racism and the Implications of History, Ideology, and Memory* (New York: Peter Lang, 2007); William H. Watkins, *The White Architects of Black Education: Ideology and Power in America, 1865–1954* (New York: Teachers College Press, 2001): 242–40; Selden, *Inheriting Shame*; Barkan, *The Retreat of Scientific Racism*.

49. *Can You Name Them?* (New York: American Committee for Democracy and Intellectual Freedom, 1939): 5.

50. *Can You Name Them?* 6.

51. *Can You Name Them?* 8.

52. *Can You Name Them?* 14.

53. *Can You Name Them?* 3.

54. *Can You Name Them?* 2.

55. "Declares School Books Teach False Race Views," *Chicago Defender*, July 29, 1939, 3. Also see Kuznick, *Beyond the Laboratory*, 198–208.

56. *Can You Name Them?* front and back cover.

57. *Can You Name Them?* 1.

58. *Can You Name Them?* 11–12.

59. ACDIF, *Can You Name Them?*

60. *Can You Name Them?* 1.

61. American Committee on Democracy and Intellectual Freedom, "Races in a Democracy," June 26, 1939, radio script. American Committee for Democracy and Intellectual Freedom, "Democracy in Education," June 5, 1939. (RSC).

62. David H. Gelernter, *1939: The Lost World of the Fair* (New York: Free Press, 1995): 357.

63. "Race Theory Blasted in Fair's Book," *Chicago Defender* September 30, 1939: 4.

64. Kuznick, *Beyond the Laboratory*, 204.

65. "Dedicatory Exercises of the American Museum of Health, Held in the Hall of Man at the New York World's Fair, June 17, 1939," folder "Osborn, Frank," AESR. Also see: Robert W. Rydell, *World of Fairs: The Century-of-Progress Exhibitions* (Chicago: University of Chicago Press, 1993): 53–58.

66. Rydell notes that Boas first publicly criticized the eugenics movement in 1916, sparking contentious relations between cultural anthropologists and their allies in genetics against eugenicists that lasted well into the 1940s, see Rydell, *World of Fairs*, 53–55. Also see Peter J. Kuznick, "Losing the World of Tomorrow: The Battle over the Presentation of Science at the 1939 World's Fair," *American Quarterly* 46, no. 3 (1994): 341–73, especially 436–347 and 364–65.

67. African Americans led a vocal and sustained opposition to the New York World Fair's racist practices and exhibits, carried on largely through the NAACP, including pickets, antifair publications, and the black press. In 1940, African Americans as well as other prominent ethnic, racial, and religious groups were invited to celebrate their folk traditions for one special week. This celebration of America's diversity was part of the fair organizers' strategy to adjust to the hastening global conflict and increased possibility of world war. See Rydell chapter 6, "African Americans and the World of Tomorrow," especially 183–87.

68. *The Genetic Basis for Democracy*, 2.

69. The public panel at the 1939 World's Fair was a close reproduction of a panel Boas had organized in January of 1939 at the Columbia Men's Faculty Club, featuring Wallace, Boas, and Superintendent of New York City Public Schools Harold G. Campbell, entitled "Racial Theories and the Genetic Basis of Democracy." "Scientists to Open Drive for Freedom," *New York Times*, January 24, 1939, 21.

70. *The Genetic Basis for Democracy*, 12.

71. "Wallace Assails Race Prejudice," *New York Times*, October 15, 1939, 48.

72. *The Genetic Basis for Democracy*, 19.

73. *The Genetic Basis for Democracy*, 20.

74. *The Genetic Basis for Democracy*, 25.

75. *The Genetic Basis for Democracy*, 25.

76. Brett Gary, *The Nervous Liberals: Propaganda Anxieties from World War I to the Cold War* (New York: Columbia University Press, 1999): 1–11. Also see Daria Frezza, *The Leader and the Crowd: Democracy in American Public Discourse, 1880–1941* (Athens: University of Georgia Press, 2007).

77. Franz Boas to Frank Trager, June 30, 1939, 1. Folder 92, Box 5. American Jewish Committee, Executive Office, Morris Waldman Papers (MWP), YIVO Institute for Jewish Research, New York. Also see Frank N. Trager to Max M. Warburg November 3, 1939. Folder 92, Box 5 MWP. The scripts of these radio shows are available in the Radio Scripts Collection, 1937–1966. Manuscripts, Archive, and Rare Books Division, Schomberg Center for Research in Black Culture, New York Public Library, New York, NY.

78. Franz Boas to Frank Trager, June 30, 1939, 2.

79. Franz Boas, "Freedom Defined," and "Freedom of Thought." A description of the lesson on race by Franz Boas in the November 1939 issue of *Teaching Biologist* can be found in Barnet S. Minters, "Biology Can Promote Tolerance," *New York Teacher* 5, no. 1 (1939): 22.

80. Franz Boas to Harry Schneiderman, May 5, 1939. Folder 92, Box 5. American Jewish Committee, Executive Office, MWP.

81. This argument is explicit in the American Jewish Committee, *Annual Reports* (New York, 1933–44). Marc Dollinger claims the AJC was the most important American Jewish organization during the first half of the twentieth century (12). A general history of the AJC is: Naomi Cohen, *Not Free to Desist: The American Jewish Committee, 1906–1966* (Philadelphia: Jewish Publication Society of America, 1972). AJC activism during this era is also treated extensively in: Marc Dollinger, *Quest for Inclusion: Jews and Liberalism in Modern America* (Princeton, NJ: Princeton University Press, 2000). Dollinger's book is particularly useful for understanding how AJC politics differed from other Jewish organizations including the American Jewish Congress, the Anti-Defamation League of B'nai B'rith, and various Jewish Federation Councils. For an analysis of Jewish activism against prejudice, including tolerance education, see Svonkin, *Jews against Prejudice*. Cheryl Lynn Greenberg analyzes the course of black-Jewish relations in America through an analysis of the AJC and the NAACP. Cheryl Lynn Greenberg, *Troubling the Waters: Black-Jewish Relations in the American Century* (Princeton, NJ: University of Princeton Press, 2006).

82. Harry Schneiderman to Frank N. Trager October 3, 1939, 1. Folder 92, Box 5. American Jewish Committee, Executive Office, MWP; Frank N. Trager to Max M. Warburg November 3, 1939. Folder 92, Box 5. American Jewish Committee, Executive Office, MWP.

83. AJC leaders are not explicit in this logic, but a close reading of their memos shows a growing concern with Boas's social activism, especially his critique that anti-Semitism was the same as other forms of racism against people of African and Asian descent. AJC documents reveal that the organization does not want to associate with this kind of broader, antiracist activism, but instead to remain focused only on anti-Semitism, which it carefully distinguished from "racism." See for example, Franz Boas to Max M. Warburg October 12, 1939. Folder 92, Box 5 American Jewish Committee, Executive Office, MWP. Harry Schneiderman to Frank N. Trager October 3, 1939, p.1. Folder 92, Box 5. MWP. Frank N. Trager to Max M. Warburg November 3, 1939. Folder 92, Box 5. MWP.

84. Kuznick, *Beyond the Laboratory*, 208–26.

85. Melville J. Herskovits, *Franz Boas: The Science of Man in the Making* (New York, Charles Scribner's Sons, 1953): 119–20. Mead, *An Anthropologist at Work*, 355.

Chapter 3

1. Margaret Mead and James Baldwin, *A Rap on Race* (Philadelphia: J.B. Lippincott Company, 1971): 8.

2. Eduardo Bonilla-Silva, *Racism without Racists: Color-Blind Racism and the Persistence of Racial Inequality in the United States*, 3rd ed. (Lanham, MD: Rowman and Littlefield Publishers, 2009); Michael K. Brown, et al. *White-Washing Race: The Myth of a Color-blind Society* (Berkeley: University of California Press, 2005).

3. Describing DuBois to Baldwin, Mead explained, "She's got a lot of quality." Mead and Baldwin, *A Rap on Race*, 7. Mead also recommends Rachel Davis DuBois's neighborhood home festival technique in Margaret Mead, "Group Living as a Part of Intergroup Education Workshops," *Journal of Educational Sociology* 18, no. 9 (1945): 526–34, page 527.

4. Mead, "Group Living as a Part of Intergroup Education Workshops," 527–28.

5. For a consideration of Benedict and Mead as educators in the broadest sense, see: Jill B. R. Cherneff and Eve Hochwald, eds., *Visionary Observers: Anthropological Inquiry and Education* (Lincoln: University of Nebraska Press, 2006). Also see Calvin Irvin Saxton, "Educating for Worldmindedness: The Theories of Harry Stack Sullivan, Ruth Benedict, and Brock Chisholm, 1945–1950." Diss. University of Connecticut, 1995. Saxton focuses on Mead's educational theories in the postwar era, but he does not consider her activism in schools or her direct work with teachers.

6. Biographies of Benedict include: Virginia Heyer Young, *Ruth Benedict: Beyond Relativity, beyond Pattern* (Lincoln: University of Nebraska Press, 2005); Lois W. Banner, *Intertwined Lives: Margaret Mead, Ruth Benedict, and Their Circle* (New York: Alfred A. Knopf, 2003); Hilary Lapsley, *Margaret Mead and Ruth Benedict: The Kinship of Women* (Amherst: University of Massachusetts Press, 1999); Judith Schachter Modell, *Ruth Benedict: Patterns of a Life* (Philadelphia: University of Philadelphia Press, 1983); Margaret Mead, *Ruth Benedict* (New York: Columbia University Press, 1974); Margaret Mead, *An Anthropologist at Work: Writings of Ruth Benedict* (Boston: Houghton Mifflin Co., 1959).

7. Ruth Benedict, *Patterns of Culture* (Boston: Houghton Mifflin Co., 1989).

8. Margaret Mead, "Preface," (1958) in Ruth Benedict, *Patterns of Culture* (Boston: Houghton Mifflin Co., 1989): xi. Warren Susman contends that *Patterns of Culture* popularized the anthropological definition of culture in the 1930s. *Culture as History: The Transformation of American Society in the Twentieth Century* (New York: Pantheon Books, 1984): 153–54. Susan Hegeman locates both Benedict and Mead within a group of Boas students who basically viewed culture as "a system of meaning making" (9). Agreeing with Susman, Hegeman explains, "It is this strain of Boasian thinking about culture that had the greatest impact on the popular imagination" (9). Susan Hegeman, *Patterns for America: Modernism and the Concept of Culture* (Princeton, NJ: Princeton University Press, 1999).

9. See Mead, "Preface," xi.

10. Merwyn S. Garbarino, *Sociocultural Theory in Anthropology: A Short History* (Prospect Heights, IL: Waveland Press, 1983): 66. For a critical analysis of Benedict's theory of culture as developed in *Patterns of Culture*, see Richard Handler, *Critics against Culture: Anthropological Observers of Mass Society* (Madison, WI: University of Wisconsin Press, 2005): 123–40.

11. Over the course of her career, Benedict worked out a unique version of Boasian culture that Richard Handler describes as a "comparative hermeneutic." Handler examines the evolution of Benedict's culture concept in the chapter "Ruth Benedict and the Modernist Sensibility" in *Critics against Culture*, 123–40. He notes that while Benedict's *Patterns of Culture* has been read by "several generations of American college students," most of these students fail to grasp the full theoretical depth of Benedict's conception of culture (137), a claim that helps to explain why it was so difficult for American school teachers in the 1940s, most of whom had very little formal training in anthropology, to accurately understand and translate what Benedict meant when she talked about "culture."

12. Mead, *An Anthropologist at Work*, 348.

13. Modell, *Ruth Benedict*, 248–49; Mead, *An Anthropologist at Work*, 350.

14. Modell, *Ruth Benedict*, 265.

15. Nicholas V. Montalto, *A History of the Intercultural Education Movement*, (New York: Garland): 133.

16. Montalto, *A History of the Intercultural Education Movement*, 138.

17. Montalto, *A History of the Intercultural Education Movement*, 137–39; Diana Selig, *Americans All: The Cultural Gifts Movement* (Cambridge, MA: Harvard University Press, 2008): 418.

18. Rachel Davis DuBois and Emma Schweppe, *The Germans in American Life* (New York: Thomas Nelson and Sons, 1936): 7–8. Also see Rachel Davis DuBois and Emma Schweppe, *The Jews in American Life* (New York: Thomas Nelson and Sons, 1935).

19. DuBois and Schweppe, *The Germans in American Life*, 8.

20. Ruth Benedict, "Privileged Classes: An Anthropological Problem," *Frontiers of Democracy* 7, no. 58 (1941):110–12.

21. See footnote on page 110, in Benedict "Privileged Classes."

22. Benedict, "Privileged Classes," 110.

23. Montalto, *A History of the Intercultural Education Movement*, 137–39; Diana Selig, *Americans All*, 418.

24. Ruth Benedict, "Anthropology and Some Modern Alarmists," 4; March 10, 1941. The Anna Howard Show Memorial Lectureship of Bryn Mawr College. Box 58, Folder 6, Ruth Fulton Benedict Papers (RFBP), Archives and Special Collections Library, Vassar College, Poughkeepsie, NY.

25. John Higham, *Strangers in the Land: Patterns of American Nativism, 1860–1925* (New York: Atheneum, 1963). Chapter 11 describes the passing of national origin laws in the 1920s and the recession of nativist sentiment after 1924. Also see Philip Gleason, "Americans All: World War II and the Shaping of American Identity," *Review of Politics* 43, no. 4 (1981): 483–518.

26. Ruth Benedict, "America's Racial Myths," 1942? 12–13. Folder 3, Box 58, RFBP.

27. Benedict, "Anthropology and Some Modern Alarmists," 4.

28. Benedict, "Anthropology and Some Modern Alarmists," 4.

29. Ruth Benedict, "American Melting Pot, 1942 Model," in Department of Supervisors and Directors of Instruction of the National Education Association, *Americans All: Studies in Intercultural Education* (Washington, DC: Department of Supervisors and Directors of Instruction, 1942): 14–24, quote page 22.

30. Benedict, "American Melting Pot, 1942 Model," 23.

31. Benedict, "American Melting Pot, 1942 Model," 22.

32. Benedict, "American Melting Pot, 1942 Model," 20.

33. Ruth Benedict, "Victory over Discrimination and Hate," *Frontiers of Democracy* 9, no. 73 (1942):

34. Benedict, "Victory over Discrimination and Hate," 81–82.

35. Ruth Benedict and Mildred Ellis, "Race and Cultural Relations: America's Answer to the Myth of a Master Race," *Problems in American Life: Unit No. 5* (Washington D.C.: National Education Association, 1942).

36. Benedict and Ellis, "Race and Cultural Relations," 44.

37. Benedict and Ellis, "Race and Cultural Relations," 45–60.

38. Violet Edwards, "Note on 'The Races of Mankind,'" in Ruth Benedict, *Race: Science and Politics* (New York: Viking, 1945): 167–68.

39. For an overview of Weltfish and her role in this publication see Earl Conrad, "A Big 'A' in Anthropology," *Chicago Defender*, April 28, 1945, 11. Also see Virginia Heyer Young, "Ruth Benedict: Relativist and Universalist," 25–54, and Juliet Niehaus, "Education and Democracy in the Anthropology of Gene Weltfish," 87–118, both in Cherneff and Hochwald, *Visionary Observers.*

40. "Army Drops Race Equality Book: Denies May's Stand Was Reason," *New York Times*, March 6, 1944, 1.

41. "Plans New Edition of Race Pamphlet," *New York Times*, March 8, 1944, 11.

42. "Hits 'Races of Mankind': House Group Says Book Army Used Has Misstatements," *New York Times*, April 28, 1944, 7.

43. Edwards, "Note on 'The Races of Mankind,'" 168. According to David Price, the FBI targeted both Benedict and Weltfish as potential "subversives" because of *The Races of Mankind.* David Price, *Threatening Anthropology: McCarthyism and the FBI's Surveillance of Activist Anthropologists* (Durham, NC: Duke University Press, 2004): 113–35.

44. Ruth Benedict and Gene Weltfish, *The Races of Mankind.* Public Affairs Pamphlet No. 85 (New York: Public Affairs Committee, 1943): 3.

45. Benedict and Weltfish, *The Races of Mankind*, 5.

46. Benedict and Weltfish, *The Races of Mankind*, 16–17.

47. Benedict and Weltfish, *The Races of Mankind*, 22.

48. In the 1940s American scientists generally recognized three racial categories: Mongoloid, Negroid, and Caucasian. Yet, within this tripartite division scientists emphasized that ideas about race were the products of history and contemporary political and social relations. They increasingly refused to associate behavior or intelligence, for example, with race. This position solidified as the dominant, but not the only, position on racial difference by the

end of World War II in disciplines like anthropology, sociology, and psychology. See Matthew Frye Jacobson, *Whiteness of a Different Color: European Immigrants and the Alchemy of Race* (Cambridge, MA: Harvard University Press, 1998): 98–111. Elazar Barkan, *The Retreat of Scientific Racism: Changing Concepts of Race in Britain and the United States between the World Wars* (Cambridge: Cambridge University Press, 1992): 279–340; Audrey Smedley, *Race in North America: Origin and Evolution of a Worldview*, 2nd ed. (Boulder, CO: Westview Press, 1999): 310–18; Thomas F. Gossett, *Race: The History of an Idea in America*, rev. ed. (New York: Oxford University Press, 1997): 409–30.

49. Benedict and Weltfish, *Races of Mankind*, 22–23.

50. "Army Drops Race Equality Book," 1.

51. "Races of Mankind" is one of many pamphlets promoted by the New York City Board of Education's Advisory Committee on Human Relations. See Series 562: Advisory Committee on Human Relations, 1945–1950, Folder 4, New York City Board of Education Records, Municipal Archives, New York. For a description of the poster series in Detroit, see Marion Edman, "Building Unity within a Community," *Elementary English Review* 21, no. 5 (1944): 179–85.

52. George F. Zook to Ruth Benedict, March 16, 1944. Folder 2, Box 19, RFBP.

53. "Intergroup Relations in Teaching Materials: Summary Statement," 1–2, January 20, 1947. Folder 2, Box 19, RFBP.

54. "Memorandum Concerning Survey of Intercultural Influences in Basic Teaching Materials," 2, May 18, 1944. Folder 2, Box 19, RFBP.

55. "Intergroup Relations in Teaching Materials: Summary Statement," 4.

56. "Intergroup Relations in Teaching Materials: Summary Statement," 4.

57. Benjamin Fine, "Survey Finds That Textbooks and Study Course Revision Could Aid Intergroup Relations," *New York Times,* January 26, 1947, E9.

58. Fine, "Survey Finds That Textbooks and Study Course Revision Could Aid Intergroup Relations."

59. Ruth Benedict, "Racism Is Vulnerable," *English Journal* 35, no. 6 (1946): 299–302.

60. Benedict, "Racism Is Vulnerable," 301.

61. Benedict, "Racism Is Vulnerable," 302.

62. Ruth Benedict, "Can Cultural Patterns Be Directed?" *Intercultural Education News* 9, no. 2 (1948): 3.

63. Margaret Mead, *Blackberry Winter: My Earlier Years* (New York: Morrow, 1984): 121–22. Also see Nancy C. Lutkehaus, *Margaret Mead: The Making of an American Icon* (Princeton, NJ: Princeton University Press, 2008); Maureen Malloy, *On Creating a Useable Culture: Margaret Mead and the Emergence of American Cosmopolitanism* (Honolulu: University of Hawaii Press, 2008); Filipe Carreira da Silva, *Mead and Modernity: Science, Selfhood, and Democratic Politics* (New York: Lexington Books, 2008); Ray McDermott, "A Century of Margaret Mead," in Cherneff and Hochwald, *Visionary Observers*, 55–86; Handler, *Critics against Culture*; Banner, *Intertwined Lives*; Clifford Geertz, *Margaret Mead, 1901–1978: A Biographical Memoir* (Washington, DC: National Academy of Science, 1989); Jane Howard, *Margaret Mead, A Life* (New York: Simon and Schuster, 1984); Rhoda Metraux, ed., *Margaret Mead: Some Personal Views* (New York: Walker and Company, 1979), especially chapter 9, "Education," 195–210.

64. The president of the AMNH in 1926 was Henry Fairfield Osborne, a committed eugenicist. Until 1945, the museum took a strong position in favor of eugenic science including selective breeding programs, however Mead's work stood in stark contrast to eugenicists like Osborne. In 1942 the museum abruptly abandoned its support of eugenics and began promoting antiracist programs of education dedicated to improving tolerance for racial minorities. For more see Selden, *Inheriting Shame: The Story of Eugenics and Racism in America* (New York: Teachers College Press, 1999); Brian Regal, *Henry Fairfield Osborn: Race, and the Search for the Origins of Man* (Lincolnshire, UK: Ashgate, 2002). Information about education programs at the AMNH can be found in American Museum of Natural

History, Annual Reports, AMNH Archives, New York. See report of the president, A. Perry Osborne, 74th annual report, 1942, 2–3 on new effort to teach scientifically accurate definitions of race to promote tolerance.

65. Margaret Mead, "Group Intelligence Tests and Linguistic Disability among Italian Children," *School and Society* 25 (1927): 465–67. In container I1, Margaret Mead Papers and the South Pacific Ethnographic Archives (MMP), Manuscript Division, Library of Congress, Washington, DC. Mead had published a similar article while completing her master's thesis on the subject at Barnard. Margaret Mead, "The Methodology of Racial Testing, Its Significance for Sociology," *The American Journal of Sociology*, 31 (July 1925–May 1926): 657–67. Container I1, MMP.

66. On social efficiency experts, IQ tests, and public school curricula see Herbert M. Kliebard, *The Struggle for the American Curriculum, 1893–1958* (New York: RoutledgeFalmer, 2004): 76–129.

67. Mead, "Group Intelligence Tests and Linguistic Disability among Italian Children," 467.

68. Margaret Mead, "The Need for Teaching Anthropology in Normal Schools and Teachers Colleges" *School and Society* 26, no. 667 (1927): 464–67, quote page 467. Container I1, MMP.

69. See pamphlet: "Backgrounds for Progressive School Units," The American Museum of Natural History in collaboration with The Metropolitan Museum of Art. Also see Mead's notes on the lecture series, "Provisional List of Primitive Units for Backgrounds Course," both in Container E106, Progressive Education Association, 1930–35, MMP.

70. Margaret Mead, *Growing Up in New Guinea: A Comparative Study of Primitive Education* (New York: W. Morrow, 1930).

71. Mead, "Backgrounds for Progressive School Units," 1.

72. Kliebard, *The Struggle for the American Curriculum*, 163. For a review of social meliorism and the PEA see 151–74.

73. American Historical Association, *Conclusions and Recommendations of the Commission on the Social Studies* (New York: Charles Scribner's Sons, 1934): 75–76.

74. Kliebard, *The Struggle for the American Curriculum*, 166. Also see Patricia Alberg Graham, *Progressive Education: From Arcady to Academe, A History of the Progressive Education Association, 1919–1955* (New York: Teachers College Press, 1967): 64–75.

75. Howard, *Margaret Mead*, 176–77.

76. V. T. Thayer to Margaret Mead, February 27, 1935, Container E106, MMP.

77. V. T. Thayer to Margaret Mead, June 5, 1935, Container E106, MMP. For an overview of the Commission on the Secondary School Curriculum and V. T. Thayer, see Graham, *Progressive Education*, 135–38.

78. Margaret Mead, Abstract of Dr. Margaret Mead's Speech to be delivered before the Progressive Education Association, General Meeting, Friday, November 23, "Youth and Civilization." Container E106 MMP.

79. Margaret Mead, "Suggestions for Working Out the Backgrounds for the Case Studies on Adolescents," 1935, p. 7, Container I8, MMP.

80. Margaret Mead, "The Student of Race Problems Can Say," *Frontiers of Democracy* 6 no. 53 (1940): 200–202: 200.

81. Mead, "The Student of Race Problems Can Say," 201.

82. Mead, "The Student of Race Problems Can Say," 202.

83. Howard, *Margaret Mead*, 232–34.

84. Margaret Mead and Kurt Lewin, "The Small Conference," in the National Research Council, Problem of Changing Food Habits, National Council Bulletin No. 108, October 1943, 113. As quoted in Howard, *Margaret Mead*, 233.

85. Margaret Mead, "Food Can Be a Bridge between Different Groups," Learning to Live in One World, April 6, 1945, Container E58, MMP.

86. Janet L. Abu-Lughod, *Race, Space, and Riots in New York, Chicago, and Los Angeles* (New York: Oxford University Press, 2007); Eduardo Obregon Pagan, *Murder at the Sleepy*

Lagoon: Zoot Suits, Race, and Riot in Wartime L.A. (Chapel Hill: University of North Carolina Press, 2006); Dominic J. Capeci Jr. and Martha Wilkerson, *Layered Violence: The Detroit Rioters of 1943* (Jackson: University of Mississippi Press, 1991); Mauricio Mazon, *The Zoot Suit Riots: The Psychology of Symbolic Annihilation* (Austin: University of Texas Press, 1988); Dominic J. Capeci Jr., *The Harlem Riot of 1943* (Philadelphia: Temple University Press, 1977).

87. Rachel Davis DuBois, "A Statement on the Aims, Works, Possibilities, and Needs of the Intercultural Education Workshop," 1943–1944, p. 7, Container E168, MMP.

88. Rachel Davis DuBois, Report of the Intercultural Education Workshop Activities for the Winter and Spring 1945, pp. 2 and 8, Container E168, MMP.

89. DuBois, Report of the Intercultural Education Workshop Activities for the Winter and Spring 1945, 2 and 8; see also Margaret Mead, "Group Living as Part of Intergroup Education Workshops," 526–34; "Wellesley School of Community Affairs," *Progressive Education* 22 no. 4 (1945):4–8.

90. Rachel Davis DuBois, *Get Together Americans: Friendly Approaches to Racial and Cultural Conflicts through the Neighborhood-Home Festival* (New York: Harper and Brothers, 1943). DuBois cites Mead on page 11. Rachel Davis DuBois, *Build Together Americans: Adventures in Intercultural Education for the Secondary School* (New York: Hinds, Hayden, and Eldredge, 1945), Mead is cited on pages x, 11, 17, 46. Rachel Davis DuBois, *Neighbors in Action: A Manual for Local Leaders in Intergroup Relations* (New York: Harper and Brothers, 1950), Mead is cited on pages 12, 27, 95–96, 102, 105, 193.

91. DuBois, Report of the Intercultural Education Workshop Activities for the Winter and Spring 1945, 6.

92. Dorothy Spaulding, "Work, Sing and Eat," *Intercultural Education News* 7 no. 3, (April 1946): 2. Container E168, MMP. See also "Your Winter Festivals" and "Bread Festival" both in *Newsletter of the Workshop for Cultural Democracy* 1, no. 2 (winter 1947): 1–2. Container E168, MMP.

93. "Bread Festival," 2.

94. "A Spring Festival," *Newsletter of the Workshop for Cultural Democracy* 1, no. 4 (spring-summer 1948): 2.

95. Rachel Davis DuBois, "Build Together Americans," (New York: Intercultural Education Workshop, 1945): 1, Container E168, MMP. (Italics in original.) Not to be confused with the textbook of the same name.

96. Mead, "Group Living as a Part of Intergroup Education," 533.

97. Downtown Community School Pamphlet, 1944, in Box 14, Folder 4, Charles James Hendley Papers, TAM 109, Tamiment Library/Robert F. Wagner Labor Archives, Elmer Holmes Bobst Library, New York, NY. Also see Carleton Mabee, "Margaret Mead and a 'Pilot Experiment' in Progressive and Interracial Education: The Downtown Community School," *New York History* 65, no. 1 (1984): 5–31.

98. Earl Conrad, "Ethnology of Jim Crow," *Chicago Defender*, February 9, 1946, 13.

99. Mabee, "Margaret Mead and a 'Pilot Experiment' in Progressive and Interracial Education," 30–31.

100. Margaret Mead, "Intercultural Relations—A Priority in 1945," The Bookshelf National Board of the Young Women's Christian Association (February 1945): 1. Container I28, MMP.

101. Rachel Davis DuBois to Margaret Mead, 16 December 1947, Container E168, MMP.

102. Library of Congress, "Margaret Mead: Human Nature and the Power of Culture." Interactive Web site, created February 16, 2006. Viewed July 13, 2010. http://www.loc.gov/exhibits/mead. Also see the Web site for the Institute for Intercultural Studies, http://www.interculturalstudies.org. Viewed July 13, 2010. The Institute for Intercultural Studies was dissolved in 2009.

103. Margaret Mead, *The School in American Culture* (Cambridge, MA: Harvard University Press, 1951).

104. Margaret Mead, Intercultural Education, 1, Container I76, MMP. See also Fannie Speiser to Margaret Mead, February 16, 1955, Container I76, MMP.
105. Margaret Mead, Intercultural Education, 2–4, Container I76, MMP.
106. Mead, Intercultural Education, 8.
107. Mead, Intercultural Education, 9.

Chapter 4

1. Margaret Gillum, "Internationalism at Home: An Experiment with Sophomores," *English Journal* 30, no. 1 (1941): 63–66, quote page 63.
2. Gillum, "Internationalism at Home," 65.
3. Gillum, "Internationalism at Home," 64.
4. Gillum, "Internationalism at Home," 65.
5. Gillum, "Internationalism at Home," 65.
6. Bruce Baum, *The Rise and Fall of the Caucasian Race: A Political History of Racial Identity* (New York: New York University Press, 2006); David R. Roediger, *Working toward Whiteness: How America's Immigrants Became White* (New York: Basic Books, 2005); Thomas A. Guglielmo, *White on Arrival: Italians, Race, Color, and Power in Chicago, 1890–1945* (New York: Oxford University Press, 2003); Gary Gerstle, *American Crucible: Race and Nation in the Twentieth Century* (Princeton, NJ: Princeton University Press, 2001); Audrey Smedley, *Race in North America: Origin and Evolution of a Worldview*, 2nd ed. (Boulder, CO: Westview Press, 1999); Matthew Frye Jacobson, *Whiteness of a Different Color: European Immigrants and the Alchemy of Race* (Cambridge, MA: Harvard University Press, 1998).
7. Annette Smith Lawrence, "The Pot's Boilin'," *Elementary English Review* 21, no. 3 (1944): 95–96, 98, quote page 95.
8. Peter Cannici, "America . . . Melting Pot of Prejudices," *New Jersey Educational Review* 18, no. 5 (1945): 156.
9. John D. Donohue, "Further Thoughts on Intercultural Education," *High Points* 27, no. 1 (1945): 14–19, quote page 19.
10. The unit "Education and Race Prejudice" is described in Donohue, "Further Thoughts on Intercultural Education," 19. Albert V. DeBonis, "Tolerance and Democracy: A Program for the English Class," *English Journal* 30, no. 2 (1941): 123–30. Clair S. Wightman, "This Hate Business," *New Jersey Educational Review* 15, no. 6 (1942): 166. The Franz Boas workshop is described on page 21 in William H. Bristow, "Intercultural Education: Problems and Solutions," *High Points* 25, no. 8 (1943): 14–26.
11. Joseph Singerman, "The Spirit of Franz Boas Lives," *Science Teacher* 10, no. 1 (1943): 20–21, quote page 28.
12. Madeline R. Morgan, "Chicago Schools Teach Negro History," *Elementary English Review* 21, no. 3 (1944): 105–9, quote page 108.
13. Jean Wagner, "An Eighth Grade Studies Racial Intolerance," *Social Education* 10, no. 2 (1946): 75–77. One pamphlet on intercultural education made this connection explicitly, and featured a photograph of a Nazi concentration camp next to a photograph of four white men chasing a lone black man down an American city street. The caption read, "This can lead to this," drawing a connection between the first photograph and the second. Flyer from the American Council on Race Relations in Chicago, no date, found in Folder 4, Box 50, Leonard Covello Papers (hereafter LCP), MSS 40, Research Library of the Balch Institute for Ethnic Studies, Historical Society of Pennsylvania, Philadelphia, PA.
14. John P. Jackson, *Social Scientists for Social Justice: Making the Case against Segregation* (New York: New York University Press, 2001); Daniel Perlstein, "American Dilemmas: Education, Social Science and the Limits of Liberalism," in *The Global Color Line: Racial and Ethnic Inequality and Struggle from a Global Perspective*, ed. Pinar Batur and Joe R. Feagin (Stamford, CT: JAI Press, 1999): 357–79; Stuart Svonkin, *Jews against Prejudice: American Jews and the Fight for Civil Liberties* (New York: Columbia University Press, 1997); Walter

A. Jackson, *Gunnar Myrdal and America's Conscience: Social Engineering and Racial Liberalism, 1938–1987* (Chapel Hill: The University of North Carolina Press, 1990).

15. "Teachers Urge Americanism in Racial Strife," *Chicago Daily Tribune*, December 5, 1943, 29.

16. M. M. Mandl, "Teaching Tolerance in the High Schools," *High Points* 23, no. 6 (1941): 61–63, quote page 61.

17. Edgar Dale, "The Price of Prejudice," *High Points* 27, no. 5 (1945): 13–17, quote page 13.

18. Daniel Kryder, *Divided Arsenal: Race and the American State during World War II* (Cambridge: Cambridge University Press, 2000); Ronald Takaki, *Double Victory: A Multicultural History of America in World War II* (Boston: Little, Brown, 2000); John W. Dower, *War without Mercy: Race and Power in the Pacific War* (New York: Pantheon Books, 1986); Philip Gleason, "Americans All: World War II and the Shaping of American Identity," *Review of Politics* 43, no. 4 (1981): 483–518. On the impact of World War II on American schools, see: Charles Dorn, *American Education, Democracy, and the Second World War* (New York: Palgrave Macmillan, 2007); Gerard Giordano, *Wartime Schools: How World War II Changed American Education* (New York: Peter Lang, 2004); Robert Shafer, "Multicultural Education in New York City during World War II," *New York History* 77, no. 3 (1996): 301–32; Thomas James, *Exile Within: The Schooling of Japanese Americans, 1942–1945* (Cambridge, MA: Harvard University Press, 1987); Isaac L. Kandel, *The Impact of the War upon American Education* (Chapel Hill: University of North Carolina Press, 1948).

19. Benjamin Fine, "Schools to Open Tolerance Drive," *New York Times*, January 16, 1938, 46. Also see: "Lesson Plans for Democracy," *New York Teacher* 4, no. 6 (1939): 171–79; "Commissioner Boosts Tolerance Programs," *New York Teacher* 4, no. 5 (1939): 1; Celia Lewis, "Schools for Tolerance," *New York Teacher* 4, no. 3 (1938): 10–11.

20. Chidnoff Arthur Studios, "Drive to Teach Tolerance Ideal," *New York Times*, March 5, 1939, D9. Also see Robert L. Fleegler, "'Forget All Differences until the Forces of Freedom Are Triumphant': The World War II–Era Quest for Racial and Religious Tolerance," *Journal of American Ethnic History* 27, no. 2 (2008): 59–84.

21. Fine, "Schools to Open Tolerance Drive," 46; Studios, "Drive to Teach Tolerance Ideal." Also see Shaffer, "Multicultural Education in New York City during World War II."

22. Diana Selig, *Americans All: The Cultural Gifts Movement* (Cambridge, MA: Harvard University Press, 2008); Daryl Michael Scott, *Contempt and Pity: Social Policy and the Image of the Damaged Black Psyche, 1880–1996* (Chapel Hill: The University of North Carolina Press, 1997): 19–40; Gleason, "Americans All"; Jackson, *Gunnar Myrdal and America's Conscience*, chapter 7.

23. Benjamin Fine, "Schools Fight Racial Hatred," *New York Times*, February 12, 1939, 58.

24. There were at least nine articles with "tolerance" in the headlines of the *New York Times* in 1938 and nineteen articles in 1939. For debates on the meaning of tolerance see "Dr. Fosdick Places Limit on Tolerance," *New York Times*, January 17, 1938, 20. On tolerance rally, "Tolerance Rally Set for April 14," *New York Times*, April 2, 1939, 29. On tolerance buttons, "Tolerance Buttons on Way," *New York Times*, April 7, 1939, 7.

25. "Roosevelt Backs Tolerance Drive," *New York Times*, June 26, 1939, 4. Also see "Class Clashes Called Path to Dictator in U.S." *Washington Post*, July 6, 1939, 6. Robert Fleegler describes FDR's initiative to promote tolerance for minorities in "Forget All Differences until the Forces of Freedom Are Triumphant," 63.

26. Fleegler, "Forget All Differences until the Forces of Freedom Are Triumphant," 62.

27. Perlstein, "American Dilemmas"; Fleegler, "'Forget All Differences until the Forces of Freedom Are Triumphant.'"

28. "Prejudice Scored as Bar to Culture," *New York Times*, May 14, 1939, 61.

29. "Bleakley Urges Loyalty," *New York Times*, December 27, 1938, 18.

30. "New York Praised for Tolerance Aid," *New York Times*, January 2, 1939, 24. On Rachel Davis DuBois's approach to intercultural education, see Selig, *Americans All*, and Nicholas

V. Montalto, *A History of the Intercultural Education Movement, 1924–1941* (New York: Garland, 1982).

31. See the special intercultural issue of the *Elementary English Review* entitled, "One Land, One Language, One People," 21, no. 3 (1944). For a sample of the new intercultural textbooks that translated social science theories on racial prejudice into classroom tolerance education, see: Alain Locke and Bernhard J. Stern, *When Peoples Meet: A Study in Race and Culture Contacts*, rev. ed. (New York: Hinds, Hayden and Eldredge, 1949); Rachel Davis DuBois, *Build Together Americans: Adventures in Intercultural Education for the Secondary School* (New York: Hinds, Hayden, and Eldredge, 1945); Hortense Powdermaker, *Probing Our Prejudices* (New York: Harper and Brothers, 1944); Rachel Davis DuBois, *Get Together Americans: Friendly Approaches to Racial and Cultural Conflicts through the Neighborhood-Home Festival* (New York: Harper and Brothers, 1943); William E. Vickery and Stewart G. Cole, *Intercultural Education in American Schools: Proposed Objectives and Methods* (New York: Harper and Brothers, 1943); Department of Supervisors and Directors of Instruction of the National Education Association, *Americans All: Adventures in Intercultural Education* (Washington, DC: Department of Supervisors and Directors of Instruction, 1942). In addition to the *Elementary English Review*, the following educational journals devoted entire issues to intercultural education: "Workshops in Intergroup Education," special issue, *Journal of Educational Sociology* 18, no. 9 (1945): 513–72; Martin D. Jenkins, ed. "Education for Racial Understanding," special issue, *Journal of Negro Education* 13, no. 3 (1944): 265–446; Everett Ross Clinchy, ed., "United We'll Stand," special issue, *Journal of Educational Sociology* 16, no. 6 (1943): 321–400.

32. Vickery and Cole, *Intercultural Education in American Schools*, 42.

33. "Confine Hatred to Hitler Only, Educators Told," *The Atlanta Constitution*, November 22, 1941, 1.

34. Sterling A. Brown, "One Language, One People," in *Sterling A. Brown's A Negro Looks at the South*, ed. John Edgar Tidwell and Mark A. Sanders (New York: Oxford University Press, 2007): 218–21, quote page 220.

35. Clarence I. Chatto, *The Story of the Springfield Plan* (New York: Barnes and Noble, 1945); James W. Wise, *The Springfield Plan* (New York: Viking, 1945); Alice L. Halligan, "A Community's Total War against Prejudice," *Journal of Educational Sociology* 16, no. 6 (1943): 374–80; Benjamin Fine, "Tolerance Plan Called Success at Springfield," *New York Times*, December 7, 1941, D6.

36. Cherry A. McGee Banks, "The Intergroup Education Movement," in James A. Banks, ed., *Multicultural Education, Transformative Knowledge, and Action: Historical and Contemporary Perspectives* (New York: Teachers College Press, 1996): 252–55.

37. Stewart G. Cole, I. James Quillen, and Mildred J. Wise, *Charting Intercultural Education, 1945–55* (Stanford, CA: Stanford University Press, 1946).

38. Herbert L. Seamans, "1945 Summer Workshops in Intergroup Education," *Journal of Educational Sociology* 18, no. 9 (1945): 569–72. This article was in a special issue of the *Journal of Educational Sociology* called "Workshops in Intercultural Education," 18, no. 9 (1945): 513–73, where every article described ongoing intercultural programs nationwide.

39. Abigail J. Stewart, "'I've Got to Try to Make a Difference': A White Woman in the Civil Rights Movement," in *Women's Untold Stories: Breaking Silence, Talking Back, Voicing Complexity*, ed. Mary Romero and Abigail J. Stewart (New York: Routledge, 1999): 195–211. Jonathan Zimmerman, "*Brown*-ing the American Textbook: History, Psychology, and the Origins of Modern Multiculturalism," *History of Education Quarterly* 44, no. 1 (2004): 46–69.

40. Results of the NEA survey were reported in: Leo Shapiro, "Intergroup Education," *Common Ground* 7, no. 1 (1946): 102–4. For a survey of intercultural programs as practiced in every school district in the state of New York, see: *Education for Unity in the*

Schools of New York State: A Report on the Program of Intergroup Education in New York State Schools (Albany: The University of the State of New York, 1947). Also see a national survey conducted by a professor of education at Teachers College: Marjorie B. Smiley et al., "Intercultural Education in English Classrooms: An Informal Survey," *English Journal* 35, no. 6 (1946): 337–49.

41. Zoë Burkholder, "From Forced Tolerance to Forced Busing: Wartime Intercultural Education and the Rise of Black Educational Activism in Boston, 1943–1965," *Harvard Educational Review* 80, no. 3 (2010): 293–326.

42. Joseph Bellafiore, "Intercultural Understanding through World Study," *English Journal* 30, no. 8 (1941): 640–44, quote page 640.

43. Rachel Davis DuBois, "Peace and Intercultural Education," *Journal of Educational Sociology* 12, no. 7 (1939): 418–24, quote page 418.

44. Ruth Bynum, "Developing World-Friendship through a Study of Immigrants," *English Journal* 29, no. 1 (1940): 61–64, quotes page 61 and 64.

45. Beatrice DeLima Meyers, "On Common Ground with Children's Books," *Common Ground* 1, no. 1 (1940): 101–3, quote page 101. Diana Selig offers a thoughtful critique of the cultural-gifts paradigm in *Americans All*; also see Michael R. Olneck, "The Recurring Dream: Symbolism and Ideology in Intercultural and Multicultural Education," *American Journal of Education* 98 (1990): 147–74.

46. William Suchy, "The High School in a New-Immigrant Community," *Common Ground* 1, no. 1 (1940): 89–91, quote page 89.

47. Suchy, "The High School in a New-Immigrant Community," 90.

48. J. M. Klotsche, "What the Schools Can Do to Promote International Goodwill," *Social Studies* 31, no. 1 (1940): 3–6, quote page 3.

49. Klotsche, "What the Schools Can Do to Promote International Goodwill," 4.

50. Max Rosenberg, "Differences and Similarities in the Study of Man," *Social Studies* 31, no. 5 (1940): 223–24; Herbert E. Bolton, "Cultural Cooperation with Latin America," *Journal of the National Education Association* 29, no. 1 (1940): 1–2; Bynum, "Developing World-Friendship through a Study of Immigrants"; Francis Hutchinson, "A Tussle with Americanism," *English Journal* 29, no. 9 (1940): 755–57.

51. Otto G. Hoiberg, "Culture-Conflict in the Public Schools," *Journal of the National Education Association* 29, no. 2 (1940): 40–41; Joshua Hochstein, "Inter-American Education at Evander Childs High School," *High Points* 22, no. 7 (1940): 54–65.

52. Jeanora Don Wingate, "Intercultural Education," *Journal of the National Education Association* 29, no. 9 (1940): 269.

53. Wingate, "Intercultural Education," 269.

54. Wingate, "Intercultural Education."

55. William Suchy, "It Can Be Done," *Common Ground* 3, no. 3 (spring 1943): 104–6, quote page 105.

56. Wingate, "Intercultural Education." For a similar lesson on teaching tolerance for Italian Americans and Jews, see Julius G. Rothenberg, "Teaching Tolerance and Democracy: A Lesson Unit on the Letter of Complaint," *English Journal* 29, no. 9 (1940): 747–51.

57. Joshua Hochstein, "Inter-Americanism Challenges Our Schools," *High Points* 24, no. 10 (1942): 35–44, quote page 35.

58. The quote on "loyal cooperation" comes from "Spread of Bigotry Seen by Educators," *New York Times*, May 12, 1940, 12. Also see, Blanche E. Door, "A Pan-American Unit on English," *English Journal* 30, no. 5 (1941): 383–86; "The People Next Door," *New Jersey Educational Review* 15, no. 2 (1941): 65; Katherine Hosmer, "I Go Pan-American," *New Jersey Educational Review* 15, no. 2 (1941): 63; "Pan American Exhibit at Seth Boyden School," *New Jersey Educational Review* 13, no. 5 (1940): 151; Paul J. Scheips, "Education, the Basis of Pan Americanism," *Journal of the National Education Association* 29, no. 9 (1940): 267–68.

59. Albert V. DeBonis, "Tolerance and Democracy: A Program for the English Class," *English Journal* 30, no. 2 (1941):123–30.

60. "Spread of Bigotry Seen by Educators," 12.

61. DeBonis, "Tolerance and Democracy," 127.

62. The following articles illustrate a diversity of intercultural education in schools nation-wide: Minneapolis, Minnesota: "High School Democracy," *Common Ground* 1, no. 13 (spring 1941): 112. Hamtramck, Michigan: "Hamtramck Experiment in Social Studies," *Common Ground* 1, no. 13 (1941): 115–16. St. Louis, Missouri: Helen Gamble "Children's Literature and Pan-American Relations," *Elementary English Review* 18, no. 8 (1941): 283–87, 290. Laramie, Wyoming: Harriet Knight Orr, "History Textbooks and International Attitudes," *Social Studies* 32, no. 6 (1941): 254–55. New York, New York: Hymen Alpern, "A Broader Base for Teaching Tolerance," *Journal of the National Education Association* 30, no. 2 (1941): 47–48.

63. Jenny L. Mayer, "One Teacher Is Doing This," *Common Ground* 1, no. 13 (spring 1941): 112–14, quote page 113.

64. Leon Lapp and Marie Atkinson, "A Study of Negro Life," *English Journal* 29, no. 8 (1940): 659–61; Floyd Simpson, "Teaching Racial Tolerance in the South," *Social Education* 4, no. 8 (1940): 549–52; J. Pope Dyer, "A Unit in Interracial Understanding," *Social Studies* 30, no. 2 (1939): 79–80; Rolphe Lanier Hunt, "What Do We Teach about the Negro," *Journal of the National Education Association* 28, no. 1 (1939): 11–12.

65. Lapp and Atkinson, "A Study of Negro Life," 660.

66. Lapp and Atkinson, "A Study of Negro Life," 661.

67. Selig, *Americans All*.

68. Myrtle Brodie Crawford, "The Negro Builds a Pyramid," *Social Studies* 32, no. 1 (1941): 27–31, quote page 27.

69. See the *Negro History Bulletin* for dozens of examples every year, published by the Association for the Study of Negro Life and History beginning in 1937 (later the Association for the Study of African American Life and History). Also see Lee F. Rodgers, "Va. Schools Observe Negro History Week," *Chicago Defender*, February 21, 1942, 11; "Negro History Week," *Chicago Defender*, February 15, 1941, 14.

70. Benjamin Fine, "Migrant War Workers Cause School Problem," *New York Times*, January 17, 1943, E7; Benjamin Fine, "Lack of Teachers Close Many Schools in Nation," *New York Times*, December 13, 1942, E7.

71. Anthony Chen, *The Fifth Freedom: Jobs, Politics, and Civil Rights in the United States, 1941–1972* (Princeton, NJ: Princeton University Press, 2009); Thomas A. Guglielmo, "Fighting for Caucasian Rights: Mexicans, Mexican Americans, and the Transnational Struggle for Civil Rights in World War II Texas," *Journal of American History* 92, no. 4 (2006): 1212–237; Dorn, *American Education, Democracy, and the Second World War*; Dorn, "'I Had All Kinds of Kids in My Classes, and It Was Fine'"; Giordano, *Wartime Schools*; Takaki, *Double Victory*; David M. Kennedy, *Freedom From Fear: The American People in Depression and War, 1929–1945* (Oxford: Oxford University Press, 1999); William L. O'Neil, *A Democracy at War: America's Fight at Home and Abroad in World War II* (Cambridge, MA: Harvard University Press, 1998); John W. Jeffries, *Wartime America: The World War II Home Front* (Chicago: Ivan R. Dee, 1996); Michael C. C. Adams, *The Best War Ever: America and World War II* (Baltimore: Johns Hopkins University Press, 1994); John Morton Blum, *V Was for Victory* (New York: Harcourt, Brace, Jovanovich, 1974); Kandel, *The Impact of the War upon American Education*.

72. Benjamin Fine, "Effects of Growing Teacher Shortage Weighed by National Convention in Pittsburgh," *New York Times*, July 9, 1944, E9.

73. Hayden S. Pearson, "Future of Education," *Washington Post*, June 2, 1945, 4. "Supreme Duty of All Teachers Is to Clear Children's Minds of Bias, Dr. Hill Declares," *Atlanta Daily World*, November 25, 1944, 6; "Education: Teacher Duty to Fight Race Bias," *New York Amsterdam News*, November 25, 1944, 4A; "Teachers Urged to Help Fight Bias," *Afro-American*,

November 18, 1944, 11; "Fighting Race Bias Held Teacher Duty," *New York Times*, November 12, 1944, 18; Marjorie McKenzie, "Pursuit of Democracy," *Pittsburg Courier*, October 14, 1944, 7; "Teachers Agree to Help Foster Racial Accord," *Chicago Defender*, December 11, 1943, 6; "Teachers Urge Americanism in Racial Strife," *Chicago Daily Tribune*, December 5, 1943, 29; "Race Relations Course Set Up," *New York Amsterdam News*, September 18, 1943, 8; Millicent Taylor, "Gaining Views of Other Lands Held Essential," *Christian Science Monitor*, July 21, 1943, 2; Johanna M. Lindlof, "Democracy Sought in Schools' Work," *New York Times*, April 25, 1943, E9; Frances H. Kohan, "Schools Program Here Adjusted to War Aims," *New York Times*, December 20, 1942, E7; "Put Emphasis on Democracy, Teachers Told," *Atlanta Constitution*, December 11, 1942, 13.

74. Commission on Wartime Policy of the National Council for the Social Studies, "The Social Studies Mobilize for Victory," *Social Education* 2, no. 1 (1943): 3–10, quote page 3.

75. Charles I. Glicksberg, "The Race Problem in the Classroom," *American Unity* 4, no. 1 (1945): 3–8, quote page 4.

76. "Ammunition," *American Unity* 5, no. 5 (1947): 12–13. Also see "New Manual Out Today: American Unity Seeks to Combat Intolerance in Schools," *New York Times*, October 1, 1942, 14.

77. Takaki, *Double Victory*, 5. The intensely racialized nature of the Pacific war in particular is confirmed and further explored by Dower, *War without Mercy*. Also see Harvard Sitkoff, "Racial Militancy and Interracial Violence in the Second World War," *Journal of American History* 58, no. 3 (1971): 661–81.

78. "Racialized rage" is Takaki's term, see *Double Victory*, 19.

79. "English Instruction and the War," *English Journal* 31, no. 2 (1942): 87–91, quote page 88.

80. Ann Ward Orr, "Round Table: The Function of English in Wartime—Continued," *English Journal* 31, no. 3 (1942): 227–29, quote page 229.

81. "Shall We Teach Them to Hate?" *Elementary English Review* 19, no. 8 (1942): 271–72, quote page 271. Also see Wightman, "This Hate Business."

82. Jim Cullen explains how perceived threats to freedom often revitalize various reiterations of the American Dream, see Jim Cullen, *The American Dream: A Short History of An Idea That Shaped a Nation* (New York: Oxford University Press, 2003). For a classroom example, see: Mary McCutchan, "The American Dream: A Unit in Junior English," *English Journal* 31, no. 3 (1942): 194–98.

83. Paul Farmer, "English Teaching during a Wartime Emergency," *English Journal* 31, no. 3 (1942): 230–31. For examples of other classrooms that used "Ballad for Americans" see Mildred C. Schmidt, "Who Are We Americans?" *English Journal* 32, no. 7 (1943): 364–69; Samuel Meyers, "The Dust Bowl Ballads," *English Journal* 30, no. 6 (1941): 492; Francis Hutchinson, "A Tussle with Americanism."

84. Department of Supervisors and Directors of Instruction of the National Education Association, *Americans All*, v.

85. Asami Kawachi, "Stranger's Rice," *Common Ground* 2, no. 4 (1942): 73–76.

86. Minnie Rugg, "In the Four Seas All Men Are Brothers," *English Journal* 31, no. 10 (1942): 719–25, quote page 719. Also see Ethel E. Ewing, "Using a Story for Chinese Children," *Social Education* 7, no. 8 (1943): 358–60.

87. Rugg, "In the Four Seas All Men Are Brothers," 719–20. A similar lesson is described in "The People Next Door," *New Jersey Educational Review* 15, no. 2 (1941): 65. In this article, photographs and captions describe how New Jersey students study the "Other Americas": "We Eat Their Food," "We Visit Their Exhibits," "We Dance Their Dances," and "We Listen to Their Broadcasts."

88. Rugg, "In the Four Seas All Men Are Brothers," 725.

89. Marie Syrkin, "Morale Begins at School," *Common Ground* 2, no. 3 (1942): 98–102, quote page 101.

90. Wightman, "This Hate Business."

91. Syrkin, "Morale Begins at School," 100.

92. Sitkoff, "Racial Militancy and Interracial Violence in the Second World War," 671. Also see Leon S. Kaiser and Leanora S. Ratner, "A Project in Inter-racial and Inter-faith Education: Finding the Road to Peace and Victory," *Elementary English Review* 21, no. 3 (1944): 81–88.

93. Wagner, "An Eighth Grade Studies Racial Intolerance," 77.

94. Esther Williams, "Facts and Democratic Values Reduce Racial Prejudice," *Social Education* 10, no. 4 (1946): 154–56, quote page 155.

95. Morgan, "Chicago Schools Teach Negro History," 108.

96. Marie Syrkin, "Jim Crow in the Classroom," *Common Ground* 4, no. 4 (1944): 24–32, quote page 25.

97. Syrkin, "Jim Crow in the Classroom," quote page 25.

98. Charles I. Glicksberg, "The Race Problem in the Classroom," *American Unity* 4, no. 1 (1945): 3–8, quote page 6.

99. Syrkin, "Jim Crow in the Classroom," 31.

100. Syrkin, "Jim Crow in the Classroom," 30–31.

101. Charles I. Glicksberg, "Education for Hate," *English Journal* 34, no. 1 (1945): 19–26, quote page 21.

102. George H. Henry, "Our Best English Unit," *English Journal* 36, no. 7 (1947): 356–62, quote page 361.

103. Pearl M. Fisher, "English, Democracy, and Color," *High Points* 24, no. 5 (1942): 5–10, quote page 5.

104. Fisher, "English, Democracy, and Color," 5–6.

105. Fisher, "English, Democracy, and Color," 10.

106. Clara A. Molendyk and Benjamin C. Edwards, "Dynamic for Democracy," *High Points* 24, no. 4 (1942): 37–46, quotes pages 40–41. A similar sentiment was expressed in John Breukelman, "What Can We Do?" *American Biology Teacher,* 4, no. 7 (1942): 209.

107. Molendyk and Edwards, "Dynamic for Democracy," 40.

108. Harry J. Walker, "Tensions in Race Relations," *Social Education* 8, no. 2 (1944): 57–61, quote page 57.

109. Horace R. Cayton, "The American Negro—A World Problem," *Social Education* 8, no. 5 (1944): 205–8, quote page 206.

110. Richard H. McFeely, "Cures for Intercultural Myopia," *Social Studies* 34, no. 6 (1943): 247–51, quote page 247.

111. McFeely, "Cures for Intercultural Myopia," 248.

112. McFeely, "Cures for Intercultural Myopia," 249.

113. See for example, W. B. Faherty, "Fostering the 'Good Neighbor' Policy," *Social Studies* 34, no. 3 (1943): 111–12; Esther Berman, "Children of the Foreign Born," *Social Studies* 34, no. 6 (1943): 252–53; Charles A. Daly, "National Unity through American Literature," *English Journal* 32, no. 8 (1943): 438–40; Robert Polglaza, "Patterson Pupils Contribute to the Good Neighbor Policy," *New Jersey Educational Review* 15, no. 5 (1942): 146.

114. "Bad Manners Can Ruin Us," *Pittsburg Courier*, August 22, 1942, 6; Sadie Mai O'Connor and Ida Nance Givens, "Department of Jeanes Supervisors of Louisiana," *Pittsburg Courier* August 22, 1942, 23, emphasis in original.

115. M. M. Mandl, "Teaching Tolerance in the High School," *High Points* 23, no. 6 (1941): 61–64, quote page 64.

116. Committee for Racial Cooperation, Benjamin Franklin High School, "Building Concepts of Racial Democracy," in Department of Supervisors and Directors of Instruction of the National Education Association, *Americans All*, test page 57. Also see, Maurice Bleifeld, "A Biology Unit Dealing with Racial Attitudes," *American Biology Teacher* 2, no. 1 (1939): 7–9.

117. Alfred Kishner, "A Scientific Approach to the Development of Tolerance," *High Points* 23, no. 7 (1941): 11–22, attitude test page 13. A similar race unit is described at the Bronx High School of Science in 1943, see: Zachariah Subarsky, "Biology Teaching in War Time: Some Suggestions for Emphasis," *American Biology Teacher* 6, no. 2 (1943): 27–30.

118. Dower offers a brief analysis of the Western tendency to associate "inferior races" with apes, see Dower, *War without Mercy,* 148–50.

119. Kishner, "A Scientific Approach to the Development of Tolerance," 18.

120. Committee for Racial Cooperation, Benjamin Franklin High School, "Building Concepts of Racial Democracy," 60.

121. Ruth Benedict and Gene Weltfish, *The Races of Mankind.* Public Affairs Pamphlet No. 85 (New York: Public Affairs Committee, 1943). More than 750,000 copies of this text were printed, and it was translated into seven languages and multiple formats including the children's book *In Henry's Backyard,* a traveling poster series prepared by the Cranbrook Institute of Science and distributed by the American Missionary Association, the comic book *There Are No Master Races* published by the Public Affairs Committee, and the animated film *Brotherhood of Man* sponsored by the United Auto Workers. Teaching journals suggest that all of these formats were popular in American schools.

122. Leonard B. Irwin, "Pamphlets and Government Publications," *Social Education* 8, no. 1 (1944): 36–37, quote page 36.

123. Norman D. Humphry, "Race Can Work toward Democracy," *Social Studies* 35, no. 6 (1944): 246–48; William H. Bristow, "Intercultural Education: Problems and Solutions," *High Points* 25, no. 8 (1943): 15–27. Also see Brian R. Sevier, "'Somewhere between Mutuality and Diversity': The Project in Intergroup Education and Teaching for Tolerance following World War II," Ph.D. dissertation, University of Colorado, Boulder, 2002: 74–90.

124. Marion Edman, "Building Unity within a Community," *Elementary English Review* 21, no. 5 (1944): 179–85, quote page 184.

125. Review of "The Races of Mankind," *American Unity* 2, no. 2 (1943): 23.

126. Wagner, "An Eighth Grade Studies Racial Intolerance," quote page 77.

127. Smiley, "Intercultural Education in English Classrooms," quote page 341.

128. Violet Edwards, "Note on the 'Races of Mankind,'" in Ruth Benedict, *Race: Science and Politics* (New York: Viking, 1945): 167–68. *American Unity,* in particular among educational journals, encouraged teachers to employ *The Races of Mankind* in tolerance programs. Among other articles, see "Cranbrook Exhibit Shows Up Race Myth," *American Unity* 2, no. 6 (1944): 14; "Races of Mankind Exhibit," *American Unity* 3, no. 6 (1945): 16; "Now in Poster Form," *American Unity* 3, no. 8 (1945): 8; Review of film "Brotherhood of Man," *American Unity* 5, no. 3 (1946): 12–13; "Ammunition," *American Unity* 5, no. 5 (1947): 12–13. For more on *The Races of Mankind* see Virginia Heyer Young, "Ruth Benedict: Relativist and Universalist," 25–54; and Juliet Niehaus, "Education and Democracy in the Anthropology of Gene Weltfish," 87–118, both in Jill B. R. Cherneff and Eve Hochwald, eds., *Visionary Observers: Anthropological Inquiry and Education* (Lincoln: University of Nebraska Press, 2006). According to David H. Price, the FBI targeted both Ruth Benedict and Gene Weltfish as potential "subversives" based on the text of *The Races of Mankind* and its reception in liberal circles. While Benedict's death in 1948 spared her the brunt of cold war investigation, Weltfish was hauled in before Senator McCarthy on April 1, 1953. Senator McCarthy quoted passages from *The Races of Mankind* as evidence of Weltfish's subversive views. See *Threatening Anthropology: McCarthyism and the FBI's Surveillance of Activist Anthropologists* (Durham, NC: Duke University Press, 2004): 113–35.

129. Humphrey, "Race Can Work toward Democracy," quote pages 246–47, emphasis in original.

130. Humphrey, "Race Can Work toward Democracy," 247.

131. Mildred Williams and W. L. Van Loan, "Education for Racial Equality," *Social Studies* 34, no. 7 (1943): 308–11, quote page 308.

132. Williams and Van Loan, "Education for Racial Equality," quote page 308.

133. Williams and Van Loan, "Education for Racial Equality," 309.

134. McFeely, "Cures for Intercultural Myopia," 251.

135. *American Unity* 1, no. 8 (1943): 7.

136. Lois M. Hutchings, Benjamin Epstein, and F. May Bullock, "High School Biology Goes to War," *American Biology Teacher* 6, no. 1 (1943): 5–8, quotes page 7–8.

137. Mayme Louise Sloat, "Science Teaching Can Develop Intercultural Understanding," *American Unity* 3, no. 9 (1945): 15–19, quote page 16.

138. Subarsky, "Biology Teaching in War Time," quote page 28, emphasis in original.

139. The play was mimeographed and distributed to teachers by the Public Affairs Committee. For a description of the play as it was put on in Minneapolis, see Leo Shapiro, "Intergroup Education," *Common Ground* 6, no. 3 (1946): 102–5. For the text of the play and a description of a performance in New York City, see Alice B. Nirenberg, "Meet Your Relatives," *Common Ground* 2, no. 4 (1944): 17–23, quotes page 17.

140. Nirenberg, "Meet Your Relatives," 20.

141. Nirenberg, "Meet Your Relatives," 20.

142. Hamill Hartman, "You Don't Teach Until You Get under Their Hides," *English Journal* 33, no. 6 (1944): 294–96, quote page 295.

143. Hartman, "You Don't Teach Until You Get under Their Hides," quote page 295.

144. William J. Mahar, *Beyond the Burnt Cork Mask: Early Blackface Minstrelsy and Antebellum American Culture* (Urbana: University of Illinois Press, 1999); William T. Lhamon Jr., *Raising Cain: Blackface Performance from Jim Crow to Hip Hop* (Cambridge, MA: Harvard University Press, 1998); Dale Cockrell, *Demons of Disorder: Early Blackface Minstrels and Their World* (London and New York: Cambridge University Press, 1997); Eric Lott, *Love and Theft: Blackface Minstrelsy and the American Working Class* (New York: Oxford University Press, 1993); Michael Rogin, Blackface, *White Noise: Jewish Immigrants in the Hollywood Melting Pot* (Berkeley: University of California Press, 1996).

145. Hartman, "You Don't Teach Until You Get under Their Hides," 296.

146. Marjorie S. Watts, "Intercultural Education: An Experiment," *English Journal* 34, no. 2 (1945): 81–87, quote page 81.

147. Watts, "Intercultural Education: An Experiment," quote page 81.

148. Watts, "Intercultural Education: An Experiment," 84.

149. Watts, "Intercultural Education: An Experiment," 85.

150. Watts, "Intercultural Education: An Experiment," 87.

151. Marie Lien, "The New Intercultural Education: Facts or Chauvinistic Myths?" *Elementary English Review* 21, no. 3 (1944): 111–13, quote page 111.

152. Edman, "Building Unity within a Community," 179.

153. Morgan, "Chicago Schools Teach Negro History," 107.

154. Morgan, "Chicago Schools Teach Negro History," 108–9.

155. E. Lawrence Palmer, "A Won World," *American Biology Teacher* 8, no. 3 (1945): 60–61, quote page 60.

156. Dale, "The Price of Prejudice."

157. Louis Schuker, "Citizenship Attitudes in a City High School," *High Points* 27, no. 1 (1945): 44–48.

158. Norma Jensen, "School Strikes in Gary, Chicago, and New York," *American Unity* 4, no. 3 (1945): 3–5. Also see Ronald D. Cohen, "The Dilemma of School Integration in the North: Gary, Indiana, 1945–1960" in *Race, Law, and American History, 1700–1990*, ed, Paul Finkelman (New York: Garland, 1992): 279–302.

159. Anonymous, "I Faced the High School Race Problem," *American Unity* 4, no. 3 (1945): 16–20, quotes pages 18 and 19.

160. Mayme Louise Sloat, "Science Teaching Can Develop Intercultural Understanding," *American Unity* 3, no. 9 (1945): 15–19, quotes pages 18 and 19.

161. Sloat, "Science Teaching Can Develop Intercultural Understanding," 17.

162. Sloat, "Science Teaching Can Develop Intercultural Understanding," 18.

163. M. F. Ashley Montagu, "Eugenics, Genetics, and Race," *Science Teacher* 12, no. 2 (1945): 24–25, 41–43.

164. Vivian E. Bergland, "A Study of Prejudice for High-School English Classes," *English Journal* 34, no. 8 (1945): 444–47, quote page 445, emphasis in original.

165. Fleegler, "'Forget All Differences until the Forces of Freedom Are Triumphant.'"

166. "Inter-cultural Education," *Chicago Defender,* June 23, 1945, 12.

167. Leo Shapiro, "Intergroup Education," *Common Ground* 6, no. 1 (1945): 95–100. This article details the various intercultural education workshops at universities, and discusses the practices of various school districts, states, and cities, as well as the support of the program by Eleanor Roosevelt and the U.S. Office of Education (both of whom publicly supported intercultural education since 1939). Leo Shapiro wrote this article in his official capacity as the director of Intercultural Relations of the Anti-Defamation League of B'nai B'rith. Also see Leo Shapiro, "Which Intercultural Education?" *Progressive Education* 25, no. 1 (1947): 232–33, 251. Reports and speeches from the annual Race Relations Institutes at Fisk University are found in the Charles S. Johnson Papers (CSJ Papers) Amistad Research Center at Tulane University, Race Relations Department, United Church Board for Homeland Ministries Archives, 1943–1970. Boxes 34–50 contain the materials from the 1944 to 1954 institutes, including details of the intercultural education workshops. Historical studies of Johnson include Patrick Gilpin and Marybeth Gasman, *Charles S. Johnson: Leadership beyond the Veil of Jim Crow* (Albany: State University of New York Press, 2003); Patrick J. Gilpin, "Charles S. Johnson and the Race Relations Institutes at Fisk University," *Phylon* 41, no. 3 (1980): 300–311; Richard Robbins, *Sidelines Activist: Charles S. Johnson and the Struggle for Civil Rights* (Jackson: University Press of Mississippi, 1996); Matthew William Dunne "Next Steps: Charles S. Johnson and Southern Liberalism," *Journal of Negro History* 83, no. 1 (1998): 1–34. The survey of New York schools' intercultural education practices was published as The University of the State of New York, *Education for Unity in the Schools of New York State: A Report on the Program of Intergroup Education in New York State Schools* (Albany: The University of the State of New York, 1947).

168. Helen J. Hanlon and Stanley Dimond, "What the Schools Can Do in Intercultural Education," *English Journal* 34, no. 1 (1945): 32–38, quote page 36.

169. Oscar Riddle, "Education for All American Youth from the Point of View of a Biologist," *American Biology Teacher* 7, no. 5 (1945): 116–20, quote page 119, emphasis in original.

170. Folders 1a, 1b, 11, Series 634. Board of Education Records, Municipal Archives (hereafter NYCBOE), City of New York, NY.

171. Herbert D. A. Donovan to Jacob Greenberg November 3, 1945. Folder 1b, Series 634. NYCBOE.

172. Carmon Ross, "Lansdowne, Pennsylvania Believes in Good Human Relations," *American Unity* 4, no. 2 (1945): 12–13.

173. The University of the State of New York, *Education for Unity in the Schools of New York State,* 63.

174. Margaret Buchanan, "An Inter-Faith Program," *Journal of the National Education Association* 34, no. 8 (1945): 182–83; Ethel E. Price, "Democratic Living: A School Experience," *Social Education* 9, no. 2 (1945): 60–62; Evelyn Simonson, "The School Assembly Program," *Elementary English Review* 22, no. 7 (1945): 257–60; Beatrice Stevens, "An International Club," *Social Education* 9 no. 6 (1945): 259–62; Charlotte Benston, "Our Lady's Tumbler," *Journal of the National Education Association* 34, no. 7 (1945): 151.

175. R. H. Eckelberry, "Intercultural Education," *Educational Research Bulletin* 24, no. 9 (1945): 229–30, quote page 229.

176. On racial liberalism, see Perlstein, "American Dilemmas"; Gary Gerstle, "The Protean Character of American Liberalism," *The American Historical Review* 99, no. 4 (1994): 1043–1073; Jackson, *Gunnar Myrdal and America's Conscience;* Ira Katznelson, "Was the Great Society a Lost Opportunity" in Steve Fraser and Gary Gerstle, *The Rise and Fall of the New Deal Order, 1930–1980* (Princeton, NJ: Princeton University Press, 1989); David W. Southern, *Gunnar Myrdal and Black-White Relations: The Use and Abuse of An American Dilemma, 1944–1969* (Baton Rouge and London: Louisiana State University Press, 1987).

Chapter 5

1. Beatrice Stevens, "An International Club," *Social Education* 9, no. 6 (1945): 259–62, quote page 259.

2. Diane Ravitch, *The Troubled Crusade: American Education, 1945–1980* (New York: Basic Books, 1983).

3. The growth of civil rights activism during World War II is well documented; see for example: Glenda Elizabeth Gilmore, *Defying Dixie: The Radical Roots of Civil Rights, 1919–1950* (New York: W.W. Norton, 2008); Thomas Sugrue, *Sweet Land of Liberty: The Forgotten Struggle for Civil Rights in the North* (New York: Random House, 2008); Glen Feldman, ed., *Before* Brown*: Civil Rights and White Backlash in the Modern South* (Tuscaloosa: University of Alabama Press, 2004); Martha Biondi, *To Stand and Fight: The Struggle for Civil Rights in Postwar New York City* (Cambridge, MA: Harvard University Press, 2003); Adam Fairclough, *Better Day Coming: Blacks and Equality, 1890–2001* (New York: Viking, 2001); Mary Dudziak, *Cold War Civil Rights: Race and the Image of American Democracy* (Princeton, NJ: Princeton University Press, 2000); Ronald Takaki, *Double Victory: A Multicultural History of America in World War II* (Boston: Little, Brown, 2000); Steven F. Lawson, *Running for Freedom: Civil Rights and Black Politics in America since 1941*, 2nd ed., (New York: McGraw-Hill, 1997); Penny M. Von Eschen, *Race against Empire: Black Americans and Anticolonialism, 1937–1957* (Ithaca: Cornell University Press, 1997).

4. Charles Dorn, *American Education, Democracy, and the Second World War* (New York: Palgrave Macmillan, 2007); Gerard Giordano, *Wartime Schools: How World War II Changed American Education* (New York: Peter Lang, 2004); Ruth Jacknow Markowitz, *My Daughter, The Teacher: Jewish Teachers in the New York City Schools* (New Brunswick, NJ: Rutgers University Press, 1993): 151–72.

5. Andrew Hartman, *Cold War: The Battle for the American School* (New York: Palgrave Macmillan, 2008); Stuart J. Foster, *Red Alert! Educators Confront the Red Scare in Schools, 1947–1954* (New York: Peter Lang, 2000); Ellen W. Schrecker, *Many Are the Crimes: McCarthyism in America* (Boston: Little, Brown, 1998); Ellen W. Schrecker, "McCarthy Era Blacklisting of School Teachers, College Professors, and Other Public Employees: The FBI Responsibilities Program File and the Dissemination of Information Policy File," *Journal of American History* 81, no. 1 (1994): 360–61; Ellen W. Schrecker, *No Ivory Tower: McCarthyism and the Universities* (New York: Oxford University Press, 1986).

6. Jonathan Zimmerman, "*Brown*-ing the American Textbook: History, Psychology, and the Origins of Modern Multiculturalism," *History of Education Quarterly* 44, no. 1 (2004): 46–69.

7. Walter A. Jackson, *Gunnar Myrdal and America's Conscience: Social Engineering and Racial Liberalism, 1938–1987* (Chapel Hill: University of North Carolina Press, 1990): 280. Yoon Pak documents the expansion of intercultural education in the postwar era in San Diego and Seattle, see: Yoon K. Pak, "'If There Is a Better Intercultural Plan in Any School System in America, I Do Not Know Where It Is': The San Diego City Schools Intercultural Education Program, 1946–1949," *Urban Education* 37, no. 5 (2002): 588–609; Yoon Pak, *Wherever I Go, I Will Always Be a Loyal American: Seattle's Japanese American Schoolchildren during World War II* (New York: Routledge, 2001). For a list of textbooks and pamphlets on intercultural education, intergroup education, and education for human relations, see the bibliography.

8. "Advertising Democracy," *The New York Times*, May 11, 1949, 28.

9. As quoted by Joseph Singerman in his introduction to the "Science for Society" section in *Science Teacher* 13, no. 2 (1946): 70.

10. Brian Sevier notes that more journal articles on intercultural education were published in 1946 than between 1929–1945 combined. Brian R. Sevier, "'Somewhere between Mutuality and Diversity': The Project in Intergroup Education and Teaching for Tolerance following World War II." Diss. University of Colorado, Boulder, 2002: 9–10. Also see: Lyle W.

Ashby, "In Peace as in War—Teamwork!" *Journal of the National Education Association* 35, no. 2 (1946): 81. Also see Irwin A. Eckhauser, "Education for International Understanding," *Social Studies* 38, no. 7 (1947): 294–95; Benjamin C. Gruenberg, "Teaching Biology after the Wars," *American Biology Teacher* 9, no. 4 (1947): 101–4; Donn V. Hart, "Education for International Understanding," *Social Studies* 38, no. 8 (1947): 344–49; Alexander Frazier, "Teaching World Citizenship: The New Realism," *Social Education* 10, no. 3 (1946); 11; Editorial Board, "And Now Let Us Highly Resolve," *New Jersey Educational Review* 19, no. 4 (1946): 152.

11. Hilda Taba and William Van Til, eds., *Democratic Human Relations: Promising Practices in Intergroup and Intercultural Education in the Social Studies*, Sixteenth Yearbook. (Washington, DC: National Council for the Social Studies, 1945): 3.

12. Over the course of the postwar period educational reformers gradually moved away from the label "intercultural education" in favor of "intergroup education" and even "education for human relations," although these names were used interchangeably by some educators. I refer to all of these curricula as intercultural education to simplify the discussion, as the same group of scholars and organizations were involved in producing these texts.

13. Stewart G. Cole, I. James Quillen, and Mildred J. Wise, *Charting Intercultural Education, 1945–55* (Stanford, CA: Stanford University Press, 1946): 3. Also see William Van Til, "The Task of Intercultural Education" *Social Education* 9, no. 8 (1945): 341–43; I. James Quillen, "The Role of the Social Studies Teacher in the Postwar World," *Social Education* 9, no. 1 (1945): 9–12.

14. Quillen, "The Role of the Social Studies Teacher in the Postwar World," 10.

15. "Pupils to Get Racial Facts in Baltimore," *Washington Post*, October 14, 1947, 4.

16. Joseph Gallant "Teaching Good Will Indirectly," *American Unity* 4, no. 4 (1946): 3–6, quote page 4. Also see Esther Williams, "Facts and Democratic Values Reduce Racial Prejudice," *Social Education* 10, no. 4 (1946): 154–56; Jean Wagner, "An Eighth Grade Studies Racial Intolerance," *Social Education* 10, no. 2 (1946): 75–77; Theodore P. Gnagey, "How Shall a Teacher Combat Prejudice?" *New Jersey Educational Review* 20, no. 3 (1946): 132–33.

17. Louise M. Rosenblatt, ed., "Intercultural Education Issue," *English Journal* 35, no. 6 (1946): 285–359.

18. Ruth Benedict, "Racism Is Vulnerable," *English Journal* 35, no. 6 (1946): 299–303, quote page 300.

19. Marjorie B. Smiley et al., "Intercultural Education in English Classrooms: An Informal Survey," *English Journal* 35, no. 6 (1946): 337–49, quote page 341.

20. Anita T. Anderson, "An Eighth Grade Gets Acquainted with the Neighbors," *American Unity* 5, no. 1 (1946): 7–13, quote page 7. Also see Allen Y. Young, "Intercultural Education in the Cleveland Social Studies Program," *Social Education* 11, no. 2 (1947): 61–64; Collins J. Reynolds, "An Interschool Project in Intercultural Education," *Social Education* 11, no. 1 (1947): 13–15.

21. National Council for the Social Studies, "Democratic Human Relations," *American Unity* 4, no. 7 (1946): 21–23, quote page 21. Also see "Characteristics of the Good Democratic Citizen," *Social Education* 14, no. 7 (1950): 310–13; Quillen, "The Role of the Social Studies Teacher in the Postwar World."

22. As quoted in Smiley et al., "Intercultural Education in English Classrooms," 339.

23. Dana W. Niswender, "Divided We Fall," *English Journal* 36, no. 6 (1947): 307–9, quote page 307.

24. Harold T. Eaton, "Round Table: A Unit on Prejudice," *English Journal* 36, no. 2 (1947): 97–98, quote page 98.

25. Reynolds, "An Interschool Project in Intercultural Education."

26. Jean Wagner, "An Eighth Grade Studies Racial Intolerance," *Social Education* 10, no. 2 (1946): 75–77, quote page 75.

27. "A Primer on Race," *Journal of the NEA* 36, no. 2 (1947): 84–85.

28. "Ammunition," *American Unity* 5, no. 5 (1947): 12–13; "Tolerance Can Be Taught" *American Unity* 5, no. 4 (1947): 12–13.

29. As featured in "Ammunition," 12–13. Many of these same pamphlets, as well as others, were used in New York City intercultural education coursesl, see Folder 4 "Printed Materials" in Series 562: Advisory Commission on Human Relations, NYCBOE. Likewise, Massachusetts published excerpts from these pamphlets in a special book for teachers called the "Scrapbook for Teachers," see: "Scrapbook for Teachers" (Boston: Governor's Committee for Racial and Religious Understanding, 1946); Also see "Scrapbook for Teachers" (Boston: Massachusetts Fair Employment Practice Commission, 1948); "Scrapbook for Teachers" (Boston: Massachusetts Fair Employment Practice Commission, 1950). Available in the Boston Public Library, Boston, MA.

30. Dirk J. Struik, "Social Responsibilities of the Scientist," *Science Teacher* 13, no. 2 (1946): 70–72, quote page 71. Also see Philip Kotlar, "Science for Freedom—An Experiment," *Science Teacher* 14, no. 1 (1947): 20–21, 39.

31. Morris Meister, "A Voice for Science Teacher," *Science Teacher* 13, no. 3 (1946): 12, 44.

32. Smiley et al., "Intercultural Education in English Classrooms," 345.

33. Collins J. Reynolds, "An Interschool Project in Intercultural Education," *Social Education* 11, no. 1 (1947): 13–15, quote page 14.

34. Young, "Intercultural Education in the Cleveland Social Studies Program," quote page 61.

35. "Pupils to Get Racial Facts in Baltimore."

36. Smiley et al., "Intercultural Education in English Classrooms," 345–46.

37. Glicksberg, "Intercultural Education: Utopia or Reality?" *Common Ground* 6, no. 4 (1946): 64–68, quote page 66.

38. Young, "Intercultural Education in the Cleveland Social Studies Program," 62.

39. See for example, Lena Denecke, "My Country in the World: A Fifth Grade Project," *Elementary English Review* 24, no. 7 (1947): 434–53; Virginia K. Neff, "Children of Other Lands: A Sixth Grade Project," *Elementary English Review* 24, no. 7 (1947): 454–68; Virginia Rider, "Modern Drama Educates for Tolerance," *English Journal* 36, no. 1 (1947): 16–22; Smiley et al., "Intercultural Education in English Classrooms."

40. Smiley et al., "Intercultural Education in English Classrooms," 346.

41. Editors, "Brotherhood Week Stimulates Study," *New Jersey Educational Review* 19, no. 5 (1946): 190.

42. Elisabeth Lasch-Quinn, *Race Experts: How Racial Etiquette, Sensitivity Training, and New Age Therapy Hijacked the Civil Rights Revolution* (New York: W.W. Norton and Company, 2001).

43. Esther Williams, "Facts and Democratic Values Reduce Racial Prejudice," *Social Education* 10, no. 4 (1946): 154–56. In a similar example, a teacher from Collingswood, New Jersey, was upset when she discovered that one of her students decided not to invite a classmate to a party because the girl was Jewish, only minutes after a special lesson on the Jewish contributions to the U.S. Supreme Court. Marie MacDonald, "The Letdown," *New Jersey Educational Review* 20, no. 2 (1946): 101.

44. Marion Edman, "We'd Better Mind the P's and Cues," *English Journal* 35, no. 6 (1946): 349–53, quote page 349.

45. Edman, "We'd Better Mind the P's and Cues," 350, emphasis in original.

46. Wagner, "An Eighth Grade Studies Racial Intolerance," 77.

47. Glicksberg, "Intercultural Education: Utopia or Reality?" quote page 63.

48. Marion Edman, "We'd Better Mind the P's and Cues," 349.

49. Frances W. MacIntire, "Appreciating Others," *Journal of the NEA* 36, no. 11 (1947): 566.

50. MacIntire, "Appreciating Others."

51. MacIntire, "Appreciating Others."

52. Sema Williams Herman, "I Teach a Way of Living," *Elementary English Review* 24, no. 7 (1947): 425–34.

53. Lena Deneke, "My Country Is the World: A Fifth Grade Project," *Elementary English Review* 24, no. 7 (1947): 435–53, quote page 436. The second article is Virginia K. Neff, "Children of Other Lands."

54. Margaret Kurtz, "Teaching Human Relations Indirectly," *Elementary English Review* 24, no. 7 (1947): 474–75, 495. Also see Azile Wofford, "Standards for Choosing Books about Other Countries," *Elementary English Review* 24, no. 7 (1947): 469–73.

55. For an exception, see "Grade Pupils Get Lesson in Race Tolerance," *American Unity* 5, no. 6 (1947): 22.

56. Leo Shapiro, "Intergroup Education," *Common Ground* 7, no. 2 (1947): 96–99.

57. George H. Henry, "Our Best English Unit," *English Journal* 36, no. 7 (1947): 356–62, quote page 361.

58. Rider, "Modern Drama Educates for Tolerance."

59. Rider, "Modern Drama Educates for Tolerance," 19.

60. Alfred G. Fisk, "Stereotypes in Intercultural Education," *Common Ground* 7, no. 2 (1947): 28–33, quote page 28.

61. Fisk, "Stereotypes in Intercultural Education," 32.

62. Fisk, "Stereotypes in Intercultural Education," 33, emphasis in original.

63. Lawrence S. Wittner, *Cold War America: From Hiroshima to Watergate*, rev. ed. (New York: Holt, Rinehart and Winston, 1978): 101.

64. Wittner, *Cold War America*, 38.

65. Schrecker describes how McCarthyism worked as a two-pronged process. First, a state or federal agency would initiate an investigation of an individual's supposed "loyalty" to the United States government. For a vast majority of American employers, including labor unions, universities, and public schools, the fact that this investigation was initiated at all was usually grounds for dismissal, no matter the evidence found to substantiate these claims. As both Andrew Hartman and Stuart Foster explain, the very way this process worked was enough to induce most teachers to censor themselves out of fear that something they did might draw enough attention to warrant investigation. See Hartman, *Education and the Cold War*, and Foster, *Red Alert!*

66. "Teachers Warned to Guard Opinions," *New York Times*, June 14, 1947, 17.

67. An Anonymous Teacher, "I'm Not Coming Back This Year," *Social Education* 16, no. 7 (1952): 319–20, quotes page 320.

68. Trevor K. Serviss, "Freedom to Learn: Censorship in Learning Materials," *Social Education* 17, no. 2 (1953): 65–70, quote page 69. Also see, Gladwin Hill, "UNESCO in Schools Los Angeles Issue," *New York Times*, April 3, 1955, 53; "Climate of Fear in Schools Denied," *New York Times*, May 21, 1953, 29; Benjamin Fine, "City Teachers Are Told That They Should Not Be Disturbed by Communist Investigations," *New York Times*, May 21, 1953, E13.

69. Zoë Burkholder, "From Forced Tolerance to Forced Busing: Wartime Intercultural Education and the Rise of Black Educational Activism in Boston, 1943–1965," *Harvard Educational Review* 80, no. 3 (2010): 293–326.

70. Herbert D. A. Donovan to Jacob Greenberg, November 3, 1945, and flyer: September 7, 1945 Inservice Credit Course for All Teachers "Promoting National Welfare through Intercultural Cooperation," both found in folder 1b, Series 634. Associate Superintendent Jacob Greenberg. Intercultural Education Course Files. 1944–1953, NYCBOE.

71. Letters of complaint about intercultural courses are on file from the editors of *The Tablet*, the Catholic Teachers Association of the Diocese of Brooklyn, the Archdiocese of New York, and the Teachers Alliance of New York. As far as I can tell, all of the letters of complaint about intercultural education programming in New York City from this period come from organizations that are either Catholic or predominantly Catholic. See folders 1a, 1b, and 11 in Series 634 NYCBOE. Also see Series 562 "The Advisory Committee on Human Relations Files, 1945–1950." The New York Teachers Guild also reported disputes with Catholic-dominated teacher associations who challenged tolerance programming. A report by the New York Teachers Guild in 1938 cautioned that "the members of the

[Teachers] Alliance and the Signpost are greatly influenced by the pronouncements in Catholic publications. I should say that 80 percent of the [Teachers] Alliance are Catholics." Auxiliary Committee on Intolerance in the Schools, Teachers Guild, Minutes, 1938, United Federation of Teachers Records, WAG 022, box 10, folder 30, Tamiment Library and Robert F. Wagner Labor Archives, Elmer Holmes Bobst Library, New York University, New York, NY.

72. Frederick Woltman, "3 Commie Course Instructors Hold City Lecture Jobs," *World-Telegram*, October 10, 1947; "City Sponsors Course by Reds for Teachers," *The Tablet*, October 11, 1947; "Another School Course Conducted by Leftists: Soviet Propaganda Institute Approved by City to Give Alertness Credit to Teachers," *The Tablet*, October 18, 1947; "Will the Bigots Take Over Our Schools? Now the Intercultural Program Is Subversive," *New York Teacher News* 8, no. 9 (1947): 4, all in Folder 11: Correspondence, January–June 1945 Intercultural Courses, Series 634. Associate Superintendent Jacob Greenberg. Intercultural Education Course Files. 1944–1953, Records of the New York City Board of Education (NYCBOE), Municipal Archives, New York, NY. For letters of protest, see: Letter, I. Alex Herskowitz, President of the New York Association of Teachers of Biological Sciences to Dr. Jacob Greenberg, October 10, 1945; Letter from Rudolf Cooper, NYC Association of Teachers of English to Superintendent John Wade October 11, 1945; Letter from Samuel Schneider, Association of the Social Studies in the City of New York to Superintendent John Wade, October 20, 1945, all in folder 1b, series 634, NYCBOE.

73. "Will the Bigots Take Over Our Schools? Now the Intercultural Program is Subversive."

74. Woltman, "City Sponsors Course by Reds for Teachers."

75. "School Superintendents Drop Course on Soviet," *The Sun*, December 11, 1947. In folder 11, Series 634 NYCBOE.

76. Leonard Buder, "School Duty Cited on Disputed Issues," *New York Times*, November 24, 1950, 34; "No Witch Hunts Is Clark's Policy," *New York Times*, May 11, 1947, 35.

77. Mary Hodge Cox, "Brotherhood: Pattern for World Peace," *English Journal* 37, no. 7 (1948): 358–61, quote pages 358–59. Also see Virginia A. Daire, "Others Fight Racial Prejudice, Do You?" *New Jersey Educational Review* 21, no. 7 (1948): 273. This article focused on the work of church groups and youth groups in promoting an international "joy of friendship" that tended to skirt over specific discussions of racial inequality or discrimination.

78. Cox, "Brotherhood: Pattern for World Peace," 358.

79. Cox, "Brotherhood: Pattern for World Peace," 359.

80. Saul Israel, "Teaching the Report of the President's Committee on Civil Rights," *Social Studies* 39, no. 3 (1948): 102–4. Also see: "To Secure These Rights," *New Jersey Educational Review* 21, no. 3 (1947): 112.

81. For exceptions see John P. Milligran, "In New Jersey Brotherhood Is Practical," *New Jersey Educational Review* 27, no. 8 (1954): 318–19, 333; Benjamin Starr and Abraham Leavitt, "School-Wide Observance of Brotherhood Week," *Social Education* 17, no. 1 (1953): 25–26; Editorial Board, "All Men Are Brothers," *New Jersey Educational Review* 24, no. 6 (1951): 210; Katherine B. Greywacz, "Superstition, Fear, and Prejudice," *New Jersey Educational Review* 23, no. 7 (1950): 246.

82. C. C. Harvey, Lewis G. Bloom, and Max Greene, "What Social Changes Should Be Reflected in the Social Studies Curriculum?" *Social Studies* 39, no. 2 (1948): 79–81, quote page 80–81.

83. Harvey, Bloom, and Greene, "What Social Changes Should Be Reflected in the Social Studies Curriculum?" 79.

84. Quote in: "Schools to Stress Democratic Living," *New York Times*, February 21, 1949, 17. Also see: "Anti-Bias Centers Slated in Schools," *New York Times*, April 21, 1949, 14; "Jansen Stresses Democracy Study," *New York Times*, February 1, 1949, 8.

85. Ralph B. Guinness, "New Viewpoints in Teaching Better Intercultural Relations," *Social Studies* 39, no. 3 (1948): 120–22, quotes page 120.

86. Guinness, "New Viewpoints in Teaching Better Intercultural Relations," 122.

87. Guinness, "New Viewpoints in Teaching Better Intercultural Relations," 121.

88. Althea Berry, "Oral Language and Inter-Group Harmony," *Elementary English Review* 25, no. 3 (1948): 161–73.

89. Daire, "Others Fight Prejudice, Do You?" 273.

90. Joseph L. Bustard, "Progress against Discrimination," *New Jersey Educational Review* 20, no. 8 (1947): 274.

91. Sema Williams Herman, "Verse and Song for Democratization," *Elementary English Review* 25, no. 6 (1948): 339–43, 388, quote page 339.

92. Herman, "Verse and Song for Democratization," 339–40.

93. Herman, "Verse and Song for Democratization," 342.

94. Herman, "Verse and Song for Democratization," 340.

95. For an exception, see Gordon H. Hullfish, "The Teacher and the Democratic Task," *Social Education* 15, no. 1 (1951): 9–12.

96. E. O. Danielson, Emily Marshall, and Alexander Frazier, "Emphases for Intergroup Education in Secondary School Science," *Science Teacher* 16, no. 1 (1949): 13–14, 41.

97. Eunice Crabtree, "Who Wants to Be Tolerated?" *Journal of the NEA* 38, no. 2 (1949): 113.

98. Sanford E. Rosen, "Not Out of Books," *Journal of the NEA* 38, no. 5 (1949): 344–45, quote page 344.

99. Rachel Davis DuBois, "A Tension Area Becomes a Neighborhood," *Journal of the NEA* 38, no. 2 (1949): 114–15.

100. NCTE Committee on Intercultural Relations, "Toward Better Human Relations" *English Journal* 38, no. 9 (1949): 527.

101. Mabel S. Finley, "The Book Approach: An Experiment in Intergroup Education," *English Journal* 38, no. 7 (1949): 384–88, quote page 384. Also see, Floreine Hudson, "How Much Grass?" *Social Education* 12, no. 6 (1948): 265–67.

102. Finley, "The Book Approach," 385.

103. Finley, "The Book Approach," 386.

104. Stanley B. Brown and George H. Chance, "E Pluribus Unum," *Social Education* 16, no. 5 (1952): 221.

105. Elisabeth Feist Hirsch, "Some Lessons about Tolerance from the Past," *Social Studies* 41, no. 7 (1950): 309–10, 315–21.

106. NCTE Committee on Intercultural Relations, "Toward Better Human Relations" *English Journal* 39, no. 1 (1950): 41; NCTE Committee on Intercultural Relations, "Toward Better Human Relations" *English Journal* 39, no. 6 (1950): 342.

107. Adelaide Schraegle, "Learning to Meet Differences in Family and Community Patterns," *Elementary English Review* 27, no. 4 (1950): 212–18, quote page 214.

108. Schraegle, "Learning to Meet Differences in Family and Community Patterns," 213–14.

109. "Democracy Study Held Inadequate," *New York Times*, September 7, 1948, 23.

110. Leonard Bude, "Freedom Stressed in Teaching Field," *New York Times*, November 28, 1952, 27.

111. Wilfred McClay explains how academic models concerning intergroup relations overflowed into popular culture and in turn generated an academic backlash by scholars who feared that individualist, inner-directed Americans were being lost in the hazy emphasis on group conformity. While scholars at the time such as David Riesman and William Whyte worried that the theoretical emphasis on group relations was harmful to American social development, it nevertheless appealed to American educators and became an important pedagogical trend in the 1950s. Wilfred M. McClay, *The Masterless: Self and Society in Modern America* (Chapel Hill: University of North Carolina Press, 1994).

112. David Mallery, "Release: A Human Relations Approach to Writing," *English Journal* 39, no. 8 (1950): 429–35, quote page 429.

113. Committee on Intercultural Education, "You've Got to Be Carefully Taught," *Elementary English Review* 27, no. 4 (1950): 219–21, 225.

114. Alice Howard Spaulding, "Intergroup Education in English Classes," *English Journal* 40, no. 9 (1951): 522–23, quote page 522.
115. Spaulding, "Intergroup Education in English Classes," 523.
116. A. C. Keller, "Tolerance—Its Function in a Democratic Society," *Social Studies* 42, no. 3 (1951): 104–10, quote page 106.
117. Elsie Butler, "Living Together in the Third Grade," *Elementary English Review* 28, no. 1 (1951): 1–13, quote page 2.
118. For a similar lesson plan from Ithaca, New York, see: Katherine Knapp, "Community Helpers: A Unit for the Second Grade," *Social Education* 17, no. 5 (1953): 199–200.
119. Sema Williams Herman, "Cooperative Living in the Classroom," *Elementary English Review* 28, no. 8 (1951): 478–81, quote page 478.
120. Herman, "Cooperative Living in the Classroom," 480.
121. Lawrence Wittner writes that thirty states required some kind of loyalty oaths from public school teachers as of 1952. See *Cold War America*, 101. Newspapers occasionally reported on politically motivated attacks on public school teachers who dared to teach racial tolerance in the 1950s, see for example: Murray Illson, "Teachers Are Out for Balking Query on Communist Ties," *New York Times*, February 1, 1952, 1; "Outsiders Hit by Talmadge," *Atlanta Daily World*, August 21, 1951, 1.
122. Malvina Lindsay, "Pussyfooting on Dissent," *Washington Post*, November 24, 1951, 8.
123. Byron L. Akers and Blaine E. Mercer, "A Legal Analysis of Segregation in Public Education," *Social Studies* 45, no. 2 (1954): 43–51; Marguerite Cartwright, "The Africa Unit," *Social Studies* 44, no. 7 (1953): 264–68; James K. Anthony, "What's New about Africa? A Recent Bibliography," *Social Education* 17, no. 5 (1953):1968; Theodore B. Johannis Jr. and Ralph A. Brown. "The Teacher and the Social Studies: IV," *Social Studies* 43, no. 6 (1952): 238–42; Jack Abramowitz, "Origins of the NAACP," *Social Education* 15, no. 1 (1951): 21–23; Isodore Starr, "Recent Supreme Court Decisions: Racial Discrimination Cases," *Social Education* 15, no. 1 (1951): 13–15; John Useem, "Social Anthropology: Recent Trends and Significant Literature," *Social Education* 14, no. 8 (1950): 347–54.
124. Margaret Taylor Burroughs, "Uncle Remus for Today's Children," *Elementary English Review* 40, no. 8 (1953): 485–92, quote page 486.
125. Ethel Newell, "The Indian Stereotype Passes," *Elementary English Review* 41, no. 8 (1954): 472–75, quote page 472.
126. William E. Martin, "Gee, I'm Glad We're All Different!" *Journal of the NEA* 43, no. 4 (1954): 219–20.
127. Diana Selig, *Americans All: The Cultural Gifts Movement* (Cambridge: Harvard University Press, 2008), 268–70; Gilbert Jonas, *Freedom's Sword: The NAACP and the Struggle against Racism in America, 1909–1969* (New York: Routledge, 2005); James T. Patterson, *Brown v. Board of Education: A Civil Rights Milestone and Its Troubled Legacy* (Oxford: Oxford University Press, 2001).
128. Charles S. Johnson. "America's Changing Racial Pattern," 2, 1952. emphasis mine. Box 48, Folder 10 in the Charles S. Johnson Papers (CSJ Papers) Amistad Research Center at Tulane University, Race Relations Department, United Church Board for Homeland Ministries Archives, 1943–1970. Charles S. Johnson received his Ph.D. in sociology from the University of Chicago, where he studied with the influential Robert E. Park. Reports and speeches from the annual institutes are found in the CSJ Papers. Boxes 34–50 contain the materials from the 1944 to 1954 institutes, including details of the intercultural education workshops. Historical studies of Johnson include Patrick Gilpin and Marybeth Gasman, *Charles S. Johnson: Leadership beyond the Veil of Jim Crow* (Albany: State University of New York Press, 2003); Matthew William Dunne, "Next Steps: Charles S. Johnson and Southern Liberalism," *Journal of Negro History* 83, no. 1 (1998): 1–34; Robbins, *Sidelines Activist: Charles S. Johnson and the Struggle for Civil Rights* (Jackson: University Press of Mississippi,

1996); Patrick J. Gilpin, "Charles S. Johnson and the Race Relations Institutes at Fisk University," *Phylon* 41, no. 3 (1980): 300–311.

129. Johnson, "America's Changing Racial Pattern," 1.

130. Folder 8 "Intergroup Committee on NY Public Schools," Series 472, NYCBOE. Also see David Ment, "Patterns of Public School Segregation, 1900–1940: A Comparative Study of New York City, New Rochelle, and New Haven," in *Schools in Cities: Consensus and Conflict in American Educational History*, ed. Ronald K. Goodenow and Diane Ravitch (New York: Holmes and Meier, 1983): 67–110.

131. *American Unity* 10, no. 5 (1952): 16.

132. *American Unity* 12, no. 1 (1953): 12–13.

Conclusion

1. Alice O'Connor, *Poverty Knowledge: Social Science, Social Policy, and the Poor in Twentieth-Century U.S. History* (Princeton, NJ: Princeton University Press, 2001): 6, 99–123; Thomas F. Pettigrew, *The Sociology of Race Relations: Reflection and Reform* (New York: Free Press, 1980).

2. Walter A. Jackson, *Gunnar Myrdal and America's Conscience: Social Engineering and Racial Liberalism, 1938–1987* (Chapel Hill: University of North Carolina Press, 1990).

3. Jonathan Zimmerman, "*Brown*-ing the American Textbook: History, Psychology, and the Origins of Modern Multiculturalism," *History of Education Quarterly* 44, no. 1 (2004): 46–69. Also see John P. Jackson, *Social Scientists for Social Justice: Making the Case against Segregation* (New York: New York University Press, 2001); John P. Jackson Jr., "The Triumph of the Segregationists? A Historiographical Inquiry into Psychology and the *Brown* Litigation," *History of Psychology* 3, no. 3 (2000): 239–61; Daryl Michael Scott, *Contempt and Pity: Social Policy and the Image of the Damaged Black Psyche* (Chapel Hill: University of North Carolina Press, 1997): 119–36; Ellen Herman, *The Romance of American Psychology: Political Culture in the Age of Experts* (Los Angeles: University of California Press, 1995): 174–207; Jackson, *Gunnar Myrdal and America's Conscience.*

4. James A. Patterson, Brown v. Board of Education: *A Civil Rights Milestone and Its Troubled Legacy* (Oxford: Oxford University Press, 2001): xxii–xxiv, 42–43, 131–36. Also see Lawrence S. Wrightsman, "Organized Psychology's Efforts to Influence the Supreme Court on Matters of Race and Education," in *Commemorating* Brown: *The Social Psychology of Racism and Discrimination*, ed. Glenn Adams et al. (Washington, DC: American Psychological Association, 2008): 25–44.

5. Daryl Michael Scott, "Postwar Pluralism, *Brown v. Board of Education*, and the Origins of Multiculturalism," *Journal of American History* 91, no. 1 (2004): 69–91.

6. Theodore Brameld, "Educational Costs," in *Discrimination and the National Welfare*, ed. R. M. MacIver (New York, 1949): 48; Also see Scott, "Postwar Pluralism, *Brown v. Board of Education*, and the Origins of Multiculturalism," 88–89.

7. Scott, "Postwar Pluralism, *Brown v. Board of Education*, and the Origins of Multiculturalism," 70.

8. Risa L. Goluboff, *The Lost Promise of Civil Rights* (Cambridge, MA: Harvard University Press, 2007); Patterson, Brown v. Board of Education, xiii–xxix; Clayborne Carson, "Two Cheers for *Brown v. Board of Education*," *Journal of American History* 91, no. 1 (2004): 26–31; Lani Guinier, "From Racial Liberalism to Racial Literacy: *Brown v. Board of Education* and the Interest Divergence," *Journal of American History* 91, no. 1 (2004): 92–118.

9. Charles M. Payne, "'The Whole United States Is Southern!': *Brown v. Board* and the Mystification of Race," *Journal of American History* 91, no. 1 (2004): 83–91, quote page 85.

10. Guinier, "From Racial Liberalism to Racial Literacy."

11. Michael Klarman argues that white backlash to *Brown* was so powerful that the ruling was actually harmful to race relations in America, see Michael J. Klarman, "How *Brown*

Changed Race Relations: The Backlash Thesis," *Journal of American History* 81, no. 1 (1994): 81–118; In contrast, most scholars are careful to point out that *Brown* was not only just, but good for American race relations in the long run. See for example the Roundtable "*Brown v. Board of Education*, Fifty Years After," in *Journal of American History* 91, no. 1 (2004): 19–118.

12. Mary Dudziak, *Cold War Civil Rights: Race and the Image of American Democracy* (Princeton, NJ: Princeton University Press, 2000). For more on the failing of the American Creed, see Jackson, *Gunnar Myrdal and America's Conscience.* Also see: Zoë Burkholder, "'Because Race Can't Be Ignored': The Failure of the Colorblind Ideal in American Schools," *Education Week* 27, no. 9, October 2007: 29, 31.

13. Adam Fairclough, "The Costs of *Brown*: Black Teachers and School Integration," *Journal of American History* 91, no. 1 (2004): 43–55; Guinier, "From Racial Liberalism to Racial Literacy," 100–116. Also see, Brian J. Daugherity and Charles C. Bolton, eds., *With All Deliberate Speed: Implementing* Brown v. Board of Education (Fayetteville: University of Arkansas Press, 2008); Lisa M. Stulberg, *Race, Schools, and Hope: African Americans and School Choice after Brown* (New York: Teachers College Press, 2008); Charles C. Bolton, *The Hardest Deal of All: The Battle over School Integration in Mississippi, 1870–1980* (Jackson: University Press of Mississippi, 2005); Ronald P. Formisano, *Boston against Busing: Race, Class, and Ethnicity in the 1960s and 1970s.* rev. ed. (Chapel Hill: University of North Carolina Press, 2004); Jerald E. Podair, *The Strike That Changed New York: Blacks, Whites, and the Ocean Hill-Brownsville Crisis* (New Haven, CT: Yale University Press, 2002); Guadalupe San Miguel, *Brown Not White: School Integration and the Chicano Movement in Houston* (College Station: Texas A&M University Press, 2001); Ruben Donato, *The Other Struggle for Equal Schools: Mexican Americans during the Civil Rights Era* (Albany: State University of New York Press, 1997); Adam Fairclough, *Race and Democracy: The Civil Rights Struggle in Louisiana* (Athens: University of Georgia Press, 1995); David S. Cecelski, *Along Freedom Road: Hyde County, North Carolina, and the Fate of Black Schools in the South* (Chapel Hill: University of North Carolina Press, 1994);

14. On the history of multicultural education see James A. Banks, ed., *Multicultural Education, Transformative Knowledge, and Action: Historical and Contemporary Perspectives* (New York: Teachers College Press, 1996); James A. Banks and Cherry A. McGhee Banks, eds., *The Handbook of Research on Multicultural Education* (New York: Simon and Schuster, 1995); Reva Joshee and Lauri Johnson, eds., *Multicultural Education Policies in Canada and the United States* (Vancouver: University of British Columbia Press, 2007); Scott, "Postwar Pluralism, *Brown v. Board of Education*, and the Origins of Multiculturalism"; Christine Sleeter, "Multicultural Education as a Social Movement," *Theory into Practice* 35, no. 4 (1996): 239–47; Becky W. Thompson and Sangeeta Tyagi, eds., *Beyond a Dream Deferred: Multicultural Education and the Politics of Excellence* (Minneapolis: University of Minnesota Press, 1993); Zimmerman, "*Brown*-ing the American Textbook."

15. Gary Orfield and Chungmai Lee, "Historic Reversals, Accelerating Resegregation, and the Need for New Integration Strategies," 5. August 2007. The Civil Rights Project, University of California, Los Angeles. http://www.civilrightsproject.ucla.edu/research/deseg/reversals_reseg_need.pdf (accessed September 14, 2007). Also see: Amy Stuart Wells, *Both Sides Now: The Story of School Desegregation's Graduates* (Berkeley: University of California Press, 2009); John Charles Boger and Gary Orfield, eds. *School Resegregation: Must the South Turn Back?* (Chapel Hill: University of North Carolina Press, 2008); Charles T. Clotfelter, *After Brown: The Rise and Retreat of School Segregation* (Princeton, NJ: Princeton University Press, 2006); Derrick Bell, *Silent Covenants:* Brown v. Board of Education *and the Unfulfilled Hopes for Racial Reform* (New York: Oxford University Press, 2005); James D. Anderson, Dara N. Byrne, and Tavis Smiley, *The Unfinished Agenda of* Brown v. Board of Education (Hoboken, NJ: John Wiley & Sons, Inc., 2004); Gary Orfield and Susan E. Eaton, *Dismantling Desegregation: The Quiet Reversal of* Brown v. Board of Education (New York: The New Press, 1996).

16. *Board of Education of Oklahoma City v. Dowell*, 498 U.S. 237 (1991), *Freeman v. Pitts*, 503 U.S. 467 (1992), *Missouri v. Jenkins* S. Ct. 2038 (1995).

17. John Higham, "Multiculturalism and Universalism: A History and Critique," *American Quarterly* 45, no. 2 (1993): 195–219, quote pages 201–2.

18. Jonathan Zimmerman, *Whose America? Culture Wars in American Schools* (Cambridge, MA: Harvard University Press, 2002): 214–16; Hasia Diner, "Some Problems With 'Multiculturalism'; or, 'The Best Laid Plans . . . ,'" *American Quarterly* 45, no. 2 (1993): 301–8; Nathan Glazer, *We Are All Multiculturalists Now* (Cambridge, MA: Harvard University Press, 1997); Higham, "Multiculturalism and Universalism."

19. See for example: Stephen May, ed., *Critical Multiculturalism: Rethinking Multiculturalist and Antiracist Education* (London: Falmer, 1999). Also see David Gillborn, "Institutional Racism in Education Policy and Practice: A View from England," in *Multicultural Education Policies in Canada and the United States*, ed. Reva Joshee and Lauri Johnson (Vancouver: University of British Columbia Press, 2007): 217–40. A popular Web site dedicated to tolerance education by the Southern Poverty Law Center www.tolerance.org uses the terms "anti-bias" and "antiracist" but not "multicultural."

20. Eduardo Bonilla-Silva, *Racism without Racists: Color-Blind Racism and the Persistence of Racial Inequality in the United States*, 2nd ed. (Lanham, MD: Rowman and Littlefield Publishers, 2006); Janet Ward Schofield, "The Colorblind Perspective in School: Causes and Consequences," in *Multicultural Education: Issues and Perspectives* 5th ed., ed. James A. Banks and Cherry A. McGee Banks (Hoboken, NJ: John Wiley and Sons, 2004): 265–88.

21. William J. Bennett, *Why We Fight: Moral Clarity and the War on Terrorism* (New York: Doubleday, 2002). Also see Gillborn: "Institutional Racism in Education Policy and Practice," 233–36.

22. Michael K. Brown, et al. *White-Washing Race: The Myth of a Color-blind Society* (Berkeley: University of California Press, 2005).

23. *Parents Involved in Community Schools v. Seattle School District No. 1*, 5 U.S. 908 (2007): 47. The ruling on this case also applied to a similar case in Kentucky: *Meredith, Custodial Parent and Next Friend of McDonald v. Jefferson County Board of Education* et al. 5 U.S. 915 (2007).

24. Goodwin Liu, "Seattle and Louisville," *California Law Review* 95, no. 1 (2007): 277–317; J. Harvie Wilkinson III, "The Seattle and Louisville School Cases: There Is No Other Way," *Harvard Law Review* 121, no. 1 (2007): 158–83.

25. George H. Henry, "Our Best English Unit," *English Journal* 36, no. 7 (1947): 356–62; Pearl M. Fisher, "English, Democracy, and Color," *High Points* 24, no. 5 (1942): 5–10; Leon Lapp and Marie Atkinson, "A Study of Negro Life," *English Journal* 29, no. 8 (1940): 659–61.

26. Walter Benn Michaels, *The Trouble with Diversity: How We Learned to Love Identity and Ignore Inequality* (New York: Metropolitan Books, 2006): 5.

27. Gloria Ladson-Billings, "It's Not the Culture of Poverty, It's the Poverty of Culture," *Anthropology and Education Quarterly* 37, no. 2 (2006): 104–9, quote page 104.

28. Marvin Lynn, "Race, Culture, and the Education of African Americans" *Educational Theory* 56, no. 1 (2006): 107–19; Jill B. R. Cherneff and Eve Hochwald, eds., *Visionary Observers: Anthropological Inquiry and Education* (Lincoln: University of Nebraska Press, 2006); John Ogbu, *Black American Students in an Affluent Suburb: A Study of Academic Disengagement* (Mahwah, NJ: Lawrence Erlbaum, 2003); George Spindler, ed., *Fifty Years of Anthropology and Education, 1900–1954: A Spindler Anthology* (Mahwah, NJ: Lawrence Erlbaum, 2000); Gloria Ladson-Billings, *The Dreamkeepers: Successful Teachers of African American Children* (San Francisco: Jossey Bass, 1994); John Ogbu, "Understanding Cultural Diversity and Learning," *Educational Researcher* 21, no. 8 (1992) 5–14; Signithia Fordham and John Ogbu, "Black Students' School Success: Coping with the Burden of Acting White," *Urban Review* 18, no. 3 (1986): 176–206; John Ogbu, "Cultural Discontinuities and Schooling," *Anthropology and Education Quarterly* 13, no. 4 (1982): 290–307.

29. Hortense Powdermaker, *Probing Our Prejudices* (New York: Harper and Brothers, 1944): vii.

30. Mike Cole, *Critical Race Theory and Education: A Marxist Response* (New York: Palgrave Macmillan, 2009); Edward Taylor, David Gillborn, and Gloria Ladson-Billings, eds., *Foundations of Critical Race Theory in Education* (New York: Routledge, 2009); Mica Pollock, ed., *Everyday Antiracism: Getting Real about Race in School* (New York: The New Press, 2008): Mica Pollock, *Because of Race: How Americans Debate Harm and Opportunity in Our Schools* (Princeton, NJ: Princeton University Press, 2008); Gloria Ladson-Billings and William F. Tate, eds., *Education Research in the Public Interest: Social Justice, Action, and Policy* (New York: Teachers College Press, 2006); Antonia Darder and Rodolfo D. Torres, "Shattering the 'Race' Lens: Toward a Critical Theory of Racism," in *The Critical Pedagogy Reader*, ed. Antonia Darder, Marta Bartodano, and Rodolfo D. Torres (New York: RoutledgeFalmer, 2003): 245–61; Daniel G. Solorzano and Dolores Delgado Bernal, "Examining Transformational Resistance through a Critical Race and LatCrit Theory Framework: Chicana and Chicano Students in an Urban Context," *Urban Education* 36, no. 3 (2001): 308–42; Gloria Ladson-Billings, "Racialized Discourses and Ethnic Epistemologies," in *Handbook of Qualitative Research*, 2nd ed., eds., Norman K. Denzin and Yvonna S. Lincoln (Thousand Oaks, CA: Sage, 2000); Daniel G. Solorzano and Tara J. Yosso, "Toward a Critical Race Theory of Chicana and Chicano Education," in *Demarcating the Border of Chicana(o)/Latina(o) Education*, ed. Carlos Tejeda, Corinne Martinez, Zeus Leonardo, and Peter McLaren (Cresskill, NJ: Hampton Press, 2000); Marvin Lynn, "Toward a Critical Race Pedagogy," *Urban Education* 33, no. 6 (1999): 606–31; Laurence Parker, Donna Deyhle, and Sophia Villenas, eds., *Race Is . . . Race Isn't: Critical Race Theory and Qualitative Studies in Education* (Boulder, CO: Westview Press, 1999).

BIBLIOGRAPHY

Manuscript Collections

American Eugenics Society Records, American Philosophical Society Library, Philadelphia, PA.

American Jewish Committee, Executive Office, Morris Waldman Papers, YIVO Institute for Jewish Research, New York, NY.

American Museum of Natural History Archives, New York, NY.

Board of Education Records, Municipal Archives, City of New York, New York, NY.

Boston School Department, City of Boston Archives, West Roxbury, MA.

Charles James Hendley Papers, TAM 109, Tamiment Library/Robert F. Wagner Labor Archives, Elmer Holmes Bobst Library, New York, NY.

Charles S. Johnson Papers, Amistad Research Center at Tulane University, Race Relations Department, United Church Board for Homeland Ministries Archives, 1943–1970, New Orleans, LA.

Franz Boas Papers, American Philosophical Society Library, Philadelphia, PA.

Franz Boas Professional Papers, American Philosophical Society, Philadelphia, PA.

Leonard Covello Papers, MSS 40, Research Library of the Balch Institute for Ethnic Studies, Historical Society of Pennsylvania, Philadelphia, PA.

Margaret Mead Papers and the South Pacific Ethnographic Archives, Manuscript Division, Library of Congress, Washington, DC.

Mildred Hodgman Mahoney Papers, 1944–1969, Schlesinger Library on the History of Women in America at Radcliffe College, Harvard University, Cambridge, MA.

Rachel Davis DuBois Papers, General/Multiethnic Collection, Immigration History Research Center, University of Minnesota, Minneapolis, MN.

Radio Scripts Collection, 1937–1966, Manuscripts, Archive, and Rare Books Division, Schomberg Center for Research in Black Culture, New York Public Library, New York, NY.

Ruth Fulton Benedict Papers, Vassar College Archives and Special Collections, Poughkeepsie, NY.

United Federation of Teachers Records, WAG 022, Tamiment Library and Robert F. Wagner Labor Archives, Elmer Holmes Bobst Library, New York University, New York, NY.

Primary Sources

PERIODICALS

American Biology Teacher, National Association of Biology Teachers, Washington, DC. 1938–1954.

American Unity, Council against Intolerance in America, New York, NY. 1942–1954.

Boston Teachers Newsletter, Boston Teachers Club, Boston, MA. 1942–1954.

Bulletin of High Points in the Work of the High Schools of New York City, New York City Board of
    Education, New York, NY. 1919–1931.
Chicago Defender, Chicago, IL. 1905–1954.
Common Ground, Common Council for American Unity, New York, NY. 1940–1949.
Elementary English Review, National Council of Teachers of English, Detroit, MI. 1924–1954.
English Journal, National Council of Teachers of English, Urbana, IL. 1912–1954.
Eugenical News: Current Record of Race Hygiene, American Eugenics Society, New York, NY. 1916–
    1953.
Frontiers of Democracy, Progressive Education Association, New York, NY. 1939–1943.
High Points in the Work of the High Schools of New York City, New York City Board of Education,
    New York, NY. 1932–1954.
The Historical Outlook: A Journal for Readers, Students, and Teachers of History, Philadelphia, PA.
    1918–1933.
History Teacher's Magazine, Philadelphia, PA. 1909–1918.
Journal of the National Education Association, National Education Association, Washington, DC.
    1921–1946.
Massachusetts Teacher, Massachusetts Teachers Federation, Boston, MA. 1938–1954.
NEA Journal, National Education Association, Washington, DC. 1946–1954.
New Jersey Educational Review, New Jersey Educational Association, Trenton, NJ. 1927–1954.
New York Teacher, Teachers Union of New York, New York, NY. 1935–1941.
New York Times, New York, NY. 1900–1954.
Science Teacher, American Science Teachers Association, Washington, DC. 1936–1954.
Social Education, National Council for the Social Studies, Arlington, VA. 1937–1954.
Social Studies, Brooklawn, NJ. 1934–1953.
Social Studies: A Periodical for Teachers and Administrators, Philadelphia, PA. 1953–1954.

BOOKS AND PAMPHLETS

American Association of School Administrators. *From Sea to Shining Sea: Administrators Hand-
    book for Intergroup Education*. Washington, DC: National Education Association of the
    United States, 1947.
American Committee for Democracy and Intellectual Freedom. *Can You Name Them?* New York:
    ACDIF, 1939.
American Committee for Democracy and Intellectual Freedom. *The Genetic Basis for Democracy*.
    New York: ACDIF, 1939.
American Committee for Democracy and Intellectual Freedom. *Science Condemns Racism:
    A Reply to the Chamber of Commerce of the State of New York*. New York: ACDIF, 1939.
Benedict, Ruth. *Race: Science and Politics*. Rev. ed. New York: Viking, 1945.
Benedict, Ruth. *Patterns of Culture*. Boston: Houghton Mifflin, 1989.
Benedict, Ruth, and Mildred Ellis. "Race and Cultural Relations: America's Answer to the Myth of
    a Master Race." In *Problems in American Life: Unit No. 5* Washington, DC: National Educa-
    tion Association, 1942.
Benedict, Ruth, and Gene Weltfish. *The Races of Mankind*. Public Affairs Pamphlet No. 85. New
    York: Public Affairs Committee, 1943.
Benedict, Ruth, and Gene Weltfish. *In Henry's Backyard: The Races of Mankind*. New York:
    H. Schuman, 1948.
Benjamin, Harold. *True Faith and Allegiance: An Inquiry into Education for Human Brotherhood and
    Understanding*. Commission for the Defense of Democracy through Education. Washington,
    DC: National Education Association, 1950.
Brameld, Theodore. *Minority Problems in the Public Schools*. New York: Harper and Brothers,
    1946.
Brown, Ina Corinne. *Race Relations in a Democracy*. New York: Harper and Brothers, 1949.
Cole, Stewart G., and Mildred Wiese Cole. *Minorities and the American Promise: The Conflict of
    Principle and Practice*. New York: Harper and Brothers, 1954.

Department of Supervisors and Directors of Instruction of the National Education Association. *Americans All: Studies in Intercultural Education*. Washington, DC: Department of Supervisors and Directors of Instruction of the National Education Association, 1942.

DuBois, Rachel Davis. *Build Together Americans: Adventures in Intercultural Education for the Secondary School*. New York: Hinds, Hayden, and Eldredge, 1945.

DuBois, Rachel Davis. *Get Together Americans: Friendly Approaches to Racial and Cultural Conflicts through the Neighborhood-Home Festival*. New York: Harper and Brothers, 1943.

DuBois, Rachel Davis. *Neighbors in Action: A Manual for Local Leaders in Intergroup Relations*. New York: Harper and Brothers, 1950.

DuBois, Rachel Davis, and Emma Schweppe, eds. *The Germans in American Life*. New York: Thomas Nelson and Sons, 1936.

DuBois, Rachel Davis, and Emma Schweppe, eds. *The Jews in American Life*. New York: Thomas Nelson and Sons, 1935.

Education for Unity in the Schools of New York State: A Report on the Program of Intergroup Education in New York State Schools. Albany: University of the State of New York, 1947.

Gilchrist, Robert S., Lothar Kahn, and Robert Haas. *Building Friendly Relations*. Columbus: Ohio State University, 1947.

Grambs, Jean D. *Group Processes in Intergroup Education: An Intergroup Education Pamphlet*. New York: National Conference of Christians and Jews, 1952.

Heaton, Margaret M. *Feelings Are Facts: An Intergroup Education Pamphlet*. New York: National Conference of Christians and Jews, 1951.

Intergroup Relations in Teaching Materials: A Survey and Appraisal. Report of the Committee on the Study of Teaching Materials in Intergroup Relations. Washington, DC: American Council on Education, 1949.

Kilpatrick, William H., and William Van Til, eds. *Intercultural Attitudes in the Making: Parents, Youth Leaders, and Teachers at Work*. Ninth Yearbook of the John Dewey Society. New York: Harper and Brothers, 1947.

Laughlin, Harry H. *Immigration and Conquest*. New York: Special Committee on Immigration and Naturalization of the Chamber of Commerce of the State of New York, 1939.

Lerman, Louis. *Winter Soldiers: A Story of a Conspiracy against the Schools*. New York: Committee for Defense of Public Education, 1941.

Locke, Alain, and Bernhard J. Stern. *When Peoples Meet: A Study in Race and Culture Contacts*. Rev. ed. New York: Hinds, Hayden, and Eldredge, 1949.

Mead, Margaret. *Blackberry Winter: My Earlier Years*. New York: Morrow, 1972.

Mead, Margaret. *Coming of Age in Samoa: A Psychological Study of Primitive Youth for Western Civilization*. New York: Morrow, 1928.

Mead, Margaret. *Growing Up in New Guinea: A Comparative Study of Primitive Education*. New York: Morrow, 1930.

Mead, Margaret. *The School in American Culture*. Cambridge, MA: Harvard University Press, 1951.

Mead, Margaret, and James Baldwin. *A Rap on Race*. Philadelphia: J.B. Lippincott, 1971.

New York City Board of Education Board of Superintendents. *Unity through Understanding*. New York: Board of Education of the City of New York, 1946.

Powdermaker, Hortense. *Probing Our Prejudices*. New York: Harper, 1944.

Taba, Hilda. *Curriculum in Intergroup Relations: Case Studies in Instruction for Secondary Schools*. Washington, DC: American Council on Education, 1949.

Taba, Hilda, Elizabeth Hall Brady, and John T. Robinson. *Elementary Curriculum in Intergroup Relations: Case Studies in Instruction*. Washington, DC: American Council on Education, 1950.

Taba, Hilda, Elizabeth Hall Brady, and John T. Robinson. *Intergroup Education in Public Schools: Experimental Programs Sponsored by the Project in Intergroup Education in Cooperating Schools: Theory, Practice, and In-Service Education*. Washington, DC: American Council on Education, 1952.

Taba, Hilda, and William Van Til, eds. *Democratic Human Relations: Promising Practices in Intergroup and Intercultural Education in the Social Studies*. Sixteenth Yearbook. Washington, DC: National Council for the Social Studies, 1945.

Van Til, William, et al. *Democracy Demands It: A Resource Unit for Intercultural Education in the High School.* New York: Harper and Brothers, 1950.

Vickery, William E., and Stewart G. Cole. *Intercultural Education in American Schools: Proposed Objectives and Methods.* New York: Harper and Brothers, 1943.

Selected Secondary Sources

Alonso, Harriet Hyman. *Peace as a Women's Issue: A History of the U.S. Movement for World Peace and Women's Rights.* Syracuse, NY: Syracuse University Press, 1993.

Anderson, James D. *The Education of Blacks in the South, 1860–1935.* Chapel Hill: University of North Carolina Press, 1988.

Anderson, James D., Dara N. Byrne, and Tavis Smiley. *The Unfinished Agenda of Brown v. Board of Education.* Hoboken, NJ: John Wiley, 2004.

Appiah, Kwame Anthony. *In My Father's House: Africa in the Philosophy of Culture.* New York: Oxford University Press, 1993.

Appiah, Kwame Anthony, and Amy Gutman. *Color Conscious: The Political Morality of Race.* Princeton, NJ: Princeton University Press, 1996.

Arnesen, Eric. "Whiteness and the Historians' Imagination." *International Labor and Working Class History* 60 (October 2001): 3–32.

Austin-Broos, Diane J., ed. *Creating Culture: Profiles in the Study of Culture.* North Sydney, Australia: Allen and Unwin, 1987.

Baker, Lee D. *Anthropology and the Construction of Race, 1896–1954.* Berkeley: University of California Press, 1998.

Banks, Cherry A. McGee. *Improving Multicultural Education: Lessons from the Intergroup Education Movement.* New York: Teachers College Press, 2005.

Banks, James A., ed. *Multicultural Education, Transformative Knowledge, and Action: Historical and Contemporary Perspectives.* New York: Teachers College Press, 1996.

Banner, Lois W. *Intertwined Lives: Margaret Mead, Ruth Benedict, and Their Circle.* New York: Alfred A. Knopf, 2003.

Barkan, Elazar. *The Retreat of Scientific Racism: Changing Concepts of Race in Britain and the United States between the World Wars.* Cambridge: Cambridge University Press, 1992.

Barrett, James R. "Americanization from the Bottom Up: Immigration and the Remaking of the Working Class in the United States, 1880–1930." *Journal of American History* 79, no. 3 (1992): 996–1020.

Baum, Bruce. *The Rise and Fall of the Caucasian Race: A Political History of Racial Identity.* New York: New York University Press, 2006.

Bederman, Gail. *Manliness and Civilization: A Cultural History of Gender and Race in the United States, 1880–1917.* Chicago: University of Chicago Press, 1995.

Bell, Derrick. *Silent Covenants: Brown v. Board of Education and the Unfulfilled Hopes for Racial Reform.* New York: Oxford University Press, 2005.

Bennett, David H. *The Party of Fear: From Nativist Movements to the New Right in American History.* Chapel Hill: University of North Carolina Press, 1988.

Biondi, Martha. *To Stand and Fight: The Struggle for Civil Rights in Postwar New York City.* Cambridge, MA: Harvard University Press, 2003.

Boger, John C., and Gary Orfield, eds. *School Resegregation: Must the South Turn Back?* Chapel Hill: University of North Carolina Press, 2008.

Bolton, Charles C. *The Hardest Deal of All: The Battle over School Integration in Mississippi, 1870–1980.* Jackson: University Press of Mississippi, 2005.

Bonilla-Silva, Eduardo. *Racism without Racists: Color-Blind Racism and the Persistence of Racial Inequality in the United States.* 3rd ed. Lanham, MD: Rowman and Littlefield, 2009.

Brinkley, Alan. *Liberalism and Its Discontents.* Cambridge, MA: Harvard University Press, 1998.

Brooks, Jennifer E. *Defining the Peace: World War II Veterans, Race, and the Remaking of Southern Political Tradition.* Chapel Hill: University of North Carolina Press, 2004.

Brown, Michael K., et al. *White-Washing Race: The Myth of a Color-Blind Society*. Berkeley: University of California Press, 2005.

Burkholder, Zoë. "From Forced Tolerance to Forced Busing: Wartime Intercultural Education and the Rise of Black Educational Activism in Boston, 1943–1965." *Harvard Educational Review* 80, no. 3 (2010): 293–326.

Capeci, Dominic J., Jr. *The Harlem Riot of 1943*. Philadelphia: Temple University Press, 1977.

Capeci, Dominic J., Jr., and Martha Wilkerson. *Layered Violence: The Detroit Rioters of 1943*. Jackson: University of Mississippi Press, 1991.

Carson, Clayborne. "Two Cheers for *Brown v. Board of Education*." *Journal of American History* 91, no. 1 (2004): 26–31.

Cecelski, David S. *Along Freedom Road: Hyde County, North Carolina, and the Fate of Black Schools in the South*. Chapel Hill: University of North Carolina Press, 1994.

Chatfield, Charles. *For Peace and Justice: Pacifism in America, 1914–1941*. Knoxville: University of Tennessee Press, 1971.

Chen, Anthony S. "'The Hitlerian Rule of Quotas': Racial Conservatism and the Politics of Fair Employment Legislation in New York State." *Journal of American History* 92, no. 4 (2006): 1238–264.

Chen, Anthony S. *The Fifth Freedom: Jobs, Politics, and Civil Rights in the United States, 1941–1972*. Princeton, NJ: Princeton University Press, 2009.

Cherneff, Jill B. R., and Eve Hochwald, eds. *Visionary Observers: Anthropological Inquiry and Education*. Lincoln: University of Nebraska Press, 2006.

Clotfelter, Charles T. *After Brown: The Rise and Retreat of School Segregation*. Princeton, NJ: Princeton University Press, 2006.

Cole, Mike. *Critical Race Theory and Education: A Marxist Response*. New York: Palgrave Macmillan, 2009.

Countryman, Matthew J. *Up South: Civil Rights and Black Power in Philadelphia*. Philadelphia: University of Pennsylvania Press, 2007.

Cullen, Jim. *The American Dream: A Short History of An Idea That Shaped a Nation*. New York: Oxford University Press, 2003.

Dagbovie, Pero Gaglo. *The Early Black History Movement: Carter G. Woodson and Lorenzo Johnston Greene*. Urbana: University of Illinois Press, 2007.

Darder, Antonia, and Rodolfo D. Torres. "Shattering the 'Race' Lens: Toward a Critical Theory of Racism." In *The Critical Pedagogy Reader*, edited by Antonia Darder, Marta Bartodano, and Rodolfo D. Torres, 245–61. New York: RoutledgeFalmer, 2003.

Daugherity, Brian J., and Charles C. Bolton, eds. *With All Deliberate Speed: Implementing* Brown v. Board of Education. Fayetteville: University of Arkansas Press, 2008.

Davila, Jerry. *Diplomas of Whiteness: Race and Social Policy in Brazil, 1917–1945*. Durham, NC: Duke University Press, 2004.

Deloria, Philip J. *Playing Indian*. New Haven, CT: Yale University Press, 1998.

Diner, Hasia. "Some Problems with 'Multiculturalism'; or, 'The Best Laid Plans. . . .'" *American Quarterly* 45, no. 2 (1993): 301–8.

Donato, Ruben. *The Other Struggle for Equal Schools: Mexican Americans during the Civil Rights Era*. Albany: State University of New York Press, 1997.

Dorn, Charles. *American Education, Democracy, and the Second World War*. New York: Palgrave Macmillan, 2007.

Dorn, Charles. "'I Had All Kinds of Kids in My Classes, and It Was Fine': Public Schooling in Richmond, California, during World War II." *History of Education Quarterly* 45, no. 4 (2005): 37–50.

Dougherty, Jack. "'That's When We Were Marching for Jobs': Black Teachers and the Early Civil Rights Movement in Milwaukee." *History of Education Quarterly* 38, no. 2 (1998): 121–41.

Douglas, Davison. *Reading, Writing, and Race: The Desegregation of the Charlotte Schools*. Greensboro: University of North Carolina Press, 1995.

Douglas, Davison. *Jim Crow Moves North: The Battle over Northern School Segregation, 1865–1954.* New York: Oxford University Press, 2005.

Dower, John W. *War without Mercy: Race and Power in the Pacific War.* New York: Pantheon Books, 1986.

Dudziak, Mary. *Cold War Civil Rights: Race and the Image of American Democracy.* Princeton, NJ: Princeton University Press, 2000.

Eagles, Charles W. "Toward New Histories of the Civil Rights Era." *Journal of Southern History* 66, no. 4 (2000): 815–48.

Fairclough, Adam. *Better Day Coming: Blacks and Equality, 1890–2001.* New York: Viking, 2001.

Fairclough, Adam. *Race and Democracy: The Civil Rights Struggle in Louisiana.* Athens: University of Georgia Press, 1995.

Fairclough, Adam. *Teaching Equality: Black Schools in the Age of Jim Crow.* Athens: University of Georgia Press, 2001.

Fairclough, Adam. *A Class of Their Own: Black Teachers in the Segregated South.* Cambridge, MA: Harvard University Press, 2007.

Feldman, Glen, ed. *Before Brown: Civil Rights and White Backlash in the Modern South.* Tuscaloosa: University of Alabama Press, 2004.

Ferguson, Ann A. *Bad Boys: Public Schools in the Making of Black Masculinity.* Ann Arbor: University of Michigan Press, 2000.

Fields, Barbara J. "Ideology and Race in American History." In *Region, Race, and Reconstruction: Essays in Honor of C. Vann Woodward,* edited by J. Morgan Kouser and James M. McPherson, 143–72. New York: Oxford University Press, 1982.

Florio-Ruane, Susan. *Teacher Education and the Cultural Imagination: Autobiography, Conversation, and Narrative.* Mahwah, NJ: Lawrence Erlbaum, 2000.

Foley, Douglas E., and Dorothy C. Holland, eds. *The Cultural Production of the Educated Person: Critical Ethnographies of Schooling and Local Practice.* Albany: State University of New York Press, 1996.

Fordham, Signithia. *Blacked Out: Dilemmas of Race, Identity, and Success at Capital High.* Chicago: University of Chicago Press, 1996.

Fordham, Signithia, and John Ogbu. "Black Students' School Success: Coping with the Burden of Acting White." *Urban Review* 18, no. 3 (1986): 176–206.

Formisano, Ronald P. *Boston against Busing: Race, Class, and Ethnicity in the 1960s and 1970s.* Rev. ed. Chapel Hill: University of North Carolina Press, 2004.

Foster, Stuart J. *Red Alert! Educators Confront the Red Scare in Schools, 1947–1954.* New York: Peter Lang, 2000.

Foucault, Michel. *The History of Sexuality: Volume 1: An Introduction.* New York: Vintage, 1990.

Fultz, Michael. "African American Teachers in the South, 1890–1940: Powerlessness and the Ironies of Expectations and Protest." *History of Education Quarterly* 35, no. 4 (1995): 401–22.

Fultz, Michael. "'The Morning Cometh': African-American Periodicals, Education, and the Black Middle Class, 1900–1930." *Journal of Negro History* 80, no. 3 (1995): 97–112.

Fultz, Michael. "Teacher Training and African American Education in the South, 1900–1940." *Journal of Negro Education* 64, no. 2 (1995): 196–210.

Gary, Brett. *The Nervous Liberals: Propaganda Anxieties from World War I to the Cold War.* New York: Columbia University Press, 1999.

Gates, E. Nathaniel, ed. *Critical Race Theory: Essays on the Social Construction and Reproduction of Race.* New York: Garland, 1997.

Gates, E. Nathaniel, ed. *Race and U.S. Foreign Policy from 1900 through World War II.* New York: Routledge, 1998.

Gerstle, Gary. *American Crucible: Race and Nation in the Twentieth Century.* Princeton, NJ: Princeton University Press, 2001.

Gerstle, Gary. "The Crucial Decade: The 1940s and Beyond." *Journal of American History* 92, no. 4 (2006): 1292–299.

Gerstle, Gary. "The Protean Character of American Liberalism." *American Historical Review* 99, no. 4 (1994): 1043–73.

Gilmore, Glenda Elizabeth. *Defying Dixie: The Radical Roots of Civil Rights, 1919–1950.* New York: W.W. Norton, 2008.

Gilpin, Patrick, and Marybeth Gasman. *Charles S. Johnson: Leadership beyond the Veil of Jim Crow.* Albany: State University of New York Press, 2003.

Gilroy, Paul. *Against Race: Imaging Political Culture beyond the Color Line.* Cambridge, MA: Belknap Press/Harvard University Press, 2000.

Giordano, Gerard. *Wartime Schools: How World War II Changed American Education.* New York: Peter Lang, 2004.

Giroux, Henry. *Pedagogy and the Politics of Hope: Theory, Culture, and Schooling; A Critical Reader.* Boulder, CO: Westview Press, 1997.

Glazer, Nathan. *We Are All Multiculturalists Now.* Cambridge, MA: Harvard University Press, 1997.

Gleason, Philip. "Americans All: World War II and the Shaping of American Identity." *Review of Politics* 43, no. 4 (1981): 483–518.

Goldstein, Eric L. *The Price of Whiteness: Jews, Race, and American Identity.* Princeton, NJ: Princeton University Press, 2006.

Goodenow, Ronald K. "The Progressive Educators, Race, and Ethnicity in the Depression Years: An Overview." *History of Education Quarterly* 15, no. 4 (1975): 365–94.

Gossett, Thomas F. *Race: The History of an Idea in America,* rev. ed. New York: Oxford University Press, 1997.

Graham, Patricia A. *Progressive Education from Arcady to Academe: A History of the Progressive Education Association, 1919–1955.* New York: Teachers College Press, 1967.

Gramsci, Antonio. *Selections from the Prison Notebooks,* edited and translated by Quintin Hoare and Geoffrey Nowell Smith. New York: International Publishers, 1971.

Greenberg, Cheryl Lynn. *Troubling the Waters: Black-Jewish Relations in the American Century.* Princeton, NJ: Princeton University Press, 2006.

Gresson, Aaron David, III. *Race and Education.* New York: Peter Lang, 2008.

Grossman, James R. *Land of Hope: Chicago, Black Southerners, and the Great Migration.* Chicago: University of Chicago Press, 1989.

Guglielmo, Thomas A. "Fighting for Caucasian Rights: Mexicans, Mexican Americans, and the Transnational Struggle for Civil Rights in World War II Texas." *Journal of American History* 92, no. 4 (2006): 1212–237.

Guglielmo, Thomas A. *White on Arrival: Italians, Race, Color, and Power in Chicago, 1890–1945.* New York: Oxford University Press, 2003.

Guinier, Lani. "From Racial Liberalism to Racial Literacy: *Brown v. Board of Education* and the Interest Divergence." *Journal of American History* 91, no. 1 (2004): 92–118.

Guterl, Matthew Pratt. *The Color of Race in America.* Cambridge, MA: Harvard University Press, 2001.

Hall, Jacquelyn Dowd. "The Long Civil Rights Movement and the Political Uses of the Past." *Journal of American History* 91, no. 4 (2005): 1233–64.

Handler, Richard. *Critics against Culture: Anthropological Observers of Mass Society.* Madison: University of Wisconsin Press, 2005.

Haney, David Paul. *The Americanization of Social Science: Intellectuals and Public Responsibility in the Postwar United States.* Philadelphia: Temple University Press, 2008.

Harris, Cheryl. "Whiteness as Property." *Harvard Law Review* 106, no. 8 (1993): 1709–91.

Harris, Marvin. *The Rise of Anthropological Theory: A History of Theories of Culture.* New York: Thomas Y. Crowell, 1968.

Harrison, Alferdteen, ed. *Black Exodus: The Great Migration from the American South.* Jackson: University Press of Mississippi, 1991.

Hartman, Andrew. *Cold War: The Battle for the American School.* New York: Palgrave Macmillan, 2008.

Hattam, Victoria. *In the Shadow of Race: Jews, Latinos, and Immigrant Politics in the United States.* Chicago: University of Chicago Press, 2007.

Hegeman, Susan. *Patterns for America: Modernism and the Concept of Culture.* Princeton, NJ: Princeton University Press, 1999.

Herman, Ellen. *The Romance of American Psychology: Political Culture in the Age of Experts.* Los Angeles: University of California Press, 1995.

Herskovits, Melville J. *Franz Boas: The Science of Man in the Making.* New York: Scribner, 1953.

Higginbotham, Evelyn Brooks. "African American Women's History and the Metalanguage of Race." *Signs* 17, no. 2 (1992): 251–74.

Higham, John. *Strangers in the Land: Patterns of American Nativism, 1860–1925.* New York: Atheneum, 1963.

Higham, John. "Multiculturalism and Universalism: A History and Critique." *American Quarterly* 45, no. 2 (1993): 195–219.

Hodes, Martha. "The Mercurial Nature and Abiding Power of Race: A Transnational Family Story." *American Historical Review* 108 (February 2003): 84–118.

Howard, Jane. *Margaret Mead, A Life.* New York: Simon and Schuster, 1984.

Howard, John. *Concentration Camps on the Home Front: Japanese Americans in the House of Jim Crow.* Chicago: University of Chicago Press, 2008.

Hyatt, Marshall. *Franz Boas Social Activist: The Dynamics of Ethnicity.* New York: Greenwood, 1990.

Ignatiev, Noel. *How the Irish Became White.* New York: Routledge, 1995.

Jackson, John P. *Social Scientists for Social Justice: Making the Case against Segregation.* New York: New York University Press, 2001.

Jackson, John P., Jr. "The Triumph of the Segregationists? A Historiographical Inquiry into Psychology and the *Brown* Litigation." *History of Psychology* 3, no. 3 (2000): 239–61.

Jackson, Walter A. *Gunnar Myrdal and America's Conscience: Social Engineering and Racial Liberalism, 1938–1987.* Chapel Hill: University of North Carolina Press, 1990.

Jacobson, Matthew Frye. *Barbarian Virtues: The United States Encounters Foreign Peoples at Home and Abroad, 1876–1917.* New York: Hill and Wang, 2000.

Jacobson, Matthew Frye. *Whiteness of a Different Color: European Immigrants and the Alchemy of Race.* Cambridge, MA: Harvard University Press, 1998.

James, Thomas. *Exile Within: The Schooling of Japanese Americans, 1942–1945.* Cambridge, MA: Harvard University Press, 1987.

Jewett, Sarah. "'If You Don't Identify with Your Ancestry, You're Like a Race without a Land': Constructing Race at a Small Urban Middle School." *Education and Anthropology Quarterly* 37, no. 2 (2006): 144–61.

Johnson, Lauri. "'Making Democracy Real': Teacher Union and Community Activism to Promote Diversity in the New York City Public Schools, 1935–1950." *Urban Education* 37, no. 5 (2002): 566–87.

Johnson, Lauri. "Multicultural Policy and Social Activism: Redefining Who 'Counts' in Multicultural Education." *Race, Ethnicity, and Education* 6, no. 2 (2003): 107–21.

Johnson, Lauri. "A Generation of Women Activists: African American Female Educators in Harlem, 1930–1950." *Journal of African American History* 89, no. 3 (2004): 223–40.

Jonas, Gilbert. *Freedom's Sword: The NAACP and the Struggle against Racism in America, 1909–1969.* New York: Routledge, 2005.

Joseph, Peniel E. *Black Power Movement: Rethinking the Black Power-Civil Rights Era.* New York: Routledge, 2006.

Joshee, Reva, and Lauri Johnson, eds. *Multicultural Education Policies in Canada and the United States.* Vancouver: University of British Columbia Press, 2007.

Kandel, Isaac L. *The Impact of the War upon American Education.* Chapel Hill: University of North Carolina Press, 1948.

Karpinski, Carol F. *A Visible Company of Professionals: African Americans and the National Education Association during the Civil Rights Movement.* New York: Peter Lang, 2008.

Kennedy, David M. *Freedom from Fear: The American People in Depression and War, 1929–1945.* New York: Oxford University Press, 1999.

Kennedy, David M. *Over Here: The First World War and American Society.* New York: Oxford University Press, 1980.

Klarman, Michael J. "How *Brown* Changed Race Relations: The Backlash Thesis." *Journal of American History* 81, no. 1 (1994): 81–118.

Kliebard, Herbert M. *The Struggle for the American Curriculum, 1893–1958.* New York: Routledge-Falmer, 2004.

Kolchin, Peter. "Whiteness Studies: The New History of Race in America." *Journal of American History* 89, no. 1 (2002): 154–73.

Kryder, Daniel. *Divided Arsenal: Race and the American State during World War II.* Cambridge: Cambridge University Press, 2000.

Kurashige, Scott. *The Shifting Grounds of Race: Black and Japanese Americans in the Making of Multiethnic Los Angeles.* Princeton, NJ: Princeton University Press, 2008.

Kuznick, Peter J. *Beyond the Laboratory: Scientists as Political Activists in 1930s America.* Chicago: University of Chicago Press, 1987.

Ladson-Billings, Gloria. *The Dreamkeepers: Successful Teachers of African American Children.* San Francisco: Jossey Bass, 1994.

Ladson-Billings, Gloria. "It's Not the Culture of Poverty, It's the Poverty of Culture." *Anthropology and Education Quarterly* 37, no. 2 (2006): 104–9.

Lapsley, Hilary. *Margaret Mead and Ruth Benedict: The Kinship of Women.* Amherst: University of Massachusetts Press, 1999.

Lasch-Quinn, Elisabeth. *Race Experts: How Racial Etiquette, Sensitivity Training, and New Age Therapy Hijacked the Civil Rights Revolution.* New York: W.W. Norton, 2001.

Lawson, Steven F. *Running for Freedom: Civil Rights and Black Politics in America since 1941*, 2nd ed. New York: McGraw-Hill, 1997.

Levinson, Bradley A., Douglas E. Foley, and Dorothy C. Holland, eds. *The Cultural Production of the Educated Person: Critical Ethnographies of Schooling and Local Practice.* Albany: State University of New York Press, 1996.

Lewis, Amanda. *Race in the Schoolyard: Negotiating the Color Line in Classrooms and Communities.* New Brunswick, NJ: Rutgers University Press, 2003.

Liss, Julia E. "Diasporic Identities: The Science and Politics of Race in the Work of Franz Boas and W. E. B. Du Bois, 1894–1919." *Cultural Anthropology* 13, no. 2 (1998): 127–66.

Liu, Goodwin. "Seattle and Louisville." *California Law Review* 95, no. 1 (2007): 277–317.

Lopez, Ian F. Haney. *White by Law: The Legal Construction of Race.* New York: New York University Press, 1996.

Lynn, Marvin. "Race, Culture, and the Education of African Americans." *Educational Theory* 56, no. 1 (2006): 107–19.

Mabee, Carleton. "Margaret Mead and a 'Pilot Experiment' in Progressive and Interracial Education: The Downtown Community School." *New York History* 65, no. 1 (1984): 5–31.

Markowitz, Ruth Jacknow. *My Daughter, the Teacher: Jewish Teachers in the New York City Schools.* New Brunswick, NJ: Rutgers University Press, 1993.

Marks, Carole. *Farewell—We're Good and Gone.* Bloomington: Indiana University Press, 1989.

May, Stephen, ed. *Critical Multiculturalism: Rethinking Multiculturalist and Antiracist Education.* London: Falmer, 1999.

McClay, Wilfred M. *The Masterless: Self and Society in Modern America.* Chapel Hill: University of North Carolina Press, 1994.

McEnaney, Laura. "Nightmares on Elm Street: Demobilizing in Chicago, 1945–1953." *Journal of American History* 92, no. 4 (2006): 1265–291.

Mead, Margaret. *An Anthropologist at Work: Writings of Ruth Benedict.* Boston: Houghton Mifflin, 1959.

Mead, Margaret. *Ruth Benedict.* New York: Columbia University Press, 1974.

Michaels, Walter Benn. *The Trouble with Diversity: How We Learned to Love Identity and Ignore Inequality.* New York: Metropolitan, 2006.

Mirel, Jeffrey. *Patriotic Pluralism: Americanization Education and European Immigrants*. Cambridge, MA: Harvard University Press, 2010.

Mirel, Jeffrey. "The Politics of Educational Retrenchment in Detroit, 1929–1935." *History of Education Quarterly* 24, no. 3 (1984): 323–58.

Modell, Judith Schachter. *Ruth Benedict: Patterns of a Life*. Philadelphia: University of Pennsylvania Press, 1983.

Montalto, Nicholas V. *A History of the Intercultural Education Movement, 1924–1941*. New York: Garland, 1982.

Mumford, Kevin. *Newark: A History of Race, Rights, and Riots in America*. New York: New York University Press, 2007.

O'Connor, Alice. *Poverty Knowledge: Social Science, Social Policy, and the Poor in Twentieth-Century U.S. History*. Princeton, NJ: Princeton University Press, 2001.

Ogbu, John. *Black American Students in an Affluent Suburb: A Study of Academic Disengagement*. Mahwah, NJ: Lawrence Erlbaum, 2003.

Ogbu, John. "Cultural Discontinuities and Schooling." *Anthropology and Education Quarterly* 13, no. 4 (1982): 290–307.

Ogbu, John. "Understanding Cultural Diversity and Learning." *Educational Researcher* 21, no. 8 (1992): 5–14.

Olneck, Michael. "The Recurring Dream: Symbolism and Ideology in Intercultural and Multicultural Education." *American Journal of Education* 98 (1990): 147–74.

Omi, Michael, and Howard Winant. *Racial Formation in the United States from the 1960s to the 1980s*, rev. ed. New York: Routledge and Kegan Paul, 1994.

Orfield, Gary, and Susan E. Eaton. *Dismantling Desegregation: The Quiet Reversal of Brown v. Board of Education*. New York: New Press, 1996.

Osur, Alan M. *Separate and Unequal: Race Relations in the AAF during World War II*. Honolulu, HI: University Press of the Pacific, 2004.

Painter, Nell Irvin. *The History of White People*. New York: W.W. Norton, 2010.

Pak, Yoon K. *Wherever I Go, I Will Always Be a Loyal American: Seattle's Japanese American Schoolchildren during World War II*. New York: Routledge, 2001.

Pak, Yoon K. "'If There Is a Better Intercultural Plan in Any School System in America, I Do Not Know Where It Is': The San Diego City Schools Intercultural Education Program, 1946–1949." *Urban Education* 37, no. 5 (2002): 588–609.

Parker, Laurence, Donna Deyhle, and Sophia Villenas, eds. *Race Is . . . Race Isn't: Critical Race Theory and Qualitative Studies in Education*. Boulder, CO: Westview Press, 1999.

Pascoe, Peggy. *What Comes Naturally: Miscegenation Law and the Making of Race in America*. New York: Oxford University Press, 2009.

Patterson, James A. *Brown v. Board of Education: A Civil Rights Milestone and Its Troubled Legacy*. New York: Oxford University Press, 2001.

Payne, Charles M. *I've Got the Light of Freedom: The Organizing Tradition and the Mississippi Freedom Struggle*. Berkeley: University of California Press, 1995.

Payne, Charles M. "'The Whole United States Is Southern!': *Brown v. Board* and the Mystification of Race." *Journal of American History* 91, no. 1 (2004): 83–91.

Perlstein, Daniel. "American Dilemmas: Education, Social Science, and the Limits of Liberalism." In *The Global Color Line: Racial and Ethnic Inequality and Struggle from a Global Perspective*, edited by Pinar Batur and Joe R. Feagin, 357–79. Stamford, CT: JAI Press, 1999.

Perry, Thelma D. *History of the American Teachers Association*. Washington, DC: National Education Association, 1975.

Pettigrew, Thomas F. *The Sociology of Race Relations: Reflection and Reform*. New York: Free Press, 1980.

Pierpont, Claudia Roth. "The Measure of America: How a Rebel Anthropologist Waged a War on Racism." *New Yorker* 80, no. 3 (2004): 48–63.

Podair, Jerald E. *The Strike That Changed New York: Blacks, Whites, and the Ocean Hill-Brownsville Crisis*. New Haven, CT: Yale University Press, 2002.

Pollock, Mica. *Because of Race: How Americans Debate Harm and Opportunity in Our Schools.* Princeton, NJ: Princeton University Press, 2008.

Pollock, Mica. *Colormute: Race Talk Dilemmas in an American School.* Princeton, NJ: Princeton University Press, 2004.

Pollock, Mica, ed. *Everyday Antiracism: Getting Real About Race in School.* New York: New Press, 2008.

Price, David. *Threatening Anthropology: McCarthyism and the FBI's Surveillance of Activist Anthropologists.* Durham, NC: Duke University Press, 2004.

Ramsey, Sonya. *Reading, Writing, and Segregation: A Century of Black Women Teachers in Nashville.* Urbana: University of Illinois Press, 2008.

Ravitch, Diane. *The Great School Wars: A History of the New York City Public Schools.* Rev. ed. Baltimore: Johns Hopkins University Press, 2000.

Ravitch, Diane. *The Troubled Crusade: American Education, 1945–1980.* New York: Basic Books, 1983.

Ravitch, Diane, and Ronald K. Goodenow. *Educating an Urban People: The New York City Experience.* New York: Teachers College Press, 1981.

Reuben, Julie. "Beyond Politics: Community Civics and the Redefinition of Citizenship in the Progressive Era." *History of Education Quarterly* 37, no. 4 (1997): 399–420.

Richardson, Theresa R., and Erwin V. Johanningmeier. *Race, Ethnicity, and Education: What Is Taught in School.* Greenwich, CT: Information Age, 2003.

Ritterhouse, Jennifer. *Growing Up Jim Crow: The Racial Socialization of Black and White Southern Children, 1890–1940.* Chapel Hill: University of North Carolina Press, 2006.

Robbins, Richard. *Sidelines Activist: Charles S. Johnson and the Struggle for Civil Rights.* Jackson: University Press of Mississippi, 1996.

Roediger, David R. *The Wages of Whiteness: Race and the American Working Class,* rev. ed. London and New York: Verso, 1999. First published 1991.

Ross, Dorothy. *The Origins of American Social Science.* Cambridge, UK: Cambridge University Press, 1991.

Ross, William. *Forging New Freedoms: Nativism, Education, and the Constitution, 1917–1927.* Lincoln: University of Nebraska Press, 1994.

Rydell, Robert W. *World of Fairs: The Century-of-Progress Exhibitions.* Chicago: University of Chicago Press, 1993.

Sacks, Karen Brodkin. *How Jews Became White Folks and What That Says about Race in America.* New Brunswick, NJ: Rutgers University Press, 1998.

San Miguel, Guadalupe. *Brown Not White: School Integration and the Chicano Movement in Houston.* College Station: Texas A&M University Press, 2001.

Sarroub, Loukia K. *All American Yemeni Girls: Being Muslim in a Public School.* Philadelphia: University of Pennsylvania Press, 2005.

Schrecker, Ellen W. *Many Are the Crimes: McCarthyism in America.* Boston: Little, Brown, 1998.

Schrecker, Ellen W. "McCarthy Era Blacklisting of School Teachers, College Professors, and Other Public Employees: The FBI Responsibilities Program File and the Dissemination of Information Policy File." *Journal of American History* 81, no. 1 (1994): 360–61.

Schrecker, Ellen W. *No Ivory Tower: McCarthyism and the Universities.* New York: Oxford University Press, 1986.

Schroer, Timothy L. *Recasting Race after World War II: Germans and African Americans in American-Occupied Germany.* Boulder: University Press of Colorado, 2007.

Scott, Daryl Michael. *Contempt and Pity: Social Policy and the Image of the Damaged Black Psyche, 1880–1996.* Chapel Hill: University of North Carolina Press, 1997.

Scott, Daryl Michael. "Postwar Pluralism, *Brown v. Board of Education,* and the Origins of Multiculturalism." *Journal of American History* 91, no. 1 (2004): 69–91.

Selden, Steven. *Inheriting Shame: The Story of Eugenics and Racism in America.* New York: Teachers College Press, 1999.

Selig, Diana. *Americans All: The Cultural Gifts Movement.* Cambridge, MA: Harvard University Press, 2008.

Sevier, Brian R. "'Somewhere between Mutuality and Diversity': The Project in Intergroup Education and Teaching for Tolerance following World War II." Ph.D. diss., University of Colorado,
Boulder, 2002.

Shafer, Robert. "Multicultural Education in New York City during World War II." *New York History*
77, no. 3 (1996): 301–32.

Sklaroff, Lauren Rebecca. "Constructing G.I. Joe Louis: Cultural Solutions to the 'Negro Problem'
during World War II." *Journal of American History* 89, no. 3 (2002): 958–83.

Sleeter, Christine. "Multicultural Education as a Social Movement." *Theory into Practice* 35, no. 4
(1996): 239–47.

Smedley, Audrey. *Race in North America: Origin and Evolution of a Worldview.* 2nd ed. Boulder,
CO: Westview Press, 1999.

Solorzano, Daniel G., and Dolores Delgado Bernal. "Examining Transformational Resistance
through a Critical Race and LatCrit Theory Framework: Chicana and Chicano Students in
an Urban Context." *Urban Education* 36, no. 3 (2001): 308–42.

Spindler, George, ed. *Fifty Years of Anthropology and Education, 1900–1954: A Spindler Anthology.*
Mahwah, NJ: Lawrence Erlbaum, 2000.

Stocking, George W. *Race, Culture, and Evolution: Essays in the History of Anthropology.* 2nd ed.
Chicago: University of Chicago Press, 1982.

Stoler, Ann Laura. *Race and the Education of Desire: Foucault's History of Sexuality and the Colonial
Order of Things.* Durham, NC: Duke University Press, 1995.

Stulberg, Lisa M. *Race, Schools, and Hope: African Americans and School Choice after Brown.* New
York: Teachers College Press, 2008.

Sugrue, Thomas. *Sweet Land of Liberty: The Forgotten Struggle for Civil Rights in the North.* New
York: Random House, 2008.

Sullivan, Patricia. *Days of Hope: Race and Democracy in the New Deal Era.* Chapel Hill: University
of North Carolina Press, 1993.

Susman, Walter I. *Culture as History: The Transformation of American Society in the Twentieth
Century.* New York: Pantheon Books, 1984.

Svonkin, Stuart. *Jews against Prejudice: American Jews and the Fight for Civil Liberties.* New York:
Columbia University Press, 1997.

Takaki, Ronald. *Double Victory: A Multicultural History of America in World War II.* Boston: Little,
Brown, 2000.

Taylor, Edward, David Gillborn, and Gloria Ladson-Billings, eds. *Foundations of Critical Race
Theory in Education.* New York: Routledge, 2009.

Theoharis, Jeanne. "'Alabama on Avalon': Rethinking the Watts Uprising and the Character of
Black Protest in Los Angeles." In *The Black Power Movement: Rethinking the Civil Rights-Black
Power Era,* edited by Peniel E. Joseph, 27–54. New York: Routledge, 2006.

Theoharis, Jeanne, and Komozi Woodward, eds. *Freedom North: Black Freedom Struggles outside
the South, 1940–1980.* New York: Palgrave Macmillan, 2003.

Theoharis, Jeanne, and Komozi Woodward, eds. *Groundwork: Local Black Freedom Movements in
America.* New York: New York University Press, 2005.

Thompson, Becky W., and Sangeeta Tyagi, eds. *Beyond a Dream Deferred: Multicultural Education
and the Politics of Excellence.* Minneapolis: University of Minnesota Press, 1993.

Tyack, David. *The One Best System: A History of American Urban Education.* Cambridge, MA:
Harvard University Press, 1974.

Tyack, David, Robert Lowe, and Elisabeth Hansot. *Public Schools in Hard Times: The Great Depression and Recent Years.* Cambridge, MA: Harvard University Press, 1984.

Van Ausdale, Debra. *The First R: How Children Learn Race and Racism.* Lanham, MD: Rowman
and Littlefield, 2002.

Von Eschen, Penny M. *Race against Empire: Black Americans and Anticolonialism, 1937–1957.*
Ithaca, NY: Cornell University Press, 1997.

Walker, Vanessa Siddle. "African American Teaching in the South: 1940–1960." *American Educational Research Journal* 38, no. 4 (2001): 751–79.

Walkowitz, Daniel. *City Folk: English Country Dance and the Politics of the Folk in Modern America.* New York: New York University Press, 2010.

Walters, Ronald G., ed. *Scientific Authority and Twentieth Century America.* Baltimore: Johns Hopkins University Press, 1997.

Ward, Jason Morgan. "'No Jap Crow': Japanese Americans Encounter the World War II South." *Journal of Southern History* 73, no. 1 (2007): 75–104.

Wells, Amy Stuart. *Both Sides Now: The Story of School Desegregation's Graduates.* Berkeley: University of California Press, 2009.

Westbrook, Robert W. "'I Want a Girl, Just Like the Girl That Married Harry James': American Women and the Problem of Political Obligation during World War II." *American Quarterly* 42, no. 4 (1990): 587–614.

Wilkinson, J. Harvie. *From Brown to Bakke: The Supreme Court and School Integration, 1954–1978.* New York: Oxford University Press, 1979.

Wilkinson, J. Harvie, III. "The Seattle and Louisville School Cases: There Is No Other Way." *Harvard Law Review* 121, no. 1 (2007): 158–83.

Williams, Vernon J., Jr. *Rethinking Race: Franz Boas and His Contemporaries.* Lexington: University Press of Kentucky, 1996.

Williams, Vernon J., Jr. *The Social Sciences and Theories of Race.* Urbana: University of Illinois Press, 2006.

Wittner, Lawrence S. *Cold War America: From Hiroshima to Watergate.* Rev. ed. New York: Holt, Rinehart, and Winston, 1978.

Yon, Daniel A. *Elusive Culture: Schooling, Race, and Identity in Global Times.* Albany: State University of New York Press, 2000.

Young, Virginia Heyer. *Ruth Benedict: Beyond Relativity, Beyond Pattern.* Lincoln: University of Nebraska Press, 2005.

Yu, Henry. *Thinking Orientals: Migration, Contact, and Exoticism in Modern America.* New York: Oxford University Press, 2001.

Zilversmit, Arthur. *Changing Schools: Progressive Education in Theory and Practice, 1930–1960.* Chicago: University of Chicago Press, 1993.

Zimmerman, Jonathan. "*Brown*-ing the American Textbook: History, Psychology, and the Origins of Modern Multiculturalism." *History of Education Quarterly* 44, no. 1 (2004): 46–69.

Zimmerman, Jonathan. "Ethnics against Ethnicity: European Immigrants and Foreign-Language Instruction, 1890–1940." *Journal of American History* 88, no. 4 (2002): 1383–404.

Zimmerman, Jonathan. *Innocents Abroad: American Teachers in the American Century.* Cambridge, MA: Harvard University Press, 2006.

Zimmerman, Jonathan. *Whose America? Culture Wars in the Public Schools.* Cambridge, MA: Harvard University Press, 2002.

INDEX

ACDIF. *See* American Committee for Democracy and Intellectual Freedom (ACDIF)
ACE (American Council on Education), 79–81
African Americans
    IQ tests, 60
    literacy skills, 36, 37
    mass migrations during World War I, 35
    as nationless race, 34–39
    and 1939 World's Fair, 61, 201*n*67
    school segregation, 35, 168, 174
    teaching associations, 5
    tolerance efforts directed toward, 13, 98, 99, 103, 107–9, 208*n*13
    See also civil rights movement; educational discourse on race; Negro History lessons
AJC (American Jewish Committee). *See* American Jewish Committee (AJC)
American Anthropological Association, 51, 60
American Biology Teacher (journal)
    on eugenics, 57–58, 200*n*46
    on tolerance education, 120, 124–25, 133–34
    as window on educational discourse, 6
American Committee for Democracy and Intellectual Freedom (ACDIF)
    Boas's involvement with, 51, 53–54, 59, 199*n*27
    founding and funding of, 63–64, 199*n*27
    1939 World's Fair exhibit, 60–61
American Council Institute of Pacific Relations, 143
American Council on Education (ACE), 79–81
American democracy
    projecting to transnational audience, 174–75
    racism as threat to, 96, 178
    tolerance education as fortification of, 4, 8, 10, 44, 45, 98, 99–100, 101–2, 108, 112, 124, 136, 151, 171
    See also Americanization programs
American Dilemma, An (Myrdal), 172

American Eugenics Society, 57, 61
American Federation of Labor, 143
American Historical Association (AHA), 85
American Indians. *See* Native Americans
Americanization programs
    assimilationist agenda of, 163, 190*n*16
    as citizenship training, 11, 16, 17–20
    cultural gifts movement as counter to, 20–23, 29
    and international education, 26
    treatment of cultural traits in, 16, 17–20
American Jewish Committee (AJC), 57, 63–64, 143, 202*n*82
American Jewish Congress, 143
American Museum of Natural History (AMNH)
    link to eugenics movement, 205*n*64
    Mead's association with, 83, 84, 85, 91, 92, 205*n*64
American Red Cross, segregation of blood, 117, 125, 126, 159, 180
Americans All—Immigrants All (radio show), 28
American Unity (journal), 110, 122, 131, 143, 168
AMNH. *See* American Museum of Natural History (AMNH)
anthropology/anthropologists
    and *Brown v. Board of Education*, 5
    campaign to undermine racism, 4–5, 10–13, 46, 60, 95, 120–23, 132, 171, 180, 182–83
    critique of eugenics movement, 58–60, 61, 201*n*66
    culture concept of, 6, 7–8, 21, 67, 181, 203*n*8
    postwar retreat from educational reform, 172, 182
    race concept, 5, 6
    See also American Anthropological Association; Benedict, Ruth; Boas, Franz; educational discourse on race; Mead, Margaret; scientific definition of race; Weltfish, Gene

243

HT 1506 .B87 2011

Burkholder, Zoë.

Color in the classroom

GAYLORD